Intersections of AI and the Freedom of Religion or Belief

Swati Chakraborty
https://orcid.org/0000-0003-0799-1954
Concordia University, Canada

IGI Global
Scientific Publishing
Publishing Tomorrow's Research Today

Vice President of Editorial Melissa Wagner
Director of Acquisitions Mikaela Felty
Director of Book Development Jocelynn Hessler
Production Manager Mike Brehm
Cover Design Jose Rosado

Published in the United States of America by
IGI Global Scientific Publishing
701 East Chocolate Avenue
Hershey, PA, 17033, USA
Tel: 717-533-8845 | Fax: 717-533-7115
Website: https://www.igi-global.com E-mail: cust@igi-global.com

Library of Congress Cataloging-in-Publication Data

Names: Chakraborty, Swati, 1985- editor
http://id.loc.gov/authorities/names/n2022036027
http://id.loc.gov/rwo/agents/n2022036027
Title: Intersections of AI and the freedom of religion or belief / edited by Swati Chakraborty.
Description: Hershey, PA : IGI Global Scientific Publishing, [2026] | Includes bibliographical references and index. | Summary: "This book explores the intersection of AI and freedom of religion or belief, unpacking the complex ways emerging technologies influence religious freedom in diverse social, cultural, and political contexts. It sheds light on both risks and the opportunities"-- Provided by publisher.
Identifiers: LCCN 2025028971 (print) | LCCN 2025028972 (ebook) | ISBN 9798337338309 hardcover | ISBN 9798337338316 paperback | ISBN 9798337338323 ebook
Subjects: LCSH: Technology--Religious aspects http://id.loc.gov/authorities/subjects/sh85133167 | Artificial intelligence--Religious aspects http://id.loc.gov/authorities/subjects/sh2024001274 | Freedom of religion http://id.loc.gov/authorities/subjects/sh85112662
Classification: LCC BL265.T4 I58 2026 (print) | LCC BL265.T4 (ebook) | DDC 323.44/2--dc23/eng/20250626
LC record available at https://lccn.loc.gov/2025028971
LC ebook record available at https://lccn.loc.gov/2025028972
British Cataloguing in Publication Data
A Cataloguing in Publication record for this book is available from the British Library.

Table of Contents

Detailed Table of Contents

The integration of Virtual Reality (VR) and Augmented Reality (AR) into Vietnam's religious practices signifies a profound fusion of technology, culture, and spirituality. This study examines cultural acceptance, community engagement, and technological deployment, revealing VR's role in enabling immersive rituals and virtual pilgrimages that transcend physical limits. AR enhances religious education through interactive storytelling, especially engaging youth and marginalized groups. Adoption faces ethical and theological challenges, including debates over virtual pilgrimage legitimacy and the preservation of traditional authority. Collaborative efforts among religious institutions, tech companies, and government foster innovation, highlighting the need for community-sensitive approaches. VR/AR promises to reshape Vietnam's religious landscape, blending digital and traditional dimensions.

In an era defined by artificial intelligence and pervasive surveillance technologies, the freedom of religion or belief (FoRB)—a cornerstone of human rights—is facing unprecedented challenges. This paper explores how AI-driven tools, including facial recognition, predictive policing, algorithmic content moderation, and data profiling, are increasingly shaping the landscape in which religious identities are expressed, regulated, or suppressed. While these technologies offer potential benefits, such as improved access to religious resources or safeguarding public safety, they also risk entrenching bias, amplifying discrimination against religious minorities, and enabling state or corporate overreach into sacred spaces and private beliefs.This interdisciplinary inquiry draws from human rights law, AI ethics, and digital sociology to examine the dual-edged role of AI in either protecting or violating FoRB.

As artificial intelligence (AI) evolves into more autonomous and affective systems, its potential to shape human cognition and spiritual life intensifies. This chapter examines the implications of next-generation AI—such as AGI, emotion AI, BCIs, and algorithmic recommendation systems—on freedom of religion or belief (FoRB), grounded in Article 18 of the UDHR. It explores how AI can influence belief formation, redefine religious authority, and challenge communal coherence through digital syncretism and AI-generated scripture. Ethical, legal, and governance concerns—including surveillance, profiling, and censorship—are critically assessed. The chapter concludes with strategic recommendations for integrating religious literacy into AI design and fostering multi-stakeholder collaboration, ensuring AI supports, rather than threats, spiritual diversity and freedom in an increasingly digitized world.

Human rights by design is an emerging framework that seeks technological systems that respect and uphold the diversity of beliefs and practices in global societies. AI-driven technologies, from automated decision-making to content moderation systems, increasingly influence individuals' ability to practice and express their religious beliefs. However, concerns have arisen regarding biases in AI algorithms, the suppression of religious content on digital platforms, in this domain require a robust framework that prioritizes human dignity, non-discrimination, and the protection of fundamental freedoms. To ensure AI systems respect religious freedom and broader human rights, designers and policymakers must address several core issues: perspectives, reinforce stereotypes, or disadvantage certain faith-based communities. Ongoing audits, diverse data representation, Automated moderation

AI technologies in India are not only transforming digital habits but also reshaping belief systems. From religious chatbots to political propaganda and tools like ChatGPT, AI now mediates truth, tradition, and trust. Drawing on sociological and media theories, this chapter explores AI as a cultural actor in India's media ecology. Based on a mixed-methods survey of 150–300 respondents and analysis of AI-mediated content, it shows how algorithms reinforce dominant narratives across caste, gender, and religion. Using concepts like habitus and mediatization, it examines how repeated AI use reshapes understandings of knowledge and authority. The chapter calls for culturally rooted AI policies and critical digital literacy, arguing that AI is emerging as an ideological force shaping belief in an automated society.

The digital age presents a paradox where unprecedented connectivity fuels the spread of religious hatred and misinformation, threatening human rights and social cohesion. This chapter explores AI's strategic role in countering these harms by moving beyond reactive content removal toward a proactive, peacebuilding approach. It highlights the limitations of manual moderation and the necessity of scalable AI solutions. We review AI's advanced capabilities, including sophisticated NLP and multimodal analysis, which are crucial for detecting nuanced hate speech and misinformation. The chapter also discusses AI's potential to foster religious tolerance through counter-narratives and dialogue platforms. However, we examine ethical challenges such as algorithmic bias, the risk of over-moderation, and the complexities introduced by generative AI. The conclusion advocates for a multi-stakeholder governance model, emphasizing "human-in-the-loop" oversight and international cooperation to ensure AI systems are technically robust, ethically sound, and culturally sensitive.

As our lives become increasingly intertwined with digital technology and way people experience and express religion is also continuously evolving. This one chapter explores how idea of FoRB is evolving in digital world over course of time, where smartphones, social media, algorithms have become everyday tools for faith, connection, control. While digital spaces can open up new opportunities for interfaith dialogue, spiritual exploration, community-building, they can also pose serious risks. Issues like online hate speech, digital surveillance, content moderation, algorithmic bias often challenge free expression of belief. This chapter will have a closer look at how FoRB operates in online environments by combining insights from international human rights law, digital sociology, case studies from around world. We here focus on examining how free belief truly is in age of internet, considering what it takes to protect that freedom when technology both connects and controls.

Preface

INTRODUCTION

In recent years, few technological developments have reshaped human experience as profoundly as Artificial Intelligence (AI). Its influence reaches beyond economics and governance, touching culture, identity, and even the deeply personal sphere of faith. *Intersections of AI and the Freedom of Religion or Belief* was conceived from a growing recognition that the conversation on AI ethics and human rights has, until now, only tentatively engaged with the question of religious freedom. Yet, as digital systems increasingly mediate how people access information, form communities, and express their beliefs, this intersection can no longer be ignored.

AI technologies—whether in search engines, social media moderation, predictive policing, or automated decision-making—are not neutral. They embody human choices, cultural assumptions, and structural power dynamics. These systems have the capacity to uplift or to marginalize, to promote interfaith understanding or to entrench bias. The same algorithms that might protect users from hate speech can also suppress religious expression. The same data analytics that promise security can be deployed for targeted surveillance of faith communities. It is within this tension that this book situates itself.

Freedom of Religion or Belief (FoRB), enshrined in Article 18 of the *Universal Declaration of Human Rights* and the *International Covenant on Civil and Political Rights*, stands as a cornerstone of human dignity. It safeguards the right of every person to believe—or not believe—and to manifest those convictions privately or publicly, alone or in community. As AI systems increasingly shape social and political life, the preservation of this right depends upon how technologies are designed, deployed, and governed.

This volume brings together a diverse group of scholars, practitioners, and advocates to explore how AI intersects with FoRB across global and local contexts. The contributions within examine both the risks—algorithmic discrimination, digital censorship, and surveillance—and the opportunities—AI-enabled tools that foster dialogue, counter online hate, and promote pluralism. Together, they illuminate urgent questions:

- Can AI be designed to respect and uphold religious freedom?
- How can algorithmic bias against faith communities be identified and mitigated?
- What legal, ethical, and policy frameworks are needed to ensure AI systems do not erode fundamental freedoms?

The intent of this collection is not merely analytical but aspirational. It calls for a vision of technological development grounded in human rights and moral responsibility—a vision where innovation serves inclusion, and progress safeguards belief.

This book is written for a wide audience: scholars of AI, law, and religion; policymakers drafting digital rights legislation; technologists seeking ethical guidance; civil society leaders advocating for human dignity; students and educators pursuing interdisciplinary understanding; and journalists shaping public narratives about faith in the digital age.

Ultimately, *Intersections of AI and the Freedom of Religion or Belief* is an invitation—to reflect, to challenge assumptions, and to act. As AI continues to redefine what it means to connect, communicate, and coexist, protecting the freedom of conscience and belief becomes not just a legal obligation, but a shared human imperative.

ORGANIZATION OF THE BOOK

Chapter 1: Virtual and Augmented Reality (VR/AR) in Religious Contexts in Vietnam: Impact and Implementation

This chapter transports readers to Vietnam, where immersive technologies are transforming spiritual life. Through an analysis of Virtual and Augmented Reality applications in religious practices, it reveals how digital rituals and virtual pilgrimages are expanding participation while raising complex ethical and theological debates. The chapter details the ways VR and AR enhance religious education, storytelling, and community engagement—particularly among youth and marginalized groups. Yet it also highlights tensions around authenticity, authority, and cultural preservation. By tracing collaborations among faith institutions, technology firms, and government agencies, this study underscores the importance of culturally sensitive innovation in reimagining religious experience in Southeast Asia.

Chapter 2: AI, Surveillance, and the Sacred: Protecting Religious Rights in a Data-Driven World

Chapter Three delves into one of the most urgent issues of the digital age—the use of AI in surveillance and its implications for religious freedom. Through an interdisciplinary lens that blends human rights law, ethics, and digital sociology, it explores how facial recognition, predictive policing, and algorithmic profiling can simultaneously serve public safety and threaten sacred privacy. The analysis reveals a tension between technological governance and spiritual autonomy, raising questions about how societies can ensure AI protects rather than infringes upon the right to belief. The chapter ultimately calls for a human rights–based framework that defends FoRB in the face of expanding data-driven control.

Chapter 3: Preparing for the Next Generation of AI Impacts on Belief Systems

As AI becomes more autonomous, emotional, and integrative, its influence on belief formation grows increasingly profound. This chapter offers a forward-looking assessment of emerging technologies—such as Artificial General Intelligence (AGI), emotion AI, brain–computer interfaces (BCIs), and recommendation algorithms—and their potential to reshape religious cognition and authority. It interrogates how AI-generated texts and digital syncretism could redefine sacredness itself, while also posing challenges to communal coherence. Through legal and ethical analysis grounded in Article 18 of the *Universal Declaration of Human Rights*, the chapter proposes strategies to embed religious literacy in AI design and governance, urging collaboration across sectors to safeguard spiritual diversity in a rapidly evolving digital world.

Chapter 4: Building Human Rights by Design: Ethical AI Development for Religious Freedom

Chapter Five advances the concept of "human rights by design" as a foundational principle for AI ethics. It argues that respect for religious freedom must be embedded from the inception of technological systems, rather than treated as an afterthought. Drawing attention to algorithmic bias, digital censorship, and the challenges of automated moderation, the chapter presents a roadmap for inclusive data practices and accountability mechanisms. By integrating perspectives from technology development, law, and human rights, it demonstrates how ethical design can prevent the marginalization of faith-based communities and ensure that digital platforms remain open spaces for authentic belief expression.

Chapter 5: Digital Dignity: Ethical AI Governance for Protecting Religious Freedom

Building on the previous discussion, this chapter focuses on governance—outlining policy deficiencies and proposing actionable solutions to ensure "digital dignity" in AI systems. It emphasizes the necessity of participatory governance models where faith leaders, policymakers, and technologists collaborate in shaping ethical standards. The author advocates for an adaptive regulatory approach rooted in transparency, fairness, and cultural sensitivity. Drawing from best practices such as IBM's fairness toolkit and municipal transparency initiatives, the chapter articulates a multi-level framework for integrating Freedom of Religion or Belief principles into the governance of AI globally.

Chapter 6: Religious Freedom in the Age of AI: A Constitutional Law Perspective

Turning to the legal domain, Chapter Seven examines how AI interacts with constitutional protections of religious freedom. It situates AI's regulatory and expressive power within constitutional frameworks, exploring issues like algorithmic bias, digital censorship, and surveillance. The analysis considers both the potential of AI to enhance interreligious dialogue and its risks to civil liberties. Through case studies and jurisprudential analysis, the author proposes a normative blueprint for aligning AI regulation with constitutional values, ensuring that technological progress reinforces rather than erodes the foundations of religious liberty.

Chapter 7: Generative AI in Contemporary Islamic Religious Education Discourse: Revelation Meets Algorithm

This chapter bridges theology and technology by examining how Generative AI (GenAI) is entering the discourse of Islamic Religious Education (IRE). By contextualizing modern innovations within Islamic epistemology, it highlights continuities between past traditions of knowledge transmission and current digital experimentation. The chapter offers a critical assessment of AI-assisted Qur'anic exegesis, hadith verification, and educational applications, while insisting on the irreplaceable role of human scholars in safeguarding spiritual authenticity. It proposes a Shariah-aligned ethical framework for responsible AI use, encouraging cautious optimism about GenAI's potential to complement, rather than replace, divine revelation in religious pedagogy.

Chapter 8: Faith, Freedom, and Artificial Intelligence: An Economic Perspective on Digital Rights and Religious Expression

Chapter Nine introduces an economic dimension to the study of AI and religious freedom. Through economic modeling and policy analysis, it evaluates how AI-driven content moderation and algorithmic systems affect religious expression, both as a cultural value and as an economic good. The chapter quantifies the costs of digital discrimination and explores how religious organizations can leverage AI for sustainability and outreach. By applying frameworks such as public goods theory and transaction cost economics, the author proposes equitable governance models that align market efficiency with human dignity, ensuring that digital economies nurture pluralism and belief diversity.

Chapter 9: Believing the Algorithm: AI and the Transformation of Popular Belief in India

This chapter turns to India to explore how AI technologies are reshaping public belief and religious identity. Drawing on sociological and media theory, it portrays AI not merely as a tool but as a cultural actor that mediates truth, authority, and trust. Through empirical data and media analysis, the author shows how algorithms reinforce social hierarchies and dominant narratives across caste, gender, and religion. The study warns of AI's growing ideological power in shaping public consciousness, advocating for culturally grounded AI policy and critical digital literacy as essential defenses of freedom in an increasingly automated society.

Chapter 10: Harnessing Artificial Intelligence to Promote Religious Tolerance and Dialogue: A Strategy to Detect and Counter Religious Hatred and Misinformation

Chapter Eleven presents a proactive vision for AI as a peacebuilding tool. Confronting the spread of online hatred and misinformation, it argues for the strategic use of AI to detect and counter digital intolerance. The chapter reviews advanced AI techniques in natural language processing and multimodal analysis capable of identifying subtle hate speech while promoting interfaith dialogue through counter-narratives. Yet, it also grapples with the ethical challenges of bias, overreach, and cultural misinterpretation. The author concludes by proposing a "human-in-the-loop" model and international cooperation to ensure that AI governance promotes empathy, pluralism, and religious coexistence.

Chapter 11: From Belief to Bandwidth: Navigating Freedom of Religion or Belief in the Age of Algorithms

In this wide-ranging exploration, the author examines how digital life is redefining the contours of religious freedom. As algorithms curate what we see, hear, and believe, the chapter asks what it truly means to have freedom of belief in an age mediated by code. Drawing from digital sociology and international law, it explores the double-edged nature of technology—its ability to connect believers across borders while also enabling surveillance, censorship, and polarization. The discussion concludes by reframing FoRB for the digital era, urging renewed protections that account for the algorithmic realities of belief and expression.

CONCLUSION

As this volume draws to a close, it becomes evident that the intersection of Artificial Intelligence (AI) and the Freedom of Religion or Belief (FoRB) is not a peripheral topic, but a defining frontier in the ethics of our digital century. The chapters gathered here—spanning disciplines, regions, and traditions—reveal a complex landscape where technology simultaneously empowers and endangers one of humanity's most fundamental rights: the freedom to believe, to doubt, to worship, and to express conviction without coercion.

Across diverse contexts, a shared theme emerges: AI is never neutral. It reflects the data from which it learns, the assumptions of those who design it, and the social structures it inhabits. Whether shaping education, governance, media, or interfaith dialogue, AI technologies hold the capacity to deepen understanding or to distort it; to protect sacred expression or to suppress it. As scholars and practitioners in this volume have shown, the ethical trajectory of AI depends not only on technical safeguards but on a moral imagination rooted in human dignity and pluralism.

The contributions within this collection remind us that FoRB must not be treated as an isolated principle but as a living standard that guides how societies design, deploy, and regulate digital systems. Ensuring religious freedom in the age of algorithms requires what several chapters describe as a *human rights by design* approach—one that embeds fairness, transparency, and accountability into every stage of technological development. It also demands the participation of voices too often excluded: faith leaders, educators, ethicists, minority communities, and those directly affected by algorithmic harms.

At the same time, this book invites cautious optimism. When guided by inclusive ethics and critical reflection, AI can serve as an ally in promoting interreligious understanding, countering hatred and misinformation, and expanding access to spiritual education. Technological progress, when aligned with compassion and justice, can reinforce rather than erode the foundations of belief and coexistence.

Ultimately, the challenge before us is one of stewardship. The task is not to halt technological innovation, but to ensure that its evolution honors the freedom of conscience that lies at the heart of humanity. In bridging the domains of AI and FoRB, we are reminded that protecting the sacred in an algorithmic world is not solely a matter of law or design—it is an act of moral responsibility.

It is my hope that *Intersections of AI and the Freedom of Religion or Belief* serves as both a scholarly resource and a call to action. May it inspire future research, informed policy, and collaborative innovation that ensure artificial intelligence remains in service to the human spirit—not the other way around.

Chapter 1
Virtual and Augmented Reality (VR/AR) in Religious Contexts in Vietnam:
Impact and Implementation

Hanh Thi Pham
https://orcid.org/0000-0001-7527-5154
Vietnam Women's Academy, Vietnam

ABSTRACT

The integration of Virtual Reality (VR) and Augmented Reality (AR) into Vietnam's religious practices signifies a profound fusion of technology, culture, and spirituality. This study examines cultural acceptance, community engagement, and technological deployment, revealing VR's role in enabling immersive rituals and virtual pilgrimages that transcend physical limits. AR enhances religious education through interactive storytelling, especially engaging youth and marginalized groups. Adoption faces ethical and theological challenges, including debates over virtual pilgrimage legitimacy and the preservation of traditional authority. Collaborative efforts among religious institutions, tech companies, and government foster innovation, highlighting the need for community-sensitive approaches. VR/AR promises to reshape Vietnam's religious landscape, blending digital and traditional dimensions.

DOI: 10.4018/979-8-3373-3830-9.ch001

1. INTRODUCTION

The integration of Virtual Reality (VR) and Augmented Reality (AR) into religious practices, worship, and cultural storytelling is a rapidly evolving field that holds significant potential for transforming how religious communities engage with their faith. In Vietnam, where cultural heritage and religious practices are deeply intertwined, the adoption of VR/AR technologies presents both opportunities and challenges. This response explores the impact of VR/AR on religious communities in Vietnam, focusing on cultural acceptance, community engagement, and religious practices. Additionally, it examines the technological development and implementation of VR/AR in Vietnam's religious settings, including local innovations, partnerships with tech firms, and government support.

Moreover, the potential of VR and AR extends beyond mere engagement; they can serve as vital tools for interfaith dialogue and cultural exchange in Vietnam's diverse religious landscape. By creating immersive experiences that allow users to explore and understand different faith traditions, these technologies can foster empathy and respect among diverse communities, potentially mitigating sectarian tensions. For instance, collaborative projects that bring together Buddhist, Islamic, and Christian narratives through shared VR experiences may encourage a broader appreciation of each tradition's unique contributions to Vietnam's cultural tapestry. This collaborative spirit aligns with the calls for innovation coalitions that leverage public and private partnerships to drive technological advancements in social contexts, emphasizing the need for inclusive approaches that respect and celebrate Vietnam's rich religious diversity. As such, the successful implementation of VR/AR in these contexts hinges on the active participation of religious leaders and community members, ensuring that technological advancements enhance rather than replace traditional practices.

Furthermore, the role of VR/AR in enhancing religious education cannot be overstated, as these technologies provide innovative pathways for engaging younger audiences who may otherwise feel disconnected from traditional teachings. By integrating interactive elements such as gamified learning experiences or virtual religious tours, educators can captivate students' interests while deepening their understanding of complex theological concepts. This approach aligns with the findings from recent studies that demonstrate the effectiveness of interactive technology in improving learning outcomes, revealing that students exposed to augmented reality systems show significantly better engagement and retention of information compared to conventional methods (Li et al., 2023). As VR/AR continues to evolve, it holds the potential to bridge generational gaps in religious understanding, fostering a more inclusive environment where all members of the community can explore and appreciate the multifaceted nature of their faith.

2. METHODOLOGY

This study adopts a mixed-methods approach to explore the impact and implementation of Virtual Reality (VR) and Augmented Reality (AR) within religious practices in Vietnam. The research methodology combines qualitative and quantitative data collection methods to gain a comprehensive understanding of how these technologies are perceived and utilized across different religious communities, including Buddhism, Islam, and Christianity.

Qualitative approach

The qualitative component of the study involves semi-structured interviews with key stakeholders within the religious communities. These stakeholders include religious leaders, scholars, and practitioners who have direct experience with or insight into the integration of VR/AR technologies in religious practices. The interviews were designed to explore the cultural, theological, and ethical implications of VR/AR in religious contexts. Questions were open-ended to allow for in-depth discussions about personal experiences, concerns, and opinions regarding the authenticity of digital religious rituals, the impact of these technologies on community engagement, and the preservation of religious traditions. The interviews were conducted in Vietnamese, with a transcription and translation process to ensure accuracy and consistency across the dataset. This qualitative data provides a rich, narrative-driven understanding of how VR/AR is being integrated into religious practices and the challenges and opportunities perceived by those directly involved.

Quantitative approach

The quantitative aspect of the research involved the distribution of surveys to a broader sample of individuals engaged in religious practices across various regions in Vietnam. The survey aimed to gauge public attitudes toward the use of VR/AR technologies in religious settings. It included questions on the respondents' level of awareness, their perceptions of the legitimacy of virtual rituals, and their openness to the use of VR/AR for religious education and community engagement. The survey also assessed the potential barriers to the adoption of these technologies, such as technological access, generational differences, and theological concerns. The quantitative data was analyzed to identify trends and correlations between demographic variables (e.g., age, religious affiliation, geographic location) and attitudes toward VR/AR technologies in religious contexts.

Case Studies

In addition to interviews and surveys, the study includes case studies of specific religious communities that have actively implemented VR/AR technologies in their practices. These case studies were selected based on their innovative use of VR/AR and their cultural significance within the Vietnamese religious landscape. Each case study examines the objectives of VR/AR implementation, the role of religious institutions and technology firms in facilitating these technologies, and the outcomes observed in terms of community participation and spiritual engagement. The case studies also highlight the ethical challenges and theological debates that arose during the integration of VR/AR, providing a nuanced perspective on the local context of technology adoption.

Ethical considerations

Given the sensitive nature of religious practices and the potential ethical concerns surrounding digital representations of sacred rituals, this research was conducted with strict adherence to ethical guidelines. All participants in interviews and surveys were informed about the purpose of the study, and their consent was obtained prior to participation. To protect participants' privacy and confidentiality, all data were anonymized, and sensitive information was handled with care. Ethical approval for the research was obtained from the institutional review board to ensure that the study met the necessary standards of academic integrity and respect for religious beliefs.

Data analysis

Data from the interviews were analyzed using thematic analysis, where recurring themes and patterns were identified and categorized. The analysis focused on understanding the cultural, theological, and social dimensions of VR/AR adoption in religious settings. Quantitative data from the surveys were analyzed using descriptive statistics to summarize trends, and inferential statistics were used to explore the relationships between demographic factors and attitudes toward VR/AR. The findings from both qualitative and quantitative analyses were triangulated to provide a holistic view of the impact of VR/AR technologies on religious practices in Vietnam.

3. CULTURAL ACCEPTANCE OF VR/ AR IN RELIGIOUS PRACTICES

3.1. Traditional vs. Digital rituals

The cultural acceptance of VR/AR in religious practices in Vietnam is influenced by the balance between traditional rituals and the integration of digital technologies. Research indicates that while VR can enhance the solemnity and immersion of digital religious rituals, it is not without limitations. For instance, the absence of multisensory integration in VR experiences may hinder its acceptance in cultures that place high value on tactile and sensory elements in religious practices (Ding-Yang, 2024). However, the potential of VR to replicate traditional temple settings and integrate key rituals, such as lighting ceremonial lamps and offering incense, suggests that it can find acceptance among certain segments of the population, particularly younger generations who are more accustomed to digital environments (Srdanović et al., 2024).

In addition to enhancing engagement through immersive experiences, the integration of VR/AR technologies in religious contexts also raises important ethical considerations that merit further exploration. For instance, the potential for misrepresentation of religious practices in digital formats could lead to misunderstandings or cultural appropriation, particularly if the narratives are not carefully curated by knowledgeable community members. This concern is underscored by the need for a collaborative framework that ensures the authenticity of religious content, allowing for a respectful representation of traditions while leveraging the benefits of technology. Furthermore, as younger generations increasingly engage with these digital platforms, there is an opportunity to cultivate a sense of digital stewardship, empowering them to navigate the complexities of faith in the digital age while preserving the core tenets of their beliefs. By fostering dialogue among stakeholders, including religious leaders, educators, and technology developers, the implementation of VR/AR can be guided by ethical principles that honor both innovation and tradition, ultimately enriching the spiritual landscape of Vietnam (Covucci et al., 2024). As the dialogue surrounding VR/AR technologies in religious contexts evolves, it is crucial to consider the broader implications of these digital innovations on cultural preservation and identity.

The intersection of technology and spirituality not only offers avenues for engagement but also poses challenges in maintaining the authenticity of traditional practices amidst rapid digitalization. For instance, the potential for cultural landscapes to be misrepresented or oversimplified in virtual formats can lead to a dilution of rich spiritual narratives, emphasizing the need for community-driven content curation that respects local customs and beliefs (Logan, 2005). Additionally, the integration of these technologies may inadvertently create a divide between those who embrace digital practices and those who adhere strictly to traditional approaches, thus necessitating ongoing dialogue and collaboration among diverse religious groups to foster a more inclusive and harmonious spiritual environment. By prioritizing ethical engagement and community involvement, the implementation of VR/AR can enhance rather than undermine the intricate tapestry of Vietnam's religious heritageThis approach not only preserves cultural heritage but also promotes interfaith dialogue, encouraging mutual respect across Vietnam's diverse religious landscape.

Moreover, as VR/AR technologies continue to evolve, their potential to facilitate interfaith dialogue and cultural exchange becomes increasingly significant, particularly in a nation as religiously diverse as Vietnam. By curating shared virtual experiences that highlight common values and narratives across different faiths, these technologies can serve as platforms for fostering understanding and empathy among various religious communities. For instance, collaborative virtual events that showcase the rituals and teachings of Buddhism, Islam, and Christianity could help dismantle stereotypes and promote a more nuanced appreciation of each tradition's contributions to Vietnam's cultural identity. This approach aligns with the growing recognition of the importance of community-driven initiatives that leverage technology to enhance social cohesion and mutual respect, emphasizing the need for inclusive practices that celebrate diversity while addressing the challenges of cultural misrepresentation and appropriation inherent in digital formats. Ultimately, the successful integration of VR/AR in religious contexts hinges on a commitment to ethical stewardship and collaborative engagement, ensuring that technological advancements enrich rather than overshadow the rich tapestry of Vietnam’s spiritual heritage.

3.2. Role of AR in religious education and practice

Augmented Reality (AR) is increasingly being recognized as a tool for religious education and practice. AR's ability to provide interactive and visual representations of religious topics makes it a valuable asset for teaching religious concepts to children, youth, and people with disabilities (Mylenka & Anhelova, 2021). In Vietnam, where religious education is often conducted through storytelling and visual narratives, AR can enhance the learning experience by bringing religious stories and symbols to life. This aligns with the broader trend of using AR to create engaging and participatory experiences in cultural and religious contexts (Srdanović et al., 2024). Moreover, the application of AR in religious education can significantly enhance inclusivity by catering to diverse learning needs, particularly for individuals with disabilities who may struggle with traditional educational methods. By utilizing AR to create multisensory experiences that engage various cognitive pathways, educators can facilitate a deeper understanding of religious concepts, making them more accessible to all learners. This approach not only aligns with the findings that underscore AR's effectiveness in improving engagement and retention but also resonates with the broader movement towards inclusive education that values diversity in learning styles (Mylenka & Anhelova, 2021). Furthermore, as AR technology continues to advance, it opens up opportunities for collaborative learning environments where students can engage with their peers in exploring religious narratives, fostering a sense of community and shared understanding that transcends individual backgrounds. Such initiatives can also serve as a bridge between generations, allowing older community members to share their insights and experiences while younger individuals contribute fresh perspectives, ultimately enriching the communal religious experience in Vietnam.

As the integration of AR in religious education evolves, it is essential to consider the role of community involvement in shaping these digital narratives. Engaging local religious leaders and educators in the development of AR content ensures that the representations of religious practices remain authentic and respectful, thereby preserving the integrity of traditions while embracing technological advancements. Furthermore, incorporating feedback from diverse community members can help mitigate potential misinterpretations or oversimplifications that may arise from a purely technological perspective, fostering a more nuanced understanding of faith practices (Ding-Yang, 2024). This collaborative approach not only empowers communities to take ownership of their narratives but also enhances the educational experience by providing a richer context that resonates with learners from various backgrounds, ultimately promoting a more inclusive and harmonious religious environment in Vietnam.

As the landscape of religious education in Vietnam continues to evolve with AR technologies, it is essential to examine the potential for these tools to not only enhance understanding but also to foster critical thinking and dialogue about faith. By encouraging students to engage in reflective practices, such as analyzing religious narratives through interactive simulations, AR can help cultivate a more discerning approach to faith that values both tradition and contemporary interpretation. This shift towards critical engagement aligns with the broader educational trend of promoting inquiry-based learning, which has been shown to significantly improve comprehension and retention among students (Mylenka & Anhelova, 2021). Furthermore, as communities increasingly adopt these technologies, there is an opportunity to create platforms for intergenerational dialogue, allowing older generations to share their interpretations and experiences while younger individuals explore innovative ways to express their beliefs. Such interactions can bridge the generational divide, ensuring that the rich tapestry of Vietnam's religious heritage is both preserved and dynamically reinterpreted in a way that resonates with all community members (Sen & Tho, 2020).

3.3. Ethical and theological considerations

The adoption of VR/AR in religious practices also raises ethical and theological questions. For instance, the use of VR for virtual pilgrimages, such as the Hajj, has been met with skepticism by some Muslim scholars who argue that it cannot replace the physical and spiritual elements of the pilgrimage (Jubba et al., 2024). Similarly, the use of AR in religious education must be carefully considered to ensure that it does not undermine the authority of religious leaders or the traditional methods of religious instruction (Mylenka & Anhelova, 2021). These concerns highlight the need for a nuanced understanding of the role of VR/AR in religious practices and the importance of involving religious leaders and scholars in the development and implementation of these technologies.

As the discourse surrounding the ethical and theological implications of VR/AR technologies in religious contexts continues to evolve, it becomes increasingly important to examine how these innovations can be harmonized with traditional teachings and practices. For instance, the potential for virtual platforms to facilitate dialogue among diverse faiths could serve as a catalyst for communal understanding and cooperation, particularly in a multicultural society like Vietnam. By creating immersive experiences that allow users to engage with various religious narratives side by side, VR/AR may not only enhance educational outreach but also promote a more profound appreciation of shared values and common goals across faiths, thus fostering interfaith harmony (Srdanović et al., 2024). However, careful consideration must be given to the design of these experiences to avoid the pitfalls of oversimplification or cultural appropriation, ensuring that they are developed in consultation with religious scholars and community leaders to maintain authenticity and respect for the traditions being represented. Ultimately, the successful integration of these technologies hinges on a collaborative approach that prioritizes ethical stewardship and community engagement, paving the way for a future where technology and spirituality coexist in a mutually enriching relationship.

As the dialogue around VR/AR technologies in religious contexts progresses, it is essential to consider their potential role in promoting mental well-being and spiritual resilience among practitioners. By offering immersive experiences that simulate sacred spaces or significant rituals, these technologies can provide individuals with a sense of connection and solace, particularly in times of crisis or isolation. For instance, virtual environments designed for meditation or prayer can help users engage in spiritual practices even when physical attendance is not possible, effectively bridging the gap between the digital and spiritual realms (Ding-Yang,

2024). Moreover, the integration of community feedback in the development of these platforms can ensure that they resonate with the emotional and psychological needs of users, thereby enhancing their therapeutic potential while remaining rooted in cultural authenticity. This approach not only supports individual spiritual journeys but also reinforces the communal bonds that are vital to religious practice, suggesting a future where technology serves as a facilitator of both personal and collective faith experiences.

4. COMMUNITY ENGAGEMENT AND VR/AR

4.1. Enhancing community participation

VRMoreover, as VR and AR technologies continue to reshape community engagement in religious contexts, they can also serve as powerful tools for social activism and awareness campaigns within faith communities. For instance, immersive experiences designed to highlight pressing social issues, such as poverty or environmental degradation, can galvanize community members to take action and foster a sense of collective responsibility. By leveraging these technologies to create participatory narratives that resonate with the values of compassion and stewardship inherent in many religious traditions, organizations can inspire a proactive response to societal challenges. This aligns with the growing emphasis on Corporate Social Responsibility (CSR) in religious institutions, which aims to enhance community welfare and address inequalities through collective action. Ultimately, the successful integration of VR/AR in promoting social engagement not only enriches the spiritual experience but also reinforces the moral imperatives of faith, encouraging adherents to actively contribute to the betterment of society.

Furthermore, the potential for VR and AR technologies to enhance community engagement extends beyond mere participation in social activism; they can also serve as platforms for fostering intergenerational dialogue and collaboration within religious communities. By creating virtual spaces where older and younger members can share their perspectives on faith, these technologies can bridge the generational divide that often exists in traditional religious settings. For instance, virtual storytelling sessions that allow elders to recount historical religious narratives while younger participants contribute contemporary interpretations can cultivate a richer understanding of shared heritage, reinforcing communal bonds and respect for diverse viewpoints. This aligns with the findings that emphasize the importance of community involvement in shaping digital narratives, ensuring that the integration of technology does not overshadow the authenticity of lived experiences and traditions. As such, VR and AR can not only enhance social engagement but also empower communities to collaboratively navigate the complexities of faith in an increasingly digital world, ultimately enriching the spiritual fabric of Vietnam's diverse religious landscape. As the integration of VR and AR technologies continues to evolve within Vietnam's religious communities, it is essential to consider the potential for these tools to enhance cultural preservation efforts, particularly in the face of globalization and urbanization. The immersive nature of VR can allow users to experience historical religious sites and rituals that may be at risk of fading from collective memory due to rapid societal changes, thus acting as a digital safeguard for cultural heritage (Lauser, 2008). Additionally, AR can facilitate the documentation and sharing of local religious practices, enabling communities to create interactive archives that celebrate their unique traditions while fostering a sense of pride and continuity among younger generations. This dual approach not only promotes the retention of cultural identity but also encourages a broader understanding of Vietnam's diverse spiritual landscape, ultimately reinforcing the importance of community-driven narratives in the digital age. By harnessing these technologies, religious groups can actively participate in shaping their representations and engage with the global discourse on cultural heritage, ensuring that their voices are heard and respected in an increasingly interconnected world.

As communities increasingly embrace VR and AR technologies, it is crucial to consider their potential in fostering mental health and spiritual resilience among practitioners, particularly in times of crisis. These immersive experiences can provide solace and connection for individuals who may feel isolated or disconnected from traditional communal practices, thereby reinforcing the importance of community bonds during challenging times. For example, virtual environments designed for meditation or prayer can serve as accessible spaces for spiritual engagement, allowing users to participate in meaningful practices regardless of physical constraints. Furthermore, the ethical development of these platforms must prioritize community feedback to ensure that they resonate with users' emotional and psychological needs, creating experiences that are both culturally authentic and therapeutically beneficial. This approach not only supports individual spiritual journeys but also strengthens communal ties, suggesting a future where technology and spirituality can coexist harmoniously, enhancing the overall well-being of Vietnam's diverse religious landscape.

4.2. Gamification and interactive learning

The integration of gamification elements into VR/AR experiences can further enhance community engagement by making religious education and practice more interactive and enjoyable. For instance, AR applications can incorporate game design principles, such as rewards and challenges, to encourage users to engage more deeply with religious content (Srdanović et al., 2024). This approach has been successfully applied in cultural heritage preservation, where gamified AR applications have been used to educate users about historical sites and artifacts (Srdanović et al., 2024). In the religious context, similar approaches could be used to teach religious stories, rituals, and values in an engaging and accessible manner.

Moreover, as the integration of VR/AR technologies continues to evolve, it is crucial to consider their implications for intergenerational dialogue within religious communities. The younger generation's familiarity with digital tools can serve as a bridge to engage older members, fostering discussions that blend traditional beliefs with contemporary practices. For example, collaborative VR experiences could allow families to explore their religious heritage together, enhancing understanding and respect across age groups. This approach not only preserves cultural narratives but also empowers youth to take active roles in their communities, potentially counteracting trends of out-migration and cultural disconnection . By creating shared experiences that resonate with both the past and present, VR/AR can play a pivotal role in revitalizing community bonds and ensuring the continuity of religious traditions in an increasingly digital world.

Such initiatives highlight the potential of VR/AR technologies to bridge generational gaps, enabling a richer understanding of cultural heritage while fostering community cohesion and spiritual engagement.These technologies can also facilitate the preservation of religious practices by documenting rituals and ceremonies in immersive formats, ensuring that cultural heritage remains accessible for future generations.The potential for VR/AR to enhance religious practices in Vietnam underscores the transformative power of technology in fostering deeper connections to cultural heritage and community engagement.Furthermore, the successful integration of VR/AR in religious contexts necessitates ongoing collaboration between technology developers, religious leaders, and community members to ensure that these innovations respect and enhance traditional practices. This collaborative approach can lead to the development of culturally sensitive VR/AR applications that honor traditional practices while embracing innovation, ultimately enriching the spiritual experience for all participants.

4.3. Bridging cultural and generational divides

One of the key benefits of VR/AR in religious contexts is its ability to bridge cultural and generational divides. By providing immersive and interactive experiences, VR/AR can make religious practices more accessible and appealing to younger generations who are accustomed to digital environments (Srdanovic et al., 2024). In Vietnam, where there is a strong emphasis on preserving cultural heritage, VR/

AR can serve as a tool for transmitting religious and cultural knowledge to future generations in a way that is both engaging and meaningful (Condell et al., 2021).

Furthermore, by incorporating elements of local culture and history into these gamified experiences, religious communities can create a more relatable and immersive educational platform that resonates with participants' identities, thus ensuring that the essence of their heritage is both preserved and dynamically engaged with in a digital context. Furthermore, the potential for VR and AR technologies to facilitate interfaith dialogue and mutual understanding among diverse religious communities in Vietnam cannot be overstated. By creating shared virtual experiences that highlight common values and narratives, these technologies can serve as platforms for fostering empathy and respect, thereby addressing sectarian tensions that may arise in a multicultural society. For instance, collaborative VR projects that allow users to experience significant rituals from different faiths side by side could not only enhance educational outreach but also promote a more nuanced appreciation of each tradition's contributions to Vietnam's cultural identity (Srdanović et al., 2024). Additionally, as communities leverage these immersive technologies, it is crucial to engage religious leaders and scholars in their development to ensure that the experiences are authentic and respectful, thus safeguarding the integrity of spiritual practices while embracing innovation. Ultimately, this commitment to ethical engagement and community involvement may pave the way for a more harmonious coexistence of technology and spirituality, enriching the overall fabric of Vietnam's diverse religious landscape.

5. IMPACT ON RELIGIOUS PRACTICES

5.1. Virtual pilgrimages and digital storytelling

Virtual pilgrimages are one of the most promising applications of VR/AR in religious contexts. By allowing individuals to virtually visit and explore sacred sites, VR/AR can provide a meaningful alternative to physical pilgrimages, which may be inaccessible due to logistical or financial constraints (Ding-Yang, 2024) (Jubba et al., 2024). In Vietnam, where pilgrimage sites such as the Perfume Pagoda and the Holy Land of Tay Ninh are significant religious and cultural landmarks, VR/AR can provide immersive experiences that allow individuals to explore these sites in detail, even from a distance. This innovative approach not only democratizes access to sacred spaces but also enriches the spiritual experiences of individuals who may otherwise be unable to undertake physical journeys.Furthermore, the use of virtual pilgrimages can redefine the concept of sacred space, allowing individuals to engage with their spirituality in novel ways that transcend geographical limitations (Dwivedi, 2020). This shift may foster a broader understanding of religious practices and enhance community connections, particularly among those unable to participate in traditional pilgrimages.

This evolution in spiritual engagement through virtual experiences highlights the need for ongoing dialogue about the authenticity and ethical implications of such practices within diverse religious communities.The exploration of virtual pilgrimages raises important questions about the spiritual legitimacy of these experiences, necessitating a dialogue among religious leaders and community members to address potential concerns.This dialogue is crucial for ensuring that virtual experiences align with the values and beliefs of the communities involved, fostering a respectful integration of technology and spirituality.This ongoing discourse will be vital in shaping how VR/AR technologies can be ethically integrated into religious practices, ensuring they complement rather than compromise traditional beliefs.As virtual pilgrimages gain traction, it is essential to evaluate their impact on traditional religious practices and community perceptions, ensuring they enhance rather than diminish spiritual engagement.

5.2. Digital storytelling and emotional engagement

Digital storytelling is another area where VRAs digital storytelling continues to evolve within religious contexts, it offers profound opportunities to deepen emotional engagement and foster a sense of belonging among practitioners. By utilizing immersive narratives that resonate with personal experiences, communities can create compelling content that not only educates but also elicits empathy and understanding across diverse faiths. For instance, AR-enhanced storytelling can bring to life significant historical events or parables, allowing users to interact with these narratives in a meaningful way, thus bridging the gap between ancient wisdom and modern interpretation (Mylenka & Anhelova, 2021). Furthermore, the incorporation of local voices and perspectives in these digital narratives ensures authenticity, empowering community members to share their unique interpretations while preserving the integrity of their traditions. Such collaborative storytelling not only enhances cultural retention but also promotes interfaith dialogue, suggesting that the future of religious engagement in Vietnam may increasingly rely on the harmonious integration of technology and spirituality to cultivate a more inclusive and interconnected community (Srdanović et al., 2024). As the landscape of VR/AR in religious contexts continues to evolve, it is crucial to explore the role of these technologies in fostering community resilience and collective identity among practitioners. By creating virtual spaces that allow for shared experiences, such as communal prayers or celebrations of significant religious events, VR/AR can reinforce social bonds and enhance a sense of belonging, particularly in an era where physical gatherings may be limited due to health concerns or social restrictions. This potential for digital engagement aligns with the broader trend of utilizing technology to promote mental well-being and social cohesion, emphasizing the importance of community support systems in navigating challenges (Benard, 1991; Blum, 2005). Furthermore, as communities actively participate in curating their digital narratives, they not only preserve their unique cultural identities but also cultivate a sense of agency, empowering individuals to shape their spiritual journeys in ways that resonate with both tradition and contemporary realities (Roffey, 2013).

5.3. Rituals and ceremonies in virtual spaces

The use of VRAs rituals and ceremonies increasingly find their place in virtual spaces, the potential for enhancing communal worship experiences also expands. For example, the integration of augmented reality can allow participants to visualize sacred symbols and narratives during online ceremonies, enriching the spiritual atmosphere and fostering a deeper connection among congregants, regardless of their physical locations. This shift not only democratizes access to religious practices but also raises questions about the evolving nature of sacredness in a digital context, challenging traditional notions of presence and participation (Ding-Yang, 2024). Furthermore, the ability to engage in real-time virtual ceremonies can facilitate interfaith collaborations, where diverse religious groups come together to celebrate shared values and beliefs, thus promoting a culture of mutual respect and understanding in Vietnam's multifaceted religious landscape (Srdanović et al., 2024). Such developments underscore the necessity for ongoing dialogue among religious leaders and community members to navigate the complexities of integrating technology with spiritual practices while ensuring that the essence of traditional rituals is preserved.

As the exploration of VR and AR in religious contexts broadens, the potential for these technologies to facilitate cross-cultural exchanges and collaborations becomes increasingly evident. For instance, virtual platforms could host interfaith dialogues where participants from various backgrounds engage in shared rituals, thereby fostering a deeper understanding of each other's beliefs and practices. Such initiatives could not only enhance mutual respect but also serve as a means of collective identity formation in an increasingly globalized world, where cultural boundaries are often blurred. Additionally, by incorporating local narratives and perspectives into these virtual experiences, communities can ensure that their unique traditions are authentically represented while simultaneously promoting a sense of belonging among participants (Srdanović et al., 2024). This approach aligns with the need for ethical stewardship in technological integration, highlighting the importance of collaborative efforts to preserve the integrity of diverse religious practices in the face of rapid digitalization. As the exploration of VR and AR technologies in religious contexts advances, it is also crucial to examine the potential implications for ritual authenticity and community identity. The reliance on digital platforms for sacred experiences may lead some practitioners to question the spiritual legitimacy of virtual participation, particularly in cultures where physical presence is deeply valued in religious observance (Jubba et al., 2024). This skepticism highlights the need for a nuanced understanding of how digital innovations can coexist with traditional practices, as well as the importance of establishing guidelines that respect the integrity of religious rituals while embracing technological advancements. Furthermore, engaging diverse voices within religious communities in the development of VR/AR content can foster a more inclusive dialogue about the evolving nature of spirituality, ensuring that the integration of technology serves to enhance, rather than dilute, the rich tapestry of cultural and religious identities in Vietnam (Srdanović et al., 2024). Ultimately, fostering a collaborative approach that prioritizes ethical considerations and community input will be essential in navigating the complexities of this digital transformation, allowing for a harmonious coexistence between tradition and innovation.

As the dialogue surrounding the integration of VR and AR in religious contexts continues to unfold, the exploration of ethical frameworks becomes increasingly vital to ensure that these technologies do not inadvertently perpetuate cultural appropriation or misrepresentation. Engaging religious scholars and community leaders in the development of digital content can help safeguard the authenticity of spiritual narratives, fostering a collaborative environment where diverse perspectives are valued and respected. This collaborative approach not only enhances the credibility of virtual experiences but also aligns with the growing emphasis on ethical stewardship within technological advancements, as highlighted by recent studies that advocate for community-driven initiatives to preserve cultural integrity (Ding-Yang, 2024; Srdanović et al., 2024). Furthermore, as practitioners navigate the complexities of faith in the digital age, the establishment of guidelines that prioritize community involvement can facilitate a more nuanced understanding of how technology can coexist with tradition, ultimately enriching the spiritual landscape of Vietnam while honoring its rich heritage.

6. TECHNOLOGICAL DEVELOPMENT AND IMPLEMENTATION

6.1. Local innovations and partnerships

The development and implementation of VR/AR technologies in Vietnam's religious settings are being driven by local innovations and partnerships with tech firms.

For example, the development of AR applications for cultural heritage preservation has demonstrated the potential for similar technologies to be applied in religious contexts (Srdanović et al., 2024). Collaborations between religious organizations, tech firms, and academic institutions can play a crucial role in the development of VR/AR applications that are tailored to the specific needs and practices of religious communities in Vietnam. These partnerships can foster a collaborative environment where technological advancements align with the spiritual and cultural values of the community, ensuring that VR/AR applications enhance rather than disrupt traditional practices.Additionally, ongoing evaluations of these partnerships are essential to ensure that the technologies developed resonate with the community's values and effectively address their unique spiritual needs.The success of these initiatives relies heavily on continuous feedback and collaboration among stakeholders, ensuring that technological innovations remain culturally relevant and ethically sound.

Moreover, as the landscape of VR/AR technologies continues to evolve, the importance of developing ethical guidelines and frameworks becomes increasingly paramount to ensure that these innovations are not only effective but also respectful of cultural sensitivities. Engaging with local religious scholars and community leaders in the design and implementation phases can foster a sense of ownership and authenticity, mitigating concerns regarding cultural appropriation and misrepresentation (Ding-Yang, 2024). For instance, establishing advisory committees composed of diverse faith representatives can facilitate ongoing dialogue about the appropriateness of digital representations of sacred texts and rituals, thereby promoting a more nuanced understanding of spiritual practices in the digital age. Additionally, as these technologies gain traction, it is crucial to assess their long-term impact on community identity and cohesion, particularly in terms of how they shape perceptions of authenticity and belonging in an increasingly interconnected world (Srdanović et al., 2024). By prioritizing ethical stewardship and community engagement, the integration of VR/AR can enhance not only religious practices but also the broader cultural landscape of Vietnam, ensuring that technology serves as a bridge rather than a barrier to spiritual connection.

6.2. Government support and policy

Government support and policy play a critical role in the development and implementation of VR/AR technologies in Vietnam. The Vietnamese government has shown a strong commitment to leveraging technology for cultural preservation and education, which has created a favorable environment for the adoption of VR/AR in religious contexts (Doukianou & Laioti, 2024). However, the implementation of these technologies must also be accompanied by ethical guidelines and policies that ensure the respectful and accurate representation of religious and cultural heritage (Doukianou & Laioti, 2024), (Barbara et al., 2021).

Engaging practitioners in the iterative design process not only fosters a sense of ownership but also ensures that the technologies resonate with the spiritual and cultural nuances of diverse faiths. For instance, by incorporating insights from local religious leaders, developers can create VR experiences that authentically represent sacred narratives and rituals, thereby addressing concerns regarding cultural appropriation and misrepresentation. Furthermore, the establishment of ethical guidelines, informed by community input, can help navigate the complexities of digital representation, ensuring that these technologies enhance rather than disrupt traditional practices. This collaborative approach not only preserves the integrity of spiritual experiences but also promotes a more inclusive dialogue about the evolving nature of faith in an increasingly digital world, ultimately enriching the communal fabric of Vietnam's diverse religious landscape.

6.3. Ethical considerations and community-centric approaches

The ethical considerations surrounding the use of VR/AR in religious contexts are complex and multifaceted. Issues such as the representation and appropriation of cultural and religious narratives, particularly involving indigenous and historically marginalized communities, must be carefully addressed (Doukianou & Lalioti, 2024). Community-centric approaches that involve religious leaders, practitioners, and other stakeholders in the development and implementation of VR/AR technologies can help ensure that these technologies are used in a way that is respectful and beneficial to all parties involved (Hamidulfuad, 2024) (Doukianou & Lalioti, 2024). This ongoing collaboration between community members and technology developers is essential for ensuring that VR/AR applications are both respectful and effective in enhancing religious practices in Vietnam. This collaborative approach not only preserves the authenticity of religious practices but also fosters a sense of shared responsibility among community members, ensuring that technological advancements align with cultural values.

As the dialogue surrounding the ethical use of VR/AR in religious contexts progresses, it is essential to consider the implications of these technologies on cultural identity and representation. The potential for VR/AR to create immersive experiences that resonate with local narratives can empower communities to reclaim their stories and assert their cultural heritage in the digital realm. For example, by involving local artisans and spiritual practitioners in the design of AR applications, communities can ensure that their unique cultural practices are accurately depicted and celebrated, fostering a sense of ownership and pride in their traditions (Hamidulfuad, 2024). This collaborative approach not only enhances the authenticity of the digital narratives but also serves as a catalyst for revitalizing interest in traditional practices among younger generations, bridging the gap between the past and the present. Furthermore, as these technologies facilitate new forms of engagement, they invite ongoing reflection on the balance between preserving authenticity and embracing innovation, ultimately enriching the spiritual landscape of Vietnam's diverse religious communities.

7. COMPARATIVE ANALYSIS OF VR/AR ADOPTION ACROSS RELIGIOUS CONTEXTS AND SWOT

7.1. Comparative analysis of VR/AR adoption across religious

The varying degrees of VR/AR adoption across different religious contexts highlight the necessity for tailored approaches that respect unique cultural and doctrinal nuances. This comparative analysis can provide insights into best practices and lessons learned that may inform future VR/AR implementations in Vietnam's religious settings, fostering a culturally sensitive approach. As the landscape of religious practices continues to evolve, understanding the interplay between technology and tradition will be vital for fostering inclusive and meaningful spiritual experiences. This dynamic interplay between technology and tradition not only enriches religious practices but also fosters a deeper understanding of cultural identity among diverse communities in Vietnam. This exploration underscores the importance of integrating ethical frameworks that respect cultural narratives while embracing technological advancements in religious practices.

The ongoing dialogue between technology and religious tradition is crucial for ensuring that innovations like VR/AR enhance rather than disrupt spiritual experiences in Vietnam's diverse religious landscape. In conclusion, the thoughtful integration of VR/AR technologies in Vietnam's religious practices can promote cultural continuity while addressing ethical concerns, ultimately fostering a more inclusive spiritual environment. This integration not only enriches the spiritual experience but also encourages a dialogue between generations, ensuring that religious traditions remain relevant in a rapidly changing world.This ongoing evolution emphasizes the need for continuous collaboration among stakeholders to navigate the complexities of integrating technology in religious contexts while preserving cultural integrity. As VR/AR technologies continue to advance, their role in shaping religious experiences and community dynamics in Vietnam will likely expand, necessitating ongoing dialogue among stakeholders to address emerging challenges.

This collaborative effort will be essential in ensuring that the integration of technology respects traditional values while enhancing the spiritual and communal dimensions of religious life in Vietnam. This integration can ultimately lead to a more vibrant and cohesive religious community, where technology serves as a bridge rather than a barrier to traditional practices. This approach not only preserves the essence of religious practices but also encourages innovation that resonates with contemporary audiences, fostering a dynamic interplay between tradition and modernity. This dynamic relationship between technology and tradition highlights the potential for VR/AR to create meaningful connections within religious communities, fostering both engagement and continuity of cultural practices.

This evolving relationship underscores the importance of balancing innovation with respect for traditional practices, ensuring that technological advancements enrich rather than replace the essence of religious experiences. The successful integration of VR/AR technologies in Vietnam's religious contexts will depend on ongoing collaboration between stakeholders, ensuring that innovations are culturally sensitive and enhance traditional practices. This collaborative process will also require the establishment of ethical guidelines that address the representation of cultural narratives, ensuring that technology serves to enhance rather than exploit religious traditions. In summary, the thoughtful integration of VR/AR technologies in Vietnam's religious practices can foster both cultural continuity and innovation, ultimately enhancing spiritual experiences for diverse communities. As Vietnam navigates this technological shift, it is imperative to prioritize ethical considerations to ensure that VR/AR applications respect and enrich the cultural and spiritual fabric of religious communities.

Table 1. Cultural and community impact of key applications of VR/AR

Religious Context	**Key Applications of VR/AR**	**Cultural and Community Impact**
Buddhist Practices	Virtual meditation, mobile apps for religious practice	Enhanced accessibility and engagement, particularly for younger generations (Connelly, 2022)
Islamic Practices	Virtual Hajj, Islamic education in the metaverse	Provides educational benefits but faces theological challenges regarding legitimacy (Jubba et al., 2024) (Popova, 2023)
Christian Practices	Virtual church services, AR storytelling	Offers new ways to engage with religious content, though theological debates persist (Mylenka & Anhelova, 2021) (Chaudhary, 2024)

(**Source:** Authors' compilation)

7.2. SWOT analysis

The application of SWOT analysis in understanding the strengths, weaknesses, opportunities, and threats of VR/AR in religious contexts can provide valuable insights for stakeholders in Vietnam's diverse religious landscape. This analysis will help stakeholders identify key areas for improvement and potential strategies for effective VR/AR implementation in religious practices across Vietnam. This analysis will also highlight the potential benefits of integrating VR/AR technologies in religious education, fostering engagement, and promoting a deeper understanding of religious teachings among practitioners. The findings from this SWOT analysis can guide religious organizations in Vietnam to effectively strategize the adoption of VR/AR technologies, ensuring that they enhance engagement while respecting traditional practices. In conclusion, the thoughtful application of SWOT analysis can guide the effective integration of VR/AR technologies in Vietnam's religious contexts, ensuring both engagement and respect for traditional practices.

This analysis emphasizes the importance of understanding the unique cultural and doctrinal nuances across different religious contexts to ensure effective implementation of VR/AR technologies in Vietnam's diverse religious landscape. In summary, the integration of VR/AR technologies in Vietnam's religious practices not only fosters engagement and accessibility but also necessitates careful consideration of cultural sensitivities and ethical implications. This analysis serves as a foundation for future research, highlighting the need for ongoing dialogue among stakeholders to ensure that VR/AR technologies are effectively and ethically integrated into religious practices in Vietnam. The adoption of VR/AR in Vietnam's religious contexts offers a promising avenue for enhancing community engagement and educational experiences, while also necessitating careful consideration of ethical implications and cultural sensitivities.

Strengths:	Weaknesses:
- Innovative Engagement: VR/AR technologies provide immersive and interactive experiences that make religious practices more accessible and engaging, especially for younger generations. **- Cultural Preservation: VR/AR can preserve religious rituals, sacred sites, and traditions by making them accessible to a wider audience, including those unable to participate in physical pilgrimages.** **- Interfaith Dialogue: These technologies have the potential to foster interfaith understanding and empathy by enabling users to experience rituals and teachings from different religious perspectives.**	**- Theological and Ethical Concerns: There are concerns about the authenticity of virtual religious experiences and the potential for misrepresentation of religious practices in digital formats.** **- Cultural Resistance: Traditional religious communities may resist the adoption of VR/AR due to concerns over undermining the authority of religious leaders and the sanctity of physical rituals.** **- Technological Barriers: The implementation of VR/AR requires significant investment in technology and infrastructure, which may not be accessible to all religious institutions, particularly in rural or economically disadvantaged regions.**
Opportunities: - **Youth Engagement**: VR/AR offers a platform to engage younger, digitally native generations who may feel disconnected from traditional religious practices. - **Global Reach**: These technologies can overcome geographical limitations, providing access to religious sites and rituals that may be otherwise inaccessible, fostering global religious exchange and learning. - **Educational Enhancement**: AR, in particular, offers opportunities to enhance religious education through interactive storytelling, gamification, and multisensory experiences, making learning more engaging and accessible.	**Threats:** - **Cultural Appropriation**: There is a risk of cultural appropriation if religious content is not curated respectfully, potentially leading to misunderstandings or dilution of sacred practices. - **Digital Divide**: Inequities in access to technology may exacerbate divides within religious communities, where only certain groups can benefit from VR/AR innovations. - **Loss of Traditional Practices**: Over-reliance on virtual experiences may threaten the continuity of traditional religious practices, potentially leading to a disconnect from the physical and communal aspects of worship.

(**Source:** Authors' compilation)

8. CONCLUSION, RESEARCH LIMITATIONS AND FUTURE RESEARCH DIRECTIONS

8.1. Conclusion

The integration of VR/AR technologies into religious practices in Vietnam holds significant potential for enhancing cultural acceptance, community engagement, and religious practices. By providing immersive and interactive experiences, VR/AR can make religious practices more accessible and appealing to a wider audience, particularly younger generations. However, the successful adoption of these technologies requires careful consideration of ethical, theological, and cultural factors, as well as collaboration between religious organizations, tech firms, and government agencies.

As VR/AR technologies continue to evolve, they are likely to play an increasingly important role in shaping the future of religious practices in Vietnam and beyond.

As the landscape of VR/AR technologies in religious contexts continues to evolve, it is crucial to consider the implications of digital engagement on community identity and cohesion. The potential for these technologies to facilitate cross-cultural exchanges can significantly enhance interfaith dialogue, allowing practitioners from different backgrounds to collaboratively explore shared values and beliefs in immersive environments. For instance, virtual workshops that combine teachings from Buddhism, Islam, and Christianity could foster mutual respect and understanding, addressing the complexities of religious diversity in Vietnam's multicultural society (Srdanović et al., 2024). However, this integration must be approached with caution, as the risk of oversimplifying or misrepresenting sacred narratives remains a concern, necessitating the involvement of local scholars and practitioners to ensure authenticity and respect for each tradition's unique context (Doukianou & Lalioti, 2024). Ultimately, the thoughtful application of VR/AR in religious practices promises not only to enrich individual spiritual experiences but also to strengthen communal bonds across Vietnam's diverse faith landscape.

As the integration of VR/AR technologies progresses, there is a growing need to consider the implications for mental health and community resilience within religious contexts. For instance, immersive experiences designed for meditation or spiritual reflection can provide solace for individuals grappling with isolation or anxiety, particularly in the wake of the COVID-19 pandemic, which has disrupted traditional communal practices (Benard, 1991; Blum, 2005). Moreover, these technologies can facilitate virtual support groups, enabling community members to connect and share their experiences in a safe, accessible environment, thus reinforcing social ties that are essential for emotional well-being. However, it is crucial to approach these innovations with sensitivity, ensuring that they complement rather than replace the invaluable human connections fostered through face-to-face interactions. By prioritizing ethical guidelines and community involvement in the development of these digital platforms, religious groups can harness the potential of VR/AR to enhance both individual spiritual journeys and collective identity, ultimately enriching the overall fabric of Vietnam's diverse religious landscape (Srdanović et al., 2024).

8.2. Research limitations

- **Sample Diversity**: While the study includes a variety of religious communities in Vietnam, the sample size may not be fully representative of all regional or ethnic groups, potentially limiting the generalizability of the findings.
- **Technological Accessibility**: The study is limited by the availability and accessibility of VR/AR technologies, particularly in rural or underdeveloped

areas, which may impact the ability of certain communities to fully engage with these technologies.

- **Evolving Nature of Technology**: As VR/AR technologies continue to evolve, the research findings may become outdated, particularly with regard to new developments in the field that were not covered during the study period.

8.3. Future research directions

- **Longitudinal studies**: Future research should explore the long-term impact of VR/AR integration on religious practices, particularly its effects on inter-generational engagement and community cohesion.
- **Cross-Cultural comparisons**: Comparative studies across different countries and religious contexts could provide valuable insights into the global applicability and challenges of VR/AR in religious settings.
- **Ethical frameworks**: There is a need for further research on the development of ethical frameworks for the use of VR/AR in religious practices, focusing on issues of authenticity, cultural respect, and the role of religious leaders in content creation.
- **Impact on religious authority**: Investigating how VR/AR technologies influence the perceived authority of religious leaders and institutions could provide deeper insights into the balance between traditional and digital forms of worship.

In conclusion, while the integration of VR/AR technologies in religious practices in Vietnam presents a promising future, it requires careful consideration of cultural, ethical, and theological factors to ensure that these innovations complement rather than replace traditional spiritual experiences. Future research should focus on refining the ethical use of these technologies, exploring their broader societal implications, and further understanding their potential to reshape religious practices in the digital age.

REFERENCES

Barbara, J., Koenitz, H., & Bakk, Á. K. (2021). *The Ethics of Virtual Reality Interactive Digital Narratives in Cultural Heritage*. DOI: 10.1007/978-3-030-92300-6_27

Chaudhary, M. Y. (2024). *Augmented Reality*. Virtual Reality, and Religion., DOI: 10.1093/oxfordhb/9780197549803.013.28

Condell, J., McShane, N., Alvarez, J., & Miller, A. (2021).*Virtual Community Heritage – An Immersive Approach to Community Heritage*. DOI: 10.5617/jomi.8791

Connelly, L. (2022). *Internet - Based Practices*. DOI: 10.1093/oxfordhb/9780190632922.013.33

Covucci, C., Confetto, M. G., Ključnikov, A., & Panait, M. (2024). Unrevealing the nexus between digital sustainability and corporate digital responsibility: A dual-track systematic literature review towards a framework of corporate digital sustainability. *Technology in Society*, *79*, 102743. DOI: 10.1016/j.techsoc.2024.102743

Ding-Yang, H. (2024). Virtual Realities in Spiritual Practices: Exploring Immersive Technologies in Digital Rituals. *International Journal of Religion*, *5*(12), 2051–2059. DOI: 10.61707/4yam2a55

Doukianou, S., & Lalioti, V. (2024, October). Ethical Extended Reality: Bridging Technology and Cultural Heritage. In *2024 IEEE International Conference on Metrology for eXtended Reality, Artificial Intelligence and Neural Engineering (MetroXRAINE)* (pp. 301-306). IEEE. doi:DOI: 10.1109/MetroXRAINE62247.2024.10796742

Dwivedi, P. S., & Narula, A. (2020). Religious communities in simulated sacred spaces: A study of pilgrimages in digital media. Journal of Content. *Community and Communication*, *11*(10), 260–267. DOI: 10.31620/JCCC.06.20/19

Jubba, H., Fernando, H., Larasati, Y. G., & Darus, M. R. (2024). *Between Reality and Virtuality: A Study of Muslim Perceptions of Metaverse Hajj as a Religious Practice*. Khazanah Theologia., DOI: 10.15575/kt.v6i1.33244

Lauser, A. (2008). Zwischen Heldenverehrung und Geisterkultur: Politik und Religion im gegenwärtigen spätkommunistischen Vietnam. *Zeitschrift für Ethnologie*.

Li, X.-Z., Chen, C.-C., & Kang, X. (2023). Religious diversity education: Raising children's awareness of religious diversity through augmented reality. *Humanities & Social Sciences Communications*, *10*(1), 708. Advance online publication. DOI: 10.1057/s41599-023-02123-w

Logan, W. (2005).*Dien Bien Phu: development and conservation in a Vietnamese cultural landscape.*

Mylenka, H., & Anhelova, A. (2021). Augmented reality in contemporary religious practice. The Journal of v N Karazin Kharkiv National University Series Philosophy Philosophical Peripeteias, 64, 104-112. DOI: 10.26565/2226-0994-2021-64-9

Popova, B. (2023, January). Embracing the Metaverse: The Future of Islamic Teaching and Learning. In 2023 20th Learning and Technology Conference (L&T) (pp. 1-7). IEEE. DOI: 10.1109/lt58159.2023.10092367

Roffey, S. (2013). Inclusive and exclusive belonging: The impact on individual and community wellbeing. *Educational and Child Psychology*, *30*(1), 38–49. DOI: 10.53841/bpsecp.2013.30.1.38

Sheh Hamidulfuad, S. N. F. (2024, August). A Collaborative Social Design Framework for Designing Spiritual Technology: Empowering the Spiritual Experiences of the Indigenous Community Through Co-Creation. In Proceedings of the Participatory Design Conference 2024: Situated Actions, Doctoral Colloquium, PDC places, Communities-Volume 3 (pp. 92-95). doi:DOI: 10.1145/3661456.3666074

Van Sen, V., & Tho, N. N. (2020). Crossing boundaries and state-building: Harmonisation and tolerance in Vietnamese religions. *IJAPS*, *16*(2), 59–83. DOI: 10.21315/IJAPS2020.16.2.4

Srdanović, P., Skala, T., & Maričević, M. (2024). InHeritage—A Gamified Mobile Application with AR and VR for Cultural Heritage Preservation in the Metaverse. *Applied Sciences (Basel, Switzerland)*, *15*(1), 257. Advance online publication. DOI: 10.3390/app15010257

Chapter 2
AI, Surveillance, and the Sacred:
Protecting Religious Rights in a Data-Driven World

Swati Chakraborty
https://orcid.org/0000-0003-0799-1954
Concordia University, Canada

ABSTRACT

In an era defined by artificial intelligence and pervasive surveillance technologies, the freedom of religion or belief (FoRB)—a cornerstone of human rights—is facing unprecedented challenges. This paper explores how AI-driven tools, including facial recognition, predictive policing, algorithmic content moderation, and data profiling, are increasingly shaping the landscape in which religious identities are expressed, regulated, or suppressed. While these technologies offer potential benefits, such as improved access to religious resources or safeguarding public safety, they also risk entrenching bias, amplifying discrimination against religious minorities, and enabling state or corporate overreach into sacred spaces and private beliefs.This interdisciplinary inquiry draws from human rights law, AI ethics, and digital sociology to examine the dual-edged role of AI in either protecting or violating FoRB.

INTRODUCTION

In an era defined by artificial intelligence (AI) and pervasive surveillance technologies, the freedom of religion or belief (FoRB)—a cornerstone of human rights—is facing unprecedented challenges. This paper explores how AI-driven tools, including facial recognition, predictive policing, algorithmic content moder-

DOI: 10.4018/979-8-3373-3830-9.ch002

ation, and data profiling, are increasingly shaping the landscape in which religious identities are expressed, regulated, or suppressed. While these technologies offer potential benefits, such as improved access to religious resources or safeguarding public safety, they also risk entrenching bias, amplifying discrimination against religious minorities, and enabling state or corporate overreach into sacred spaces and private beliefs. Drawing on human rights law, AI ethics, and digital sociology, this interdisciplinary inquiry examines the dual-edged role of AI in either protecting or violating FoRB and offers recommendations to uphold digital dignity and religious freedom in the algorithmic age.

Freedom of religion or belief (FoRB) represents one of the oldest and most foundational rights recognized under international human rights law. Enshrined in Article 18 of the Universal Declaration of Human Rights and the International Covenant on Civil and Political Rights (ICCPR), FoRB protects not only the right to have or adopt a belief but also to manifest it individually or collectively, publicly or privately. However, as societies move deeper into the age of artificial intelligence and surveillance capitalism, the exercise of religious freedom has become increasingly mediated through digital technologies.

AI systems—once heralded as tools of neutrality and efficiency—now function as powerful instruments of social control and classification. They collect, analyze, and predict patterns of human behavior, including those linked to religious identity and practice. This paper investigates the ethical, legal, and sociological implications of such technologies on FoRB, arguing that algorithmic systems often mirror and magnify the prejudices embedded in society and governance structures.

THE DIGITAL TURN AND THE CHANGING CONTEXT OF FORB

The digital transformation has fundamentally altered how religion is experienced and expressed. Online worship, virtual communities, and AI-assisted translations of sacred texts have expanded religious accessibility and inclusion. Yet, these same tools operate within data ecosystems that commodify human behavior, leaving religious expression vulnerable to manipulation and surveillance.

Governments and corporations increasingly deploy AI-driven surveillance systems to monitor populations under the pretext of national security, public health, or counterterrorism. In certain contexts, such as China's Xinjiang region, facial recognition and predictive policing technologies have been used to track and repress Uyghur Muslims—illustrating how digital infrastructures can become instruments of religious persecution.

The advent of digital technologies has fundamentally reshaped the landscape of freedom of religion or belief (FoRB). Religious expression, historically anchored in physical spaces such as temples, mosques, churches, and synagogues, now increasingly occurs in digital environments. The digital turn has introduced both unprecedented opportunities and significant risks for religious communities worldwide (Bielefeldt, Ghanea, & Wiener, 2016).

EXPANDING ACCESS AND PARTICIPATION

Digital technologies have democratized access to religious knowledge and practice. Platforms enabling online worship, livestreamed services, and virtual pilgrimages allow individuals who are geographically isolated, differently-abled, or otherwise restricted from attending physical congregations to participate in religious life. AI-assisted translation and text recognition tools further facilitate the engagement of diverse populations with sacred texts, enabling interlingual access to religious teachings and promoting cross-cultural understanding.

Virtual communities—whether on social media, forums, or messaging platforms—create new forms of belonging and mutual support. For minority faith communities, these spaces can serve as safe havens, fostering solidarity and resilience in contexts where offline expression may be constrained.

SURVEILLANCE AND THE COMMODIFICATION OF BELIEF

Despite these benefits, the same digital infrastructures operate within data ecosystems that commodify human behavior. Religious expression online generates extensive data—ranging from participation in digital rituals to engagement with faith-based content—which can be collected, analyzed, and monetized by corporations and governments alike. This data is often fed into AI systems that predict behavior, classify users, or target them with algorithmically curated content (Zuboff, 2019).

Such systems can reshape the ways religious identities are experienced, often subtly. For instance:

- **Algorithmic recommendations** may privilege majority or mainstream religious content, marginalizing minority faith narratives.
- **Targeted advertising** can exploit religious practices for commercial purposes, blending spiritual experience with consumerist imperatives.
- **Predictive profiling** can influence which individuals are deemed trustworthy, safe, or potentially "risky," affecting their access to services or digital platforms.

State Surveillance and the Threat to FoRB

Governments increasingly deploy AI-driven surveillance under the guise of national security, counterterrorism, or public health. While such measures may be justified in some contexts to protect public safety, they often disproportionately impact religious minorities and vulnerable communities.

A stark example is China's Xinjiang region, where Uyghur Muslims have been subjected to intensive digital monitoring. Facial recognition cameras, biometric data collection, predictive policing algorithms, and social credit systems are used to track religious behavior, monitor gatherings, and enforce state-prescribed religious conduct. Reports indicate that individuals have been penalized for attending mosques, observing religious holidays, or expressing beliefs deemed incompatible with state ideology. This illustrates how digital infrastructures can be weaponized to repress religious practice, transforming surveillance into a tool of coercion rather than protection (Floridi & Taddeo, 2016).

CORPORATE SURVEILLANCE AND PLATFORM GOVERNANCE

The private sector also plays a critical role in shaping the digital context of FoRB. Social media companies and tech platforms, through algorithmic content moderation, AI-based recommendation systems, and user analytics, wield enormous influence over what forms of religious expression are visible, amplified, or censored. These corporate decisions, often opaque and driven by proprietary algorithms, can entrench bias against minority religious groups, limit pluralism, and inadvertently create online environments hostile to free belief.

Duality of the Digital Turn

The digital transformation thus presents a dual-edged reality for FoRB:

- **Opportunity:** Increased accessibility, interfaith engagement, and the preservation of religious knowledge.
- **Risk:** Surveillance, profiling, commodification, and the potential criminalization or suppression of minority beliefs.

Recognizing this duality is essential for developing ethical and human rights–centered approaches to AI governance. Protecting FoRB in the digital era requires not only legal safeguards and technological transparency but also community empowerment through digital literacy, inclusive design, and participatory governance.

The digital turn has redefined the spatial, social, and epistemic dimensions of religious life. While technology offers new avenues for expression, it also introduces complex vulnerabilities. Understanding these dynamics is critical for scholars, policymakers, and technologists committed to safeguarding religious freedom in an era of pervasive AI and surveillance.

ALGORITHMIC BIAS AND RELIGIOUS DISCRIMINATION

AI systems are not value-neutral; they are trained on datasets that reflect social inequalities. Algorithmic bias occurs when training data or decision-making processes reproduce patterns of discrimination. For instance, automated content moderation platforms have disproportionately removed posts related to minority religious practices, mistaking ritual images or attire for "extremist content."

Religious minorities often become "invisible" in AI datasets, leading to underrepresentation and misclassification. Predictive policing algorithms, when fed biased data, may associate ethnic or religious groups with higher security risks. This dynamic reinforces structural discrimination and deepens distrust between religious communities and the state.

The advent of digital technologies has fundamentally reshaped the landscape of freedom of religion or belief (FoRB). Religious expression, historically anchored in physical spaces such as temples, mosques, churches, and synagogues, now increasingly occurs in digital environments. The digital turn has introduced both unprecedented opportunities and significant risks for religious communities worldwide.

Expanding Access and Participation

Digital technologies have democratized access to religious knowledge and practice. Platforms enabling online worship, livestreamed services, and virtual pilgrimages allow individuals who are geographically isolated, differently-abled, or otherwise restricted from attending physical congregations to participate in religious life. AI-assisted translation and text recognition tools further facilitate the engagement of diverse populations with sacred texts, enabling interlingual access to religious teachings and promoting cross-cultural understanding.

Virtual communities—whether on social media, forums, or messaging platforms—create new forms of belonging and mutual support. For minority faith communities, these spaces can serve as safe havens, fostering solidarity and resilience in contexts where offline expression may be constrained.

Surveillance and the Commodification of Belief

Despite these benefits, the same digital infrastructures operate within data ecosystems that commodify human behavior. Religious expression online generates extensive data—ranging from participation in digital rituals to engagement with faith-based content—which can be collected, analyzed, and monetized by corporations and governments alike. This data is often fed into AI systems that predict behavior, classify users, or target them with algorithmically curated content.

Such systems can reshape the ways religious identities are experienced, often subtly. For instance:

- **Algorithmic recommendations** may privilege majority or mainstream religious content, marginalizing minority faith narratives.
- **Targeted advertising** can exploit religious practices for commercial purposes, blending spiritual experience with consumerist imperatives.
- **Predictive profiling** can influence which individuals are deemed trustworthy, safe, or potentially "risky," affecting their access to services or digital platforms.

State Surveillance and the Threat to FoRB

Governments increasingly deploy AI-driven surveillance under the guise of national security, counterterrorism, or public health. While such measures may be justified in some contexts to protect public safety, they often disproportionately impact religious minorities and vulnerable communities.

A stark example is China's Xinjiang region, where Uyghur Muslims have been subjected to intensive digital monitoring. Facial recognition cameras, biometric data collection, predictive policing algorithms, and social credit systems are used to track religious behavior, monitor gatherings, and enforce state-prescribed religious conduct. Reports indicate that individuals have been penalized for attending mosques, observing religious holidays, or expressing beliefs deemed incompatible with state ideology. This illustrates how digital infrastructures can be weaponized to repress religious practice, transforming surveillance into a tool of coercion rather than protection.

Corporate Surveillance and Platform Governance

The private sector also plays a critical role in shaping the digital context of FoRB. Social media companies and tech platforms, through algorithmic content moderation, AI-based recommendation systems, and user analytics, wield enormous influence over what forms of religious expression are visible, amplified, or censored. These corporate decisions, often opaque and driven by proprietary algorithms, can entrench bias against minority religious groups, limit pluralism, and inadvertently create online environments hostile to free belief.

Duality of the Digital Turn

The digital transformation thus presents a dual-edged reality for FoRB:

- **Opportunity:** Increased accessibility, interfaith engagement, and the preservation of religious knowledge.
- **Risk:** Surveillance, profiling, commodification, and the potential criminalization or suppression of minority beliefs.

Recognizing this duality is essential for developing ethical and human rights–centered approaches to AI governance. Protecting FoRB in the digital era requires not only legal safeguards and technological transparency but also community empowerment through digital literacy, inclusive design, and participatory governance.

The digital turn has redefined the spatial, social, and epistemic dimensions of religious life. While technology offers new avenues for expression, it also introduces complex vulnerabilities. Understanding these dynamics is critical for scholars, policymakers, and technologists committed to safeguarding religious freedom in an era of pervasive AI and surveillance.

SURVEILLANCE, SACRED SPACES, AND THE EROSION OF PRIVACY

Pervasive surveillance technologies blur the line between public security and private belief. When congregations, mosques, temples, or churches are monitored using facial recognition or location tracking, the sacredness of worship spaces is compromised. Individuals may refrain from participating in religious gatherings for fear of being identified, profiled, or targeted.

The erosion of spiritual privacy challenges the core of FoRB: the autonomy of conscience. Religious belief, by its nature, requires a protected space of reflection and choice. When surveillance penetrates this realm, it effectively coerces conformity and silences dissenting or minority beliefs.

The Promise of AI for Advancing Forb

Despite its risks, AI also holds transformative potential for advancing religious freedom. Machine learning tools can facilitate interfaith dialogue through real-time translation, preserve endangered languages used in sacred texts, and enhance accessibility for people with disabilities in worship contexts.

Moreover, AI-driven data analysis can help human rights organizations detect and document patterns of religious persecution, providing empirical evidence for advocacy and policy reform. When guided by ethical frameworks and human rights standards, AI can be leveraged to protect rather than persecute (Latonero, M. (2018)).

TOWARDS AN ETHICAL FRAMEWORK FOR DIGITAL RELIGIOUS FREEDOM

To safeguard FoRB in the age of AI, a multi-layered ethical and legal framework is needed. This framework should include:

1. **Human Rights Impact Assessments (HRIAs)** before deploying surveillance technologies in religiously sensitive contexts.

Human Rights Impact Assessments (HRIAs) are systematic tools designed to evaluate the potential effects of laws, policies, or technologies on the enjoyment of human rights. In the context of artificial intelligence and surveillance, HRIAs serve as preventive mechanisms to identify and mitigate risks *before* technologies are implemented—particularly in contexts where religious identities, practices, and beliefs are involved.

Conducting an HRIA before deploying surveillance technologies in religiously sensitive spaces—such as places of worship, pilgrimage sites, or community gatherings—helps ensure that technological interventions do not inadvertently infringe upon the freedom of religion or belief (FoRB) guaranteed under Article 18 of the *Universal Declaration of Human Rights (UDHR)* and the *International Covenant on Civil and Political Rights (ICCPR).*

A well-designed HRIA for FoRB-sensitive contexts should include the following components:

1. **Contextual Risk Analysis:**

Evaluate the socio-political and religious environment in which the technology will be deployed. In societies with histories of religious discrimination or state surveillance, even "neutral" AI systems may exacerbate mistrust and fear among minority groups.

2. **Stakeholder Consultation:**

Engage religious leaders, community representatives, civil society organizations, and human rights experts in participatory dialogue. Their insights help identify potential harms that may not be visible through technical assessments alone.

3. **Assessment of Algorithmic Bias:**

Analyze whether the training data or design of AI systems reflects religious, ethnic, or cultural biases. For example, facial recognition systems may misidentify individuals wearing religious attire or symbols, leading to wrongful targeting or exclusion.

4. **Privacy and Data Protection Review:**

Examine whether data collected through surveillance could reveal individuals' religious affiliation, attendance at places of worship, or online expressions of belief. Such information should be treated as *sensitive data* and safeguarded under robust privacy frameworks.

5. **Remediation and Accountability Measures:**

Establish transparent procedures for redress if FoRB violations occur because of technological misuse or error. Accountability mechanisms must include independent oversight bodies capable of halting or reviewing AI deployments that endanger religious rights.

6. **Ongoing Monitoring and Public Reporting:**

HRIAs should not be one-time exercises but continuous processes that adapt to technological evolution and community feedback. Publicly reporting findings fosters trust, legitimacy, and democratic accountability.

By institutionalizing HRIAs as a precondition for the deployment of AI-based surveillance, governments and private entities can demonstrate their commitment to respecting religious diversity, protecting spiritual autonomy, and aligning digital innovation with the moral imperatives of human rights.

1. **Transparency and Accountability Mechanisms** for algorithmic decision-making processes that affect religious identity or expression.

Transparency and accountability are foundational principles of ethical AI governance. When algorithmic systems influence or regulate expressions of religious identity—such as through content moderation, surveillance analytics, or predictive policing—their opacity poses serious threats to the freedom of religion or belief (FoRB). Without visibility into how these systems operate, it becomes nearly impossible to determine whether violations of FoRB result from intentional bias, systemic design flaws, or data-driven discrimination.

THE CHALLENGE OF ALGORITHMIC OPACITY

Many AI systems function as "black boxes," making decisions based on complex models that are often inaccessible to the public, policymakers, or even their creators. This opacity can obscure patterns of harm—such as disproportionate removal of religious content online or misidentification of individuals in surveillance footage due to religious attire. In such cases, the lack of transparency prevents affected individuals and communities from seeking justice or appealing wrongful actions.

Transparency as a Democratic Safeguard

Transparency ensures that technological systems are open to scrutiny, audit, and contestation. For FoRB-related contexts, this involves:

- **Disclosure of AI Purpose and Scope:** Institutions deploying AI should publicly clarify the purpose, data sources, and operational boundaries of technologies that might impact religious expression or assembly.
- **Explainability and Right to Information:** Individuals must have the right to understand how algorithmic decisions are made about them—particularly when such decisions concern religious symbols, attire, gatherings, or online speech.
- **Open Access to Impact Assessments:** Reports from Human Rights Impact Assessments (HRIAs) should be made publicly available, fostering informed debate and civic oversight.

Accountability Through Oversight and Redress

Accountability requires that decision-makers and system developers bear ethical and legal responsibility for the outcomes of AI applications. In the context of FoRB, this means establishing:

- **Independent Oversight Bodies:** Multi-stakeholder institutions comprising human rights experts, technologists, and representatives of faith communities should monitor AI deployments that affect religious life.
- **Auditability and Traceability:** Algorithms should be subject to regular audits by independent third parties to ensure that their outputs do not perpetuate religious bias or discrimination. Audit trails must be preserved to trace how and why particular decisions were reached.
- **Grievance and Redress Mechanisms:** Individuals whose FoRB rights are violated by algorithmic actions—such as the wrongful deletion of faith-based content or profiling of worshippers—should have access to transparent complaint systems and remedies.

CORPORATE AND GOVERNMENTAL RESPONSIBILITY

Both state and private actors must adhere to the UN Guiding Principles on Business and Human Rights, which affirm that corporations have a duty to respect human rights, including FoRB, across their operations and digital platforms. Governments, in turn, should integrate transparency obligations into regulatory frameworks governing AI deployment. Mandatory disclosure of algorithms used for surveillance, public service delivery, or online moderation ensures that technological power remains accountable to human rights standards.

Building Public Trust Through Ethical AI

Transparent and accountable AI systems not only protect FoRB but also strengthen public confidence in digital governance. When people understand how technology interacts with their religious identities and beliefs, they are more likely to engage in online and offline religious expression without fear. In this sense, transparency is not only a procedural requirement—it is a moral and civic imperative that upholds dignity, trust, and social cohesion in an increasingly data-driven world.

2. **Data Protection Laws** that explicitly recognize religious belief as sensitive personal information, prohibiting its collection without informed consent.

In the digital age, personal data has become a primary currency of power. Artificial intelligence systems and surveillance technologies thrive on vast datasets that include behavioral, biometric, and demographic information. Within this ecosystem, religious belief—once considered a private matter of conscience—can now be inferred or extracted from digital traces such as social media activity, attendance at worship spaces, or online expression of faith. The absence of strong data protection laws that recognize religious affiliation as *sensitive personal information* exposes individuals and communities to discrimination, stigmatization, and persecution.

THE LEGAL FOUNDATIONS OF DATA PROTECTION AND FORB

The right to privacy is intrinsically linked to the freedom of religion or belief (FoRB). Article 17 of the *International Covenant on Civil and Political Rights (ICCPR)* protects individuals from "arbitrary or unlawful interference with privacy," while Article 18 safeguards the inner freedom of conscience. Collecting or processing data about a person's religion without their explicit consent violates both principles, as it undermines the autonomy to hold or change belief without coercion or surveillance.

Modern data protection frameworks—such as the EU General Data Protection Regulation (GDPR)—explicitly classify religious belief as a *special category of sensitive data*. Under Article 9 of the GDPR, the processing of such data is strictly prohibited unless it meets narrow exceptions, such as explicit consent or public interest based on law. However, many countries outside the EU lack equivalent safeguards, allowing governments and corporations to gather religious information indirectly through algorithmic inference.

Risks of Religious Data Profiling

AI-driven systems can infer religious identity without direct disclosure. For example:

- Facial recognition algorithms can identify individuals wearing religious attire or symbols.
- Social media analysis can track engagement with faith-based content.
- Predictive analytics can cluster users based on holiday observance, dietary preferences, or community participation.

These seemingly innocuous datasets can be weaponized to profile, monitor, or exclude individuals based on their beliefs—particularly in authoritarian contexts or conflict-prone regions. Such practices not only violate privacy but also chill the free expression of faith in digital and physical spaces.

The Principle of Informed Consent

To uphold FoRB, informed consent must be central to any data collection process involving religious information. This entails:

- **Explicit and Voluntary Consent:** Individuals should be fully aware of what religious data is being collected, for what purpose, and how it will be used. Consent must be freely given, not coerced or implied.
- **Right to Withdraw and Erasure:** Individuals must have the right to withdraw consent and demand the deletion of their religious data ("the right to be forgotten").
- **Purpose Limitation and Data Minimization:** Data collectors should limit processing strictly to what is necessary and relevant for a clearly defined purpose, avoiding unnecessary aggregation or sharing.

Strengthening Legal and Institutional Frameworks

Governments must integrate explicit protections for religious data into national privacy and data protection laws. This includes:

- Defining *religious belief* as a sensitive data category, requiring special handling.
- Establishing independent data protection authorities (DPAs) empowered to investigate and penalize misuse.
- Requiring human rights due diligence for any technology or AI system that processes data potentially linked to religious identity.

Moreover, corporations and digital platforms should adopt internal compliance policies aligned with international human rights standards. These policies must include data anonymization, encryption of sensitive records, and routine ethical audits to prevent misuse or unauthorized disclosure.

PROTECTING THE SACRED IN THE DIGITAL SPHERE

Recognizing religious belief as sensitive personal information is not merely a technical adjustment—it is a reaffirmation of the sacredness of human conscience.

Informed consent represents the digital expression of religious freedom: the individual's right to control how their beliefs are known, shared, or concealed. Data protection laws thus become a moral as well as legal safeguard, ensuring that digital technologies serve human dignity rather than exploit spiritual identity.

2. **Inclusive AI Design**, ensuring that religious minorities are represented in datasets and consulted during system development.

Artificial intelligence systems derive their power from data—but also their prejudice. When datasets fail to reflect the diversity of human experience, including religious and cultural pluralism, they risk producing technologies that are blind to or biased against marginalized groups. Inclusive AI design is therefore essential to ensuring that freedom of religion or belief (FoRB) is protected, not undermined, in an algorithmically governed world.

The Problem of Exclusion and Misrepresentation

AI systems are only as fair as the data that trains them. In practice, data used for facial recognition, natural language processing, or online content moderation often excludes or misrepresents religious minorities. For example:

- Facial recognition algorithms misclassify individuals wearing religious head coverings or symbols, leading to higher rates of false identification.
- Content moderation tools disproportionately flag posts by minority faith groups as "extremist" or "inappropriate," reflecting cultural bias in training datasets.
- Voice recognition systems fail to accurately interpret languages or dialects used in minority religious communities.

These forms of exclusion perpetuate digital invisibility, where religious minorities are either misrepresented or entirely absent from technological systems that increasingly shape public life.

REPRESENTATION AS A HUMAN RIGHTS IMPERATIVE

Inclusion in AI design is not simply a technical concern—it is a human rights obligation. Article 18 of the *Universal Declaration of Human Rights* guarantees equal protection for all beliefs, while the *UN Declaration on the Rights of Persons Belonging to National or Ethnic, Religious and Linguistic Minorities* (1992) emphasizes participation in decisions affecting minority groups. When religious minorities are excluded from the design and governance of AI systems, their right to equal participation in social, cultural, and technological development is violated.

PRINCIPLES OF INCLUSIVE AI DESIGN

Building AI systems that respect religious diversity requires deliberate action at every stage of development. Key principles include:

- **Diverse and Representative Datasets:**

Data collection must intentionally include individuals from varied religious, ethnic, and cultural backgrounds. This can prevent the dominance of majority-group norms in training data and reduce systemic bias.

- **Participatory Design Processes:**

Religious minorities should be consulted as stakeholders in the design, testing, and deployment of AI systems. Participatory engagement ensures that the lived realities of diverse faith groups inform system functionality and ethical safeguards.

- **Cultural and Religious Sensitivity Training:**

AI developers, engineers, and data scientists should receive training in human rights, intercultural communication, and religious literacy. Understanding the nuances of belief systems helps prevent algorithmic design choices that inadvertently offend or marginalize.

- **Ethical Review Panels with Minority Representation:**

Institutional review boards or AI ethics committees should include representatives from minority faith communities and human rights organizations. Their perspectives add moral depth and contextual awareness to technical evaluations.

FROM DIVERSITY TO JUSTICE IN AI DEVELOPMENT

True inclusion goes beyond representation—it seeks justice in how technology shapes human experience. Merely adding diverse data points to a biased system is insufficient if underlying power structures remain unchallenged. Inclusive AI design should therefore be guided by intersectional ethics, recognizing how religious identity intersects with gender, race, and socioeconomic status to influence digital vulnerability (Crawford, 2021).

Furthermore, AI companies and governments should adopt a "nothing about us without us" approach—ensuring that those most affected by technological decisions have a voice in shaping them. This participatory ethos transforms inclusion from a procedural checkbox into a democratic right.

Towards an Ethically Plural Digital Future

Inclusive AI design recognizes the world's religious and cultural pluralism as a source of richness, not risk. When diverse voices are embedded in the technological imagination, AI systems become more just, empathetic, and responsive to human complexity.

Incorporating religious minorities into data governance and system design is, ultimately, an act of technological peacebuilding—fostering coexistence, trust, and mutual respect in a data-driven society. By making inclusion a design principle rather than an afterthought, the digital future can reflect humanity's sacred diversity rather than erase it.

3. **Digital Literacy Programs** empowering religious communities to understand and mitigate surveillance risks.

In an age where digital technologies mediate nearly every aspect of human interaction, digital literacy has become an essential element of citizenship and rights awareness. For religious communities, especially minorities and marginalized groups, digital literacy is not only a technical skill—it is a form of empowerment that enables the protection of freedom of religion or belief (FoRB) in surveillance-prone environments. By equipping individuals and faith-based organizations with the knowledge to recognize and mitigate digital risks, societies can foster resilience, autonomy, and informed participation in the digital public sphere.

The Knowledge gap and its Consequences

Many religious communities operate with limited understanding of how surveillance technologies and AI systems collect, analyze, and use data. This knowledge gap exposes them to various vulnerabilities:

- **Unwitting Data Exposure:** Congregants may share personal or group information online—such as event photos, location tags, or live streams—without realizing that these can be used for tracking or profiling.
- **Manipulation through Targeted Algorithms:** AI-powered recommendation systems can amplify divisive or extremist content, creating internal fragmentation within faith communities.
- **Chilling Effects on Worship and Expression:** When individuals suspect that their digital interactions are monitored, they may self-censor, withdraw from online faith discussions, or avoid digital worship spaces altogether.

Addressing these gaps requires moving beyond reactive measures toward proactive education that builds digital confidence and awareness rooted in human rights principles.

The Role of Digital Literacy in Protecting Forb

Digital literacy programs serve as preventive tools that strengthen community resilience against both state and corporate surveillance. They help individuals:

- Understand how data is collected through devices, apps, and online platforms.
- Recognize the implications of algorithmic profiling for religious identity and privacy.
- Learn practical security measures, such as data encryption, anonymity tools, and privacy settings.
- Exercise informed consent when interacting with digital platforms that gather sensitive information.
- Engage in advocacy for ethical technology governance that respects religious diversity.

When integrated into community learning spaces—such as faith-based schools, interreligious forums, and civil society workshops—digital literacy becomes an instrument for human rights education and social empowerment.

Designing Culturally Sensitive Literacy Initiatives

For digital literacy initiatives to be effective, they must be contextually and culturally appropriate. Key elements include:

- **Community-Led Curriculum Development:** Programs should be co-created with religious leaders and educators who understand the community's cultural and theological sensitivities.
- **Gender-Inclusive Approaches:** Women and girls in religious communities often face compounded digital barriers; programs must ensure equal access and address gender-specific risks, such as online harassment or surveillance of religious attire.
- **Interfaith Collaboration:** Cross-faith literacy initiatives encourage solidarity and collective advocacy, reinforcing shared values of dignity, compassion, and justice in digital spaces.
- **Practical Skill Building:** Training should emphasize hands-on skills—using secure messaging apps, understanding privacy settings, or recognizing misinformation campaigns that exploit religious sentiment.

Institutional Partnerships and Policy Support

Governments, civil society organizations, and technology companies all have roles to play in advancing digital literacy for FoRB protection.

- **Governments** can fund national digital rights education programs that integrate freedom of religion as a learning module.
- **Tech Companies** can support user-friendly privacy tools, multilingual awareness materials, and transparent data use policies for faith-based communities.
- **Universities and NGOs** can develop specialized training for religious leaders, helping them guide their communities responsibly in digital spaces.

Collaborative efforts ensure that digital literacy transcends technical instruction to become a broader movement for ethical digital citizenship.

From Awareness to Agency

Ultimately, digital literacy is a pathway from awareness to agency. It empowers individuals to navigate digital life without fear, assert their rights online, and hold institutions accountable for intrusive or discriminatory technological practices.

For religious communities, this empowerment is deeply connected to the essence of FoRB: the freedom to believe, to express, and to assemble without coercion or surveillance. By investing in digital literacy, societies affirm that technological progress must be accompanied by moral progress—where every believer, skeptic, and seeker can participate safely and equally in the digital age. By embedding FoRB considerations into AI governance, societies can balance technological innovation with ethical responsibility.

CONCLUSION

Artificial intelligence and surveillance technologies represent a paradox for religious freedom. They can both illuminate and obscure the sacred, empower and oppress, protect and persecute. As states and corporations expand their reliance on data-driven governance, it is imperative to reaffirm the spiritual and ethical dimensions of human dignity. The future of FoRB will depend not merely on technological design but on moral choice—whether societies choose to use AI as a tool of emancipation or as an instrument of control. Protecting religious rights in the digital age demands vigilance, interdisciplinary collaboration, and a renewed commitment to the sanctity of conscience in the face of algorithmic power.

The rapid evolution of artificial intelligence and surveillance technologies has transformed not only how societies function but also how fundamental freedoms are experienced, expressed, and contested. Among these, the freedom of religion or belief (FoRB) stands as a critical frontier in the digital human rights landscape. Once rooted in physical spaces of worship and conscience, FoRB is now increasingly negotiated within algorithmic infrastructures, data ecosystems, and digital governance systems. This transformation presents both profound opportunities and unprecedented risks.

AI and data-driven technologies have the potential to enhance religious freedom—by improving accessibility to sacred knowledge, fostering interfaith dialogue, and supporting inclusive communication across borders. Yet, when deployed without ethical safeguards, these same technologies can become instruments of surveillance, bias, and suppression. Algorithmic profiling, facial recognition, and predictive policing have demonstrated the ability to entrench discrimination against religious minorities, erode privacy in sacred spaces, and chill the open manifestation of belief. These practices not only violate human rights norms but also corrode the moral foundations of pluralistic societies.

The interdisciplinary analysis presented in this paper underscores the urgent need for a human right–centered governance framework for AI and surveillance technologies. Such a framework must recognize the sanctity of belief as integral to human dignity and autonomy. To that end, five interrelated strategies have been proposed:

1. **Human Rights Impact Assessments (HRIAs)** ensure that the deployment of surveillance and AI systems in religiously sensitive contexts is preceded by careful evaluation, participatory consultation, and transparent oversight.

2. **Transparency and Accountability Mechanisms** open the "black box" of algorithmic decision-making, allowing individuals and communities to understand, contest, and seek redress for FoRB-related violations.
3. **Data Protection Laws** that explicitly classify religious belief as *sensitive personal information* are essential to prevent coercive or exploitative data collection without informed consent.
4. **Inclusive AI Design** guarantees representation of religious minorities in datasets and decision-making processes, transforming AI systems into tools of equity rather than exclusion.
5. **Digital Literacy Programs** empower faith communities to recognize, mitigate, and resist the subtle encroachments of digital surveillance, fostering resilience and agency in the face of technological power.

Together, these pillars articulate a vision of ethical technological pluralism, in which innovation and human rights coexist rather than collide. By embedding FoRB into the ethical DNA of digital governance, societies can ensure that technological progress serves the cause of liberation, not control.

Ultimately, the protection of FoRB in the age of AI is not merely a legal or technical challenge—it is a moral and philosophical imperative. It demands that we reassert the primacy of conscience over code, and of human dignity over data. As machines increasingly shape the conditions of human freedom, it becomes essential to ask not only *what technology can do*, but *what it should do* in service of justice, empathy, and the sacred.

In reclaiming the sacred in the algorithmic age, humanity affirms that even amid digital complexity, the freedom to believe, doubt, and worship remains inviolable—the timeless core of human rights and the foundation of a truly ethical digital future.

REFERENCES

Bielefeldt, H., Ghanea, N., & Wiener, M. (2016). *Freedom of religion or belief: An international law commentary*. Oxford University Press. DOI: 10.1093/law/9780198703983.001.0001

Crawford, K. (2021). *The Atlas of AI: Power, politics, and the planetary costs of artificial intelligence*. Yale University Press.

Floridi, L., & Taddeo, M. (2016). What is data ethics? *Philosophical Transactions. Series A, Mathematical, Physical, and Engineering Sciences*, *374*(2083), 20160360. DOI: 10.1098/rsta.2016.0360 PMID: 28336805

Latonero, M. (2018). *Governing artificial intelligence: Upholding human rights & dignity*. Data & Society Research Institute.

Zuboff, S. (2019). *The age of surveillance capitalism: The fight for a human future at the new frontier of power*. PublicAffairs.

Chapter 3
Preparing for the Next Generation of AI Impacts on Belief Systems

Satya Subrahmanyam
https://orcid.org/0000-0003-0441-2742
Holy Spirit University of Kaslik, Lebanon

ABSTRACT

As artificial intelligence (AI) evolves into more autonomous and affective systems, its potential to shape human cognition and spiritual life intensifies. This chapter examines the implications of next-generation AI—such as AGI, emotion AI, BCIs, and algorithmic recommendation systems—on freedom of religion or belief (FoRB), grounded in Article 18 of the UDHR. It explores how AI can influence belief formation, redefine religious authority, and challenge communal coherence through digital syncretism and AI-generated scripture. Ethical, legal, and governance concerns—including surveillance, profiling, and censorship—are critically assessed. The chapter concludes with strategic recommendations for integrating religious literacy into AI design and fostering multi-stakeholder collaboration, ensuring AI supports, rather than threats, spiritual diversity and freedom in an increasingly digitized world.

INTRODUCTION

The rapid and exponential evolution of artificial intelligence (AI) has significantly reshaped multiple aspects of human life, penetrating deeply into domains traditionally perceived as the bastions of human agency, such as social, political, and religious spheres. Initially confined to computational tasks and automation, AI has evolved through machine learning, deep learning, and now into more sophisticated

DOI: 10.4018/979-8-3373-3830-9.ch003

and complex territories including generative models, affective computing, artificial general intelligence (AGI), and neuro-symbolic systems. These advancements signify a transition from narrow, task-specific AI to more general, adaptable, and emotionally responsive technologies that hold the potential to engage with deep human dimensions such as belief, spirituality, and conscience.

This transformation is not merely technological but socio-cultural. The deepening integration of AI into societal frameworks challenges conventional understandings of identity, autonomy, and rights. AI-driven content moderation affects freedom of speech; biometric surveillance technologies impact privacy; and algorithmic bias influences socio-political representation. Consequently, as AI technologies become more nuanced and pervasive, their implications on *freedom of religion or belief* (FoRB) - a fundamental human right enshrined in international law - become increasingly salient. The digitalization of belief systems, AI's potential role in religious interpretation or proselytization, and the surveillance of religious communities are examples where AI intersects directly with FoRB concerns.

The Case for Exploring Next-Generation AI

The decision to focus on next-generation AI technologies is not arbitrary but emerges from a necessity to anticipate and critically evaluate future challenges before they become entrenched realities. Technologies such as AGI—which aspires to match or surpass human cognitive capacities—pose unique philosophical and ethical dilemmas. If machines can think or reason like humans, questions emerge about their potential influence on moral reasoning, theological discourse, and spiritual practices. Affective computing, which allows machines to recognize and simulate human emotions, introduces a new dynamic in human-machine interactions. In religious settings, where emotional resonance and moral empathy are essential, affective AI might be deployed in roles such as digital clergy, pastoral care bots, or religious educators, potentially reshaping the spiritual landscape.

Generative models like GPT (Generative Pre-trained Transformers) and image-generation systems such as DALL·E have already demonstrated the capability to create religious texts, hymns, or visual iconography, blurring the lines between sacred authorship and machine-generated content. Neuro-symbolic systems—AI architectures that combine the strengths of symbolic reasoning with neural networks—offer prospects for more robust and interpretable decision-making, possibly affecting ethical deliberation in interfaith dialogues or judicial arbitration on religious matters.

As these technologies evolve, they bring forth both risks and opportunities. On the one hand, they could enhance interreligious understanding, provide access to religious resources in marginalized areas, and assist in preserving endangered spiritual traditions. On the other hand, they could exacerbate religious surveillance, automate theological gatekeeping, and manipulate religious sentiments for political gains. Therefore, the urgency of addressing these concerns is not merely academic but imperative to safeguarding fundamental freedoms in an AI-influenced world.

Purpose and Scope of the Chapter

A topic that has garnered little but increasing academic interest in the field of artificial intelligence ethics, freedom of religion or belief (FoRB) is the focus of this chapter, which seeks to investigate and foresee the effects of future AI technologies on FoRB. The chapter aims to contribute to theoretical discourse and policy development by critically examining the intersection of advanced AI systems with the right to practice, change, or manifest religion or belief. In various cultural and legal settings, it will delve into many ways artificial intelligence technology might influence religious expression, accessibility, and government.

Three primary aspects are covered throughout the chapter's scope. To begin, it will lay the groundwork conceptually by going over the ethical principles and legal frameworks that support FoRB in international human rights documents including the ICCPR and Article 18 of the UN Declaration of Human Rights. Additionally, it will provide an overview of next-gen AI systems, focusing on their salient characteristics and its uses in theological contexts.

Second, the chapter will delve into specific case studies and scenarios where AI is likely to intersect with FoRB. These include AI-assisted religious content generation, algorithmic filtering of religious expression on social media, and biometric profiling of religious minorities under the guise of national security. Each case will be analyzed to illustrate both the enabling and constraining effects of AI on religious freedom.

Third, the chapter will propose a forward-looking framework for ensuring that AI development and deployment respect and promote FoRB. This will include recommendations for policy-makers, religious leaders, technologists, and civil society actors to collaboratively develop AI governance models that are inclusive, transparent, and culturally sensitive. Ethical design principles, algorithmic accountability, and participatory technology assessment will be explored as part of this normative framework.

In essence, the chapter is both diagnostic and prescriptive. It seeks to diagnose potential threats and opportunities posed by AI to FoRB and prescribe concrete actions to mitigate harm while maximizing benefits. Through interdisciplinary analysis and a rights-based approach, the chapter will underscore the need for vigilance, adaptability, and ethical foresight as we transition into a future where AI is not just a tool but a co-participant in shaping the contours of belief and spirituality.

CONCEPTUAL FOUNDATIONS

The accelerating development of artificial intelligence (AI) and its integration into spheres of belief and identity necessitates a clear understanding of the foundational concepts underpinning this discourse. To critically explore the relationship between AI and *freedom of religion or belief* (FoRB), it is essential to define and contextualize key terms such as AI (in its narrow and general forms), belief systems (religious, spiritual, and secular), and FoRB itself as articulated in international human rights law. A historical and philosophical exploration of the intersection between technology and belief provides important context for the current and future implications of AI on belief systems.

Artificial Intelligence: From Narrow Systems to General Intelligence

Machines with artificial intelligence can learn and reason just like humans, and they can perceive and interpret language and solve problems just like humans. Narrow AI, often called weak AI, and general AI, sometimes called AGI, are the two main types of artificial intelligence. Narrow AI systems work within established boundaries and are meant to do specialized tasks, including language translation, face recognition, or recommendation engines. These systems have already had a big impact in fields like digital communication, content moderation, and surveillance, and they control the present scene of AI applications (Russell & Norvig, 2021).

In contrast, *Artificial General Intelligence* (AGI) aims to replicate human cognitive abilities across a wide range of tasks and contexts, potentially surpassing human intelligence in some areas. AGI remains largely theoretical but is a central focus of emerging AI research. Technologies under development - such as neuro-symbolic systems, affective computing, and large language models - move toward greater autonomy, flexibility, and contextual awareness. These capabilities introduce new ethical and epistemological questions when deployed in contexts tied to personal identity, morality, and spiritual beliefs (Subrahmanyam, 2025a).

Belief Systems: Religious, Spiritual, and Secular Ideologies

Belief systems encompass the frameworks through which individuals interpret existence, morality, purpose, and the nature of the universe. These systems include organized *religions* such as Christianity, Islam, Hindutva, and Buddhism; *spiritual* beliefs, often individualized and eclectic, emphasizing personal experience of the transcendent; and *secular ideologies*, which may espouse humanist, atheistic, or materialist worldviews. Each belief system, religious or otherwise, provides not only metaphysical narratives but also ethical codes and social structures that influence behavior, community life, and identity.

In contemporary societies, belief systems exist in pluralistic configurations. Individuals and groups may derive meaning from overlapping or hybrid sources of belief, challenging the traditional dichotomy between the religious and the secular. The increasing digital mediation of belief - through social media, virtual communities, and AI-generated content - further complicates this landscape, influencing how beliefs are formed, expressed, and regulated (Campbell & Tsuria, 2021).

Freedom of Religion or Belief (FoRB): Legal and Ethical Dimensions

Freedom of Religion or Belief (FoRB) is a universally recognized human right that protects the individual's ability to adopt, change, and manifest belief. It is enshrined in major international legal instruments, notably *Article 18 of the Universal Declaration of Human Rights* (UDHR), which states:

> *"Everyone has the right to freedom of thought, conscience and religion; this right includes freedom to change his religion or belief, and freedom, either alone or in community with others and in public or private, to manifest his religion or belief in teaching, practice, worship and observance" (United Nations, 1948).*

This foundational right is further articulated in *Article 18 of the International Covenant on Civil and Political Rights* (ICCPR), which elaborates on the scope and limitations of FoRB. It emphasizes non-coercion, non-discrimination, and the importance of pluralism in democratic societies. FoRB encompasses not only traditional religions but also atheistic, agnostic, and other non-religious belief systems, thus providing protection for a broad spectrum of ideological orientations (OHCHR, 1966).

The digital transformation and the rise of AI create new contexts for the exercise of FoRB. AI-driven surveillance in authoritarian regimes can target individuals based on religious affiliation, violating privacy and inhibiting free expression of belief. AI tools can also be designed to promote religious literacy, interfaith dialogue, and access to sacred texts, thereby enhancing FoRB.

Historical and Philosophical Intersection of Technology and Belief

The interaction between technology and belief is not a novel phenomenon. Historically, technologies have shaped the transmission, organization, and experience of religious life. The invention of the printing press in the 15th century revolutionized religious communication, facilitating the Protestant Reformation and democratizing access to sacred texts (Eisenstein, 1979). Radio and television later became tools for evangelism and spiritual outreach, while the internet has enabled the rise of "cyber-religion" and virtual worship spaces.

Philosophically, the relationship between technology and belief has been both complementary and contested. On one hand, thinkers such as Martin Heidegger warned of technology's capacity to enfranchise instrumental rationality at the expense of deep existential reflection (Heidegger, 1977). On the other hand, proponents of *technological determinism* and *transhumanism* argue that technology can extend human potential and even contribute to spiritual transcendence. This line of thought sees AI as a potential collaborator in the moral and metaphysical evolution of humanity (Kurzweil, 2005).

In contemporary discourse, AI is increasingly portrayed as both a tool and a symbol. As a tool, it can support religious education, translation of sacred texts, and even simulate ritual interactions. As a symbol, AI evokes theological questions about consciousness, soul, and divine creation. Religious traditions are beginning to grapple with these issues, with some scholars debating whether AI entities could possess moral agency or spiritual significance (Coeckelbergh, 2020).

The conceptual foundations outlined above demonstrate the complexity and urgency of examining the interface between AI and belief. As AI systems evolve in capacity and scope, their influence on belief systems—religious, spiritual, or secular—will likely grow. Understanding AI in its technical and philosophical dimensions, contextualizing belief as a pluralistic and dynamic phenomenon, and grounding the discussion in international legal standards on FoRB are crucial for navigating this emerging frontier.

A historical awareness of how previous technologies have transformed religious expression, coupled with critical engagement with the philosophical implications of AI, provides the analytical tools necessary to assess both the risks and opportunities ahead. The next chapters will delve deeper into these dynamics, exploring specific scenarios, challenges, and governance frameworks to ensure that technological progress upholds, rather than undermines, the right to freedom of religion or belief.

MAPPING THE NEXT GENERATION OF AI

As artificial intelligence continues to evolve at an exponential pace, we find ourselves on the precipice of a transformative era shaped by emerging paradigms that redefine how technology interacts with human cognition, emotion, and belief. The next generation of AI technologies—including Artificial General Intelligence (AGI), Brain-Computer Interfaces (BCIs), affective computing, hyper-personalization, and AI-driven sociotechnical systems—herald a future where AI moves from being a tool to an autonomous co-actor in social and ideological spheres. These advances not only pose profound technical and ethical challenges but also introduce new dynamics in the realm of *freedom of religion or belief* (FoRB), influencing belief systems, religious practices, and the very formation of human identity.

Emerging AI Trends

Artificial General Intelligence (AGI)

Creating AI systems with general-purpose cognitive abilities on par with or better than humans are what we mean when we talk about artificial general intelligence (AGI). The goal of AGI is to reason, plan, learn, and understand on a broad scale, in contrast to narrow AI that is tailored to specific tasks like language translation or image recognition (Goertzel & Pennachin, 2007). Concerns about autonomy, agency, and accountability arise when considering the possibility of artificial general intelligence (AGI) mimicking or even surpassing human cognition, particularly in settings involving moral or religious judgment. There is a risk that AGI entities could pose a threat to established religious leadership and institutions if they are able to reason theologically or interpret holy texts (Bostrom, 2014).

Brain-Computer Interfaces (BCIs)

Technologies that allow for direct contact between the brain and external equipment are known as brain-computer interfaces. Rapid advancements in both invasive and non-invasive BCIs are empowering users to control prosthetics, engage with digital systems, and possibly even convey emotions and thoughts (Lebedev & Nicolelis, 2017). When combined with AI, BCIs have the potential to bring algorithmic processing and human consciousness together in a seamless manner. This coming together has the potential to open up new avenues for spirituality, such as collective neuronal involvement in worship activities, real-time moral feedback, or immersive spiritual experiences. Ienca and Andorno (2017) note that this development does, however, bring up important moral concerns about cognitive liberty, consent, and the value of personal thinking.

Emotion AI and Affective Computing

Affective computing, or emotion AI, is the study and creation of computer systems with the ability to detect, understand, mimic, and even influence human emotions. According to Picard (1997), affective AI is able to personalize interactions based on users' emotional states by analyzing physiological data, facial expressions, and speech data. This has the potential to revolutionize religious and spiritual practices by creating lectures that hit close to home, personalized spiritual instruction, or prayers crafted by artificial intelligence with the intention of evoking certain feelings. There is a danger of emotional manipulation and the commercialization of holy experiences, even if these innovations could increase user involvement and accessibility.

Hyper-Personalization and Predictive Algorithms

Modern AI systems increasingly rely on vast datasets and machine learning techniques to anticipate user preferences, behaviors, and beliefs. Hyper-personalization, driven by predictive algorithms, customizes digital content to align with users' past actions, inferred desires, and emotional states (Zuboff, 2019). In a religious context, this could translate into curated spiritual content, tailored doctrinal interpretations, or even algorithmically matched faith communities. However, such personalization may lead to ideological echo chambers, reinforce biases, and reduce exposure to pluralistic worldviews—ultimately undermining the principles of FoRB, which emphasize autonomy, diversity, and open inquiry.

AI-Driven Sociotechnical Systems and Autonomous Agents

AI is increasingly embedded in sociotechnical systems—complex networks where human and machine actors interact to perform tasks or achieve social goals. Examples include autonomous social robots, algorithmic governance tools, and AI-enabled content moderators. These agents can mediate access to religious information, regulate speech, and enforce digital norms, sometimes without transparent human oversight (Floridi et al., 2018). As autonomous agents become more influential in shaping public discourse and managing religious spaces online, concerns arise over algorithmic bias, censorship, and the erosion of communal agency in belief formation.

Implications for Cognitive and Emotional Influence

Persuasion Technologies and Belief Shaping

The convergence of AI and behavioral psychology has led to the rise of persuasion technologies—systems designed to influence human attitudes, decisions, and actions through tailored content and interaction. Drawing data from social media, biometric sensors, and user profiles, AI can identify cognitive vulnerabilities and deploy strategies to modify belief and behavior (Tegmark, 2017). In spiritual or ideological contexts, these tools could be used to guide religious conversion, reinforce doctrinal adherence, or suppress dissent. While such applications may be beneficial in promoting certain ethical values, they can also infringe on cognitive autonomy and violate the principle of non-coercion central to FoRB (UNHRC, 2020).

Of particular concern is the potential deployment of AI for mass persuasion by state or corporate actors with ideological agendas. If algorithms can be weaponized to subtly shift belief systems or stigmatize certain faiths, the foundational right to freedom of conscience may be undermined without users' awareness. Religious groups themselves may adopt AI-driven persuasion tools, raising questions about authenticity, consent, and the ethics of spiritual influence.

AI-Generated Religious/Spiritual Content and Synthetic Prophets

AI's capacity to generate coherent, context-sensitive text and audio has given rise to the phenomenon of AI-generated religious content. Natural language processing models such as GPT-4 can produce sermons, prayers, and theological treatises that are indistinguishable from those created by humans. Virtual avatars can deliver religious messages with emotional resonance, and AI systems can simulate sacred dialogue in real-time (McCormack et al., 2022). This raises the possibility of "synthetic prophets" - AI entities perceived as spiritually enlightened or divinely inspired, either by design or public perception.

The rise of synthetic prophets presents several dilemmas. On one hand, they may democratize religious knowledge, increase access for marginalized groups, and foster interfaith understanding. On the other, they risk trivializing sacred traditions, introducing doctrinal confusion, or fostering cultic behavior around charismatic digital entities. Without clear guidelines on authorship, accountability, and theological integrity, AI-generated content may disseminate harmful ideologies or reinforce extremism under the guise of spiritual authority.

In response, religious institutions and policy makers must consider new frameworks for the authentication and governance of digital religious content. Questions around the legitimacy of AI spiritual guidance, its alignment with traditional doctrines, and its impact on communal practices will need careful examination to protect FoRB while embracing technological innovation.

The next generation of AI technologies introduces unprecedented opportunities and challenges in the realm of belief, cognition, and emotional influence. AGI, BCIs, emotion AI, and hyper-personalization represent a significant leap in AI's ability to interact with the most intimate aspects of human identity and spirituality. While these systems can enhance religious expression, broaden access to belief systems, and foster spiritual exploration, they also raise serious concerns about manipulation, authenticity, and agency.

Figure 1. The next generation of AI (Author, 2025)

As AI becomes a more active participant in shaping belief and behavior, the principles of *freedom of religion or belief* must be rearticulated and safeguarded within the context of this new technological landscape. Regulatory bodies, religious communities, technologists, and human rights advocates must collaborate to ensure that innovation does not erode individual dignity, diversity of belief, or cognitive freedom.

Future discourse should not only anticipate the ethical and legal implications of these technologies but also offer visionary pathways for coexistence, where AI supports rather than supplants the spiritual and moral dimensions of human life.

PROJECTED IMPACTS ON BELIEF SYSTEMS

As artificial intelligence continues to embed itself more deeply into society, its potential to transform religious, spiritual, and ideological landscapes becomes increasingly evident. Emerging AI technologies are reshaping the very foundations of religious authority, belief formation, and freedom of conscience. From AI-driven spiritual leaders to algorithmically curated belief systems, and from enhanced surveillance of religious practices to the hyper-personalization of spiritual content, the implications for traditional belief systems are both expansive and profound. This section explores how AI might reconfigure epistemological foundations, democratize or fragment religious experiences, and challenge freedom of religion or belief (FoRB) through new forms of surveillance and control.

Reshaping of Religious Authority and Epistemology

Algorithmic Spiritual Leaders and AI-Guided Rituals

One of the most significant shifts on the horizon is the potential emergence of algorithmic spiritual leaders. These are AI systems capable of delivering sermons, interpreting sacred texts, offering spiritual guidance, and even leading rituals. Driven by natural language processing and affective computing, such AI systems can simulate empathetic responses, recognize emotional states, and provide tailored spiritual counsel, sometimes surpassing the availability and scalability of human clergy (McCormack et al., 2022).

While this technological innovation may provide spiritual access to isolated individuals or those in underserved regions, it also poses challenges to traditional epistemology within religious frameworks. Religious authority has historically been grounded in human experiences, communal traditions, and interpretations handed down through generations. AI, by contrast, derives its authority from algorithmic logic, statistical modeling, and vast databases of text, potentially disrupting long-standing interpretative hierarchies. The shift from human to machine-led spiritual discourse could weaken the credibility of traditional institutions and foster alternative, algorithmically sanctioned theologies (Turek, 2020).

AI-guided rituals—ceremonies or practices led or augmented by AI—could redefine the experience of worship itself. Virtual reality combined with AI could simulate sacred spaces, recreate pilgrimage experiences, or generate interactive liturgical performances tailored to individual sensibilities. These innovations might enhance participation but also raise concerns about the authenticity and commodification of sacred practices (Campbell, 2017).

Challenges to Traditional Interpretation and Institutional Authority

AI's interpretive power, particularly through large language models, enables it to analyze and synthesize religious texts across traditions at a scale unimaginable for any individual scholar or theologian. The interpretive neutrality of such models is questionable, as they inherently reflect the biases embedded in their training data (Bender et al., 2021). As a result, AI interpretations might favor dominant or mainstream perspectives, marginalizing minority doctrines or unorthodox beliefs.

Traditional religious institutions may find their epistemological authority diluted as believers turn to AI for spiritual insight. This raises critical questions: Who determines the legitimacy of AI-generated interpretations? How are doctrinal disputes adjudicated when the source is not a person but an algorithm? The decentralization of spiritual authority could lead to theological disorientation and institutional fragmentation.

AI and the Democratization or Fragmentation of Belief

Online Platforms, Echo Chambers, and Filter Bubbles

Digital platforms empowered by AI recommendation systems increasingly mediate the consumption and dissemination of religious content. These platforms prioritize engagement, often reinforcing users' pre-existing beliefs through echo chambers and filter bubbles (Pariser, 2011). Consequently, rather than fostering interfaith dialogue or religious literacy, AI-driven algorithms may exacerbate sectarianism and ideological polarization.

The algorithmic curation of belief content often favors emotional or sensational material, privileging charismatic digital figures or controversial doctrines. This dynamic could elevate fringe movements while sidelining more nuanced or traditional voices, thereby reshaping public perceptions of religious legitimacy and orthodoxy (O'Callaghan et al., 2015).

Social media's viral dynamics, combined with AI's predictive capabilities, enable the rapid propagation of pseudo-religious ideologies or digitally constructed faith systems. These new belief formations, unmoored from communal oversight or theological depth, contribute to a fragmented spiritual marketplace where individuals become isolated nodes in algorithmically constructed worlds of meaning.

Customizable Religious Experiences and Digital Syncretism

AI technologies enable highly customizable religious experiences. Through data-driven insights, users can tailor spiritual journeys that align with their preferences, cultural background, emotional state, and philosophical inclinations. Platforms may recommend prayers, meditations, or religious readings based on behavioral patterns, effectively transforming belief into a consumer-oriented product (Zuboff, 2019).

While this hyper-personalization democratizes access to spiritual content and empowers individual autonomy, it also risks undermining the communal and transcendent dimensions of faith. Religious syncretism - blending elements from various traditions - may be facilitated not through reflective theological engagement but via algorithmic mashups. The resulting spiritual experiences may be shallow or incoherent, lacking the depth and continuity provided by traditional religious education and mentorship.

Theological integrity and coherence may be difficult to maintain in a landscape dominated by algorithmic curation. Believers may come to view faith not as a lived tradition but as an aesthetic or therapeutic choice among many digital options. This transformation of belief into a modular, customizable product challenges long-held notions of commitment, authority, and community in religious life.

AI, Surveillance, and Religious Freedom

Biometric and Behavioral Monitoring of Religious Practices

AI-enhanced surveillance systems - often deployed under the guise of public safety or social governance - have the capacity to monitor biometric and behavioral data related to religious activity. Facial recognition, gait analysis, voice identification, and other forms of digital tracking can identify individuals participating in religious services, rituals, or prayer sessions (Harari, 2018).

While these technologies can be used benignly, such as improving crowd management during pilgrimages, they are equally capable of facilitating intrusive surveillance, particularly in authoritarian regimes. In China, for example, AI is used to track the activities of Uighur Muslims, including attendance at mosques and religious gatherings (Mozur, 2019). These practices not only violate privacy but can have a chilling effect on religious participation, expression, and community cohesion.

Potential for Religious Profiling, Discrimination, or Social Scoring

The integration of AI into state and corporate governance raises the specter of religious profiling and discrimination. When AI systems are used to assign social scores or monitor "desirable" behavior, individuals may be penalized for religious expressions that deviate from sanctioned norms. This has implications for employment, education, mobility, and civic rights (Feldstein, 2019).

Religious minorities are particularly vulnerable to being misclassified or disproportionately targeted by biased algorithms. Predictive policing tools may identify religious gatherings as potential security risks based on flawed data or prejudiced training inputs. The opacity of AI decision-making processes - often described as the "black box" problem - complicates efforts to challenge such biases or seek redress.

The erosion of anonymity in religious practice, particularly in digital spaces, also undermines a core tenet of FoRB: the right to manifest belief privately or communally, openly or in solitude. When digital footprints can be analyzed to infer religious affiliation, individuals may lose the freedom to explore or change their beliefs without surveillance or reprisal.

Figure 2. Impacts on belief systems (Author, 2025)

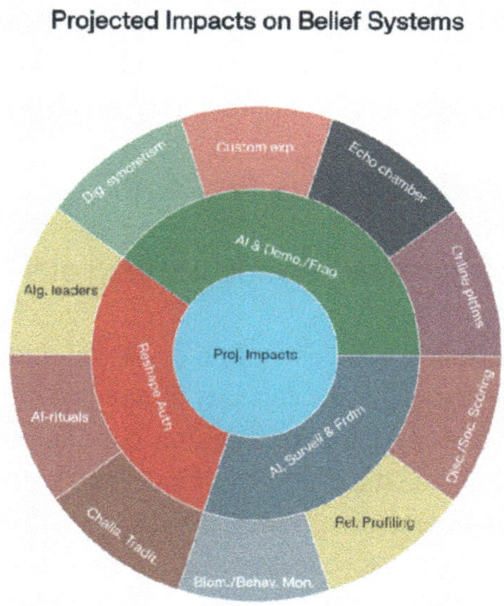

The next generation of AI technologies presents a paradox for belief systems: the potential to enrich and expand religious experience is counterbalanced by profound risks of epistemic instability, fragmentation, and surveillance. Algorithmic spiritual leaders and AI-curated rituals could reshape the contours of religious authority, while hyper-personalization and digital syncretism might redefine spiritual autonomy at the cost of theological coherence and community.

AI-driven surveillance and profiling threaten core elements of religious freedom, particularly for marginalized communities. The challenge lies in navigating these complex dynamics to ensure that technological progress aligns with human rights, ethical reflection, and pluralistic values. Policymakers, religious leaders, and technologists must work collaboratively to safeguard integrity, diversity, and freedom of belief in the AI age.

ETHICAL AND LEGAL CONSIDERATIONS

As artificial intelligence (AI) continues to be woven into the fabric of modern society, its intersection with religion presents complex ethical and legal challenges. AI technologies—from predictive policing and surveillance systems to content moderation algorithms—can directly or indirectly impinge on the fundamental right to freedom of religion or belief (FoRB). The rapidly evolving capabilities of AI often outpace current legal frameworks, resulting in regulatory gaps and ambiguities in accountability. The application of AI ethics principles, including transparency, fairness, and non-maleficence, becomes particularly crucial when addressing sensitive issues like religious pluralism, belief-based expression, and spiritual identity.

Potential Conflicts Between AI and FoRB

Predictive Policing and Religious Expression

Predictive policing tools, which leverage AI to forecast potential criminal activity based on historical and real-time data, have raised significant concerns about their implications for religious freedom. In particular, these systems may disproportionately target religious communities that are already marginalized or perceived as security threats, thereby chilling religious expression and participation. AI-driven surveillance has been deployed to monitor religious gatherings, analyze facial and biometric data of worshippers, and flag individuals attending places of worship—actions that can violate both privacy and FoRB rights (Feldstein, 2019).

Such predictive systems, trained on biased or incomplete datasets, risk embedding systemic prejudices against certain faith groups, such as Muslims, Sikhs, or other religious minorities. When AI systems use religious affiliation as a proxy for potential radicalization, it reinforces harmful stereotypes and undermines the presumption of innocence, a cornerstone of both ethical AI use and human rights law (Eubanks, 2018). The result is a conflict between the technological aims of predictive safety and the constitutional and moral obligation to protect religious liberty.

AI in Content Moderation vs. Freedom of Religious Speech

Content moderation algorithms used by social media platforms and other digital services often fail to distinguish between hate speech and legitimate religious discourse. These AI systems, which are tasked with removing harmful content, are not always equipped with the cultural, linguistic, or theological nuance necessary to accurately interpret religious expression (Gorwa, Binns, & Katzenbach, 2020).

Hence, sermons, prayers, or religious commentary - particularly from non-dominant faiths - may be erroneously flagged or removed.

This can have a disproportionate effect on religious communities that rely heavily on online platforms for outreach and worship, especially during crises like the COVID-19 pandemic. The absence of human oversight in many content moderation decisions amplifies this issue, leaving users with limited avenues for appeal or clarification. While the intent of content moderation is often to reduce harm and hate, without sufficient transparency and cultural competency, it risks suppressing legitimate religious expression and further marginalizing vulnerable communities.

Table 1. Potential conflicts between AI and FoRB

AI Application	Description	FoRB Conflict	Key Concerns
Predictive Policing	AI forecasts criminal activity based on past data	Targets marginalized religious groups	Religious profiling, loss of privacy, biased datasets, surveillance of worshippers
AI-driven Surveillance	Monitors religious gatherings, uses facial/ biometric data	Suppresses religious participation	Chilling effect on freedom of worship, erosion of privacy
Content Moderation Algorithms	Automated removal of harmful or offensive online content	Misclassification of legitimate religious speech	Lack of theological nuance, cultural insensitivity, overreach, censorship of non-dominant faiths
Platform Dependence for Worship	Online worship spaces increasingly reliant on algorithm-driven platforms	Content moderation affects religious access	Disproportionate impact on religious minorities, limited appeal mechanisms

Regulatory Gaps and Challenges

Existing Legal Protections vs. Technological Capabilities

The right to religious freedom is guaranteed by several legal systems worldwide, including the United States' First Amendment and Article 18 of the Universal Declaration of Human Rights. The capabilities and repercussions of AI technology may not be fully addressed by these legal rules, which were designed before the digital era. Algorithmic profiling, data collection from religious material, and the automation of belief-based decision-making are all areas that conventional legal safeguards fail to address.

This misalignment creates a significant regulatory gap, where AI systems can influence or infringe upon religious rights without clear mechanisms for accountability or redress. Legal scholars argue that the current reactive, fragmented approach to AI regulation is ill-suited to handle such nuanced and evolving challenges, especially when transnational platforms and surveillance tools are involved (Brkan, 2019).

The global nature of AI applications complicates legal accountability. A content moderation algorithm developed in one country may censor religious speech in another where such expression is protected. Cross-border data flows and jurisdictional inconsistencies further hinder effective governance, highlighting the urgent need for harmonized international standards.

Accountability in AI Systems Affecting Belief-Based Decisions

AI systems that make or influence decisions based on religious belief - whether in employment, access to services, or surveillance - must be subject to strict accountability mechanisms. Most current AI systems lack meaningful transparency, explainability, and human oversight. This is particularly problematic when algorithms influence high-stakes outcomes, such as religious asylum determinations, employment discrimination cases, or decisions related to religious accommodations (Wachter et al., 2017).

The "black box" nature of many AI models means that affected individuals may not understand why or how their religious affiliation played a role in an algorithmic decision. This opacity not only erodes public trust but also makes it difficult to challenge unjust or biased outcomes, undermining procedural fairness and access to justice.

Table 2. Regulatory gaps and challenges in addressing AI and FoRB

Issue	Current Status	Gap/Challenge	Implications
Legal Protections (e.g., UDHR, 1st Amendment)	Enshrined in constitutions and international law	Designed for pre-digital era, not aligned with AI capabilities	Inadequate coverage of profiling, automated decision-making, surveillance
Transnational AI Platforms	Operate across jurisdictions	Regulatory inconsistency and jurisdictional conflicts	Religious speech censored globally based on foreign norms
Algorithmic Decision-Making in Religion	AI used in asylum, hiring, and service access	Lack of transparency and oversight	Procedural unfairness, hidden discrimination, difficulty appealing biased outcomes
Accountability Mechanisms	Limited or non-existent in many AI deployments	AI decisions difficult to audit or explain	Public distrust, legal ambiguity, barriers to justice

Human Rights, AI Ethics, and Religious Pluralism

Applying AI Ethics Principles in Religious Contexts

To address the ethical challenges of AI in religious contexts, developers and policymakers must apply core AI ethics principles—such as transparency, fairness, and non-maleficence—in ways that are sensitive to religious diversity and pluralism.

Transparency demands that AI systems be auditable and explainable, particularly when they impact belief-based expression. Users should be informed when AI is moderating religious content or analyzing religious behavior, and they should have access to clear appeal processes.

Fairness requires the mitigation of algorithmic bias that may disadvantage religious minorities. This involves diverse training data, culturally aware model design, and inclusive testing across different religious traditions and languages (Binns, 2018). Ethical AI must ensure that no group is disproportionately harmed or misrepresented due to algorithmic decisions.

Non-maleficence, or "do no harm," obliges designers and regulators to proactively assess and prevent harms associated with AI use in religious domains. This includes avoiding the deployment of AI in ways that enable discrimination, erode spiritual autonomy, or incite interreligious tension.

Importantly, these principles must be embedded within an overarching commitment to religious pluralism - the recognition and respect for diverse belief systems. AI governance models should not privilege dominant religious narratives or secular assumptions but must instead uphold the right of individuals and communities to express, practice, and develop their beliefs freely.

Table 3. AI ethics principles in religious contexts

AI Ethics Principle	Application in Religious Context	Specific Recommendations	Goal
Transparency	AI systems affecting religion must be explainable and auditable	Notify users when AI moderates religious content or behavior; provide clear appeals	Promote informed consent, procedural clarity
Fairness	Ensure algorithms do not disadvantage religious minorities	Use diverse training data; test for bias across faith groups; include theological experts	Prevent systemic bias and unequal treatment
Non-maleficence	AI should avoid harming spiritual autonomy or inciting religious conflict	Conduct ethical risk assessments; limit harmful deployments (e.g., religious profiling)	Preserve dignity, autonomy, and peaceful coexistence
Religious Pluralism	Respect and uphold the diversity of belief systems in AI design and policy	Avoid privileging dominant or secular views; support pluralistic frameworks	Ensure equal rights and cultural sensitivity in digital religious spaces

The ethical and legal considerations of AI's interaction with religion are multifaceted and urgent. Predictive policing and automated content moderation risk infringing on religious expression and participation. Legal frameworks lag behind the technological capabilities of AI, creating vulnerabilities for religious communities - especially minorities. A robust ethical approach grounded in human rights principles and attuned to the realities of religious pluralism is essential. As AI continues to shape the digital and societal landscape, proactive governance, inclusive design, and rights-based regulation are critical to ensuring that freedom of religion or belief is not a casualty of technological progress.

CASE SCENARIOS AND FUTURE POSSIBILITIES

As artificial intelligence (AI) continues to mature and infiltrate domains previously governed by human intuition and cultural tradition, its potential roles in spiritual and religious contexts demand critical attention. Both hypothetical and real-world scenarios illustrate the complex dualities - opportunity and risk, empowerment and control - embedded in AI's integration with belief systems. From AI-powered spiritual chatbots to government surveillance of religious gatherings, the implications for civil liberties, freedom of religion or belief (FoRB), and cultural integrity are profound and far-reaching.

AI-Powered Chatbot as a Spiritual Guide

Imagine a highly sophisticated AI chatbot trained on theological texts, spiritual philosophies, and ethical teachings from a wide range of religious and spiritual traditions. This AI, branded as a "universal spiritual guide," becomes widely accessible through smartphones and smart speakers. It offers daily prayers, meditation routines, scriptural explanations, and even advice on moral dilemmas tailored to individual users' belief systems.

Benefits of such a system include enhanced accessibility to spiritual resources, especially for those in remote or secular environments who lack access to traditional religious institutions. It can serve as a supportive tool for spiritual exploration, interfaith understanding, and even mental health, especially when integrated with affective computing technologies that allow the chatbot to respond empathetically to users' emotional states (McStay, 2020).

Risks are equally significant. First, there is the problem of epistemological authority—users may over-rely on AI-generated spiritual guidance, mistaking algorithmic interpretations for divine or doctrinal truths. This challenges the role of religious leaders and scholars who interpret sacred texts within specific socio-cultural contexts. Second, such a chatbot could become a vehicle for ideological manipulation, especially if developed by actors with commercial, political, or theological agendas. The system's design choices - such as prioritizing certain faiths over others or filtering controversial interpretations - may invisibly steer users' beliefs (O'Neil, 2016).

The data privacy implications are grave. Users disclosing personal beliefs, confessions, or spiritual concerns to a digital entity open themselves up to surveillance, profiling, or exploitation - particularly in regions where religious expression is sensitive or criminalized.

Government Use of AI to Monitor Minority Religious Gatherings

In a hypothetical nation grappling with interreligious tensions, the government deploys AI-enabled drones and surveillance software to monitor all public gatherings for "security" purposes. Minority religious groups, particularly those deemed politically or socially subversive, find their events disproportionately targeted. Facial recognition systems and behavioral analysis tools log attendance, record interactions, and detect anomalies.

Implications for civil liberties are deeply troubling. Such surveillance violates not only the right to privacy but also FoRB as outlined in Article 18 of the Universal Declaration of Human Rights (United Nations, 1948). When individuals fear that their religious participation may lead to government scrutiny, job discrimination, or social exclusion, it constitutes a form of chilling effect on religious expression (Feldstein, 2019).

Algorithmic errors - such as false positives in identifying "suspicious" behavior - could lead to wrongful arrests or persecution. These systems often lack transparency and accountability, making it difficult for citizens to challenge their classification or seek redress. If such technologies become normalized, democratic societies risk sliding toward **digital authoritarianism**, where AI enforces ideological conformity under the guise of national security (Mozur, 2019).

AI in Content Recommendation and Radicalization

AI-driven recommendation systems, used by platforms such as YouTube and Facebook, play a pivotal role in shaping user engagement with spiritual, ideological, and religious content. These algorithms are designed to maximize watch time and interaction, often pushing users toward more emotionally charged or extreme content.

While some individuals report positive spiritual transformations after engaging with religious videos or guided meditations discovered through recommendations, the same algorithms have also been implicated in cases of online radicalization. Users seeking content on spirituality or religion may be funneled into echo chambers that reinforce sectarian ideologies or even promote hate speech and conspiracy theories (Tufekci, 2018).

This dynamic underscore the ethical tension between personalization and manipulation. The line between enabling spiritual discovery and engineering ideological outcomes is thin—and often crossed. Regulatory oversight remains minimal, and the lack of algorithmic transparency makes it difficult to understand how religious content is being filtered, promoted, or suppressed (Gorwa, Binns, & Katzenbach, 2020).

Social Robots in Religious Ceremonies and Caregiving

Social robots are increasingly being used in religious and spiritual contexts, particularly in East Asia and parts of Europe. In Japan, robots like "Pepper" have been programmed to perform Buddhist funeral rites, chant sutras, and interact with mourners. In Christian contexts, robotic prayer assistants and sermon bots are being explored to support congregational life, especially in aging or rural communities (Gonzâlez, 2020).

In caregiving settings, robots that integrate spiritual caregiving - offering religious music, guided prayer, or scriptural readings - are being trialed in elderly care homes. These innovations highlight the potential benefits of integrating AI into spiritual caregiving, such as reducing loneliness, enhancing spiritual well-being, and maintaining ritual continuity where human clergy are unavailable.

Critics question the authenticity of robotic spirituality and warn of ritual commodification. Replacing human spiritual leadership with machines risks reducing sacred rituals to mechanical performances, stripping them of emotional resonance and communal meaning. There is also the risk of technological determinism, where religious institutions may feel pressured to adopt AI innovations to remain "relevant," even if they conflict with theological principles (Coeckelbergh, 2020).

These case scenarios and real-world examples reveal a spectrum of possibilities in the convergence of AI and religion—from empowering new forms of spiritual engagement to threaten civil liberties and eroding traditional religious authority. The AI-powered spiritual chatbot offers inclusiveness and accessibility but raises deep concerns about epistemological integrity and data ethics. State surveillance of religious gatherings illustrates the risks of digital repression. Meanwhile, real-world instances of algorithmic content recommendation and social robots in religious life highlight the complex interplay of commercialization, innovation, and spiritual authenticity.

As the boundary between the sacred and the synthetic blurs, it is essential for policymakers, religious leaders, technologists, and ethicists to work collaboratively.

The goal must be to ensure that AI technologies serve to enhance—not erode—freedom of religion or belief in an increasingly digital world.

STRATEGIES FOR PREPAREDNESS AND RESILIENCE

As artificial intelligence (AI) becomes increasingly integrated into societal, political, and spiritual landscapes, its influence on belief systems and religious freedoms demands preemptive strategies. Preparedness and resilience must go beyond reactive measures to proactive design, ethical consideration, and inclusive dialogue. This section outlines four essential strategies: multistakeholder engagement, designing AI with religious literacy, fostering education and digital literacy among believers, and developing ethical guidelines and safeguards to uphold Freedom of Religion or Belief (FoRB).

Multistakeholder Engagement

To ensure that AI technologies serve rather than subvert religious diversity and FoRB, it is critical to foster inclusive multistakeholder engagement. This includes collaboration among religious leaders, AI developers, ethicists, civil society actors, and policymakers. Each brings a unique and necessary perspective.

Religious leaders offer insights into doctrinal sensitivity, ritual practices, and moral values that can guide AI development in spiritually respectful ways. Their involvement is essential for preventing algorithmic misinterpretations of sacred texts and ensuring that AI does not promote biased or exclusionary views.

Technologists and AI developers, on the other hand, must be sensitized to the social and cultural implications of the systems they build. Without an understanding of religious pluralism and context, they risk embedding unconscious biases or engineering systems that unintentionally marginalize minority beliefs (Boddington, 2017).

Ethicists help interrogate the normative dimensions of AI design and deployment, including what constitutes harm, fairness, and moral accountability. Meanwhile, policymakers play a pivotal role in creating legal infrastructures that can uphold human rights, including FoRB, within digital environments.

Collaborative frameworks like UNESCO's "Recommendation on the Ethics of Artificial Intelligence" (2021) underscore the need for participatory governance in AI systems. Creating formal platforms for these stakeholders to interact - such as interfaith-AI councils, regulatory advisory boards, or ethics review panels - can institutionalize this engagement and lead to more equitable technological outcomes.

Designing AI with Religious Literacy

Another crucial strategy is designing AI systems with religious literacy - the capacity to recognize and respect diverse worldviews, religious practices, and spiritual doctrines. Religious literacy in AI development entails more than avoiding overt offense; it requires actively accounting for the symbolic, ethical, and ritual dimensions of faith in a nuanced manner.

This can be achieved by:

1. **Diverse training data**: Ensuring that datasets used to train AI systems include content from a wide array of religious and cultural backgrounds. This avoids the overrepresentation of dominant traditions and supports more balanced algorithmic outputs (Subrahmanyam, 2025b).
2. **Context-aware natural language processing (NLP)**: Developing AI that can discern theological nuance, historical context, and linguistic subtleties is vital when working with sacred texts or belief-based queries. This reduces the risk of blasphemous or reductive interpretations.
3. **User-centered design**: Engaging believers in the development process allows for customization without commodification. Systems can be built to support diverse expressions of faith while avoiding prescriptive or manipulative functionalities (Latif et al., 2021).

By fostering religious literacy in design, AI technologies can become tools for interreligious dialogue, comparative theology, and spiritual education rather than instruments of misunderstanding or exclusion.

Education and Digital Literacy for Believers

In the face of AI-mediated belief systems, digital literacy and critical engagement are essential for resilience among religious communities. As individuals increasingly turn to digital platforms for spiritual guidance, they must be equipped with the tools to navigate and question algorithms shaping their beliefs.

Digital religious literacy refers to the ability to discern between authentic religious content and AI-generated imitations or ideological propaganda. Believers should understand how recommender systems work, how their data is used, and how to critically evaluate AI-driven spiritual content. Without such skills, there is a risk of over-reliance on AI "prophets," leading to spiritual disempowerment and epistemic confusion (Campbell & Tsuria, 2021).

Religious institutions and educational bodies can play a key role by:

- Incorporating digital ethics and AI awareness into religious education curricula.
- Hosting workshops or online modules that explain algorithmic bias and data privacy.
- Partnering with tech organizations to create resources tailored for spiritual audiences.

The aim is to foster informed autonomy - helping individuals maintain agency in their spiritual journeys, even within AI-mediated environments.

Developing Ethical Guidelines and Safeguards

To prevent future AI developments from infringing on religious rights or freedoms, the establishment of ethical guidelines and safeguards is non-negotiable. These frameworks must align with both international human rights standards and principles of AI ethics.

The right to freedom of thought, conscience, and religion is affirmed in both the Universal Declaration of Human Rights (Article 18) and the International Covenant on Civil and Political Rights (Article 18). When developing, implementing, and overseeing artificial intelligence systems that interact with religious or philosophical tenets, these rights must be considered.

Key ethical principles to embed include:

- **Transparency**: Systems interacting with spiritual or religious content should clearly disclose their artificial nature, data sources, and algorithmic logic to prevent confusion or manipulation.
- **Fairness and Non-Discrimination**: AI systems must treat all belief systems equitably, avoiding favoritism or exclusion, particularly in pluralistic societies.
- **Non-maleficence**: Preventing harm should be a foundational design goal. This includes psychological harm (e.g., algorithmic manipulation), social harm (e.g., stereotyping), and legal harm (e.g., criminalization of certain beliefs).
- **Accountability**: Clear mechanisms must exist for challenging, reviewing, or correcting AI systems that produce biased or harmful outcomes. This is especially critical when AI is used in surveillance, moderation, or policy enforcement contexts (Jobin, Ienca, & Vayena, 2019).

Incorporating these principles into AI policy documents, design codes of conduct, and interfaith charters can offer concrete protections against the misuse of technology in religious life.

The future convergence of AI and belief systems presents both profound opportunities and significant risks. Ensuring preparedness and resilience demands a multi-pronged strategy that includes inclusive engagement, religiously literate design, public education, and ethical safeguards. By anticipating the spiritual dimensions of AI's influence, societies can uphold both technological innovation and fundamental freedoms.

Rather than seeing religion and AI as inherently antagonistic, this approach envisions a constructive coexistence—where belief informs design, technology supports spiritual agency, and governance preserves the sanctity of conscience. The time to build this future is now.

CONCLUSION

As artificial intelligence becomes deeply embedded in the fabric of society, its intersection with belief systems presents both unprecedented challenges and transformative possibilities. Emerging trends—such as Artificial General Intelligence (AGI), brain-computer interfaces (BCIs), and emotion-aware AI—are reshaping not only the processing of information but also the formation, expression, and experience of faith. The proliferation of AI-generated spiritual content, algorithmic prophets, and predictive religious interfaces signifies a new frontier in which belief is increasingly mediated through technological systems.

These developments call for urgent attention to the ways AI may influence epistemology, challenge traditional religious authorities, or fragment belief communities through filter bubbles and hyper-personalization. Equally pressing are concerns surrounding surveillance, religious profiling, and the erosion of privacy—all of which could undermine the foundational human right to Freedom of Religion or Belief (FoRB).

To meet these challenges, proactive governance, ethical foresight, and inclusive dialogue across cultural and spiritual boundaries are imperative. Designing AI systems with religious literacy, fostering digital resilience among believers, and engaging religious leaders in technological policymaking are not optional but essential. Such strategies ensure that AI supports rather than supplants spiritual inquiry, community, and conscience.

The path ahead demands a shared commitment to shaping a future in which AI enhances, rather than erodes, the plurality and dignity of belief. By aligning technological innovation with the values of transparency, fairness, and inclusivity, we can build a digital ecosystem that honors both spiritual autonomy and social cohesion. This is a call to action for scholars, policymakers, technologists, and faith communities alike: to co-create an ethical, respectful, and inclusive digital future for all expressions of human spirituality.

REFERENCES

Bender, E. M., Gebru, T., McMillan-Major, A., & Shmitchell, S. (2021). On the dangers of stochastic parrots: Can language models be too big? In *Proceedings of the 2021 ACM Conference on Fairness, Accountability, and Transparency* (pp. 610–623). DOI: 10.1145/3442188.3445922

Binns, R. (2018). Fairness in machine learning: Lessons from political philosophy. *Proceedings of the 2018 Conference on Fairness, Accountability and Transparency*, 149–159.

Boddington, P. (2017). *Towards a code of ethics for artificial intelligence*. Springer. DOI: 10.1007/978-3-319-60648-4

Bostrom, N. (2014). *Superintelligence: Paths, dangers, strategies*. Oxford University Press.

Brkan, M. (2019). Artificial intelligence and human rights: A business and human rights perspective. *Cambridge International Law Journal*, *8*(2), 241–258.

Campbell, H. A. (2017). *Digital religion: Understanding religious practice in new media worlds*. Routledge.

Campbell, H. A., & Tsuria, R. (2021). *Digital religion: Understanding religious practice in digital media*. Routledge. DOI: 10.4324/9780429295683

Coeckelbergh, M. (2020). *AI ethics*. MIT Press. DOI: 10.7551/mitpress/12549.001.0001

Eisenstein, E. L. (1979). *The printing press as an agent of change*. Cambridge University Press.

Eubanks, V. (2018). *Automating inequality: How high-tech tools profile, police, and punish the poor*. St. Martin's Press.

Feldstein, S. (2019). *The global expansion of AI surveillance*. Carnegie Endowment for International Peace.

Floridi, L., Cowls, J., Beltrametti, M., Chatila, R., Chazerand, P., Dignum, V., Luetge, C., Madelin, R., Pagallo, U., Rossi, F., Schafer, B., Valcke, P., & Vayena, E. (2018). AI4People—An ethical framework for a good AI society: Opportunities, risks, principles, and recommendations. *Minds and Machines*, *28*(4), 689–707. DOI: 10.1007/s11023-018-9482-5

Goertzel, B., & Pennachin, C. (Eds.). (2007). *Artificial general intelligence*. Springer. DOI: 10.1007/978-3-540-68677-4

González, F. (2020). Robot priests and funeral rituals: When technology meets religion. *Religion and Digital Society*, *12*(1), 21–35.

Gorwa, R., Binns, R., & Katzenbach, C. (2020). Algorithmic content moderation: Technical and political challenges in the automation of platform governance. *Big Data & Society*, *7*(1), 2053951719897945. DOI: 10.1177/2053951719897945

Harari, Y. N. (2018). *21 lessons for the 21st century*. Spiegel & Grau.

Heidegger, M. (1977). *The question concerning technology and other essays* (W. Lovitt, Trans.). Harper & Row.

Ienca, M., & Andorno, R. (2017). Towards new human rights in the age of neuroscience and neurotechnology. *Life Sciences, Society and Policy*, *13*(1), 5. DOI: 10.1186/s40504-017-0050-1

Jobin, A., Ienca, M., & Vayena, E. (2019). The global landscape of AI ethics guidelines. *Nature Machine Intelligence*, *1*(9), 389–399. DOI: 10.1038/s42256-019-0088-2

Kurzweil, R. (2005). *The singularity is near: When humans transcend biology*. Viking.

Latif, S., Qayyum, A., Usama, M., Qadir, J., & Williams, M. J. (2021). Artificial intelligence for religious studies: The potential and the risks. *AI & Society*, *36*(1), 123–135.

Lebedev, M. A., & Nicolelis, M. A. (2017). Brain-machine interfaces: From basic science to neuroprostheses and neurorehabilitation. *Physiological Reviews*, *97*(2), 767–837. DOI: 10.1152/physrev.00027.2016

McCormack, J., Gifford, T., & Hutchings, P. (2022). The Rise of AI Religions: Spiritual Implications of Autonomous Text and Ritual. *AI & Society*.

McStay, A. (2020). *Emotional AI: The rise of empathic media*. SAGE Publications.

Mozur, P. (2019). One month, 500,000 face scans: How China is using A.I. to profile a minority. *The New York Times*. https://www.nytimes.com

O'Callaghan, D., Greene, D., Conway, M., Carthy, J., & Cunningham, P. (2015). Down the (white) rabbit hole: The extreme right and online recommender systems. *Social Science Computer Review*, *33*(4), 459–478. DOI: 10.1177/0894439314555329

O'Neil, C. (2016). *Weapons of math destruction: How big data increases inequality and threatens democracy*. Crown Publishing.

OHCHR. (1966). *International Covenant on Civil and Political Rights*. United Nations. https://www.ohchr.org/en/instruments-mechanisms/instruments/international-covenant-civil-and-political-rights

Pariser, E. (2011). *The filter bubble: What the Internet is hiding from you*. Penguin Press.

Picard, R. W. (1997). *Affective computing*. MIT Press. DOI: 10.7551/mit-press/1140.001.0001

Russell, S., & Norvig, P. (2021). *Artificial intelligence: A modern approach* (4th ed.). Pearson.

Subrahmanyam, S. (2025a). Integrating AI and AR Into Teaching and Scholarly Communication. In Vrba, J., & Huynh, T. (Eds.), *Revolutionizing Academic Research With AI and Augmented Reality* (pp. 179–212). IGI Global Scientific Publishing. DOI: 10.4018/979-8-3373-1414-3.ch006

Subrahmanyam, S. (2025b). Qualitative Research Designs in Higher Education. In Mdikana, A. (Ed.), *Social Implications of Research in Higher Education* (pp. 263–296). IGI Global Scientific Publishing. DOI: 10.4018/979-8-3373-0654-4.ch010

Tegmark, M. (2017). *Life 3.0: Being human in the age of artificial intelligence*. Penguin.

Tufekci, Z. (2018). YouTube, the great radicalizer. *The New York Times*. https://www.nytimes.com

Turek, M. (2020). Theological ethics and artificial intelligence: New challenges and responses. *Ethics and Information Technology*, *22*(3), 163–174.

UN. (1948). *Universal Declaration of Human Rights*. United Nations General Assembly. https://www.un.org/en/about-us/universal-declaration-of-human-rights

UNESCO. (2021). *Recommendation on the ethics of artificial intelligence*. https://unesdoc.unesco.org

UNHRC. (2020). *Freedom of thought report*. United Nations Human Rights Council.

United Nations. (1948). *Universal Declaration of Human Rights*. https://www.un.org/en/about-us/universal-declaration-of-human-rights

Wachter, S., Mittelstadt, B., & Floridi, L. (2017). Transparent, explainable, and accountable AI for the public sector. *Computer*, *50*(5), 56–65.

Zuboff, S. (2019). *The age of surveillance capitalism: The fight for a human future at the new frontier of power*. PublicAffairs.

KEY TERM AND DEFINITIONS

AI-Driven Sociotechnical Systems: These are systems where AI is integrated into social and technical infrastructures to influence decision-making and behavior. In religious life, such systems may impact access to worship spaces, religious education, and communal practices through automated moderation or surveillance.

AI-Human Symbiosis: This term describes the close collaboration between humans and AI in cognitive, emotional, or decision-making processes. In religious contexts, it raises questions about the role of AI as a spiritual co-agent or advisor.

Algorithmic Spiritual Leadership: The emergence of AI systems that function as spiritual leaders—offering guidance, rituals, or doctrinal advice—presents a paradigm shift in religious authority and community dynamics, often challenging traditional clergy roles.

Artificial General Intelligence (AGI): AGI refers to a theoretical form of artificial intelligence that possesses the ability to understand, learn, and apply knowledge across a wide range of tasks at a human or superhuman level. Unlike narrow AI, AGI could independently engage in theological reasoning or moral deliberation, impacting religious and philosophical discourse.

Belief-Shaping Algorithms: These are AI algorithms that subtly influence user beliefs and values through curated content, predictive suggestions, or emotional manipulation. They can shift moral and religious outlooks, often without user awareness.

Digital Rituals: These are religious or spiritual practices facilitated or mediated through digital technologies, including AI. Examples include AI-led meditation, virtual prayer gatherings, or automated sacraments, which provoke debates about legitimacy, embodiment, and sacred presence.

Digital Syncretism: Digital syncretism is the blending of diverse religious and spiritual traditions through online platforms or AI interfaces. It challenges traditional theological boundaries and creates new, often customizable, belief systems.

Emotion AI: A subset of affective computing, emotion AI is designed to detect human emotions through facial expressions, voice tone, and physiological signals. In faith contexts, it can be applied to enhance spiritual experiences or monitor emotional engagement during religious activities.

Freedom of Religion or Belief (FoRB): FoRB is a fundamental human right enshrined in international law, including Article 18 of the Universal Declaration of Human Rights, granting individuals the freedom to practice, change, or abstain from religion or belief without coercion. Emerging AI technologies pose new threats and opportunities for FoRB.

Hyper-Personalization: This refers to the use of AI to tailor content and experiences to individual preferences based on behavioral data. In religious life, hyper-personalization can lead to fragmented belief systems, "religion-as-a-service" models and potentially reinforce echo chambers.

Neuro-Symbolic AI: This approach combines the learning capabilities of neural networks with the reasoning strengths of symbolic AI. In religious domains, it could potentially simulate theological reasoning or analyze complex belief structures.

Religious Profiling: Religious profiling involves identifying or discriminating against individuals based on perceived religious affiliation using AI tools such as facial recognition, voice analysis, or online behavior monitoring. It threatens FoRB, particularly in authoritarian regimes.

Chapter 4
Building Human Rights by Design: Ethical AI Development for Religious Freedom

Kannan Kunnathully
https://orcid.org/0000-0001-6467-2146
Vinayaka Mission's Law School, Vinayaka Mission's Research Foundation, Chennai, India

M. Jinesh
https://orcid.org/0009-0008-9891-691X
School of Law, Vels Institute of Science, Technology, and Advanced Studies, Chennai, India

Pamarthi Satyanarayana
https://orcid.org/0009-0008-4041-3674
VEL TECH University, India

V. Esther
https://orcid.org/0009-0002-5956-7397
Saveetha Institute of Medical and Technical Sciences, India

Ganesh Pathak
https://orcid.org/0000-0003-0427-2145
Sri Balaji University, Pune, India

P. Selvakumar
https://orcid.org/0000-0002-3650-4548
Department of Science and Humanities, Nehru Institute of Technology, Coimbatore, India

T. C. Manjunath
https://orcid.org/0000-0003-2545-9160
Rajarajeswari College of Engineering, India

ABSTRACT

Human rights by design is an emerging framework that seeks technological systems that respect and uphold the diversity of beliefs and practices in global societies.AI-driven technologies, from automated decision-making to content moderation systems, increasingly influence individuals' ability to practice and express their religious beliefs.

DOI: 10.4018/979-8-3373-3830-9.ch004

However, concerns have arisen regarding biases in AI algorithms, the suppression of religious content on digital platforms, in this domain require a robust framework that prioritizes human dignity, non-discrimination, and the protection of fundamental freedoms. To ensure AI systems respect religious freedom and broader human rights, designers and policymakers must address several core issues: perspectives, reinforce stereotypes, or disadvantage certain faith-based communities. Ongoing audits, diverse data representation, Automated moderation systems deployed by social media platforms often struggle to differentiate between harmful content and legitimate religious discourse.

INTRODUCTION TO HUMAN RIGHTS BY DESIGN: THE INTERSECTION OF AI, ETHICS, AND RELIGIOUS FREEDOM

Human rights by design is an emerging framework that seeks technological systems that respect and uphold the diversity of beliefs and practices in global societies.AI-driven technologies, from automated decision-making to content moderation systems, increasingly influence individuals' ability to practice and express their religious beliefs. However, concerns have arisen regarding biases in AI algorithms, the suppression of religious content on digital platforms, in this domain require a robust framework that prioritizes human dignity, non-discrimination, and the protection of fundamental freedoms.Key Considerations in Human Rights by DesignTo ensure AI systems respect religious freedom and broader human rights, designers and policymakers must address several core issues: perspectives, reinforce stereotypes, or disadvantage certain faith-based communities. Ongoing audits, diverse data representation, and bias mitigation strategies are essential for fairness(Azenkot et al., 2011).. Freedom of Expression and Content Moderation: (Azenkot et al., 2011) Automated moderation systems deployed by social media platforms often struggle to differentiate between harmful content and legitimate religious discourse. There is a need for transparent content moderation policies that protect free expression while preventing online hate speech and discrimination.. Privacy and Surveillance Concerns: AI-powered surveillance tools have been used to track religious groups, raising concerns about mass surveillance and the infringement of privacy rights. Safeguards must be put in place to prevent the misuse of AI for oppressive purposes. Inclusive AI Development: AI ethics guidelines should involve religious and ethical scholars, human rights organizations, and diverse communities in decision-making processes to ensure that religious freedoms are protected in digital environments. to prevent the erosion of fundamental rights in the digital age. rights by design principles. Ethical AI governance should incorporate diverse cultural and religious perspectives, ensuring that technological advancements contribute to a more inclusive and rights-respecting global society.y design(Barocas and Selbst, 2016). By embedding(Beck et al., 2001) fundamental rights into AI systems from the outset, policymakers, technologists, and human rights advocates can work together to create a future where technological progress aligns with ethical values and religious freedoms remain protected in the digital era.I've expanded the introduction to cover the intersection of AI, ethics, and religious freedom within the human rights by design framework. Let me know if you'd like any refinements or additional insights!

The Importance of Religious Freedom in the Digital Age: Challenges and Opportunities

where communication, social interaction, and even religious practices increasingly take place online, ensuring the protection of religious freedom has become more complex and urgent. While digital platforms dialogue, they also introduce significant challenges related to censorship, bias, surveillance, and discrimination. Content Moderation and Censorship: (Beck et al., 2001)Social media platforms and search engines use AI-driven content moderation systems to detect and remove harmful content. However, these systems sometimes misclassify religious speech as hate speech, extremism, or misinformation, leading to the unjust suppression of religious voices. The lack of transparency in moderation policies and algorithmic decision-making further exacerbates the issue..(Barocas & Selbst, 2016) This is particularly concerning in automated hiring processes, advertising algorithms, and social media content ranking systems, where religious affiliation or beliefs may unintentionally affect outcomes..(Broeders et al., 2017) Digital Surveillance and Privacy Violations: Governments and private entities increasingly use AI-powered surveillance technologies to monitor religious communities, sometimes under the pretext of national security. discourse, they have also become spaces where religious minorities face cyber harassment, threats, and organized misinformation campaigns. Addressing these challenges requires more robust protections against digital discrimination while safeguarding free expression. The digital divide, particularly in developing regions, limits the ability of marginalized religious groups to engage in online discourse, access virtual religious services, or connect with broader faith-based communities. Interfaith Dialogue and Global Connectivity:(Broeders et al., 2017) Digital platforms enable unprecedented levels of interfaith communication and collaboration. Social media, virtual events, and online forums provide opportunities for diverse religious groups to engage in meaningful dialogue, reducing misunderstandings and fostering mutual respect.. AI for Inclusive Religious Expression: AI can be leveraged to develop tools that promote religious diversity and inclusion. For example, AI-driven translation services can help make religious texts accessible to a broader audience, and sentiment analysis tools can identify and addressreligious discrimination in online spaces.. Decentralized and Secure Religious Practices: Blockchain technology and decentralized platforms offer new ways for religious communities to practice their faith securely, free from governmental or corporate interference. Secure digital identities can help individuals access religious services while protecting their privacy..(Cavoukian, 2008) Ethical AI Governance and Human Rights by Design: By integrating religious freedom protections into AI governance frameworks, policymakers and technology companies can develop more ethical and transparent systems that respect diverse faith traditions.(Cavoukian, 2008) This includes refining content moderation policies, ensuring algorithmic fairness, and strengthening data protection laws. Digital Advocacy and Awareness Campaigns: Religious organizations, human rights groups, and civil society actors can harness digital tools to advocate for religious freedom. Online petitions, social media campaigns, and digital storytelling can bring global attention to religious persecution and promote policies that protect faith-based rights., and human rights. This requires increased transparency in AI decision-making, stronger legal frameworks for protecting online religious expression, and greater public awareness of digital rights and freedoms.

The Role of AI in Shaping Religious Freedom: Benefits, Risks, and Ethical Considerations

AI-driven technologies influence religious expression, access to faith-based content, and interactions within religious communities. While AI presents numerous benefits, such as increased accessibility to religious knowledge and enhanced interfaith dialogue, it also introduces significant risks, including algorithmic bias, digital censorship, and surveillance. Understanding the complex role AI plays in shaping religious freedom requires careful examination of its benefits, risks, and ethical considerations.(Citron and Pasquale, 2014)Benefits of AI in Promoting Religious Freedom. Enhanced Accessibility to Religious Texts and Teachings: AI-powered translation and transcription tools enable wider access to religious scriptures, sermons, and teachings in multiple languages, making religious knowledge more inclusive and available to diverse populations.(Citron & Pasquale, 2014) AI-Driven Personalization for Faith-Based Content: Recommendation algorithms on digital platforms help users discover religious content tailored to their beliefs and interests, fostering deeper engagement with faith-based materials and communities.. Interfaith Dialogue and Digital Inclusivity: AI-driven chatbots and virtual assistants facilitate discussions on religious topics, helping bridge gaps between different faith communities and encouraging interfaith understanding.. Automated Religious Services and Virtual Worship: AI enhances religious experiences through virtual congregations, prayer assistants, and automated sermon generation, enabling people to practice their faith remotely, especially in times of crisis or geographical constraints..(Davis and Nathan, 2015) Protection(Davis & Nathan, 2015) Against Religious Discrimination Online: AI-based monitoring tools help detect and prevent online hate speech, misinformation, and targeted harassment against religious groups, contributing to a safer digital space for faith-based discussions. religious discourse as hate speech or extremist content, leading to the wrongful suppression of religious voices on social media and digital platforms. Digital Censorship and Content Manipulation: Governments and private entities can use AI to control the visibility of religious perspectives, either by promoting specific ideologies or restricting access to faith-based materials that challenge dominant narratives.urveillance and Targeting of Religious Communities: AI-powered surveillance technologies have been used to monitor religious groups, track faith-based activities, and identify individuals based on religious affiliations, raising serious privacy and human rights concerns.. Deepfake and Misinformation Risks: AI-generated deepfake videos and synthetic religious content can be used to spread misinformation, manipulate religious teachings, or incite religious conflicts, potentially undermining trust within faith communities.

Designing AI Systems that Respect Religious Freedom: Principles, Guidelines, and Best Practices

Designing AI systems that respect religious freedom requires a structured approach that incorporates ethical principles, practical guidelines, and best practices to mitigate risks such as bias, censorship, and surveillance while fostering inclusivity and fairness.Principles for AI Systems that Uphold Religious Freedom.(Eykholt et al., 2018) Non-Discrimination and Fairness: AI systems should be designed to treat all religious beliefs equitably, avoiding biases that favor or disadvantage specific faith communities.. Transparency and Explainability: AI algorithms should be transparent in how they process religious content, ensuring users understand how information is prioritized, moderated, or filtered.. Privacy and Data Protection: AI should not be used to monitor, track, or discriminate against individuals based on religious beliefs. Strong privacy safeguards must be in place to prevent the misuse of religious data.(Eykholt et al., 2018) Freedom of Expression: AI content moderation systems should distinguish between legitimate religious discourse and harmful speech, ensuring that faith-based expressions are not unfairly suppressed.. Inclusivity and Representation: Faith-based communities should be involved in the AI development process to ensure that diverse religious perspectives are reflected in system design. Ethical AI Governance: Governments, tech companies, and human rights organizations should establish oversight mechanisms to ensure AI upholds religious freedoms without being used for discrimination or repression. Consultation with Religious (Flanagan et al., 2008)Experts and Ethicists: Collaborate with theologians, ethicists, and religious leaders to assess how AI policies affect religious expression and freedom.. Balanced Content Moderation Policies: Develop AI moderation guidelines that prevent hate speech while protecting legitimate religious discussions and practices.. Data Minimization Practices: Avoid unnecessary collection of religious affiliation data and implement strict consent protocols for data usage.. Accessible and Inclusive AI Design: Ensure AI tools accommodate religious needs, such as supporting diverse linguistic, cultural, and doctrinal interpretations.. User Control and Appeal Mechanisms: (Vijayakumar et al., 2024)Provide users with mechanisms to challenge AI decisions that restrict religious content or participation in faith-based discussions. Training AI with Diverse Religious Data: Incorporate datasets that reflect a broad spectrum of religious traditions, texts, and cultural perspectives to improve AI's ability to interpret faith-based content accurately.. Developing AI Ethics Committees:(Flanagan et al., 2008) Establish advisory boards with religious scholars, civil rights advocates, and AI researchers to oversee AI's impact on religious freedom.. Building AI Tools for Religious Inclusion: Encourage the development of AI applications that support religious practices, such as language translation for scriptures, virtual prayer assistants, and interfaith dialogue platforms.. Public Reporting and Transparency:(Franzke, 2016) AI developers should release transparency reports detailing how religious content is moderated, flagged, or restricted to promote accountability.. Preventing AI-Enabled Religious Persecution: Governments and international bodies must ensure AI is not used for oppressive purposes, such as profiling religious minorities or restricting access to places of worship.. Promoting Digital Literacy in Religious Communities: Educate religious groups on AI's influence on faith-based interactions and empower them to navigate AI-driven environments responsibly.Future Directions for AI and Religious FreedomAs AI evolves, ongoing research and collaboration among technologists, policymakers, and religious communities will be necessary to refine AI systems that uphold religious freedom. Developing robust regulatory (Wakabayashi, 2018) frameworks, enhancing AI literacy, and fostering interfaith dialogue will be key to ensuring AI remains a tool for empowerment rather than exclusion.I've expanded the discussion on designing AI systems that respect religious freedom, covering key principles, guidelines, and best practices. Let me know if you'd like any refinements!

The Importance of Transparency, Accountability, and Explainability in AI Decision-Making for Religious Freedom

These systems risk reinforcing biases, restricting religious expression, or enabling discrimination against faith communities. Establishing clear standards for transparency, accountability, and explainability can help prevent such negative outcomes while fostering trust in AI systems.

. Clear AI Policies and Guidelines: Organizations deploying AI should publicly disclose how their systems interact with religious content, including content moderation criteria and algorithmic decision-making processes. Open AI Models and Data Sources:(Franzke, 2016) AI systems should be transparent about the datasets used for training and whether they include diverse religious perspectives to prevent algorithmic biases. Content Moderation Transparency Reports: Tech companies should release periodic reports detailing how AI moderates religious content, including statistics on flagged or removed materials User Access to AI Decisions: Users should have access to explanations when their religious content is flagged or restricted, along with clear reasoning for the AI's decision (Gerards, 2019)Public Consultation and Collaboration(Zhu et al., 2018): AI developers should engage religious scholars, ethicists, and civil society organizations in discussions about how AI impacts religious freedom and expression.countability in AI Systems Affecting Religious Freedom. Ethical AI Oversight Bodies: Independent committees consisting of religious leaders, human rights advocates, and AI researchers should monitor how AI impacts religious freedom.. Appeals and Redress Mechanisms: Users must have the ability to challenge AI decisions that negatively impact their religious expression, ensuring a fair review process..(Gerards, 2019) Legal and Regulatory Frameworks: Governments should establish policies that hold AI developers and platforms accountable for AI-related infringements on religious freedom.. Human-in-the-Loop Systems: AI should not operate without human oversight in sensitive cases, particularly when determining the permissibility of religious speech or practices.Ethical Responsibility of AI Developers: Engineers and AI professionals should adhere to ethical guidelines that emphasize human rights and religious freedom in their AI design and deployment. Explainability in AI Decision-Making for Religious Freedom. Interpretable AI Models: AI models should be designed in a way that makes their decision-making logic understandable to users and policymakers.. User-Friendly Explanations: AI systems should provide comprehensible explanations for decisions affecting religious content rather than using opaque technical language.. AI Literacy Programs for Religious Communities: Faith groups should be educated on how AI systems work, how they may impact religious expression, and how to navigate AI-driven environments responsibly.. Algorithmic Bias Audits: Regular assessments should be conducted to identify and mitigate biases in AI that could disproportionately impact religious communities.Future Considerations for AI and Religious(Halbertal, 2015) FreedomAs AI continues to evolve, developing standards for transparency, accountability, and explainability will be crucial for ensuring religious freedom in digital spaces. Ongoing collaboration between governments, tech companies, religious institutions, and civil society organizations will be necessary to create ethical

AI governance frameworks. By prioritizing openness and fairness in AI decision-making, we can protect religious diversity while fostering inclusive and respectful digital environments.religious freedom in the digital age. AI systems that impact religious expression must be designed with ethical safeguards that promote fairness, prevent discrimination, and allow for meaningful human oversight. By fostering a culture of openness and responsibility, AI can be leveraged as a tool for religious inclusivity rather than exclusion, ensuring that faith communities worldwide can freely express their beliefs in an increasingly digitalized world.

Figure 1. Human Rights-Based Approach – AI and Equality

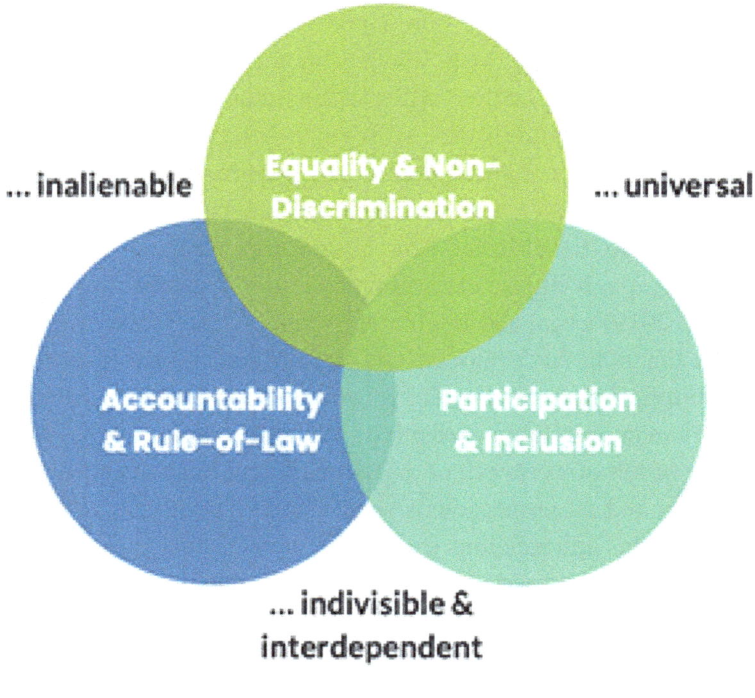

Addressing Bias and Discrimination in AI Systems: Ensuring Fairness and Equality for Religious Minorities

As artificial intelligence increasingly shapes digital interactions, decision-making, and societal norms, concerns regarding bias and discrimination in AI systems have grown. AI-driven platforms, including content moderation systems, (Zuiderveen Borgesius, 2018)facial recognition technologies, and recommendation algorithms, have demonstrated the potential to reinforce existing societal biases, including those affecting religious minorities. Without proactive measures, AI systems may unintentionally marginalize religious communities, restrict access to religious content, or perpetuate stereotypes. Addressing bias and discrimination in(Halbertal, 2015) AI is crucial to ensuring fairness, inclusivity, and equal treatment for religious minorities in an increasingly digital world.. User Interaction Bias: AI systems trained on user-generated content may adopt biases present in online discussions, reinforcing negative stereotypes.. Lack of Representation: If religious minorities are underrepresented in training datasets(Kosinski et al., 2013), AI may struggle to recognize their needs and perspectives accurately.. Automated Content Moderation Bias: AI moderation tools may disproportionately flag religious expressions as inappropriate, leading to suppression of religious discourse.Ensuring Fairness and Equality in AI for Religious Minorities. Diverse and Representative Training Data: AI developers must ensure training datasets include a broad spectrum of religious perspectives to mitigate exclusionary biases.. Bias Audits and Regular Evaluations: Continuous assessment of AI algorithms can help identify and rectify biases that impact religious communities..(Halbertal, 2015) Human Oversight and Ethical Review Boards: AI decisions, particularly those related to content moderation and religious expression, should involve human review to prevent automated dcrimination.. Transparency in AI Decision-Making: Religious communities should have access to explanations regarding AI decisions affecting their content, with clear guidelines for contesting unfair actions. Algorithmic Fairness Testing: AI systems should undergo rigorous testing to measure their impact on religious minorities and ensure equal treatment.. Context-Aware AI Models: AI should be designed to recognize the cultural and religious context of expressions, preventing wrongful suppression of religious discourse.Addressing Discrimination in AI Deployment. Inclusive AI Development Practices: AI teams should include diverse professionals with expertise in religious studies, ethics, and human rights to prevent exclusionary biases.2. Public Collaboration and Stakeholder Engagement: Religious leaders, civil society organizations, and advocacy groups should be involved in discussions about AI's impact on religious freedom.. Equitable Access to AI Benefits: Religious communities should have the opportunity to leverage AI technology for language preservation, education, and cultural expression.nisms to detect and counteract biases that disproportionately affect religious groups.(Kosinski and Wang, 2018) Future Directions in AI Fairness for Religious MinoritieAs AI continues to shape global communication and decision-making, efforts to ensure fairness and equality for religious minorities must evolve.

This requires ongoing research, collaboration, and policy advancements to address emerging challenges. The future of AI fairness includes:. Developing More Ethical AI Standards: AI governance frameworks should prioritize religious inclusivity and non-discrimination.. Enhancing AI Explainability: AI systems should be transparent about their decision-making processes, allowing religious groups to understand how AI impacts their communities.. Promoting AI Literacy Among Religious Communities: Educational initiatives should empower religious groups to engage with AI technologies and advocate for their digital rights.. Leveraging AI for Religious and Cultural Preservation: (Leese, 2014)AI tools should be used to support endangered religious languages, cultural traditions, and historical documentation.. Strengthening Global AI Policy Coordination: International collaboration can help create standardized policies to address bias and discrimination in AI systems worldwide. Digital platforms enable unprecedented levels of interfaith communication and collaboration. Social media, virtual events, and online forums provide opportunities for diverse religious groups to engage in meaningful dialogue, reducing misunderstandings and fostering mutual respect.. AI for Inclusive Religious Expression: AI can be leveraged to develop tools that promote religious diversity and inclusion. For example, AI-driven translation services can help make religious texts accessible to a broader audience, and sentiment analysis tools can identify and addressreligious discrimination in online spaces.. Decentralized and Secure Religious Practices: Blockchain technology and decentralized platforms offer new ways for religious communities to practice their faith securely, free from governmental or corporate interference. Secure digital identities can help individuals access religious services while protecting their privacy. Ethical AI Governance and Human Rights by Design: By integrating religious freedom protections into AI governance frameworks, policymakers and technology companies can develop more ethical and transparent systems that respect diverse faith traditions. This includes refining content moderation policies, ensuring algorithmic fairness, and strengthening data protection laws. Digital Advocacy and Awareness Campaigns: Religious organizations, human rights groups, and civil society actors can harness digital tools to advocate for religious freedom. Online petitions, social media campaigns, and digital storytelling can bring global attention to religious persecution and promote policies that protect faith-based rights., and human rights. This requires increased transparency in AI decision-making, stronger legal frameworks for protecting online religious expression, and greater public awareness of digital rights and freedoms.

Case Study: Developing AI-Powered Tools for Monitoring and Analyzing Religious Freedom Violations

Natural Language Processing (NLP) for Content Analysis: NLP algorithms analyze news reports, government statements, social media discussions, and human rights reports to detect religious discrimination patterns.Sentiment Analysis for Hate Speech Detection: AI tools identify online hate speech and discriminatory narratives targeting religious groups, enabling early intervention and policy recommendations. Geospatial Analysis and Mapping: AI-powered platforms track religious freedom violations geographically, providing real-time visual insights into regions with rising religious intolerance. Machine Learning for Predictive Analytics: AI models process historical data to predict potential religious conflicts or policy changes that may impact religious communities. Automated Data Collection and Classification: AI scrapes and categorizes religious freedom-related content from multiple sources, creating structured datasets for analysis. Facial Recognition and Biometrics for Persecution Monitoring: Some AI tools employ facial recognition technology to document cases of religious persecution, though this raises ethical concerns regarding privacy and misuse.Challenges in Developing AI for Religious Freedom AnalysisWhile AI offers transformative potential in monitoring religious freedom violations, several challenges must be addressed:. Misinformation and Disinformation Detection: AI must differentiate between credible human rights reports and fabricated information, a complex challenge given the rise of deepfake content and propaganda.. Privacy and Data Security: AI-driven monitoring must balance surveillance concerns with ethical data collection practices to protect religious communities at risk.. Linguistic and Cultural Barriers: Religious freedom violations occur in diverse linguistic and cultural contexts, requiring AI models to be trained in multiple languages and cultural nuances.. Government Censorship and Restrictive Policies: In authoritarian regimes, governments may restrict data access, limiting AI's ability to track religious freedom violations.. Ethical Use of AI: AI should be used as a tool for advocacy and transparency, rather than as a means for surveillance or religious profiling by oppressive regimes.Ethical (Leese, 2014)Considerations in AI-Powered Religious Freedom MonitoringEnsuring ethical AI use in religious freedom monitoring requires adherence to key principles:. Transparency and Explainability: AI decision-making processes should be clear and interpretable to avoid unjust accusations or misinterpretations.. Human Oversight and Expert Validation: AI findings must be reviewed by human rights experts and researchers to verify accuracy and prevent misclassification.. Informed Consent and Anonymity: (Kosinski & Wang, 2018)Data collection should prioritize the protection of at-risk religious groups by anonymizing sensitive information.. Preventing AI-Driven Discrimination: AI systems must be designed to detect and mitigate bias rather than reinforce existing discrimination.. Stakeholder Engagement: Collaboration with religious organizations, policymakers, and human rights groups ensures AI development aligns with ethical and legal frameworks.Real-World Applications of AI in Religious Freedom MonitoringAI-powered tools are already being implemented in various human rights initiatives worldwide. Some notable applications include:. The United Nations' AI-Driven Human Rights Analysis: AI models process vast datasets to detect religious freedom violations reported in global human rights documentation.

Example of AI-Driven Initiative for Promoting Interfaith Dialogue and Understanding

This initiative leverages machine learning, natural language processing (NLP), and ethical AI frameworks to enhance mutual respect and cooperation among diverse faith traditions.(Lim et al., 2008)The Interfaith Harmony AI Platform operates as a digital ecosystem where religious scholars, community leaders, and individuals from different faiths can engage in constructive dialogue. It employs sophisticated NLP models that analyze religious texts, interpret sentiments, and generate respectful and inclusive responses. This ensures that conversations remain objective, fact-based, and sensitive to various religious perspectives. Additionally, the AI is trained on a vast corpus of religious and philosophical literature, enabling it to facilitate discussions with historical and theological accuracy.(Sugumaran et al., 2024)A central feature of the platform is its AI-driven moderation system, which detects and mitigates hate speech, misinformation, and inflammatory rhetoric. By utilizing deep learning algorithms, the system identifies potentially harmful content and either flags it for human review or suggests alternative wording to maintain the integrity of discussions. This proactive approach creates a safer environment where individuals can engage in faith-based discussions without fear of harassment or misrepresentation.The platform also incorporates real-time translation tools, allowing participants from different linguistic backgrounds to communicate effortlessly. By leveraging AI-driven speech and text translation technologies, (Mann and Matzner, 2019)the initiative ensures that interfaith dialogues are inclusive and accessible, overcoming language barriers that traditionally hinder global discussions on religion and spirituality.Moreover, AI-powered chatbots and virtual assistants are integrated into the platform to provide instant responses to theological inquiries, clarify misconceptions, and guide users towards scholarly resources. These intelligent agents are programmed to be unbiased and are constantly updated with the latest interfaith research and religious studies, ensuring that the information they provide is accurate and relevant.One of the groundbreaking aspects of the Interfaith Harmony AI Platform is its use of sentiment analysis to gauge the emotional tone of conversations. By analyzing user interactions, the AI can detect signs of hostility, tension, or misunderstanding and intervene with diplomatic prompts or suggest calming narratives.

This feature is particularly useful in de-escalating conflicts and ensuring that interfaith discussions remain productive and respectful.The initiative also hosts AI-curated virtual events, such as interfaith dialogues, webinars, and panel discussions featuring religious leaders, scholars, and activists.(Tubella et al., 2019) The AI helps in selecting topics that resonate with current global religious discourse, curating diverse perspectives, and even moderating sessions to ensure balanced and insightful discussions.Users can engage with interactive courses that explore various religious traditions, historical interfaith movements, and contemporary issues in religious harmony. These courses are tailored to individual learning preferences and provide AI-generated quizzes, discussion prompts, and multimedia content to enhance understanding.Furthermore, the initiative collaborates with religious institutions, universities, and peace organizations to expand its reach and credibility. By integrating AI-driven analytics, the platform provides insights into global interfaith trends, sentiment shifts, and emerging challenges in religious discourse. (Sreenivasulu et al., 2022)These data-driven insights assist policymakers, educators, and religious leaders in shaping strategies for fostering interfaith cooperation and combating religious intolerance groundbreaking discussions on AI ethics, religious values, and moral considerations in technology, paving the way for more inclusive and ethically sound AI development.Challenges remain in the implementation of AI-driven interfaith initiatives, including biases in AI training data, ethical concerns regarding automation in religious discussions, and resistance from traditional religious communities. However, through continuous improvement, human (Van de Poel, 2013)oversight, and ethical AI development, initiatives like the Interfaith Harmony AI Platform are demonstrating how technology can serve as a bridge rather than a barrier in fostering global religious understanding.In conclusion, AI-driven initiatives for interfaith dialogue and understanding represent a significant advancement in leveraging technology for social good. By integrating AI with theological discourse, these initiatives promote a more inclusive, respectful, and knowledge-driven approach to religious conversations. As AI continues to evolve, its potential to foster peace and unity among diverse faith communities will only grow, making interfaith harmony an achievable goal in the digital age.

Challenges and Limitations of Ethical AI Development for Religious Freedom: Addressing Technical, Social, and Cultural Concerns

The development of ethical artificial intelligence (AI) for promoting religious freedom presents numerous challenges and limitations that span technical, social, and cultural dimensions. While AI has the potential to foster interfaith dialogue, protect religious minorities, and counteract religious discrimination, it also raises critical concerns regarding bias, ethical governance, and cultural sensitivities. Addressing these concerns requires a multidisciplinary approach that incorporates technological advancements, social awareness, and policy interventions religious affiliation data must ensure robust security measures to prevent misuse or surveillance. (Vijayakumar et al., 2024)In some regions, governments or organizations may exploit AI-generated data to monitor religious groups, leading to increased persecution or suppression of religious freedoms. Ensuring data protection through decentralized

(Mantelero, 2018)AI models and secure encryption is essential to mitigating these risks.l interpretations or spiritual guidance, but they lack the human empathy and nuanced understanding that religious discussions require. Relying too heavily on AI in religious matters may erode the role of traditional faith leaders, diminishing the depth of interpersonal engagement and spiritual mentorship.Additionally, the digital divide remains a major concern. AI-based solutions for religious freedom and interfaith dialogue may be inaccessible to communities with limited technological literacy or infrastructure. Marginalized religious groups, particularly in underdeveloped regions, may struggle to engage with AI-driven platforms, further exacerbating inequalities(Wakabayashi, 2018) in religious representation and discourse.generated misinformation can distort religious teachings, spread false narratives, or manipulate interfaith dialogues to incite conflict. Deepfake technology, if misused, could create fraudulent religious proclamations or misattribute controversial statements to religious leaders, escalating tensions and undermining trust in faith-based institutions. Furthermore, some religious communities may resist (Zhu et al., 2018)AI-driven interventions due to doctrinal objections. Certain faith traditions emphasize human-led spiritual guidance and may view AI-driven religious tools as incompatible with their theological beliefs. Ethical AI development must respect these perspectives and ensure that AI remains an optional, supportive tool rather than a replacement for human-led religious discourse.(Madgule et al., 2023)The risk of AI inadvertently exacerbating sectarian divides is another cultural challenge. AI algorithms that categorize religious content may reinforce sectarian biases by amplifying echo chambers, where individuals are only exposed to content that aligns with their pre-existing beliefs. This could hinder interfaith understanding rather than promote it, necessitating careful design and oversight of AI-driven recommendation systems. traditions, is crucial in mitigating bias. moderation or recommendation processes, and enabling human oversight in religiously sensitive applications.surveillance and exploitation. (Zuiderveen Borgesius, 2018)Implementing decentralized AI models, encryption protocols, and ethical data governance practices will help safeguard religious freedoms in digital spaces.ls can assist faith leaders in research, content dissemination, and community engagement, but they should not supplant the role of human interpretation, empathy, and spiritual guidance.Lastly, cross-disciplinary collaboration between technologists, religious scholars, ethicists, and policymakers is essential. Ethical AI development for religious freedom requires input from diverse stakeholders to ensure that AI systems align with religious, ethical, and human rights principles.

Future Directions in Ethical AI Development for Religious Freedom: Emerging Trends and Opportunities

However, as AI becomes more integrated into global governance, digital platforms, and security systems, it is essential to ensure that its deployment aligns with ethical principles that protect religious expression and diversity. The future of ethical AI development for religious freedom is marked by several emerging trends and opportunities that could redefine how technology interacts with faith communities worldwide. identify common theological themes, and generate respectful discussions that promote mutual understanding. Chatbots and virtual assistants trained on diverse religious perspectives can assist individuals in learning about different faith traditions, breaking down misconceptions, and fostering peaceful coexistence.Algorithmic bias has been a longstanding concern in AI ethics, particularly when AI models inadvertently favor one religious perspective over others.(Raso et al., 2018) Future AI development must focus on creating more adversarial training and bias-detection algorithms, can help mitigate unintended discrimination and ensure equitable representation of all faiths. AI models offer a promising solution. Blockchain-based AI systems can ensure secure, private, and tamper-proof data management for faith-based organizations and religious individuals. By giving users greater control over their data, decentralized AI reduces the risk of state or corporate exploitation of religious affiliations and practices.Social media and digital platforms frequently rely on AI to moderate religious content, but these systems often struggle to differentiate between hate speech, theological critique, and legitimate religious discourse. Future advancements in explainable AI (XAI) and human-in-the-loop moderation approaches can enhance accuracy and fairness in content moderation. AI systems that incorporate cultural sensitivity training and community feedback mechanisms will be better equipped to uphold both free speech and responsible discourse. Future AI systems will likely leverage augmented reality (AR) and virtual reality (VR) to create immersive interfaith experiences, allowing users to explore religious sites, rituals, and historical events in a more interactive and inclusive manner.

These technologies can help bridge gaps between faith communities and promote deeper understandingAI's predictive analytics and data-driven insights can be leveraged to monitor religious freedom violations and advocate for policy changes. AI-driven platforms can analyze global trends in religious persecution, track incidents of faith-based discrimination, and generate reports that inform human rights organizations and policymakers.(Raso et al., 2018) By providing real-time data, AI can serve as a tool for religious advocacy groups to mobilize action and influence legislative protections for religious minorities. ethicists, and scholars from diverse religious traditions. Interdisciplinary collaboration can help refine AI's understanding of theological concepts, religious sensitivities, and the ethical implications of its applications. (Ramakrishnan et al., 2022)AI ethics committees that include religious representatives can guide the development of inclusive and respectful AI models. establish standardized best practices for AI deployment in religious contexts, ensuring consistency across different legal and cultural landscapes.hostility in online discussions and suggest diplomatic interventions. AI-assisted mediation tools can also be used by conflict resolution specialists to facilitate peaceful negotiations between religious groups experiencing disputes.language interpretation systems can enhance inclusivity in religious services, ensuring that all members of faith communities can participate fully in worship and spiritual life.preservation projects can provide future generations with access to invaluable religious knowledge and history.. AI chatbots and virtual assistants can also provide emotional and spiritual support to displaced individuals seeking religious guidance during crises.

Recommendations for Developing AI Systems that Respect Religious Freedom: A Human Rights-Based Approach

Developers should implement fairness-aware algorithms and conduct rigorous bias audits to identify and mitigate any discriminatory tendencies in AI systems. Additionally, inclusivity in AI design means recognizing and accommodating religious diversity. AI-powered platforms should support multilingual and multicultural perspectives, ensuring that religious content is accurately represented. Features such as customizable(Santoni de Sio et al., 2014) AI assistants that cater to different religious practices and beliefs can enhance inclusivity and user trust. or policy recommendations are affected. Explainable AI (XAI) techniques can be employed to ensure that users can access clear explanations of how and why AI systems reach specific conclusions.Regulatory bodies should require AI developers to maintain comprehensive documentation of training data sources, decision-making frameworks, and algorithmic changes. Independent audits and third-party assessments can help verify that AI systems align with ethical and human rights standards.. (Ramakrishnan et al., 2022)Protecting Religious Privacy and Data Securit discriminatory profiling. Legal frameworks, such as the General Data Protection Regulation (GDPR), should be extended to explicitly cover the ethical handling of religious data by AI systems. religious expression and content deemed inappropriate under community guidelines. Overly aggressive moderation may lead to the suppression of religious discourse, while lax moderation could enable hate speech under the guise of religious rhetoric.To strike a balance, AI moderation tools must integrate human-in-the-loop mechanisms, where trained experts—particularly those familiar with religious contexts—review AI-generated decisions. AI developers should also establish community-driven moderation policies, enabling diverse religious groups to provide input on content guidelines.(Nissenbaum, 2005) that explicitly recognize religious freedom as a fundamental right. These frameworks should provide clear guidelines on preventing religious discrimination in AI systems and ensuring equitable treatment of religious communities.(Sreenivasulu et al., 2022)Organizations such as UNESCO and the United Nations Human Rights Council (UNHRC) can play a pivotal role in setting international AI ethics standards that incorporate religious freedom protections. Public and private AI stakeholders should commit to these frameworks, ensuring compliance through regular evaluations and accountability measures.gious leaders, ethicists, policymakers, AI researchers, and human rights organizations. Engaging faith-based organizations in AI policy discussions can provide valuable insights into the ethical considerations of religious AI applications.Academic institutions and technology firms should conduct interdisciplinary research exploring the intersection of AI, religion, and human rights. By fostering open dialogue and knowledge-sharing, stakeholders can identify best practices for responsible AI governance. understanding and cooperation.(Madgule et al., 2023) AI-driven platforms can facilitate interfaith dialogue, provide educational resources on world religions, and support initiatives that counter religious intolerance.Machine learning models can be used to detect early signs of religious discrimination or violence, alerting human rights organizations and policymakers to take preventive action. AI-powered translation tools can help bridge communication gaps between different religious communities, fostering more inclusive global conversations on faith and spirituality.t AI-driven religious discrimination, establish redress mechanisms for individuals whose religious rights are violated by AI systems, and ensure accountability for AI developers.Independent regulatory bodies should oversee AI applications that impact religious freedoms, ensuring that companies and institutions comply with human rights standards. These regulatory frameworks should be adaptable, evolving alongside advancements in AI technology to address emerging ethical concerns.

FINAL THOUGHTS: THE IMPORTANCE OF A HUMAN RIGHTS-BASED APPROACH IN AI DEVELOPMENT FOR PROMOTING RELIGIOUS FREEDOM AND SOCIAL JUSTICE

As artificial intelligence continues to redefine human interactions, governance, and societal structures, ensuring its alignment with fundamental human rights—especially religious freedom and social justice—becomes a moral and ethical imperative. AI has the potential to serve as a tool for empowerment, fostering interfaith dialogue, reducing discrimination, and enhancing religious expression in digital spaces. However, without a deliberate human rights-based approach, AI can just as easily become a mechanism of exclusion, oppression, and bias, threatening the very freedoms it has the potential to protect. technology corporations, civil society, and religious institutions to establish ethical(Tubella et al., 2019) AI frameworks that prevent religious discrimination, ensure access to digital spaces for all faith communities, and mitigate algorithmic bias. religious beliefs but should instead create an equitable environment where diverse religious and non-religious perspectives can coexist harmoniously. AI-driven content moderation tools must be developed with sensitivity to cultural and religious nuances, ensuring that faith-based discourse is not unjustly censored. Additionally,(Mann & Matzner, 2019) AI systems deployed in governance, law enforcement, and public services must be scrutinized for their potential impact on religious minorities, ensuring that digital tools do not contribute to structural inequalities or social injustices.Furthermore, AI's role in social justice extends beyond religious freedom. It intersects with broader issues of equity, dignity, and human rights. Ethical AI development must prioritize marginalized communities, providing them with access to digital resources, preventing algorithmic true plurality of human experiences and beliefs. must not be sacrificed at the altar of technological progress; instead, AI should be harnessed as a force for good, promoting a more inclusive, just, and tolerant global society. AI-driven technologies have the potential to support religious pluralism, foster interfaith dialogue, and combat discrimination. However, without deliberate safeguards, they can also reinforce biases, enable digital censorship, and inadvertently suppress religious expression. Thus, integrating human rights by design in AI development is essential to preserving and promoting religious freedom in the digital age.The key findings underscore the necessity for a collaborative, multi-stakeholder approach where governments, corporations, civil society, and faith-based organizations work together to create AI systems that respect religious liberties. Governments must establish clear regulatory frameworks that enforce ethical AI principles while ensuring that AI applications do not infringe on religious rights. Corporations must take responsibility for designing AI algorithms that promote fairness, transparency, and inclusivity while mitigating biases in content moderation, data collection, and automated decision-making. Civil society, including religious institutions, human rights groups, and academics, must advocate for accountability, educate the public, and monitor AI's impact on religious freedom globally.AI impact assessments must become standard practice, ensuring that religious groups are neither marginalized nor excluded by automated processes. The responsibility falls on all stakeholders—policymakers, technologists, academics, and religious leaders—to ensure that AI is developed and deployed in ways that uphold human dignity, protect fundamental freedoms, and foster a world where diversity is not just tolerated but celebrated. By embedding human rights principles into AI governance, we can create a future where technology serves humanity, rather than undermining its most cherished values.

Future Research Directions: Exploring the Intersection of AI, Ethics, and Human Rights in Promoting Religious Freedom and Social Justice

As artificial intelligence continues to shape societies, its intersection with ethics and human rights demands deeper academic inquiry and interdisciplinary collaboration. AI's impact on religious freedom and social justice presents both opportunities and challenges, necessitating a forward-looking research agenda that ensures technological advancement aligns with fundamental human rights principles. Future research must explore(Vijayakumar et al., 2024) AI's potential to support religious pluralism, counter discrimination, and uphold social justice while mitigating risks related to bias, censorship, and exclusion(Sugumaran et al., 2024). One critical area of future research is the analysis of bias in AI systems, particularly in how religious beliefs and practices are represented in training datasets. Many AI models, particularly those Developing fairness-aware machine learning models to reduce bias in AI decision-making.Examining how religious texts and traditions are incorporated into AI training data.Studying the effects of algorithmic content moderation on religious discourse.AI-driven tools can foster interfaith dialogue by bridging linguistic and cultural barriers. Future research should explore how AI applications, such as machine translation and virtual dialogue platforms, can facilitate meaningful exchanges between religious communities. Key questions include:How can AI enhance interfaith education and mutual understandingWhat ethical considerations must be addressed in AI-assisted religious discourse?Can AI-driven mediation tools help resolve religious conflicts and promote peace?The regulatory landscape surrounding AI and religious freedom remains fragmented(Mantelero, 2018). Future studies should focus on developing comprehensive legal and ethical frameworks that guide AI's deployment in ways that respect religious liberties. Research areas include:Comparative analyses of global AI governance models and their impact on religious rights.The role of international organizations in setting AI ethics standards.Mechanisms for ensuring accountability and redress for AI-related religious discrimination. AI and the Protection of Religious MinoritiesReligious minorities often face systemic discrimination, and AI can either exacerbate or alleviate these injustices. Research is needed to determine how AI can be used to:Detect and prevent religious persecution through predictive analytics.Support religious minority representation in digital spaces.Ensure equitable access to AI-driven services regardless of faith background.. AI Ethics in Religious and Social Justice MovementsAI's role in social justice activism, particularly in religious contexts, is an emerging field of study. Researchers should examine:The ethical implications of AI-driven surveillance on religious activism.How AI can empower faith-based social justice initiatives.The balance between free religious expression and the prevention of hate speech through AI moderation(Lim et al., 2008). Ethical AI Deployment in Faith-Based OrganizationsReligious institutions are increasingly adopting AI for community engagement, security, and administration. Future research should investigate:he ethical considerations of AI usage in religious settings.How AI can enhance religious outreach while preserving human agency.Potential risks of AI-driven religious profiling or exclusion.

CONCLUSION

As artificial intelligence continues to shape societies worldwide, ensuring its alignment with fundamental human rights principles—particularly religious freedom—has become a matter of urgent ethical responsibility. AI-driven technologies have the potential to support religious pluralism, foster interfaith dialogue, and combat discrimination. However, without deliberate safeguards, they can also reinforce biases, enable digital censorship, and inadvertently suppress religious expression. Thus, integrating human rights by design in AI development is essential to preserving and promoting religious freedom in the digital age.The key findings underscore the necessity for a collaborative, multi-stakeholder approach where governments, corporations, civil society, and faith-based organizations work together to create AI systems that respect religious liberties. Governments must establish clear regulatory frameworks that enforce ethical AI principles while ensuring that AI applications do not infringe on religious rights. Corporations must take responsibility for designing AI algorithms that promote fairness, transparency, and inclusivity while mitigating biases in content moderation, data collection, and automated decision-making. Civil society, including religious institutions, human rights groups, and academics, must advocate for accountability, educate the public, and monitor AI's impact on religious freedom globally.AI impact assessments must become standard practice, ensuring that religious groups are neither marginalized nor excluded by automated processes. Emerging trends in ethical AI development signal a shift towards responsible innovation, emphasizing transparency, stakeholder inclusion, and proactive bias mitigation. Opportunities exist to leverage AI as a force for good—using it to enhance religious education, enable multilingual interfaith communication, and develop AI-assisted tools that foster respectful dialogue across diverse faith traditions. Ethical AI certification programs, industry-wide best practices, and international agreements on AI governance can further strengthen the commitment to religious freedom in digital spaces.. By upholding ethical principles, fostering cooperation among stakeholders, and continuously evaluating AI's societal impact, we can ensure that technological advancements contribute to a world where religious freedom is protected, respected, and enhanced by AI rather than threatened by it. The path forward requires vigilance, commitment, and a shared vision for a future where human rights and AI innovation coexist harmoniously.I've prepared a comprehensive conclusion on building human rights by design in AI development for religious freedom. Let me know if you'd like any refinements or additions.

REFERENCES

Azenkot, S., Prasain, S., Borning, A., ... (2011) Enhancing independence and safety for blind and deaf-blind public transit riders. In: Proceedings of the 2011 annual conference on Human factors in computing systems - CHI '11, New York, NY, 2011, pp.3247–3256. New York: ACM. DOI: 10.1145/1978942.1979424

Barocas, S., & Selbst, A. D. (2016). Big Data's disparate impact. *California Law Review*, *104*(3), 671–732.

Beck, K., Beedle, M., Van Bennekum, A., ... (2001) Manifesto for Agile Software Development. Available at: https://agilemanifesto.org/ (accessed 16 August 2019).

Broeders, D., Schrijvers, E., & Hirsch Ballin, E. (2017) Big Data and security policies: Serving security, protecting freedom. Available at: https://english.wrr.nl/binaries/wrr-eng/documents/policy-briefs/2017/01/31/big-data-and-security-policies-serving-security-protecting-freedom/WRR_PB6_BigDataAndSecurityPolicies.pdf (accessed 31 July 2019).

Cavoukian, A. (2008). Privacy in the clouds. *Identity in the Information Society*, *1*(1), 89–108. DOI: 10.1007/s12394-008-0005-z

Citron, D. K., & Pasquale, F. A. (2014). The scored society: Due process for automated predictions. *Washington Law Review (Seattle, Wash.)*, *89*, 1–33.

Davis, J., & Nathan, L. P. (2015). Value Sensitive Design: Applications, adaptations, and critiques. In Van den Hoven, J., Vermaas, P. E., & Van de Poel, I. (Eds.), *Handbook of Ethics, Values, and Technological Design* (pp. 11–40). Springer. DOI: 10.1007/978-94-007-6970-0_3

Eykholt, K., Evtimov, I., Fernandes, E., ... (2018) Robust physical-world attacks on deep learning models. In: 2018 IEEE/CVF conference on computer vision and pattern recognition, Salt Lake City, UT, 18–22 June 2018, pp.1625–1634. IEEE.

Flanagan, M., Howe, D. C., & Nissenbaum, H. (2008). Embodying values in technology: Theory and practice. In Van den Hoven, J., & Weckert, J. (Eds.), *Information Technology and Moral Philosophy* (pp. 322–353). Cambridge University Press. DOI: 10.1017/CBO9780511498725.017

Franzke, A. S. (2016). *Big Data Ethicist - What Will the Role of the Ethicist Be in Advising Governments in the Field of Big Data?* Utrecht University.

Gerards, J. (2019). The fundamental rights challenges of algorithms. *Netherlands Quarterly of Human Rights*, *37*(3), 205–209. DOI: 10.1177/0924051919861773

Halbertal, M. (2015) Three concepts of human dignity. Available at: https://youtu.be/FyEvREFZVvc (accessed 8 August 2019).

Kosinski, M., Stillwell, D., & Graepel, T. (2013). Private traits and attributes are predictable from digital records of human behavior. *Proceedings of the National Academy of Sciences of the United States of America*, *110*(15), 5802–5805. DOI: 10.1073/pnas.1218772110

Kosinski, M., & Wang, Y. (2018). Deep neural networks are more accurate than humans at detecting sexual orientation from facial images. *Journal of Personality and Social Psychology*, *114*(2), 246–257. DOI: 10.1037/pspa0000098

Leese, M. (2014). The new profiling: Algorithms, black boxes, and the failure of anti-discriminatory safeguards in the European Union. *Security Dialogue*, *45*(5), 494–511. DOI: 10.1177/0967010614544204

Lim, Y.-K., Stolterman, E., & Tenenberg, J. (2008). The anatomy of prototypes: Prototypes as filters, prototypes as manifestations of design ideas. *ACM Transactions on Computer-Human Interaction*, *15*(2), 1–27. DOI: 10.1145/1375761.1375762

Madgule, M., Vinayaka, N., Sonkhaskar, Y. M., Patel, D. R., Karthikeyan, R., & Selvakumar, P. (2023). Mechanical properties and microstructure of activated TIG welded similar joints of Inconel alloys by desirability approaches. *Materials Today: Proceedings*, *77*, 528–533.

Mann, M., & Matzner, T. (2019). Challenging algorithmic profiling: The limits of data protection and anti-discrimination in responding to emergent discrimination. *Big Data & Society*, *6*(2), 1–11. DOI: 10.1177/2053951719895805

Mantelero, A. (2018). AI and Big Data: A blueprint for a human rights, social and ethical impact assessment. *Computer Law & Security Review*, *34*(4), 754–772. DOI: 10.1016/j.clsr.2018.05.017

Nissenbaum, H. (2005). Values in technical design. In Mitcham, C. (Ed.), *Encyclopedia of Science, Technology and Ethics* (pp. lxvi–lxx). Macmillan.

Ramakrishnan, T., Mohan Gift, M. D., Chitradevi, S., Jegan, R., & Subha Hency Jose, P. Nagaraja, Rajneesh Sharma H.N., Selvakumar P., Sintayehu Mekuria Hailegiorgis, (2022). "Study of Numerous Resins Used in Polymer Matrix Composite Materials", Advances in Materials Science and Engineering, vol. 2022, Article ID 1088926, 8 pages, 2022. DOI: 10.1155/2022/1088926

Raso, F., Hilligoss, H., Krishnamurthy, V., ... (2018) Artificial intelligence & human rights: Opportunities & risks. Available at: https://cyber.harvard.edu/publication/2018/artificial-intelligence-human-rights (accessed 22 August 2019).

Santoni de Sio, F., Robichaud, P., & Vincent, N. A. (2014). Who should enhance? Conceptual and normative dimensions of cognitive enhancement. HUMANA. *MENTE Journal of Philosophical Studies*, *7*(26), 179–197.

Sreenivasulu, A., & Manimozhi, T. Satheesh kumar P., Selvakumar P. and Singh P.,(2022). "The Model of Smart Sensing Device For Sensitive Nanoclusters Modification in Sensing Properties," 2022 2nd International Conference on Advance Computing and Innovative Technologies in Engineering (ICACITE), Greater Noida, India, 2022, pp. 1043-1047, DOI: 10.1109/ICACITE53722.2022.9823846

Sugumaran, K. M. D., Pandiyarajan V., Y. B S, Selvakumar P. and M. S, (2024). "Analysis of Electromyography Signals for Control of Mechanical Prosthesis using Machine Learning Techniques," 2024 2nd International Conference on Intelligent Data Communication Technologies and Internet of Things (IDCIoT), Bengaluru, India, 2024, pp. 1059-1067, DOI: 10.1109/IDCIoT59759.2024.10467707

Tubella, A. A., Theodorou, A., & Dignum, F.. (2019) Governance by glass-box: Implementing transparent moral bounds for AI behaviour. In: *Proceedings of the twenty-eighth international joint conference on artificial intelligence AI for improving human well-being*, 10–16 August 2019, pp.5787–5793. IJCAI.

Van de Poel, I. (2013). Translating values into design requirements. In Michelfelder, D. P., McCarthy, N., & Goldberg, D. E. (Eds.), *Philosophy and Engineering: Reflections on Practice, Principles and Process* (pp. 253–266). Springer. DOI: 10.1007/978-94-007-7762-0_20

Vijayakumar, G., Rajkumar, M., Rajiv Chandar, N., Selvakumar, P., & Duraisamy, R. (2024). Muniyandi Rajkumar, Rajiv Chandar N, Selvakumar P and Ramesh Duraisamy, (2024). Environmentally friendly TDS removal from waste water by electrochemical ion exchange batch-type recirculation (EIR) technique. *Environmental Science. Water Research & Technology*, *10*(4), 826–835. DOI: 10.1039/D3EW00793F

Wakabayashi, D. (2018) Self-driving Uber car kills pedestrian in Arizona, where robots roam. The New York Times, 19 March.

Zhu, H., Yu, B., Halfaker, A., & Terveen, L. (2018). Value-sensitive algorithm design. *Proceedings of the ACM on Human-Computer Interaction*, *2*(CSCW), 1–23. DOI: 10.1145/3274463

Zuiderveen Borgesius, F. (2018) Discrimination, artificial intelligence and algorithmic decision-making. Available at: https://rm.coe.int/discrimination-artificial-intelligence-and-algorithmic-decision-making/1680925d73 (accessed 17 August 2019).

Chapter 5
Digital Dignity:
Ethical AI Governance for Protecting Religious Freedom

Kishore Selva Babu
https://orcid.org/0000-0003-4113-3849
Christ University, India

Suhash Swaminathan
https://orcid.org/0009-0009-3546-4255
Christ University, India

ABSTRACT

The chapter describes how artificial intelligence intersects with freedom of religion or belief through an analysis of policy deficiencies followed by proposed guidelines to address biases and discriminatory practices and cultural sensitivity problems. The implementation of a "human rights by design" method should become the standard practice by incorporating diverse data collection and bias assessment procedures and processes that explain artificial intelligence protocols and require collaboration between stakeholders. The chapter supports faith leader participation in AI development processes through a design method that also requires an adaptive governance system adapted to evolving religions and technologies. The integration of FoRB into AI ethics requires the analysis of best practices from IBM's fairness toolkit alongside Boston's transparency policies and the development of cross-border coordination systems that admit oversight mechanisms as an immediate requirement.

DOI: 10.4018/979-8-3373-3830-9.ch005

INTRODUCTION

The increasingly profound incorporation of artificial intelligence (AI) into the framework of modern society requires serious examination of its intricate interaction with the existing systems of human rights, and specifically the right to Freedom of Religion or Belief (FoRB), which is often viewed as minor yet provokes cancerous growth in modern society. The chapter is a critical analysis of this juncture, transcending beyond principle to precisely pinpoint gaps in policy systems within the current regulatory and ethical AI frameworks (Fjeld et al., 2020) and, subsequently, develop specialized, practical guidelines that could be used to reduce or avoid particular harm. The existing landmark efforts, including the European Union-proposed world-first AI Act and the UNESCO Recommendation on the Ethics of Artificial Intelligence, have been shown to contain no explicit protections or guarantees of FoRB, introducing a dangerous vacuum into governance (Jobin et al., 2019). Such neglect is reflected in very practical, harmful ways: AI models often have a severe failure to recognize religious imagery, clothing, behavior, and material with a resulting incorrect censorship, filtering-based discrimination (Ali et al., 2021), or improper labeling that stigmatizes believers. Moreover, the introduction of AI-enhanced surveillance and monitoring systems, in the name of security or content control, unfairly target and investigate minority religious groups, suppressing religious freedom of speech and assembly, creating an atmosphere of distrust, and providing the opportunity to persecute. On top of that, most state-of-the-art AI systems suffer a dire lack of transparency and explainability ("black box" nature) (Veliz and Murphy, 2025), meaning that it is impossible to explain how they made their decision, and persons or communities adversely affected by religious bias would have no meaningful explanation or way to contest the fairness of the negative consequences.

In order to preventively manage such complex challenges and incorporate FoRB protections into the very design of AI creation and implementation, the authors advocate an inclusive approach of human rights by design (HRbD). The given approach stipulates that FoRB considerations are to be embedded in AI system design starting at the conceptual level. It requires participatory and representative data gathering standards which are deliberately inclusive of the overwhelming religious diversity of the world, including religious minorities and their opinions, and which are thereby an active opposition to the leveling forces of popular datasets. It needs strict, continuous bias measurement and reduction measures designed particularly to identify and correct religious discrimination, through technical audits (Veale & Binns, 2017), as well as socio-legal analyses. Most importantly, it requires the deployment of powerful AI explanation systems (XAI) that can offer interpretable explanations on decisions that affect religious expression or practice. At the most basic level, HRbD requires authentic community collaboration, including consultation and cooperation with a wide variety of faith leadership, academics, and practitioners through the entire AI lifecycle in order to produce systems that are culturally aware, contextually sensitive, and theologically mindful. It is on the basis of HRbD that the authors advance a three-pillar strategic model that is critical in safeguarding religious diversity and agency of the individual in the epoch of AI. First, company-geged technology reviews should become obligatory, with special FoRB impact analyses added to the current risk assessments, with such tools and methods as bias detectors and religious expertise on ethics review boards. Second, the law has to change to identify the FoRB as an essential aspect of AI ethics and non-discrimination legislation, requiring the application of HRbD principles, banning religious profiling through AI, and providing clear remedies in case of its occurrence. Third, the global standards currently being developed and adopted by international organizations to create consistency across borders are urgently needed; institutions such as the UN Human Rights Council, OSCE, and the suggested Global AI Observatory should immediately issue specific guidelines and monitoring tools related to the effect of AI on religious freedom, instead of making generic statements on human rights. To bring these strategies into practical reality, the authors proceed to make two specific, future proposal: the institutionalization of standard protocols of faith leader and community involvement in the AI development process, theological and cultural expertise directly informing system design, training data curation, and evaluation criteria; and the development of active, real-time observatory systems explicitly aimed at monitoring AI effects on FoRB in a variety of contexts, a combination of automated recognition of religious bias cases and community reporting, to allow regulatory regimes and mitigation measures to adapt in real-time to the co-evolving worlds of technology and religion. Hypothetical examples of how the implementation could be achieved through case studies focusing on the shortcomings and possibilities of using such tools as the AI Fairness 360 toolkit developed by IBM to detect religious bias, as well as the discussion of the municipal efforts like the algorithmic transparency policies adopted in Boston that may soon be expanded to include FoRB-related concerns, can illustrate the viable implementation routes. The need to act with determination is categorical; global governance institutions, transnational organizations, national oversight authorities, technology companies and civil society should make it their collective priority to ensure that clear, binding FoRB protections are integrated into the mainstream of international AI ethics and regulation policies to avoid the further entrenchment of religious disadvantages and the further undermining of this most critical human right in the digital era.

EXISTING POLICIES AND THEIR LIMITATIONS

Institutional Discrimination against FoRB in Substantive Rule Tools

The modern environment of artificial intelligence regulation, although showing noble progress in covering general ethical imperatives, such as non-discrimination, privacy, and accountability, has a catastrophic flaw in its structure: the systematic omission of Freedom of Religion or Belief (FoRB) as a regulatory category. This is not a matter of oversight, but it is more of a fundamental omission with far-reaching international consequences. Pioneering legislation such as the European Union Artificial Intelligence Act (AIA) (Jobin et al., 2019; Fjeld et al., 2020) with its innovative risk-based approach does not mention FoRB as a separate protected category. Including religious freedom as a subcategory of unspecified "fundamental rights" or "non-discrimination" provisions, the AIA does not require Fishbowl-On-Religion-Specific impact analyses, special mitigation measures, or protection against algorithmic underrepresentation of minority religious information. Equally, the Ethics of AI Recommendation, although promoting cultural diversity by UNESCO, approaches FoRB as an implied element of human rights, without practical instructions. Instead, the lack of such concretizations makes possible the AI-facilitated monitoring of religious minorities or algorithm-based suppression of valid theological debate, leaving a governance gap within which religious discrimination can run free.

Multi Stakeholder Ethical Frameworks Illiteracy

The second main weakness, common in multi-stakeholder groups, like the Partnership on AI (PAI), is the lack of contextual religious literacy on how principles of fairness may be operationalized. The guidelines provided by PAI as part of the drive towards inclusive AI do not include the mechanism of dealing with faith-based weaknesses. One of the examples of such failure is the continuous incorrect recognition of religious items (hijabs, turbans, kippahs) as facial recognition software (Buolamwini & Gebru, 2018), leading to the denial of service and social stigmatization. Automated content moderation takes this a step further; making mistakes of false positives; believing sacred texts, theological controversies or minorities practices to be hate speech. The effect of these errors is that it compels groups that are marginalized to appeal processes that are not clear, which discourage legal speech. The problem is that the frameworks are monolithic in viewing religion rather than putting into account the sectarian particularities, power asymmetries of history, and culturally specific manifestations of bigotry. Ethical rules are theoretically right but in practice, wrong without theological expertise in-built in the provisions of fairness.

Jurisdictional Fragmentation and Accountability Deficits

The regulatory problem presented by the transnational character of AI consists in the fact that it creates a problem of jurisdiction fragmentation. Complex computer software designed by international companies stretches the law to such extents that it forms gaps in the legislation. Three features make even those jurisdictions that have excellent anti-discrimination laws unable to combat AI-based FoRB violations:

Technical Opacity

Black box systems ensure that the decision channels are unobservable, and hence religious discrimination is therefore hard to prove.

Black Boxes of Discrimination

Instead of operating in a discriminatory way that is easy to see (e.g., using houses of worship as crime potential predictors), prejudice usually works in a structurally controversial way that is hard to determine.

Digital Borderlessness

The acts of violation committed in the cybernetic space (e.g. algorithmic defunding of religious content) are not covered by the territorial jurisdiction. When it comes to the victims, there are no redresses when they suffer harm, i.e., when the person who was discriminated against based on his or her religious affiliation assigned based on analyzing his or her behavioral data, does not receive a job, or when a community under the surveillance of surveillance AI is profiled. Even in a scenario where liability is distributed using the law concerning these invisible harms produced by algorithms, legal regimes do not have the technical details to do so (Jeroen, 2023).

Technological-Theological Inapplicability of the Existing Mitigation Tools

Three inadequacies with regard to the current prevailing forms of governance:

Tool Inadequacy Generic Bias

The existing fairness criteria on race or gender is not micro-grained as the identity of religion. Sentiment analysis technologies impose negative meaning on the neutral religious concepts (e.g. the term jihad is incorrectly identified as violent extremism). Hate speech algorithms are defined as the pathological forms of theological debates characteristic of some traditions. The policies are partisan without auditing structures that is appropriate to theological ontologies and power relations.

Amnesia of Religious Knowledge

Governance models Governance models rarely consider faith communities in the involvement of AI development. This blind spot is constructed in an omission, which creates a deficit in Indigenous spiritual activity in datasets (Crawford, 2021; Mohamed et al., 2020), algorithmic time that is unaware of holy days, or religious iconography content filters (Khan & Srinivasan, 2024. The systems representatives of majoritarian opinions are promoted by the absence of communal participation forceful assurances. New generative AI threat vectors: The large language models (LLMs) and other upcoming technologies come with new threat vectors that have not been seen before: o Synthetic Disinformation: Deepfakes of religious figures in the appeal to sectarian violence. o Micro-targeted Manipulation: Artificial intelligence-driven hate speech that is exercised against specific denominations. o Doctrinal Distortion: Algorithms of scriptural interpretation containing the extremist thinking into the mass (Boddington & Černy, 2024).

Communal Profiling

Using network analysis to make the inferences of religious affiliations to monitor or socially control. The policies which exist do not have adaptive alternatives to these changing threats.

The Road to Religious Discrimination as an Institutionnalized Practice

Otherwise, these constraints will enshrine religious disparities of the past in the software of the present. The intersection of generic structures, jurisdictional gaps and AI capabilities growing exponentially pose a threat of automating religious oppression: the marginalization will be algorithmically formalized, the surveillance will be blessed by predictive analytics, and the culture erasure will be continued with the help of synthetic media. This curve is turning AI, which was a tool of empowerment, into a structure of discrimination, and therefore poses a threat to the human right of autonomy of belief, which is the basis of many other human rights. The inertia of policy has hitherto frozen a future in which technological advancement will require religious concession - a price too high to pay by the pluralistic communities.

GAPS IN FORB PROTECTIONS

Machine Learning Promotion of Historic Religious Biases

The deep disparities in safeguarding the Freedom of Religion or Belief (FoRB) do not begin in the present-day neglect but in the technological legacy of centuries-old biases and systematic prejudices and the colonialism power layouts that are entrenched in training data and decision-making logic (Crawford, 2021; Zhang & Lee, 2025). This is most perniciously reflected in the algorithmic capture of Islamophobic discourse, in which historical Orientalist motifs and post-9/11 security frameworks are statistically encoded in the form of scraped datasets of biased news archives, security databases and online discussion.

In that way, AI systems apply the following distortions: predictive policing algorithms over-represent Muslim-majority communities as "high-risk" areas through false positives in the correlation between religious density and crime rates; content moderation algorithms engage in digital McCarthyism by automatically censoring Arabic text, images of mosques, or theological notions like "jihad" because of excessively broad models of "violent extremism"; sentiment analysis begins to pathologize discourses about Islamic scholarship as hate speech.

This widespread stigmatization, which is hiding under the notion of algorithmic neutrality, justifies surveillance apparatus, suppresses religious life, and bolsters the patterns of anti-Muslim persecution across the world. At the same time, epistemic erasure strikes Indigenous spiritualities: training datasets provided by the Global North, text-based, institutionalized religions are virtually devoid of any oral tradition, land-based ceremony, and sacred topography representation. Heritage AI labels Indigenous ritual objects as artifacts instead of living sacred objects; knowledge graphs label creation stories as mythology; resource extraction algorithms ignore spiritual relations to the land, making it possible to desecrate the environment. It is a digital assimilation, which continues the colonial dispossession, making cosmologies, which have been developed over millennia, algorithmically invisible.

The Techno-Hermeneutic Failure in the Religious Recognition

The dominant AI systems have an inherent lack of hermeneutic ability - the ability to comprehend context-sensitive religious meaning (Tsuria & Yemini, 2024). Theoretical frameworks that depend on the Western, Abrahamic-driven taxonomies diminish the spiritual diversity of the world to coarse classificatory grids, with disastrous effects of misrecognition that have worldly effects: Symbolic & Dress Misidentification: Sikh turbans, Jewish kippot or Muslim hijabs are pathologized as an anomaly by facial recognition systems and can initiate a security lockdown or access denial. Hindu tilak marks are coded as stains, Ash Wednesday ashes as dirt or Indigenous ceremonial paint as war symbols by image classifiers.

Linguistic & Ritual Misinterpretation

NLP technologies recognize sacred texts (Quranic verses, Buddhist sutras) or theological debates as hate speech. The algorithmic moderators have their accounts suspended, in one case due to posting Sabbath meal preparations (misdescribed as "weaponized content"), and the other due to posting Indigenous chants (described as "nonsensical").

Ontological Reductionism

Recommendation engines are foisting syncretic religions (e.g., Vodun, Candombl Fe) on pillarized taxonomies (e.g. "Animism") and are not including non-institutionalized spirituality (e.g. eco-paganism, personalized mysticism).

The reason behind this failure lies in three vices, namely, statistical models based on frequency rather than meaning; lack of embedded anthropological/theological knowledge; and inability to see how the same expression may have different significances in different cultures (e.g., head coverings may indicate modesty, piety or cultural identity depending on the context). What we have as a outcome is an algorithmic imperialism that imposes majoritarian religious norms.

The Opacity of Corporate and Accountability Vacuum across Nations

The international supply chain of AI products and services presents a jurisdiction black hole when it comes to the implementation of FoRB (Jeroen, 2023). The way it is working is that multinational technology companies are designing systems in locations that have strong protection of rights (e.g., EU, US) and are then implementing them through cloud computing architecture in states where there is active persecution based on religion (e.g., China, Saudi Arabia).

This kind of division is armed with deliberate corporate opacity:

Data Obscurity

Companies conceal the source of religious training data (e.g. scraping interfaith forums without consent) and sanitize data provenance records.

Architectural Secrecy

The mass of models, decision thresholds using a "risk" score, and content moderation parameters are all deemed to be "proprietary" and guard against criticism of algorithmic sectarianism.

Audit Theater

The internal bias tests, where such exist, have no FoRB-related indicators, theological feedback, or openness. There are impassable obstacles to victims: a Uyghur Muslim labeled by the surveillance AI in China has no means to sue the European facial recognition provider selling the algorithm; a Hindu loan seeker rejected by the credit-scoring AI on caste-biased Indian data has no cause of action under US anti-discrimination law; minority religious groups delisted by secretive moderation systems have no resources to pursue cross- border litigation. The international human rights mechanisms (e.g. UN Treaty Bodies) have no technical capacity or enforcement abilities, and domestic courts face the challenge of extraterritoriality and the black box problem.

The Existential Threats Enhanced by Generative AI

Generative AI is added to the FoRB expansion loopholes and inventions new vectors of persecution:

Synthetic Sacrilege

LLMs might be taught on blasphemous text and imagery to create in the image of spiritual leaders (e.g. deepfake Popes blessing heresy, fake Imams declaring jihad), delegitimizing spiritual authority and causing violence (Papadopoulos, 2025; Boddington & Cerny, 2024). Micro-targeted disinformation the specifics of theology can also be turned against those who possess it: micro-targeted disinformation campaigns can spread AI-generated fatwas by nonexistent Sunni clerics throughout Shia populations, or deepfake videos of practices by minor sects can be circulated, presented as satanic.

Doctrinal Sabotage

The casual followers of any religion can be radicalized by allowing a personalized scripture interpolator application, which is already primed on extremist data, to guide them via a radicalizing reading of scripture without having to go through the gatekeepers of a given religion religious establishment.

Communal Profiling

AI-based network analysis can project religious affiliation onto social ties, enabling state agents to locate and monitor underground religious communities (e.g., house churches in Iran, Baha'i networks in Egypt). The existing regimes of governance are completely not ready for these threats.

Regulatory Lag

This means that genocidal speech (e.g. anti-Rohingya deepfakes in Myanmar) can be boosted without hindrance, and content moderation systems will not be able to tell the difference between genuine religious unhate and AI-generated hate. The lack of FoRB-focused red-teaming, live sacred content moderation systems and cross-border synthetic media regulations place religious populations at the mercy of algorithmic destruction.

THE CONFLUENCE: TOWARDS ALGORITHMIC THEOCRACY

This cluster of gaps, which include historical bias amplification, hermeneutic failure, corporate impunity and generative escalation, forms a constellation of gaps that make a perfect storm. AI is not just religious discrimination, it industrializes it. The predictive policing algorithms have made anecdotal prejudices mathematically objective suppression; the content moderators have made the state censorship of minority religions automated and generative tools have made theology a weapon on a mass scale. AI systems can easily turn into the infrastructure of digital inquisition without the binding FoRB-specific safeguards:

Spiritual Identity Suppression

Ostracizing of religious attire/paraphernalia due to algorithmic profiling (e.g., Sikhs choosing to take off their turbans in order to run through airport scanners).

Communal Fragmentation

AI-driven echo chambers exacerbate sectarianism (ex: recommendation engines pushing Hindu nationalist content to diasporic audiences).

Sacred Space Invasion

Biometric monitoring of temples/mosques affecting ritual privacy (e.g., facial recognition in prayer). The way ahead cannot be made of merely technical fixes, but a take-down of the epistemic colonialism coded into the AI, and a corresponding re-building of governance with theological integrity as its foundation.

THE NEED FOR FORB-SPECIFIC AI GUIDELINES

Foundational Imperative for Specialized Frameworks

The fundamental insufficiency of the current AI regulation systems in mitigating the vulnerability of religious freedom implies that there is an urgent need to design and implement specific FoRB guidelines. They should go beyond token representation in generic human rights standards and make FoRB a non-derogable foundation of AI ethics. Holistic operational requirements ought to cut across all of the lifecycle phases: data sourcing and model design; deployment and monitoring (Lu et al., 2025; Dignum, 2020). Such specialization is needed to combat special harm generators such as algorithmic discrimination of religious minority content, biometric Identification at places of worship, and artificial intelligence enabled doctrinal manipulation. In the absence of these customized structures, the present governance voids allow systemic discrimination to fail the test of pluralistic democracy by allowing theocracy-as-biased-by-technology to eat the foundations of the Compatibility of Pluralistic Democracy with Technology.

Architecting Religious Autonomy Protections

The core of these principles is the vehement protection of religious liberty - the affirmative right to determinate belief without the algorithmic pressure. That will necessitate an outright prohibition of belief manipulation through AI (e.g. (de)conversion therapy algorithms that homer in on particular beliefs). Manipulation of the doctrines by non- transparent religious instruments of interpretation. Replacement of the faith-based organizational principles in the algorithms of the public service. Notably, the principles must provide meaningful human oversight and binding opt-out control over AI judgments that influence religious practice. This involves rights to disapprove, Algorithmic scheduling which intrudes on inflexible holy days. Facial recognition at the temples (biometric authentication in sanctified places). Filtering of religious material of significance by computers. AI-made judgments concerning the eligibility of faith-based programs depending on discriminatory proxies (Khan & Srinivasan, 2024)

Recognition and Defense Mechanisms for Minority Faiths

Values ought to mandate a revolution in the majoritarian data paradigms to participatory representation through Culturally Sovereign Data Collection: Binding rules to collaborative data collection with Indigenous elders and minority scholars employing participatory mapping and community-developed annotation standards that epistemic violence (Zhang & Lee, 2025).

Contextual Intelligence Systems

AI applied cumulative with superior symbolic recognition skills, integrating anthropological knowledge graphs and ritual-sensitive multimodal learning to disambiguate polysemic religious forms (e.g. disambiguating Sikh kirpans as items of faith, rather than as weapons).

Expert Anti-Discrimination Processes

Introduction of specialized bias detection, theological adversarial testing (e.g. testing loan algorithms on name-based discrimination against minority religions) and on-line disparate impact monitoring with Community access to reporting.

Operational Infrastructure for Implementation

Mandatory FoRB Impact Assessments: Unlike generic human rights assessments, Mandatory FoRB Impact Assessments should examine threats of doctrinal manipulation, sacred symbol erasure and surveillance disproportionality though methodologies jointly designed with religious scholars.

Formalized Community Partnership

Formalized processes that integrate various faith leaders into all stages of AI development - in requirement definition as well as in the design of redress pathways - so that cultural awareness is prioritised before code.

Theologically Legible Explainability

XAI needs that are faith-first (e.g., converting an algorithmic decision into terms and concepts that can be understood by a theological misinterpretation). Specialized Redress Ecosystems: Autonomous adjudication mechanisms that have the power to order corrections of systems, reparations and non-repetition assurances in case of violations.

Multilevel Governance Enforcement Architecture

Principles on FoRB must be implemented internationally in coordination,

International Standardization

UNESCO/OCHCR must plan monitoring systems that place FoRB somewhere other than in the margins of AI ethics statements.

Regional Regulatory Translation

EU AI Act (Jobin et al., 2019; Fjeld et al., 2020), amendments introducing FoRB-specific high-risk categories; OSCE/OAS considering binding conformity assessments.

National Legislative Internalization

Domestic Laws that mandate FoRB to be followed concerning public/privately owned AI and other regulatory entities.

Corporate Accountability

Self-regulation in the industry with independent audit of reduction of religious bias.

EXISTENTIAL CONSEQUENCES OF INACTION

These specialized guidelines are the only solutions to ensuring that AI will not eternally magnify historical religious biases, digitally erase Indigenous spiritualities through assimilation, and cause daily damages through algorithmic exclusion. A lack of binding structures permits transnational impunity of atrocities such as bio metric desecration of sacralized places or artificial intelligence aided oppression of

Uighur Muslims. Suchundermining of the autonomy of conscience poses a threat to the ethical underpinnings of civilization - compelling religious liberty to become little more than an algorithmic allowance as opposed to an inalienable right. The implementation therefore does not consist in a technical readjustment, but in a civilizational self-preservation: the least guarantee that technology will remain the servant of the spiritual variety of mankind, and not its homogenizing reduction to computationally convenient data points.

OPERATIONALIZING FORB IN AI DEVELOPMENT

Community-Led Data Co-Creation Frameworks

Optimal operationalization of FoRB-specific AI guidelines will require structured, ethics-informed frameworks of representative dataset development, directly transferring participatory approaches of healthcare (Community-Based Participatory Research - CBPR) and education (Culturally Sustaining Pedagogy), (Rahwan, 2018; Zhang & Lee, 2025). That requires actual co-ownership in which religious communities, also those marginalized and Indigenous, are epistemic partners at the starting point. Cooperation should include: the co-definition of culturally sensitive data collection procedures; the development of annotation taxonomies that capture theological subtly (e.g., the distinctiveness of sect-specific understandings of religious dress, the accurate characterization of non-Western ceremony), the co-determination of ethical limits to sacred knowledge, and the co-production of data through community-driven digital storytelling, participatory photography/videography of ceremonies (with rigid controls on consent), and collaborative ethnography. Formal governance read more by doing so, this would make the datasets have contextual authenticity, which would reduce the epistemic violence and create a sense of community ownership of digital religious representation.

Permanent Multidisciplinary Oversight Bodies

Ongoing algorithmic religious discrimination surveillance can only be achieved by developing standing supervisory committees that bring together a variety of skills: data scientists, theologians, FoRB ethicists, anthropologists, religion historians, human rights lawyers, and most importantly, faith representatives (leaders, practicing, youth). Such bodies should: co-design contextually specific harm measures based in theological reality (e.g., developing error rates of facial recognition on religious clothing across environmental conditions; false positives of minority faith terms in content moderation); undertake routine adversarial testing with religiously literate situations (e.g., testing loan algorithms with minority faith profiles); and undertake longitudinal impact studies to track impacts on communal integrity/access to sacred space; and monitor and enforce remedial measures (Tsuria & Yemini, 2024; Agbese et al., 2023). This changes technical compliance bias mitigation into a continuous ethical enhancement based upon humanistic and theological insights.

Faith-Centric Explainability (XAI) Requirements

Guidelines are needed to support religious autonomy and algorithmic accountability, and these strict requirements should be provided by the so-called Faith-Centric XAI. Reasons behind the decisions that affect religious practices (e.g., visa denials to religious pilgrimages, content removals of scriptural exegesis) need to go beyond technical jargon, either explaining particular factors in terms that are theologically meaningful (Dignum, 2020). An example: Visa Denials: "Marked: Short term travel patterns to [X countries] which are assessed as risk factors- not religious travel affiliation." Content Removal: "[specific quote] + historical context markers related to violent rhetoric in training data. The technical innovations have to feature religiously meaningful counterfactuals ("Your visa will be approved, as long as you spent 6 months in Country X before you applied") and culturally sensitive natural language interfaces designed in collaboration with religious communication specialists, permitting religiously significant theological examination and challenge.

Conscientious Opt-Out Rights & Implementation

Principles should entrench universal accessible opt-out privileges against AI engagements that breach bona fide religious beliefs, free of any penalty. Such potential crisis situations are: Biometric systems (facial recognition/iris scanning) in holy places (temples, pilgrimage sites) or during holy days. Analytics of behavior in secret religious counseling, AI-generated religious text and content that goes against the authority of doctrine. Algorithms choosing in highly personal religious aspects (e.g. marriage matching) To implement, it would need: redundant alternative channels (human proxies to conduct visa interviews, non-biometric access); civic education in religious circles; legal safeguards against discrimination by opting-out; and means of group opt-outs (e.g. banning aerial surveillance of private rituals). These alternatives have to be built into technical architectures.

IMPLEMENTATION INFRASTRUCTURE & GLOBAL ENFORCEMENT

To actualize this framework requires: standardized FoRB impact assessment forms that include all pillars; special funding to support community AI literacy; global standards to support cross-border opt-out enforcement (Jeroen, 2023); and autonomous auditing institutions that also have the power to sanction. Supportive frameworks are needed to make sure that the guidelines are no longer a dream but a reality and can be applied as society-level protection against religious oppression in the algorithmic era.

RECOMMENDATIONS FOR STAKEHOLDERS

Developer Imperatives: Embedding FoRB-by-Design

The introductory stakeholder obligation rests with system developers that should incorporate stringent, uninterrupted FoRB risk evaluation as part and parcel of the whole AI lifecycle, including the preparation of the system design and data gathering to model training and deployment, as well as post-deployment observing.

Such evaluations should specifically analyze possible biases in algorithmic decision-making that can take the form of religious discrimination, including: visual mislabeling of religious symbols by computer vision systems (e.g. Sikh turbans being triaged as an abnormality), content moderation that has a disproportionate impact on minority faiths (e.g. automatic deletion of Indigenous spiritual imagery), and biased resource triaging in government services that disproportionately impact religious people. Such assessment must proceed in parallel with assessing the dangers of surveillance bias towards religious minorities (e.g., predictive policing algorithms learning mosque attendance patterns), unintentional amplification of historical religious biases in training data (e.g., anti-Semitic stereotypes in language models), and cultural ignorance in natural language processing (e.g. theological text mistaken as aggression).

That requires making domain-specific evaluation frameworks in collaboration with religious studies researchers, theologians, and ethicists in order to detect context-sensitive weaknesses that generic bias tools miss (Mohamed et al., 2020; Rahwan, 2018). More importantly, project teams should have permanent and empowered representatives of different religious traditions, Indigenous spiritual leaders, minority faith advocates, representatives of secular belief systems, involved directly in serving on ethical review boards, design sprints, and bias audits. This takes token consultation to substantial co-creation: requirement definition supported by theological insights, inclusive religious data sets managed by community control, evaluation criteria which are culturally sensitive and the interpretation of audit findings through hermeneutical prisms. This kind of integration would entrench pluralistic considerations in the architectural DNA of the AI and ensure that the systemic results of exclusion that are so problematic in existing systems would be avoided.

Corporate Accountability & Radical Transparency

To supplement in-house governance, entities creating or implementing high-FoRB-impact AI should actively endeavor to promote the results of thorough bias audits, as well as more detailed disclosures of the criteria by which an algorithm makes its decisions.

It includes publishing: the detailed procedures that were followed to conduct religious bias testing protocols (e.g., adversarial scenarios testing hijab recognition under varying lighting conditions), demographic analyses of error rates that affect religious groups specifically (e.g. false positives in Muslim content moderation), records of mitigation steps and their quantified effect, and theologically meaningful characterizations of how automated decisions, which affect religious activities, are computed.

Examples that would demand such transparency are visa algorithm approvals of pilgrimages (Hajj/Kumbh Mela), content removals of scriptural content, and eligibility checks of faith-based social services. The disclosures should be made public in easy-to-read formats and languages that serve affected populations so that affected people can scrutinize them independently, following the examples of the algorithmic transparency registry in San Jose (Agbese et al., 2023). This municipal-level model - requiring AI purpose, data provenance, risk assessment and oversight to be publicly documented - should be taken worldwide through knowledge-sharing fora such as the OECD.AI Policy Observatory, and religious bias surveillance (e.g. special reporting categories when sacred material is removed).

Governmental Regulatory Enforcement Mechanisms

At the same time, national governments have to implement GDPR-like regulatory frameworks with FoRB safeguards expressly imposed as obligations in AI policies. It requires: legislative bans on algorithmic religious discrimination that have extraterritorial reach; the mandatory impact assessment of FoRB on high-risk AI systems in the public sector in migration control, law enforcement, and social benefit allocation; the establishment of independent regulatory bodies, equipped with forensic auditing abilities and the power to require algorithmic documentation, as well as the power to impose sanctions, including fines proportional to revenues and the mandatory recall of systems (Jeroen, 2023). Regulatory agencies should also be given the power by statute to look into cross-border FoRB abuses, such as the misrecognition of hijab-wearing women by facial recognition systems at international border checkpoints, by transcending jurisdictional gaps via mutual legal assistance treaties modified to suit algorithmic responsibility. To overcome chronic weaknesses in small religious groups unable to marshal institutional resources, there should be long-term government funding of interdisciplinary studies of AI disparate impacts, along with earmarked appropriations towards: community-based AI literacy trainings, subsidies to bring strategic lawsuits against discriminatory algorithms, and the design of culturally specific bias mitigation strategies (e.g., adversarial testing guidelines in Druze spirituality settings). The results of the research are to be enshrined in regulatory norms which are to be spread through such organizations as UN Alliance of Civilizations.

International Governance & Multilateral Standardization

At the international level, the United Nations and OECD should immediately improve the AI ethics frameworks with FoRB-specific measures and evaluation procedures. These would require: standardized indicators, to measure algorithmic religious bias (e.g., disparity indices to faith-based service access, misclassification rates of minority religious content); mandatory reporting forms, to describe FoRB protections to signatory states; and specially designated monitoring committees, with expert representation by theological institutions and human rights NGOs, to evaluate compliance (Lu et al., 2025).

These actions would bring FoRB to a level higher than its current peripheral references in various documents, such as the AI Ethics Recommendation of UNESCO, to a pillar that can be actively grasped. This initiative should be complemented by officially widening the mandate of the UN Special Rapporteur on FoRB to systematic observation of AI governance aspects, allowing thematic reporting on novel threats (e.g., generative AI deepfakes sparking sectarian violence), and state AI system investigations upon country visits, as well as supporting country AI strategy technical assistance in collaboration with the UN Tech Envoy. Most importantly, best practices in operations, such as the transparency registry developed in San Jos, will need to be selectively adopted to religious bias monitoring and distributed through networks such as GPAI, accompanied by capacity-building measures targeting policymakers in areas of highest risk and legislative model clauses to facilitate enforcement at the municipal level, where religious populations are most likely to interact with governmental AI.

SYNCHRONIZED IMPLEMENTATION FOR ALGORITHMIC PLURALISM

But the overarching requirement of FoRB protection as a whole is the coordinated movement on all levels of stakeholders: developers institutionalizing FoRB-by-design with inclusive co-creation and auditable transparency; governments implementing robust regulatory frameworks with the GDPR-like enforceability; researchers focusing on marginalized belief communities via context-specific interventions; international organizations integrating FoRB-quantifiable standards in global governance; and local innovators scaling context-sensitive transparency technologies. It is a multistakeholder ecosystem that needs to be dynamically driven by the experiences of religious people living in automated public spaces more and more. Then and only then can AI be repurposed as a force of religious liberation, as opposed to a force of religious oppression: by ensuring that algorithmic regimes are integrated, enforceable partnerships between the digital and the physical, such that algorithmic systems serve to reinforce, rather than undermine, the bulwarks of democratic pluralism by introducing a rigorous defense of autonomy of conscience along the entire digital-physical spectrum of religious existence.

BUILDING HUMAN RIGHTS BY DESIGN: ETHICAL AI FOR RELIGIOUS FREEDOM

Preemptive FoRB Impact Assessment in High-Risk Contexts

The first HRbD principle requires transformative embedding of FoRB protections that starts with obligatory, thorough FoRB Impact Assessments (FoRB-IAs) prior to system implementation, particularly in military/security processes where mistakes in algorithms result in irreparable damage. Sincere FoRB-IAs should analyze:

- Direct Risks: Targeting systems powered by AI misidentifying religious structures as military targets because of biased geospatial databases; surveillance systems labeling minority religious dialects as being "suspicious" because of defective language models.
- Systemic Risks: Predictive analytics that relate religious demographics (e.g., mosque attendance patterns) with threat indicators disproportionately, justifying discriminatory profiling; autonomous systems desecrating sacred spaces by physically intruding into them. That forces defense planners and intelligence agencies to integrate theological knowledge and direct access to faith leaders in the requirement specification process, designing algorithmic

constraints to avoid sacred sites, developing real-time human override procedures, and preventing ethical breaches in the architectural level instead of remediating them after deployment.

Institutionalized Religious Co-Design Across the AI Lifecycle

In addition to high-risk situations, a preventative culture must involve structured engagement of different faith groups (Indigenous leaders, minority scholars, secular representatives) in the entire lifecycle of a product: in brainstorming and crafting an ethical charter, in the monitoring of deployment, and in continuously refining and improving it. This goes beyond advisory groups with Governance Structures: Rotating religious representative seats on ethics boards with a veto of FoRB-crucial decisions; community-based data stewardship committees with power over the ethical sourcing/annotation of religious data. Embedded Expertise: Theological liaisons in engineering teams offering real-time advice on cultural sensitivity (e.g., warning against Indigenous regalia being misinterpreted as costumes in image databases). Hermeneutic Integration: Pro-active stewardship of systems by lived realities and contextual vulnerabilities of affected communities, that AI does not discriminate against cyclical religious calendars in publicly used service algorithms, nor what is called hermeneutic violence in NLP systems handling sacred texts.

Adaptive Governance for Evolving Techno-Religious Threats

In order to be effective in such fast-changing environment, FoRB-by-design policies need to be calibrated dynamically to, Shifting Religious Landscapes: Emerging movements, reinterpreted doctrines, evolving persecution patterns. Generative AI deepfakes Neuroadaptive interfaces Ubiquitous biometrics. Prescriptive review periods (in alignment with UN human rights reporting or catalyzed by breakthroughs must: include threat intelligence (e.g., AI-enhanced disinformation along sectarian fault lines); and feedback from international FoRB monitors; and renew technical standards of bias detection, transparency, and human control (Agbese et al., 2023). Such agility deals with new vectors, such as hyper-personalized manipulation of religious sentiment by algorithmic means or AI-powered exclusion of groups who engage in religiously mandated behaviors (e.g., Sabbath-observant workers being punished by productivity algorithms), (Papadopoulos, 2025).

Specialized Bias Mitigation & Radical Transparency Protocols

Technical FoRB-by-design Technical FoRB-by-design would require adapting generic fairness tools to become specialized by, Context-Sensitive Metrics: Co-designed with theologians to quantify disparate impact on the basis of different doctrinal interpretations (e.g. different error rates between Orthodox and Reform Jewish content moderation) or to quantify the extent of "hermeneutic bias" in the processing of sacred texts. Adversarial Religious Datasets: Synthetic data with syncretic spiritual practices, Indigenous ceremonies, or theological discussions currently underrepresented in major corpora (Tsuria & Yemini, 2024). Bias Mitigation Techniques: Counterfactual augmentation that produces stereotype-free religious expressions; fairness constraints that promote equal resources to meet convergent religious requirements (e.g., halal/kosher meal options in AI-optimized welfare programs). At the same time, radical transparency would require all public-facing AI to be publically disclosed: purpose/legal authority; religious demographic representation gaps; error rates broken down by faith characteristics (e.g., hijabs/turbans misidentification rates); decision thresholds impacting FoRB (e.g., variables in visa adjudication); and FoRB-IAs summaries availability. Following the examples of San Jose and its registry, published in community-specific languages, religious vetting of registries becomes possible, such as immigration algorithms or "extremist content" flaggers.

Architecturally Embedded Human Safeguards

The HRbD model concludes with binding forms of human oversight, Human-in-the-Loop (HITL) Mandates: In high-stakes areas (employment, visa processing, sacred space access), authoritative reviewers, educated in the discrimination law of religion, should have clear override powers. The real-time explanation interfaces should mark indicators of bias (e.g., "Resume score deducted because of being affiliated with an Organization X related to [Religious Group Y])). Right to Opt-Out Responsibly: People should have the right to refuse biometric identification in consecrated areas (e.g., facial recognition in temples breaching ritual privacy) or AI-based determinations that fundamentally clash with their beliefs (e.g., algorithmic matching in religious matchmaking services). Fail-Safe Protocols: Avoiding algorithmic theocracy by leaving the final decision on issues which affect religious autonomy to human actors, who are ethics-trained, especially where communal integrity is concerned (e.g., autonomous systems in the vicinity of pilgrimage sites). This systemic embedding across proactive evaluation, institutionalized co-design, adaptive governance, specialist bias engineering, extreme transparency and human-centric safety nets create an ethical layer in which FoRB becomes non-negotiable and guarantees that the inalienable right to conscience, belief and community religious practice is not undermined by technological progress.

SAFEGUARDING RELIGIOUS FREEDOM ALGORITHMICALLY

The Non-Negotiable Urgency of FoRB Protections in AI Governance

The widespread digitalization of human life, which is irreversibly accompanied by the adoption of artificial intelligence, makes the active inclusion of Freedom of Religion or Belief (FoRB) safeguards in the architecture of AI governance systems more than an ethical desire but a practical necessity to maintain the human dignity of the 21st century and achieve the long-term fair implementation of technology in different societies. The poorly exposed lack of intentional, binding FoRB protections in the modern AI paradigms is an algorithm of systematic discrimination: overrepresenting the religious minorities in the algorithmic misidentification (misfiring facial recognition on Sikh turbans or Islamic hijabs as security anomalies), unwarranted surveillance (ai predictive policing profiling areas based on religious demographics), and economic disadvantage (biased credit rating extrapolating risk based on religious adherence). At the same time, legitimate religious expression is being stifled by excessive content moderation that mistakenly censors theological discussion, religious texts, or minority practices under the banner of "hate speech," deteriorating the foundations of democratic pluralism by delegitimizing communal self-determination, discouraging religious expression in the fear of inadvertent censorship, and splintering social cohesion due to algorithmic reinforcement of sectarian division and historical bigotry encoded in training sets. That turns AI, which could become a tool to human flourishing, into a carrier repeating and magnifying age-old patterns of religious marginalization, endangering the very fiber of inclusive societies.

Constructing Rights-Based Infrastructure: From Harm to Empowerment

Addressing these existential risks will need responsible development of infrastructural systems of rights that will need system developers to move beyond ad hoc fixes of bias in systems and instead re-engineer the AI lifecycle. This would require: the incorporation of FoRB Impact Assessments (FoRB-IAs) into the design stage; the adoption of ongoing transparency procedures publicly announcing algorithmic standards which impact religious expression (after the model of San Jose registry); and the creation of permanent co-governance mechanisms which grant active, empowered involvement of the religious communities and groups impacted by a project, including marginalized and Indigenous traditions, through the development, auditing, and deployment stages. This changes communities as passive subjects of algorithmicplace to active creators of digital religious futures. The suggested all-encompassing system includes strict technical auditing with the help of theologically expertise-based religious bias indicators; policy assessment requiring FoRB-specific adherence in national AI strategies and international ethics frameworks (OECD, UNESCO), which can be enforced via GDPR-based regulatory frameworks with penalties; and deep institutional shifts towards tech corporate religious literacy, regulatory bodies with forensic audit powers, and extended UN Special Rapporteur on FoRB remits. Such practical steps will provide the stakeholders with a visible roadmap that can lead to AI systems that proactively consider religious diversity (V Eliz & Murphy, 2025; Chowdhury & Williams, 2024).

Multi-Stakeholder Implementation Framework for Algorithmic Pluralism

When implemented by stakeholders, tech leaders embracing FoRB-by-design principles, policymakers introducing binding protective measures, international organizations establishing aligned standards, civil society organizations overseeing their observance, AI can fulfill its potential as a tool of inclusion on a grand scale. This generates digital spaces in which technology can bridge the divide between people of different faiths via interreligious dialogue forums; give voice to the voiceless by prioritizing persecution counter-narratives using secure communication systems; and ensure equal access to religious resources by means of fair algorithmic curation. The result is a shift of technological advancement and religious liberty as an expanding sphere of tension into mutually supportive pillars of a thriving global village where the freedom of conscience is non-negotiable and pluralism is digitally fostered.

Emerging Threat Landscape and Adaptive Resilience Imperatives

Such future security will need unblinking vigilance with the understanding that the protection of FoRB is not a static, one-time undertaking but rather an ongoing effort to keep up with the ever-changing technological capacity and the co-evolution of the global religious Landscapes. New risks require constant research, policy revising itself kept in step with technological breakthroughs, and responsive governance systems that get ahead of new harm vectors before they have a chance to metastasize: generative AI creating blasphemous deepfakes to drive sectarian violence; hyper-personalized disinformation campaigns playing on religious divides; neuroadaptive interfaces that can manipulate religious experiences; biometric surveillance that desecrates houses of worship. Sustaining protection is a transnational, trans sectoral, responsibility, Governments should establish legally binding safeguards: a specific ban on algorithmic religious discrimination; a mandatory FoRB-IA on all AI in the public sector; research funding on the effects of AI on vulnerable belief groups; independent regulatory bodies with investigative powers and authority to sanction. Technology Companies need to bake in high levels of religious literacy: permanent theological advisory boards; investment in context-specific religious bias detection algorithms; transparent publication of faith-group-disaggregated performance data; institutionalized community co-design, conception through to post-market surveillance. Civil Society Organizations should become watchdogs (independent audits, accessible grievance channels, strategic litigation) and, at the same time, strategic collaborators (facilitating the technologist-faith community dialogue, religious institution AI literacy curriculum, culturally responsive educational resource co-design). International Bodies (UN, OECD) should promote FoRB to a central status, to define measurable standards/monitoring procedures, coordinate cross-border application through mutual recognition of sanctions, and promote international best-practice sharing (e.g. using municipal transparency registries to oversee FoRB).

Toward Techno-Religious Pluralism: Fulfilling Technology's Purpose

To realize the fulfilment of the primary mission of technology to serve human welfare, dignity and potential requires a holistic, long-term stakeholder cooperation that is consciously focused AI innovation to develop systems that actively respect, protect, and honor the true beliefs, practices, and identities inherent in all spiritual traditions. Only together can we make sure that our digital future looks so that algorithms become stewards of pluralism, keepers of conscience, and facilitators of the great tapestry of belief that makes up humanity, as an inalienable right to find meaning in accordance with the deepest convictions, a non-negotiable pillar of common life in the algorithmic era.

THE CONVERGENCE OF THREE CATASTROPHIC GAPS NECESSITATES IMMEDIATE INTERVENTION

Epistemic Violence in Data and Design

By training on data filled with stories of orientalism and colonial views on top of post 9/11 security models, AI systems then inherit and magnify centuries old biases. It leads to the algorithmic disappearance of Indigenous cosmologies (incorrectly and pejoratively relabelled as "mythology" in knowledge graphs) and the systematic stigmatization of Islam (via "violent extremism" classifiers on Arabic terms), (Crawford, 2021; Mohamed et al., 2020).

Hermeneutic Failure in Algorithmic Recognition

The dominating models possess no theological literacy to read contextualized religious meaning and thus reduce the variance of spiritual expressions to coarse taxonomies. This is expressed through symbolic mistaking (Hindu tilak marks identified as "stains"), ritual misunderstanding (Sabbath preparations tagged as "weaponized content"), and ontological reductionism (syncretic traditions such as Vodun crammed into "Animism" boxes), (Tsuria & Yemini, 2024).

Transnational Accountability Vacuum

A combination of corporate secrecy (black box algorithms, hidden training data) and territorial division of responsibility lets multinational tech companies off the hook. Chinese AI-powered surveillance Uyghur Muslims cannot sue European sellers; Hindu loan seekers rejected by caste-based algorithms have no redress in Western anti-discrimination legislations (Jeroen, 2023).

The blueprint for redemption lies in architecting "Human Rights by Design" (HRbD) into AI's core:

- Preemptive FoRB Impact Assessments (FoRB-IAs) should be required prior to deployment, particularly in high-risk situations such as military operations, and should assess both direct risks (e.g., misclassification of religious sites as targets) and systemic risks (e.g. algorithmic profiling of worship patterns). They need theological competence and advice of faith leaders during the design stage.
- Instead of extractive data practices, Culturally Sovereign Data Co-Creation has to be implemented. Following approaches used in the healthcare (Community-Based Participatory Research) and education (Culturally Sustaining Pedagogy), religious communities should co-own the development of datasets by using participatory ethnography, documentation of rituals, and community-established annotation guidelines.
- Faith-Centric XAI should cross the bridge of technical language: Visa rejections of pilgrimages should give non-religious reasons (e.g., "temporary travel behavior to X nations"); scripture content removals should reference the specific phrases mistake as violent.
- Conscientious Opt-Out Rights should become universal: People should not be punished because they refuse biometric identification in temples, AI-

based matching in religious services, or algorithmic counseling that breaches the confessional privilege.

Generative AI's Escalating Threats Make Delay Catastrophic

Large Language Models (LLMs) have brought new vectors of persecution that have never been seen before:

- Synthetic Sacrilege: Deepfakes of religious figures promoting heresy or with calls to violence.
- Doctrinal Sabotage: Extremist interpretations of the scripture by the so-called personalized scripture interpreters.
- Communal Profiling: Underground mapping of faith groups by network analysis to be surveyed by the state. In the absence of FoRB-dedicated red-teaming, religious content verification standards, and international laws on synthetic media, religious societies will be helpless (Boddington & Černy, 2024).

The Path Forward is Clear, Urgent, and Non-Negotiable

We are at a crossroad of civilizations. With policy paralysis continuing as it is, AI will enshrine a digital inquisition: spiritual identities policed via algorithmic profiling (Sikhs being forced to remove their turbans at airports); sacred places assaulted by biometric surveillance; communal relationships splintered by AI-powered sectarianism. On the other hand, when stakeholders put this blueprint collectively:

- Algorithms turn into bridges- inter-religious dialog and fair use of religious resources.
- Societies re-assert control - co-creating systems that accommodate ritual calendar, spiritual iconography and theological subtlety. Technology is in the service of dignity- technology should oppose the computational homogenization of humanity in honor of its reducibility to spiritual plurality (Khan & Srinivasan, 2024).
- The imperative is not merely technical re-adjustment; it is the preservation of human meaning as such. Because in the algorithmic era, the right to pursue meaning based on the most profound beliefs is not a privilege that can be negotiated, but the foundation of the pluralistic vitality. And let it be our covenant, to create not the architectures of discrimination, but the digital ecosystems in which every turban, hijab, tilak, and prayer will be acknowledged not as the data point to be processed, but as the reminder of the divine autonomy

that makes us all the same. Then only will AI range fulfil its real potential not as a means of control but as a means of uplift to the human soul.

The digitized world of today requires the FoRB protections to be embedded in the AI governance as they are now necessary not only on moral grounds but also due to the practical requirements of implementation. The absence of control of AI systems has been shown to perpetuate discrimination against religious minorities alongside the suppression of legitimate religious expression and undermining of democratic pluralistic systems in societies. Such possible risks can be handled when the developers of systems develop rights-based infrastructure where the process is transparent and has active participation of the affected communities. The suggested system comprising technical auditing and policy assessment and institutional changes gives detailed procedures for overcoming these problems. Those stakeholders who embrace such steps will shield AI not to become a tool of exclusion such that technology would be linked to empowerment of everyone and both progress and religious liberty would coexist.

The future of FoRB matters demands continuous monitoring of the development of the situation in the areas of AI and the global religious organization. The safeguarding of FoRB in the AI age turns into a shared responsibility that necessitates various segments and global boundaries to collaborate. Government protections that can be enforced come alongside the needed inclusion of religious literacy by technology firms as civil society acts as watchdog and strategic collaborator in these efforts. To realize the fulfillment of the purpose of technology to serve human welfare, there must be an all-inclusive stakeholder collaboration to create systems that acknowledge true beliefs across all spiritual traditions.

CONCLUSION

The utmost importance of artificial intelligence as an embedded aspect of human lives requires no less than a fundamental restructuring of the governance systems to enshrine the sacred right of Freedom of Religion or Belief (FoRB). The future of AI as it is headed in terms of development and implementation, with little to no regard to religious freedom implications, is therefore an existential threat to the pluralistic democracy, community self-determination, and the spiritual dignity of the individual, as this analysis has clearly shown. The lack of clear, binding FoRB protections in revolutionary regulatory frameworks, such as the AI Act in the EU and ethical guidelines in UNESCO has left a dangerous governance gap that allows algorithmic systems to reproduce historical biases, tear at sectarian fault lines and enforce discrimination of religious minorities and Indigenous spiritual practices.

It is not a theoretical danger but a reported fact: facial recognition systems pathologize the Sikh turban and Islamic hijab as security anomalies; content moderation algorithms mistakenly censor theological discussion as "hate speech"; predictive policing technologies disproportionally police neighborhoods with religious prices; and generative AI can create blasphemous deepfakes that violent mobs will use as an excuse to attack the vulnerable. They are not accidental failures but the signs of a more fundamental techno-ethical crisis the brashness of AI-driven, explanations-seeking logic against the subtle, context-specific, and highly individualized aspects of religious identity and practice.

REFERENCES

Agbese, M., Alanen, H.-K., Antikainen, J., ... (2023). Governance in ethical and trustworthy AI systems: Extension of the ECCOLA method for AI ethics governance using GARP. *e-Informatyka*. https://www.e-informatyka.pl/index.php/einformatica/volumes/volume-2023/issue-1/article-1/

Ali, M., Sapiezynski, P., Bogen, M., Korolova, A., Mislove, A., & Rieke, A. (2021). Discrimination through optimization: How Facebook's ad delivery can lead to skewed outcomes. *Proceedings of the ACM on Human-Computer Interaction*. DOI: 10.1145/3479598

Boddington, P., & Černý, D. (2024). The moral machines: How generative AI challenges freedom of thought and conscience. *Minds and Machines*. https://link.springer.com/journal/11023/volumes-and-issues/34-3

Buolamwini, J., & Gebru, T. (2018). Gender shades: Intersectional accuracy disparities in commercial gender classification. *Proceedings of Machine Learning Research*. http://proceedings.mlr.press/v81/buolamwini18a/buolamwini18a.pdf

Chowdhury, R., & Williams, J. (2024). Artificial intelligence and socioeconomic forces: Transforming the landscape of religion. *Humanities & Social Sciences Communications*, *11*(1), 602. Advance online publication. DOI: 10.1057/s41599-024-03137-8

Crawford, K. (2021). The atlas of AI: Power, politics, and the planetary costs of artificial intelligence. *AI & Society*. Advance online publication. DOI: 10.1007/s00146-021-01349-z

Dignum, V. (2020). Responsibility and artificial intelligence. *Oxford Handbook of Ethics of AI*, 215–231. DOI: 10.1093/oxfordhb/9780190067397.013.12

Fjeld, J., Achten, N., Hilligoss, H., Nagy, A., & Srikumar, M. (2020). Principled artificial intelligence: Mapping consensus in ethical and rights-based approaches. *Berkeley Journal of Law & Technology*. https://doi.org/DOI: 10.15779/Z38M32N851

Jeroen, T. (2023). Artificial intelligence and religious freedom. In Oxford University Press eBooks. DOI: 10.1093/law/9780192882486.003.0004

Jobin, A., Ienca, M., & Vayena, E. (2019). The global landscape of AI ethics guidelines. *Nature Machine Intelligence*, *1*(9), 389–399. Advance online publication. DOI: 10.1038/s42256-019-0088-2

Khan, A., & Srinivasan, R. (2024). Algorithmic pluralism: Designing for religious diversity in public-service AI. *Journal of Social Computing*. Advance online publication. DOI: 10.23919/JSC.2024.0003

Lu, Y., Cao, Y., Wang, B., & Yang, S. (2025). AI governance: A systematic literature review. *AI and Ethics*, *5*(3), 3265–3279. Advance online publication. DOI: 10.1007/s43681-024-00653-w

Mohamed, S., Png, M. T., & Isaac, W. (2020). Decolonial AI: Decolonial theory as sociotechnical foresight in artificial intelligence. *Philosophy & Technology*, *33*(4), 659–684. Advance online publication. DOI: 10.1007/s13347-020-00405-8

Papadopoulos, T. (2025). Artificial intelligence in religious education: Ethical, pedagogical, and theological perspectives. *Religions*, *16*(5), 563. Advance online publication. DOI: 10.3390/rel16050563

Rahwan, I. (2018). Society-in-the-loop: Programming the algorithmic social contract. *Ethics and Information Technology*, *20*(1), 5–14. Advance online publication. DOI: 10.1007/s10676-017-9430-8

Tsuria, R., & Yemini, A. (2024). Artificial intelligence's understanding of religion: Investigating the moralistic approaches presented by generative artificial intelligence tools. *Religions*, *15*(3), 375. Advance online publication. DOI: 10.3390/rel15030375

Veale, M., & Binns, R. (2017). Fairer machine learning in the real world: Mitigating discrimination without collecting sensitive data. *Big Data & Society*, *4*(2). Advance online publication. DOI: 10.1177/2053951717743530

Véliz, C., & Murphy, T. (2025). Artificial intelligence and its "slow violence" to human rights. *AI and Ethics*, *5*(3), 2265–2280. Advance online publication. DOI: 10.1007/s43681-024-00547-x

Zhang, W., & Lee, M. K. (2025). Decolonizing AI ethics: Indigenous cosmologies and algorithmic bias mitigation. *AI & Society*. Advance online publication. DOI: 10.1007/s00146-024-01935-x

Chapter 6
Religious Freedom in the Age of AI: A Constitutional Law Perspective

Tridipa Sehanobis
School of Law, Christ University, Bengaluru, India

Mohammad Saleem
https://orcid.org/0009-0000-4777-3113
Faculty of Law, Marwadi University, Rajkot, India

Karun Sanjaya
https://orcid.org/0009-0005-1647-1549
Symbiosis Law School, Symbiosis International University, Pune, India

Abhishek Benedict Kumar
https://orcid.org/0000-0002-3998-3150
Symbiosis Law School, Symbiosis International University, Pune, India

ABSTRACT

This chapter examines the developing linkage between religious freedom and artificial intelligence (AI) in the field of constitutional law. As AI systems play a growing role in filtering access to information, censoring speech, and shaping governance, they pose remarkable opportunities while also constituting major challenges to the freedom of religion or belief (FoRB). The chapter considers how AI can improve religious expression and inter-religious dialogue, and then it identifies concerns, such as algorithmic bias, digital censorship, and surveillance of religious groups. It also examines constitutional structures and case laws, with special attention to the balance between technological innovation and fundamental rights protection. By promoting ethically designed AI systems, inclusive governance and effective

DOI: 10.4018/979-8-3373-3830-9.ch006

legal protections, this chapter suggests elements of such a normative blueprint to ensure that religious freedom continues to be affirmed in the digital era. It ends with future-oriented approaches and how AI regulation could be aligned with FoRB standards globally.

INTRODUCTION

AI (Artificial Intelligence) has accelerated a great transformation in the way how human life functions today. AI technologies have transformed societal structures, governance models, the way we communicate and express ourselves and many other aspects of everyday life. With these changes, core human rights are being re-examined and challenged in these new surroundings. Amongst these is the most intimate and politically explosive, the freedom of religion or belief (FoRB). Historically rooted in constitutional law and protected by a combination of legal, political and societal mechanisms, FoRB now faces a series of threats and opportunities presented by AI technologies.

Religious freedom, after all, goes beyond a mere policy of tolerance. It involves the freedom of persons and communities to exercise, affirm or change religious or non-religious beliefs, without the threat of discrimination, repression or violence (Ashraf, 2021). Such a right is a fundamental aspect of the dignity and identity of every man and the basis of the principle of democracy and the community of social life as well as of a pluralistic society. Such rights can be found in numerous constitutional forms in countries around the world, ranging from non-establishment clauses to religious expression defenses to prohibitions of religious discrimination. But the terrain of how we exert those rights is recklessly shifting as AI goes mainstream.

AI technologies do not appear out of a vacuum, however, they are designed and developed in a particular context, trained on human-generated data and implemented into human societies. So, they are in themselves a reflection of what human needs is and perhaps can even amplify the current social norms, biases and inequalities. These tensions particularly manifest at the intersection of AI and religion. One example is the facial recognition technology, till date it has been observed that how this technology is highly exploitative of communities of faith, with potential for discriminatory targeting. That is, perhaps in employment or education, some are unintentionally discriminated by algorithmic decision-making since the latent religious bias in the biased training data is learned by the model during the learning process. AI moderated social networks might over filter or under police religious content. These are serious, urgent constitutional matters. Is AI subject to human rights-based scrutiny, akin to that of Governments? What does it mean when private tech companies that is, not state actors that police religious speech with the use of opaque algorithms? What can court and legislatures do to prevent basic rights from being washed into digital backwaters that defy old notions of state power and public regulation? These are not academic questions alone, but they are the pressing legal and ethical questions which demand immediate careful constitutional analysis.

But for all that, what is perhaps even more interesting is that AI can also be an effective tool to stand up for and promote religious freedom. It can promote gaining access to the religious literature, facilitate the communication between diverse faiths, using advanced translation and telecommunication facilities and can bridge between the separated religious human beings by a distance (Ahmed et al, 2024). It can also serve to identify and counter religious hate speech online, to produce inclusive school materials which represent a range of religious voices and to ensure that faith communities are actively involved in shaping technological change through religious AI agents and ethical guidelines.

Constitutional law should be simultaneously a shield and rudder that helps our society navigate through these changes, protecting against harmful deployments of AI and enabling beneficial applications of AI that are attentive and that do not undermine human dignity and pluralism. To match the era of AI, government and societal reform we need constitutions that can evolve, be replaced and updated to reflect a new reality while preserving the central truths of law and justice. But legal institutions will themselves have to find their way around this complex and entangled battlefield surrounding jurisdiction, accountability and technological proficiency if they are to remain effective gatekeepers of justice in the digital age.

The chapter below provides an in-depth analysis of the convergence between AI and religious freedom based on constitutional law. This starts with setting out a theoretical understanding of FoRB in constitutional law systems and its minimum fundamental principles for legal protection. It subsequently presents the particular threats that AI poses to religious freedom, in areas such as surveillance, algorithmic discrimination and the privatization of regulatory power (Paya, 2023). These menaces that AI pose are set against the backdrop of the prevailing court readings and developing doctrinal trends to discuss specific ways in which the judiciary and the legislature are starting to react.

The chapter also identifies the ways in which AI can contribute to the advancement of religious freedom, specifically through religious practice, dialogue and community. It highlights regulatory and policy environments that embed constitutional values into AI governance, such as legislative protections, international human rights jurisprudence and participatory policymaking. The chapter also looks forward and discusses the future course of constitutional law in an era defined by AI and stresses on the imperative of flexible, ethically guided and internationally focused religious freedom protections for the digital age. The development of AI calls for analogous evolutions in our legal and constitutional doctrine. The potential of AI should not be at the cost of human rights. Instead, through responsible governance, inclusive dialogue and robust constitutional protections, AI can be a tool to uphold and enrich the right to freedom of religion or belief for all.

CONCEPTUAL FOUNDATIONS: FREEDOM OF RELIGION OR BELIEF (FORB) AND CONSTITUTIONAL NORMS

Definition and Scope of FoRB

Freedom of religion or belief (FoRB), a key right in the constitutional traditions of democratic states, is an established principle in international human rights law. It is not just about being free to follow one or any religion or belief but stands for when anyone wanting to convert or give up a certain religion, wanting to manifest one's religion, alone or with others, in public or in private, practice, worship and observance of any religion (Scharffs 2024). This relationship is evident from primary global instruments such as Article 18 of the UDHR and the ICCPR which elucidates the domestic constitution of a nation.

In constitutional regimes, FoRB tends to have both individual and collective aspects. The right to individual conscience allows people to be free to follow their own conscience based on their deeply held personal beliefs without interference or forcing. The social dimension protects institutional religious communities' autonomy to organize and conduct their affairs, from property rights to religious education and the administration of their own internal affairs. It is important to note again that FoRB is not an absolute right. Belief and faith are regarded as sacrosanct and absolute, though manifestations of belief may be subject to constitutional limitation. Such restrictions must be provided for by law, serve a legitimate interest, public safety, order, health or the rights of others and be necessary and proportionate for that interest. These principles, including those developed in constitutional jurisprudence and human rights case law, serve to mitigate the tension that exists between individual freedoms and societal rights.

Historical and Philosophical Underpinnings

Religious freedom has been defined as the civil rights of individuals to receive or to be free from public interference or coercion in exercising their religion. From the granting of toleration in the Edict of Milan (313 CE) that recognized Christian worship as a legitimate activity in the Roman Empire, through the Protestant Reformation and the Enlightenment views of thinkers such as John Locke and Voltaire to the formalization of the idea as a right that could be litigated by individuals, the expression of religious liberty has been the transition of the concept from a gift of the state to something that can be enforced through the courts. In Locke's Letter Concerning Toleration, for instance, the notion that civil government should not infringe on the spiritual domain helped to establish an intellectual rationale for modern secularism and pluralism (Bielefeldt et al., 2022).

The men who framed important constitutional text were motivated by these philosophical commitments. In the United States, the First Amendment prevents the government from establishing religion while also protecting the freedom to worship, creating a two-tier system intended to safeguard people from either the state forcing them to be religious or for the state to interfere with their religion. Likewise, numerous decolonized African, South Asian, and Latin American constitutions included clauses on religious freedom that borrowed from both international human rights standards and domestic struggles for cultural and religious autonomy (Witte, 2020).

Structural and Doctrinal Elements in Constitutional Law

While constitutions typically feature a combination of positive guarantees and negative prohibitions to protect FoRB, they often also contain doctrine to assess when and how that right may be limited. Positive guarantees include the right to worship, the right to conscientious objection and mandates to ensure religious education and religiously prescribed attire. Negative prohibitions include prohibitions on government establishment of religion, religious tests for public office and religious discrimination. Doctrinally, courts utilize a variety of interpretive tools to assess FoRB restrictions. The 'strict scrutiny' standard in US constitutional law demands that a law burdening religious freedom must serve a state's compelling interest and that it be narrowly tailored to achieve it. European constitutional systems and the ECHR frequently rely on proportionality analysis to balance religious freedom against other fundamental rights and public policy interests. In pluralistic societies, these legal categories are increasingly challenged by the variety and intersectionality of religious identity and discrimination. Cases such as those involving religious minority rights, gendered religious expression claims such as headscarf bans, and intra-religious divides test the limits of law and require more of a nuanced adjudicative approach.

Religion and the Role of the State

One of the most longstanding issues for any constitutional democracy is identifying the proper relationship between the state and religion. From the almost absolute prohibition of religious involvement in public affairs in France, to cooperation between government and a particular religion or all religions, most constitutional democracies have developed several options. The difference is largely due to the normative framework. France's laïcité stands for the state's absolute neutrality in matters of belief with an emphasis on the positive neutrality of the state toward any religious belief. In turn, Germany, employs an active neutral model, which requires the state to cooperate with religious institutions using all facilitation and means, which includes financial support, if they comply with the values of pluralism and non-discrimination (Agus Handoko, 2024). The normative framework determines how constitutional norms and standards of FoRB should be applied in practice, identifying possible areas of their conflict associated with the aforementioned tension between the norms. Given the use of AI in an increasing number of areas of state functions such as education, law enforcement, and public services, new forms of challenges appear. Whether the state through the automated system meets the FoRB standards when filtering religious content in digital classrooms of public schools or an algorithm denying fewer benefits to persons wearing religious attire, these are the issues regulated by the constitutional suffrage.

Non-State Actors and the Expansion of Constitutional Norms

It is a relatively a recent and new development. Traditionally, constitutional rights applied to state actions or actions reasonably attributable to the state. The digital age has blurred the line between public and private power, not only because high-tech corporations increasingly act as state-like platforms of expression, community, and commerce. Hence, these 'private companies' perform content moderation, data procession, and internal policy enforcement, often resulting in more or less direct limitations of religious expression by their users. Therefore, constitutional scholars and courts increasingly acknowledge the need to develop doctrines addressing this emerging shift of power (Gómez, 2025). In many jurisdictions, the notion of 'horizontal effect' is adopted, which means that constitutional norms, especially fundamental rights like FoRB, affect private relations and private duties. In other cases, more indirect mechanisms were used, such as anti-discrimination statutes or digital rights acts. For example, AI-driven content moderation helps companies to hide the mechanism of flagging religious content, suppressing or boosting it, thus creating a number of ways for covert religious censorship and discrimination. Even though private actors are almost never directly limited in their power by constitutional free speech and FoRB provisions in the way governments are, their action can sometimes void the essence and function of these doctrines.

Global Trends and Comparative Constitutionalism

Constitutions globally adopt diverse approaches in regard to the protection of FoRB. In particular, India's Article 25 of the Constitution guarantees the freedom of conscience and the right to freely profess, practice, and propagate religion, subject to public order, morality, and health. In Canada, religious freedom is included in the Charter of Rights and Freedoms under Section 2 under the category of freedom of thought, belief, opinion, and expression. In Canada, it has increasingly been interpreted very broadly, covering both belief and practice. Furthermore, shortly after the end of apartheid, South Africa adopted a new constitution with an emphasis on equality and dignity. Among others, the document lists religious diversity among core democratic values. Comparative constitutionalism related insights would be especially relevant in investigating conflict dimensions associated with advancements in AI in multi-faith societies or societies that have recently experienced religious conflicts. In the context of AI governance, the most relevant insights could be applied to developing models of integration with constitutional rights protection. Some countries are already considering constitutional amendments or digital rights charters that include specific stipulations related to AI and digital platforms responsibilities in upholding the fundamental human right to religious freedom (Çapar, 2024).

THREATS TO RELIGIOUS FREEDOM IN THE AGE OF AI

With AI technologies being integrated into virtually all areas of human life, they pose not only immense opportunities but also serious threats to fundamental rights, and one of them refers to freedom of religion or belief. These threats may be indirect or direct, aimed at the rights of both the persons and the religious communities (He, 2024).

Following are some of the key challenges that are inherent to AI influence on religious freedom and structures:

Surveillance and Discrimination

AI-based surveillance, such as facial recognition, predictive policing and surveillance of social media have equally broad implications for restrictions on religious freedom, particularly when it comes to weakly or non-democratic state regimes. Some governments have used these tools to surveil, suppress and persecute religious groups that they consider a threat. For instance, machine learning surveillance systems have also been used to surveil the activities and movements of Uyghur Muslims in China, limiting the religious freedoms of those people and infringing both their privacy and the right to assembly. Even in the contexts of a state where democratic liberalism prevails, cases pertaining to police targeting minority religious communities with AI-powered surveillance, techniques like algorithmic profiling on suspected demographic elements, are utilized. Such policing can be seen coercive, threatening and unreasonable to the public. As a matter of fact, this kind of enforcement is often done in the dark, without any transparency, accountability or judicial supervision and that creates serious constitutional problems around due process of law and equal protection of law.

Algorithmic Bias and Data Discrimination

AI is as good as the data sets on which it is trained, and data sets have an ugly tendency to reproduce the cultural biases of the societies in which they are produced. To the extent that the training data set is naturally inclined to omit or misrepresent particular religious groups, AI is likely to re-create and accentuate that bias (Munir, 2025). For instance, hiring algorithms could keep candidates with information about their religion (like membership in a religious-based organization) down in the hiring funnel, reasoning that the data makes them controversial or not a good cultural fit for a company.

On platforms such as YouTube or Facebook or TikTok, content recommenders might similarly under-expose or mis-represent religious content. This might leave out voices of minority spokesperson for religion, or it might accentuate too much an outdated or overly negative view of one or another religious tradition. This sort of automated decision is often made without the people it affects even hearing about it and without any obvious avenue for recourse.

Biasness AI algorithms do more than sustain inequality, it conflicts with constitutional values of neutrality and non-discrimination. It is especially lethal in pluralistic societies in which laws and institutions already protect the rights of all religious groups.

Suppression and Over-Moderation of Religious Content

AI is deployed widely for content moderation on platforms such as social media, to take down hate speech, misinformation or extremist propaganda. While these goals are commendable, the blunt tools of automated moderation regularly deploy and make millions of pieces of legitimate religious speech disappear. For instance, references to religious writings or theological doctrine could fall under the hate speech moniker when viewed outside the algorithms of content moderation.

Moderating religious speech is both a legal and a moral conundrum. What counts as appropriate religious speech has a real impact on religious liberty in the digital environment (Parmar & Murari, 2025). Irrespective of this the problem people face is not that they do not have effective mechanisms to challenge such decisions, but the process by which they can do so is often unclear, with rights violated and silence imposed. Such overreach not only steps upon the rights of the faithful to act as individuals, it also can scuttle broader religious conversation and community building. Inability to express religious opinions freely on social media could result in cultural immobility, a silencing of diverse opinions and public ignorance about different faiths.

Deterring Effects and Self-Censorship

Certainly, one of the dangerous consequences of censorship to an extreme level is the creation of a 'deterring effect' from AI-powered surveillance and moderation where people being scared to even express themselves out of worry that they would be watched or reprimanded. Religions followers might not like to talk about their religion online or join online prayer circles or share religious content. Particularly, if a community has been historically targeted or stigmatized, they may be even more unwilling to express anything online.

These deterring effects dampen the vitality of corporate religious speech as well as the ability to develop and sustain community (Daruwala, 2025). The collective acts and the free conversations are the bedrock of religious identity. This is not just freedom from oppression, but freedom to see the conviction to one's beliefs, the core of a person and a community, realized. Constitutionally, this portends as alarming threat to the freedom of speech and of religion. However, legal frameworks will also need to evolve to account for how digital spaces are regulated, AI can coercively exert social pressure so as to discourage free and voluntary religious expression.

State-Private Hybrid Power Dynamics

One novelty in the governance of AI is the mix of public authority and private agencies. Governments tend to outsource the construction and maintenance of AI infrastructure to private technology companies, which are generally left unregulated in how they build and maintain such systems. From the perspective of religious liberty, this presents substantial questions around accountability and the limits of constitutional rights. When a government outsources content moderation to a tech platform or uses privately developed AI to spy on us, questions arise about whether the protection of law applies to such activities (Menkel-Meadow & Schneider, 2025).

Do users have rights not to be discriminated against on religious grounds and not to be spied upon arbitrarily by algorithms that were created or deployed by nonstate actors? Do private platforms have to allow religious speech, as public forums do? These questions challenge the traditional doctrinal dichotomies between state and private action. As AI mediates religious governance, courts or lawmakers might have to come to terms with new concepts of responsibility and how to extend constitutional norms to these new hybrids of power. That includes figuring out whether private companies should serve as gatekeepers of human rights. rules for transparency, accountability and due process in such instances.

There are countless, deeply systemic threats to freedom of thought and expression posed by AI and these are often hidden deep within multiple layers of technical infrastructure. From surveillance to profiling to discrimination and then from biased decision-making to oppression and ultimately, to the dissolution of public-private distinctions. AI creates mechanisms of governance unimagined by earlier constitutional systems. It is not as if these are mere hypotheticals rather, they are already happening in ways that threaten to marginalize and demean individual believers and religious communities, emboldening perpetrators of violence or exclusion targeting those who strive to remain not just devout but also civically engaged.

We need legal doctrines and technical standards that adhere to these constitutional principles to safeguard FoRB in the age of AI. That will involve the continued strengthening of safeguards against discrimination, the promotion of transparency and accountability in algorithmic systems, and ensuring that all have the opportunity to express, practice and share their beliefs, among other things. Law can fulfill these demands, as a promise within this zone of anticipatory dialogue in which constitutional law already exist as the promise keeper of freedom and justice which is the need of the future emergent world.

AI AS A TOOL FOR ENHANCING RELIGIOUS FREEDOM

Although a lot of focus has been on the dangers of AI and rightly so to religious freedom, the positive potential for AI to contribute to and at the same time defend the right to FoRB is also worth highlighting. From use in religious practices to inculcating pluralism and enhancing legal protections, emerging AI technologies, if responsibly designed and implemented can be catalysts for religious liberty (He, 2024b). This article covers five particular aspects where AI could create a positive impact towards the fulfillment of religious freedom in the digital world.

Figure 1. Meta's hate speech problem (Zandt, 2024)

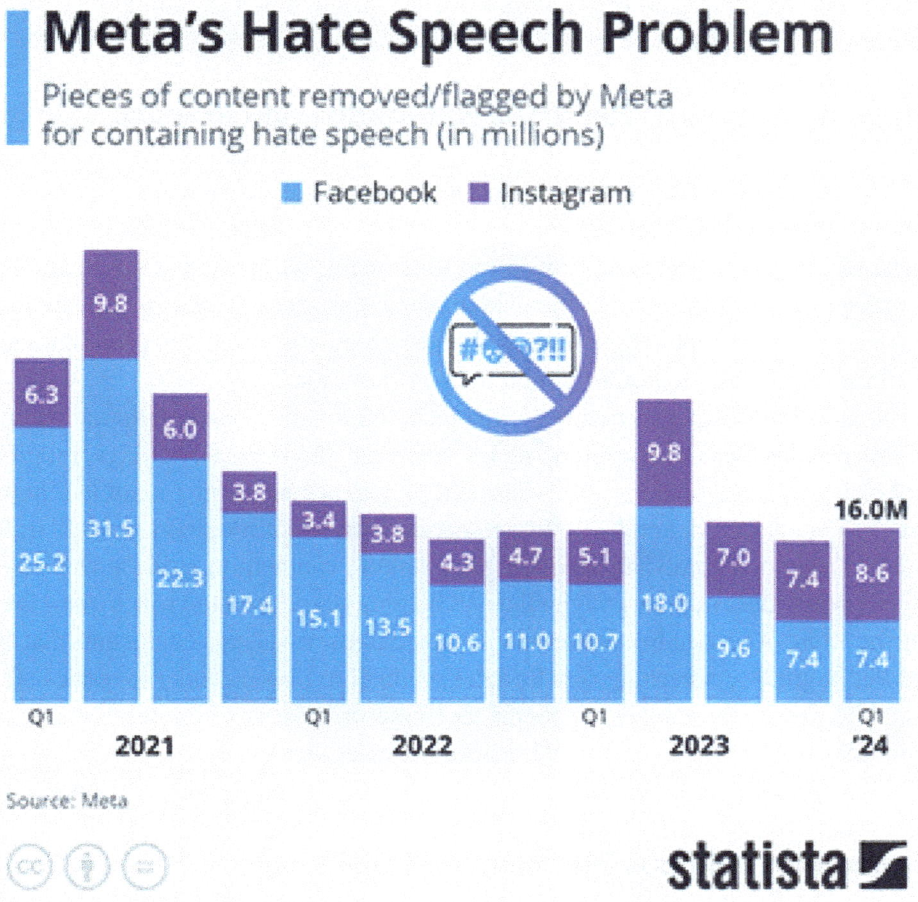

In the above Figure 1, from Q4 2017 to Q3 2023, Facebook significantly ramped up the rate at which it is moderating hate speech. In the first half of 2024, Meta (Facebook and Instagram) either flagged or took down about 16 million hate-related pieces of content which is a major benchmark in its moderation efforts. However, trend evaluation revealed an increasing trend in the number of removals per quarter which is consistent with an increased use of AI-based detection systems. The rise peaked in circa late 2022, with a softening around late 2023, possibly indicating refinements in the algorithms or changes in platform priorities.

These figures underscore Metas increasing emphasis on content moderation and the company's two-track effort i.e. to enforce its rules at scale, while risking overreach and errors. Large scale proactive takedowns are made possible through the use of automated systems, however accuracy and transparency issues yet persist. What that means is that the data offers both a glimpse of the scope of Facebooks moderation footprint and of the effectiveness, fairness, and accountability of AI-driven content control.

Enabling Access to Religious Knowledge and Practice

There are some easy to identify steps AI could take that would improve religious freedom. Chief among them is to further democratize access to religious texts, teaching and practice. Translation tools using AI can put sacred texts and commentaries into the hands of people in many languages, removing the language barriers that have kept people from probing the teaching across religious lines and even for those with an inquiry within their own tradition.

Natural Language Processing (NLP) techniques can be used to do annotation, summarization and cross referencing of scriptures, theological writings, religious and jurisprudential sources (Abdullah, 2022). For instance, an AI can facilitate a user to read across denominational or sect boundaries of a certain passage in the Bible, Yazan or Torah. This technological venture can help to face the challenges in religious education, refining belief and helping the faithful to grow in their faith. Furthermore, AI can help us develop virtual religious assistants or chatbots that can answer inquiries concerning rituals, dates on the liturgical calendar, or ethics. This could be especially valuable to members living in isolated or oppressive cultures who may not be able to easily visit leaders or institutions of the faith. Four of her creations provide inclusivity, accessibility and spiritual independence for everyone.

Promoting Religious Pluralism and Dialogue

Artificial intelligence (AI) based platforms could also encourage interfaith dialogue and religious tolerance by presenting alternative religious perspectives, emphasizing shared values and connecting individuals following different religious traditions. Anti-echo-chamber and anti-filter-bubble algorithms can support the curation of information that presents users with alternative views of the world in a respectful and educational way. For example, an AI driven network could be structured to encourage positive conversation between Christians, Muslims, Jews, Hindus, Buddhists, atheists and others around common concerns like ethics, justice and peace. This kind of engagement not only encourages religious tolerance but also cultivates civic virtues of pluralism and living together.

Indeed, these types of AI are even in line with constitutional principles that protect the free exchange of ideas and foster an environment that is a marketplace of ideas (Makridakis, 2017). Through partnerships between governments and civil society organizations and developers, AI systems will develop, rather than undermine, all these values.

Safeguarding Religious Rights Through Legal and Policy Tools

AI is increasingly becoming part of law research, case profiles and judgments digests. We can use these tools to follow trends in religious liberty jurisprudence, red-flag potential violations, and bolster policy responses. Legal AI is able to analyse vast data sets of court judgments and legislation to pinpoint trends in discriminatory rulings, anomalies in the application of FoRB principles or emerging legal threats (Kumar, Sanjaya, & Saleem, 2025). For instance, an AI system that is trained on constitutional case law could alert civil rights organizations to judicial opinions that are narrowing the scope of religious exemptions or that are defining religious liberty in a majoritarian rather than accommodating way. On the basis of such understanding, advocates can develop tailored legal strategies and public education efforts to protect those who are hit hardest.

Governments can also use AI to take action against violators before something happens as a means to ensure that religious accommodations are being followed in public sector institutions like schools, prisons and workplaces. AI is an enforcement, a literal and not merely interpretive enforcement, of the constitutional commitment to religious freedom.

Strengthening Community Engagement and Civic Participation

Religious organizations have much to gain through AI for the public good and philanthropy. Analysis powered by AI has the potential to allow religious groups to understand the needs of their community better and offer a more bespoke spiritual aid and the most effective distribution of resources. For instance, machine learning apps could analyze social media sentiment or demographic data to identify underserved communities or emerging mental health issues among congregants.

Religious groups are using AI more often to coordinate disaster relief actions, activate network of interfaith community and ensure large scale gathering of heterogeneous people. These practices not only are operationally sound, but they also acknowledge the positive role for religion in public life. It is simply that a rich democratic ecology is one in which religious communities are flourishing and doing a great deal to foster social harmony. AI is an enabler of religious vitality and democratic resilience, each of which is protected under constitutional orders.

Mitigating Bias and Enhancing Inclusion Through Ethical Design

One way in which advanced AI can support FoRB in the future is by helping to overcome the very biases that compromise religious freedom. By adopting inclusive design principles and responsible AI development practices, developers can construct systems that recognise the plurality of religious life and seek to prevent discrimination.

For example, religious ethicists, theologians or human rights activists may be involved in the creation of AI in order to warrant the consideration of religious norms and values. AI could in principle be trained on input which is as diverse as those multiple religious traditions and that includes more than one language, more than one cultural system, so that we do not reach algorithms that produce global belief structures or one that marginalized minority societies (Kumar & Karun Sanjaya, 2025).

Furthermore, explainable AI (XAI) techniques might help to make more transparent as to how religious content is ranked, flagged or promoted on certain digital platforms. This transparency enables users to understand and challenge the algorithmic determinations that affect their religious discourse. Algorithmic audits and fairness testing would be helpful in this arena as well to prevent the Vedic voices from being systematically underrepresented or mis-represented. Regulators and constitutional courts can encourage or mandate ethical AI use through non-discrimination, inclusion and freedom of expression under laws and policies. If we align technological innovation with constitutional values, we can ensure that our AI systems mirror, and enable, religious freedom. AI is neither a friend nor an enemy, of religious freedom but rather a tool that can be used for good or for ill, depending upon how it is created, used and governed.

AI can be well utilized in increasing access to religious literacy to strengthen dialogue, to power legal advocacy, to educate about inclusion. AI can be instrumental in fighting and maintaining the constitutional religious liberty. Technologists need to combine forces with legal scholars, policymakers and religious communities. If combined, these two would be the thing that can create a spiritual autonomous AI ecosystem so that everyone could practice freedom and let diversity thrive so that people can manifest their beliefs in a more complete manner in this digital world.

RECONCILING AI GOVERNANCE WITH CONSTITUTIONAL PROTECTIONS OF RELIGIOUS FREEDOM

As AI technologies continue to enter public and private life, the challenge for constitutional democracies is how to reconcile that governance framework for AI with the broad protection of human rights which is enshrined in constitutional law (Kumar & Mohanty, 2024). Nowhere is this more pressing than in the area of FoRB, because even well-intentioned technologies and legislation can come into conflict with religious rights. This section addresses this necessary task of reconciling AI governance with constitutional rights of religious freedom. It analyses normative tensions, instruments of regulation, institutional competences and models of adjudication that should shape the integration of AI in constitutional democracies.

Normative Tensions Between Technocratic Governance and Constitutional Freedoms

One of the initial difficulties of integrating AI governance with constitutional FoRB protections is the inherent conflict between technocratic decision-making and a notion of fundamental rights adjudication. Machine learning and AI usually work by optimising, predicting and general reasoning to a conclusion, whereas constitutional freedoms are grounded in values like dignity, pluralism and individual self-government. Rights-based models would in turn be brought to the fore when such paradigms do come into conflict.

AI content moderation system which discourages religious expression that is controversial or non-mainstream according to most relevant user preferences may be misguided from a platforms perspective of driving engagement while running afoul of constitutionally protected free exercise and freedom of speech. From a constitutional standpoint, the design and assessment of algorithmic systems should be conducted with regard to not only technical benchmarks but also human rights norms.

To help bridge this gap, constitutional governance should contain legal mechanisms which can be enforced and that emphasize rights in the development, use and regulation of AI systems. Public deliberation and judicial review are crucial devices for bringing normative disagreement to the surface and for resolving them.

Embedding FoRB Standards into AI Regulation and Policy

Attaching constitutional FoRB norms to AI laws, regulations and institutions is a vital part of this overall AI governance strategy that seeks to ensure that AI governance is in line with constitutional and another relevant FoRB guarantees (Ashraf & Mustafa, 2024). National and supranational entities should mandate respect for religious rights within the AI design, data collection, training, deployment and evaluation process.

This can be implemented in various ways:

i. Religion should also be designated as a protected class with race, sex and disability in non-discrimination legislation in AI regulation.
ii. Privacy laws should prohibit the gathering or processing of sensitive religious knowledge unless the individual has been informed and consented to such gathering or processing.
iii. Public sector AI procurement rules should require compliance with constitutional FoRB standards (especially in contexts such as law enforcement, education and health).

The European Union's AI Act, for instance, labels some uses of AI 'high-risk' and subject to stricter scrutiny. A constitutional FoRB framework would mean applying similar scrutiny to systems that affect religious speech, religious worship or the recognition of religious identity.

Role of Courts in Interpreting and Enforcing Constitutional Safeguards

For constitutional courts to play a central role in developing how FoRB applies to new technologies like AI is crucial. Through constitutional litigation and judicial review, courts can serve as impartial arbiters in the allocation of responsibility between states, non-state actors and AI in the violation of religious rights. Precedents in various legal systems like religious attire, faith-based education or conscientious objectors, can be applied to AI-mediated ones. For example, courts might analyze whether algorithmic decisions present an undue burden upon religious practice or might fall within the realm of de facto discrimination, under the equal protection guarantee of the constitution (Kumar & Karun Sanjaya, 2025).

All these are challenges mentioned, directly have to do with making our legal structures capable of understanding the technical functioning of AI systems, as well as their sociopolitical effects. Amicus briefs by technologists, ethicists and businesses that specialize in religious freedom can fill the gap of knowledge along with judicial training on AI.

Supervision by Independent Regulatory Bodies and Civil Society

A comprehensive AI governance framework should be established through joint contributions by independent supervision bodies like data protection authority, human rights commissions, technology ethics boards and so on. These bodies would have the power to enforce adherence of AI systems to religious freedom safeguards and provide remedy to those that have been impacted (Hartmann et al., 2024).

Civil society groups, especially those concerned with religious freedom, are considerably playing their role as an alert watchdog. They can further audit AI systems, file complaints about AI systems, do strategic litigation and advocate for rights-based policy that takes on an AI system. Interreligious coalitions, in particular, have the potential to be conduits for discussion among and between various faith communities, paving way for an inclusive and pluralistic model of AI governance. Further, public participation in the design of regulations through consultations, hearings or participatory policymaking mechanisms can democratize AI governance in manner that reflects religious diversity in the decision-making.

International Norms and Comparative Constitutional Practice

International human rights law and comparative constitutional jurisprudence can offer valuable insights to guide governance of AI to promote FoRB. Instruments like the ICCPR and regional covenants sufficiently deal with freedom of religion and could serve as a model for countries. Comparative practices in jurisdictions for countries like Germany, Canada, India and South Africa, reveal an array of constitutional strategies to the governance of the religion-state dimension in the society where technology induced changes is a given norm (Romana & Santiago, 2024). These cases may also be taken as a reminder of the usefulness of context-sensitive, but principled governance. For example, South Africa's constitutional recognition of human dignity and equality has framed judicial protection for minority groups in public spaces. In Canada, the Charter is interpreted to include secularism and multicultural inclusion. These approaches can help to inform AI policy conforming to both local practices and universal rights.

Developing Constitutional Metrics for AI Accountability

For AI governance to be reconciled with constitutional protection of FoRB, more robust standards of accountability will have to be developed. These have to be more than simply technically sound and include metrics around human rights impact. Some suggestions may include:

i. Percentage of algorithm decisions reviewed for religious bias.
ii. Cases and consequences of FoRB related complaints and court cases involving AI.
iii. Religions are transparent in content moderation and censorship.
iv. Protecting religious minorities in AI development and supervision.

These types of metrics can be included in transparency reports, regulatory audit and academic appraisal. They offer an empirical basis for assessing whether AI systems are fulfilling constitutional guarantees. The reconciliation of AI governance and the constitutional protection of religious freedom is not just an engineering problem but rather one with constitutional responsibility. While AI continues to influence public discourse, how institutions operate and how individuals identify, it all must remain grounded in responsible and rights-based governance.

Incorporating FoRB norms into legal foundations, creating strong judicial and institutional review, promoting open policymaking and using international legal standards will help to ensure that AI technologies are utilised to uphold rather than undermine the values of pluralism, dignity and religious freedom. The long-term objective is to build an AI governance system that works under the principles of constitution-based democracy, constitutional principles and a democracy which enables technological advancement without sacrificing the core right to believe, worship and behave according to one's conscience.

WAY FORWARD AND FUTURE DIRECTIONS

The confluence of AI and religious freedom is an important issue of the twenty-first century. But digital technologies now mediate and used in speech, identity, for use of public and private goods and almost everything. Therefore, they are bound to influence on the impact it creates in the mind of individuals and communities. This chapter suggests some ways that policy makers, technologists, legal scholars, religious groups and civil society actors could put in use when protecting and promoting freedom of religion or belief (FoRB) in the age of AI.

Reaffirming Constitutional Commitments in a Technological Era

At the center of any democratic reaction to the rise of AI lies the reassertion of constitutional principles, including the unalienable right to religious freedom. Constitutions are not historic museum pieces but vibrant texts that are intended to help shape societies as they go through as time changes. They need to be interpreted dynamically to face emerging challenges presented by algorithmic decision-making, automated surveillance and digital content regulation (Abiri, 2024). Keeping this in mind, it will be upon the parliaments and courts to ensure that constitutional protections of FoRB are not undermined through technological or bureaucratic obfuscation. Governments should encourage jurisprudence that supports the notion that freedom of religion entails not only private belief but public expression, even in an algorithmically driven world.

Ethical and Human Rights-Centered AI Design

To ensure protection of religious freedom in future, tech needs to be built with a lot of emphasis on ethics and human rights. This includes reliable fairness, transparency, accountability and non-discrimination being embedded between the AIs code lines, particularly in cases when these systems are expected to shape religious practices, identities or the access to faith-based services (Kumar & Mohanty, 2024).

Developers and companies have a legal and perhaps even more a moral imperative to develop technologies that do not oppress or misrepresent religious communities. Ethical audits, religious diversity impact assessments and interdisciplinary advisory boards can help ensure that normative commitments inform technical decisions.

Inclusive Multistakeholder Governance Models

No one actor will be able to safeguard FoRB in the age of AI. Instead, what is required is a multistakeholder model of governance that includes governments, technology companies, faith communities, civil society organizations, academic bodies and international human rights agencies. Each actor can have a unique role:

i. Governments can enact protection with an oversight commission.
ii. Technology companies could design for rights and redress.
iii. Religious communities can also voice the needs of their communities and serve as cultural stewards.
iv. Academics and ethicists can work on frameworks and the implications for systems.

Collaborative governance mechanisms, like global AI ethics initiatives, interfaith digital roundtable discussions or national human rights commission which can help to ensure that decisions regarding AI are informed by multiple values, including religious values.

Safeguarding Pluralism in the Digital Public Sphere

The matter is made far worse by AI acting as an increasingly dominant cultural gatekeeper, curating and filtering public discourse, leading people to see certain things, to believe certain things and to say certain things. This presents opportunities for religious mediatization but also new forms of inclusion, stereotyping, and silencing. one should make a pluralistic digital space where various religious voices can have their say without fear of being suppressed by algorithms or attacked (Schlesinger, 2024).

It is therefore imperative not to allow content moderation systems to be prejudiced against specific religious symbols, speech or practices. Appeal mechanisms have to be open and easy to access. More generally, constitutional principles of viewpoint neutrality, proportionality and equal treatment should guide the regulation of platforms.

Strengthening Global Norms and Transnational Protections

Since AI systems frequently cross national borders, legal and ethical safeguards for religious freedom need to do the same. International human rights law that includes, most notably the Universal Declaration of Human Rights and the International Covenant on Civil and Political Rights (ICCPR) establishes standards that states and companies must meet.

In future the international and regional organizations should encourage efforts to harmonize AI laws to mention FoRB-specific regulation. The United Nation (UN), Council of Europe (COE), African Union (AU) and Association of Southeast Asian Nations (ASEAN) can provide capacity building, peer learning support and adopt regional charters or principles on AI and religious freedom. Cross-border legal instruments such as data protection agreements, non-discrimination treaties and freedom of expression compacts must also adapt to the new reality in which AI acts as an intermediary even for basic freedoms.

Empowering Individuals and Communities Through Digital Literacy

Providing citizens, in particular religious minorities and marginalized communities with the necessary tools to comprehend, critique and shape AI is key to democratic resilience. Efforts to teach digital literacy need to include instruction on how AI operates, what are user rights and how to seek redress for violations. Houses of worship, religious schools and community centers can be key nodes for digital rights education. Interfaith tech fellowships or training programs for clergy on AI ethics, could further narrow the divide between centuries-old religions and cutting-edge technologies.

Creating Mechanisms for Redress and Restoration

A comprehensive strategy to protect religious freedom would also include a means of recourse when violations take place. The victims of algorithmic discrimination should have access and available avenues of remedy, whether by courts or regulators, by ombudspersons or by internal company processes. Reparative actions such as community consultations, public apologies or compensation schemes, can also be a response not only to material harms, but to symbolic and spiritual injuries of religious injustice in the digital era.

CONCLUSION

Freedom of religion is one of the cornerstones of democratic constitutions. We can raise it higher than the private conscience to embrace public articulations, institutional autonomy, and cultural self-comprehension. It's a freedom inflected with danger and possibility on a topography of complexity, as amplified by the data-powered AI systems that increasingly mediate our encounter with the world on a scale and temperament that was never seen before in human history. AIs potential is not inherently at odds with religious liberty, but there are challenges when it comes to using the technology responsibly. AI should be supported one must also ensure that it is also helping to raise up human dignity and spiritual flourishing, rather than diminish it (Van den Hoven et al., 2024).

A comprehensive strategy to protect FoRB in an age of AI must begin with an acknowledgment that constitutional rights are not frozen in time, but evolve in response to changing social, technological, and political conditions. Therefore, this analysis is crucial, and it needs to be rigorous, fact based and forward leaning. It will take jurisprudential innovation to accommodate how AI has transformed the religious speech landscape, whether through the programmed censorship of religious discourse on digital platforms, the discriminatory profiling of religious minorities by surveillance technologies or the algorithmic imbalances in supplying assistance to faith-based groups.

Similarly important is the principle of subsidiarity, religious freedom considerations in AI governance should be made at the lowest level possible to those impacted groups. In practice, this looks like lifting up the voices of religious minorities, indigenous faith traditions and other underrepresented communities in conversations around tech policy. The governance of AI cannot simply be left to technocrats or to companies, it has to be participatory, and it must occur in a framework of democratic deliberation, sensitive to culture and respectful of religion. AI systems are growing in their international reach, however, this also means that violation of religious rights abroad can resonate far beyond borders. Algorithms tuned for one cultural context, for the east, may not know how to spot or treat religious symbols or speech in the west. Technologies that are exported while not well protected against their potential misuse may make the entire suppression of religious freedom by authoritarian governments. Here, international human rights law should set out a minimum standard and pave the way forward towards aspirational standards for promoting and protecting FoRB.

They should support legal harmonisation and transnational cooperation to ensure that FoRB is embedded in policy and regulation of AI at all levels. Regional instruments such as the EU AI Act do offer us some welcome examples of how to bake HRAs into the governance of technology. At the same time, law instruments, such as the Organisation for Economic Co-operation and Developments (OECD) AI Principles and The United Nations Educational, Scientific and Cultural Organizations (UNESC) AI Ethics Recommendation, can serve as valuable gear to establish norms and to cultivate peer review, especially in countries with lower thresholds in institutional checks.

We must develop cultural and theological approaches toward technology, as machine intelligence is defining more and more of the world in which we live. Religious traditions are supported by deep wells of wisdom concerning ethical discernment, human agency and the sanctity of personhood. It is not that religious leaders and communities are simply to acclimate to AI but to be involved in the co-creation and critiquing of it. That includes training clergy and laity to understand the implications of new technologies, investing in faith-shaped programs for tech literacy and cultivating moral imagination in digital design. There Interfaith organizations, Universities and Seminaries have a particular role to play in leading and contributing to interdisciplinary research and pedagogy on the co-habitation of AI and religion. There is good reason to think that if we pool our scholarly resources, we can get closer to an understanding of how people in different religious traditions across the globe think about what is fair, who is responsible and what counts as human well-being in a world that is technologized. It may also pave the way of formulating culturally contextualized AI ethics frameworks that transcend the Western liberal value system and resonate with the people worldwide. We must keep in mind that defending religious liberty in the age of AI will demand strong accountability safeguards. Systemic remedies, such as the establishment of independent regulatory bodies, ombuds and class action devices, are required to monitor, prevent and redress such infringements. Industries must be held responsible for what constitutes their standard of due diligence on transparency and public disclosure, particularly when applying technologies that have known impacts on freedom of religion.

This chapter has sought to at least sketch out an agenda, grounded in constitutional doctrine, but sensitive to the ethical, cultural and geopolitical implications of AI.

Because ultimately what we want is not only to prevent harm, but to build a future where technology helps us develop our ability to understand, love, be passionately moved by the beauty around us, feel deeply connected to the entire world. It is also a test of whether our societies can maintain their highest values in the face of radical technological change.

REFERENCES

Abdullah, M. A. (2022). Islamic Religious Education Based on Religious Intersubjectivity: Philosophical Perspectives and Phenomenology of Religion. *Jurnal Pendidikan Agama Islam, 19*(1), 141–164. DOI: 10.14421/jpai.2022.191-11

Abiri, G. (2024). Public Constitutional AI. *ArXiv (Cornell University), 2*(1). Cornell University. /arxiv.2406.16696DOI: 10.2139/ssrn.4874670

Ahmed, S., Sumi, A. A., & Aziz, N. A. (2024). Exploring Multi-Religious Perspective of Artificial Intelligence. *Theology and Science, 23*(1), 1–25. Taylor & Francis online. DOI: 10.1080/14746700.2024.2436783

Ashraf, C. (2021). Exploring the impacts of artificial intelligence on freedom of religion or belief online. *The International Journal of Human Rights, 26*(5), 1–35. Taylor & Francis online. DOI: 10.1080/13642987.2021.1968376

Ashraf, Z. A., & Mustafa, N. (2024). AI Standards and Regulations. *Advances in Healthcare Information Systems and Administration Book Series*, 325–352. DOI: 10.4018/979-8-3693-7051-3.ch014

Bielefeldt, H., Pinto, T. A., & Petersen, M. J. (2022). Introduction: Freedom of Religion or Belief as a Human Right. *The Review of Faith & International Affairs, 20*(2), 1–12. DOI: 10.1080/15570274.2022.2065799

Çapar, G. (2024). Global Constitutionalism and Legitimate International Authority. *Jus Cogens, 6*(3), 223–243. Advance online publication. DOI: 10.1007/s42439-024-00093-4

Daruwala, N. A. (2025). Social media, expression, and online engagement: A psychological analysis of digital communication and the chilling effect in the UK. *Frontiers in Communication, 10*, 1565289. Advance online publication. DOI: 10.3389/fcomm.2025.1565289

Gómez, O. A. (2025). The State as a Humanitarian Actor: Opportunities and Challenges in Decolonizing Humanitarianism. *Yearbook of International Humanitarian Law*, 43–73. DOI: 10.1007/978-94-6265-663-5_2

Handoko, A. (2024). Paradigm Of The Relationship Of Religion And The State. *Asian Journal of Engineering Social and Health, 3*(2), 271–284. DOI: 10.46799/ajesh.v3i2.243

Hartmann, D., de Pereira, J. R. L., Streitbörger, C., & Berendt, B. (2024). Addressing the regulatory gap: moving towards an EU AI audit ecosystem beyond the AI Act by including civil society. *AI and Ethics, 1*(1). Springer Nature Link. DOI: 10.1007/s43681-024-00595-3

He, Y. (2024a). Artificial intelligence and religious freedom: Divergent paths converging on economic expansion. *Humanities and Social Sciences Communications, 11*(1), 1–12. *Humanities & Social Sciences Communications*. Advance online publication. DOI: 10.1057/s41599-024-02642-0

He, Y. (2024b). Artificial intelligence and socioeconomic forces: Transforming the landscape of religion. *Humanities & Social Sciences Communications, 11*(1), 602. Advance online publication. DOI: 10.1057/s41599-024-03137-8

Kumar, A. B., & Sanjaya, K. (2025). Advances in Social Networking and Online Communities Book Series. AI and Social Justice., DOI: 10.4018/979-8-3693-9904-0.ch008

Kumar, A. B., & Mohanty, A. (2024). Artificial Intelligence. *Advances in Human and Social Aspects of Technology Book Series*, 35–62. DOI: 10.4018/979-8-3693-3334-1.ch002

Kumar, A. B., Sanjaya, K., & Saleem, M. (2025). Justice in the Age of Algorithms. *Advances in Computational Intelligence and Robotics*, •••, 191–210. DOI: 10.4018/979-8-3693-9395-6.ch009

Makridakis, S. (2017). The Forthcoming Artificial Intelligence (AI) revolution: Its Impact on Society and Firms. *Futures*, *90*(90), 46–60. DOI: 10.1016/j.futures.2017.03.006

Menkel-Meadow, C. J., & Schneider, A. K. (2025). International Conflict Resolution Processes. SSRN *Electronic Journal*. SSRN. DOI: 10.2139/ssrn.5168799

Munir, B. (2025). Islamophobic Artificial Intelligence in the USA: A Critical Analysis of Religious Bias in Datasets. *The Law Library Journal, 1*(1). *SSRN*. DOI: 10.2139/ssrn.5265355

Parmar, H., & Murari, U. K. (2025). Adapting AI Moderation. *Advances in Computational Intelligence and Robotics*, •••, 29–54. DOI: 10.4018/979-8-3373-0335-2.ch002

Paya, A. (2023). Is AI a threat to faith? How could we maintain human freedom, autonomy, and agency in the age of rising AI power? The Perspective of a Shi'a Muslim. *Journal of Shi'a Islamic Studies, 16*(3-4), 185–208. DOI: 10.1353/isl.2023.a942954

Romana, F., & Santiago, F. (2024). A Comparative Analysis of Artificial Intelligence Regulatory Law in Asia, Europe, and America. *SHS Web of Conferences, 204*(1), 07006–07006. SHS Web of Conference. DOI: 10.1051/shsconf/202420407006

Scharffs, B. G. (2024). Building Bridges between Freedom of Religion and Belief and Other Fundamental Human Rights. *Routledge EBooks*, 117–128. DOI: 10.4324/9781003519188-9

Schlesinger, P. (2024). The Post-Public Sphere and Neo-Regulation of Digital Platforms. *Javnost (Ljubljana), 31*(1), 1–25. Taylor & Francis online. DOI: 10.1080/13183222.2024.2311010

Van den Hoven, J., Stauch, M., Musiani, F., Ferrer, J. D., Ruggieri, S., Pratesi, F., Trasarti, R., & Comandé, G. (2024). Democracy in the Digital Age. *Hal.science*. DOI: 10.15488/18259

Witte, J. (2020). The Right of Freedom of Religion: An Historical Perspective from the West. In Ferrari, S. (Eds.), *Routledge Handbook on Freedom of Religion and Belief*. SSRN Electronic Journal., DOI: 10.4324/9780203732625-4

Chapter 7
Generative AI in Contemporary Islamic Religious Education Discourse:
Revelation Meets Algorithm

Mussa Saidi Abubakari
https://orcid.org/0000-0003-3782-281X
Dig Connectivity Research Laboratory (DCRLab), Uganda & Universiti Brunei Darussalam, Brunei

ABSTRACT

The chapter explores the integration of Generative Artificial Intelligence (GenAI) in contemporary Islamic Religious Education (IRE), exploring the intersections between Islamic theology, pedagogy, and AI. It begins by addressing foundational Islamic epistemology, highlighting historical precedents of technological assimilation in Muslim scholarship, followed by a technical overview of GenAI capabilities and limitations. Practical applications in IRE, such as AI-assisted Qur'anic exegesis and hadith verification, are critically discussed. The chapter further dives into pedagogical and theological considerations by emphasising that the human roles are irreplaceable, ethical authenticity, and the spiritual dimensions of education are critical. Challenges within IRE contexts are outlined, proposing a Shariah-aligned framework for responsible AI integration. We conclude and recommend strategies for educational stakeholders, policymakers, and technologists, advocating cautious optimism in balancing tradition with innovations.

DOI: 10.4018/979-8-3373-3830-9.ch007

INTRODUCTION

Background

The rise of generative artificial intelligence (GenAI) in recent years has ushered in profound changes in education. Tools like Claude and OpenAI's ChatGPT and DALL·E can produce human-like text and images, offering new ways to deliver personalised learning materials at scale (Yan et al., 2024). In mainstream education, GenAI promises to enhance learning experiences by providing on-demand tutoring, instant feedback on student work, and diverse creative content. However, alongside these opportunities come significant challenges – model inaccuracies, ethical dilemmas, and disruptions to traditional teaching methods (Yan et al., 2024). Educators worldwide are thus grappling with how to integrate GenAI in classrooms responsibly. This challenge is especially acute in Islamic Religious Education (IRE), where preserving the sanctity of knowledge and moral values is paramount. The urgency for IRE to respond to AI integration stems from GenAI's fast-growing influence on how learners access information and religious guidance. Muslim educators and institutions increasingly recognise that ignoring AI is not an option; instead, they must actively shape its use in alignment with Islamic principles (Abubakari, Shafik, et al., 2024; Djazilan et al., 2024). As one recent case study in Indonesia noted, AI is already enhancing Quranic learning and ethical discussions in Islamic schools, yet it must "complement rather than replace traditional teacher-led instruction" to maintain spiritual and moral development (Djazilan et al., 2024). This highlights the delicate balance IRE faces: embracing innovation while safeguarding tradition.

Exploring GenAI through an Islamic lens is especially significant because Islamic education is not value-neutral; it is rooted in a worldview where knowledge (*ilm*) is sacred and closely tied to ethics and spirituality. The integration of any innovative technology, therefore, must be evaluated not only for efficacy but also for its impact on faith and character (Abubakari, Zakaria, et al., 2024; Abubakari & Kalinaki, 2024). Contemporary scholars argue that Western secular paradigms have predominantly shaped the global discourse on AI ethics, and there is a need for pluralistic perspectives that include Islamic ethical frameworks (Elmahjub, 2023). By drawing on Islamic sources, both textual (Qur'ān and Sunnah) and scholarly (*fiqh, u ūl al-fiqh*), educators can benchmark AI use against principles of *masla a* (public welfare), justice, and moral accountability (Achruh et al., 2024; Elmahjub, 2023). This chapter's approach is to articulate those connections, thereby contributing to an emerging conversation about 'Islamic AI ethics.'

The chapter's purpose is to explore the intersection of GenAI with Islamic pedagogy and theology. We aim to examine how "revelation meets algorithm" – that is, how foundational Islamic principles can guide the ethical use of AI in religious education, and conversely, how AI might transform the practice of teaching and learning about Islam. The scope includes both practical applications (such as AI tools for Qur'ān study or fatwa guidance) and deeper pedagogical and theological considerations (such as the role of human teachers, authenticity of knowledge, and alignment with Islamic Sharīʿah values). Through the survey of the latest peer-reviewed research and thought leadership across fields, including Islamic studies, education technology, and AI ethics, this chapter provides a comprehensive overview of GenAI's promises and pitfalls in the context of IRE.

Chapter Structure and Methodology

The chapter progresses from theory to practice. In what follows, we first lay the foundations by discussing Islamic epistemology (how knowledge and technology have historically interacted in Muslim thought). We then provide a primer on Generative AI technologies and their general educational applications. Next, we delve into specific applications of GenAI in IRE, from Quranic chatbots to AI tutors. We subsequently address pedagogical and theological considerations, examining risks like misinformation and the irreplaceable role of human educators in spiritual development. The chapter also tackles ethical and legal challenges unique to Muslim contexts, such as aligning AI with Islamic values of modesty, truthfulness, and justice. Finally, we propose a framework for integrating GenAI into Islamic education, guided by *Maqā id al-Sharī ah* (the objectives of Islamic law), and conclude with reflections on future directions. By combining insights from Muslim education scholars and AI experts, this chapter sheds light on how revelation (divine guidance) and algorithm (machine intelligence) can coexist and co-create the future of Islamic education.

Specifically, Section 2 discusses Islamic epistemology and historical perspectives on science/technology in Islam. Section 3 explains what GenAI is and how it works. Section 4 surveys current and potential AI applications in IRE settings. Section 5 examines key pedagogical and theological issues raised by those applications. Section 6 considers ethical/legal challenges in Muslim societies. Section 7 present guiding principles and an integral model for integrating GenAI into Islamic education. Section 8 offers insights for practical recommendations and identifies areas for future research and collaboration. Finally, the last section provides concluding remarks of the chapter. Through this structure, the chapter demonstrates a cautious optimism: GenAI can be a beneficial tool for IRE if used wisely, but the rich moral and pedagogical traditions of Islam must deliberately frame its adoption.

For research methods, the chapter utilised a comprehensive literature search, collection, and evaluation of relevant studies to find the themes related to the chapter's objectives. Thus, various scholarly databases, such as Scopus, Springer Link, and Google Scholar, among others, were surveyed to find the relevant studies. The search prioritised recent works that discussed AI and religious studies, especially Islamic education, by using keywords like "Islamic religious education and AI," "Artificial intelligence and religion," and "AI and Education," among other keywords.

CONCEPTS AND FOUNDATIONS: ISLAMIC EPISTEMOLOGY AND TECHNOLOGY

Islamic epistemology is grounded in the belief that all true knowledge comes from God and is attained through both revelation and reason. The primary sources of knowledge in Islam are the Qur'ān (considered the direct word of God) and the Sunnah (the teachings and example of the Prophet Muhammad) (Butt et al., 2024). These revealed sources form the textual foundation for understanding reality and guiding life. In addition, classical Islamic scholarship recognises consensus (*ijmā*) and analogical reasoning (qiyās) as important epistemic tools to derive rulings for new situations based on the primary texts. Together, Qur'ān, Sunnah, *ijmā* , and qiyās constitute a holistic system of knowledge validation in Islam (Daun & Arjmand, 2018). This system inherently values both preservation of authenticity (through *isnād*: chains of transmission for hadith) and creative reasoning to extend principles to novel circumstances. For instance, the rigorous science of hadith verification – classifying narrations as *a ī* (authentic), *asan* (good), *a īf* (weak), and so on – reflects a deep commitment to truthfulness and accuracy in knowledge transmission (El Ganadi et al., 2025; Mghari et al., 2022). The ethical imperative is clear: conveying religious knowledge is a trust (*amānah*), and Muslim scholars historically developed meticulous methods to fulfil that trust without alteration or error.

Historically, the Islamic worldview has been enthusiastic about knowledge and science, seeing no inherent conflict between divine revelation and the exploration of the natural world. Classical Islamic civilisation (8th–12th centuries CE) witnessed a golden age of science, mathematics, medicine, and technology, precisely because early scholars saw all knowledge as an extension of understanding God's creation (Daun & Arjmand, 2018, 2021). The Qur'ān itself contains over 750 verses urging believers to reflect on nature, the cosmos, and their own intellect, thereby stimulating and encouraging Muslims to engage in activities that lead to the development of science (Hidayat et al., 2020). Islam does not traditionally compartmentalise "religious" vs "secular" knowledge; rather, it posits a unified epistemology under which studying geology or astronomy can be a form of worship if done with the right intention. As one study puts it, in Islam, one never looks at the science of religion and general knowledge separately, because both come from one source, namely God Almighty (Hidayat et al., 2020). Revealed knowledge (e.g., scripture like the Qur'an) and acquired knowledge (e.g., empirical science) are seen as complementary – revelation provides guiding principles and values, while human reason and observation explore the specifics of the world. This integration meant that Muslim scholars like Ibn Sina (Avicenna) and Ibn al-Haytham made groundbreaking scientific contributions without feeling they were leaving the fold of faith (Karagözoğlu, 2017). Indeed, many viewed their scientific work as tafakkur (contemplation), an act of piety.

Despite this generally harmonious view of science and faith, Islamic thought has also grappled with tensions between divine revelation and human innovation. For example, medieval theological debates (such as between the Mu'tazila and Ashʿarī schools) revolved around the roles of reason vs. literal scriptural interpretation. Thinkers like Abū āmid al-Ghazālī critiqued overreliance on Hellenistic philosophy, fearing it could lead to heretical ideas, while others like Ibn Rushd (Averroes) championed philosophy and logic as necessary tools to understand religion deeply (Gyagenda, 2024). Nonetheless, even those debates took place on the common premise that truth cannot contradict truth – what is genuinely established by sound reasoning or observation cannot ultimately conflict with the Qur'ān, since the same God authored both the universe and the scripture. This principle underlies the long tradition of Islamic science and technology: Muslims engaged with technologies from paper-making to architecture to astronomy as manifestations of human creativity endowed by God (Daun & Arjmand, 2018). The classical era saw inventions such as ingenious water clocks, astrolabes, and medical instruments in the Muslim world, reflecting an embrace of technological advancement. Many scholars were at once religious jurists and scientists (e.g. al-Bīrūnī, who wrote on fiqh and physics), epitomising the integrated epistemology of Islam.

Throughout Islamic history, scholars have also set ethical parameters for knowledge transmission and innovation. Knowledge (*ilm*) is not merely an intellectual commodity; it has a moral purpose – to benefit humanity and help individuals fulfil their duties to God and society. Thus, the concept of *adab al- ilm* (the proper etiquette of seeking and imparting knowledge) was developed (Tamuri, 2021). This includes sincerity of intention (*niyyah*) – seeking knowledge for the sake of truth and service, not for arrogance or worldly gain – and honesty in teaching (not withholding or distorting knowledge). We see this ethic in practice in how teachers and students relate in the traditional madrasah or *halaqah* setting: the student shows reverence and humility, the teacher demonstrates care and moral example, and knowledge is passed with a sense of sacred trust (Daun & Arjmand, 2021). The chain-of-transmission model for hadith is a concrete mechanism to ensure accountability for knowledge – every narrator had to be evaluated for integrity and accuracy (El Ganadi et al., 2025; Mghari et al., 2022). In modern terms, one might say Islamic epistemology has long stressed what we now call "source verification" and "information integrity." This is highly relevant in the age of AI, as we later discuss: an AI system generating Islamic information without accountability or clear sourcing challenges this traditional ethic. Another ethical parameter is the principle of no harm (*lā arar*): innovations in knowledge or technology should not cause net harm to faith, life, intellect, lineage, or property, which correspond to the five *Maqā id al-Sharī ah* (objectives of Islamic law) (Mohadi & Tarshany, 2023). Historically, when innovative ideas or tools emerged, Muslim jurists examined them through the lens of maqā id, asking whether they serve public welfare (*maslahah*) or entail harms that must be mitigated. This principle is even more crucial when evaluating GenAI in IRE: does it preserve or undermine the religious values and well-being of students?

In sum, Islam's epistemological foundations provide a rich framework for engaging with technology. Islamic thought celebrates knowledge acquisition through both revelation and exploration, expects ethical stewardship of knowledge, and has mechanisms (like consensus and analogy) to extend guidance to new matters. As we stand in the fourth industrial revolution, with AI as a defining technology, these foundations will help ensure that as "human innovation" advances, it remains in harmony with "divine revelation", not at odds with it (Hidayat et al., 2020). The next section builds on this foundation by explaining what generative AI is, before we then analyse how it might be applied in the context of Islamic education.

UNDERSTANDING GENERATIVE AI IN EDUCATION

Conceptualising GenAI Technologies

Generative AI (GenAI) refers to a class of artificial intelligence systems designed to produce new content, such as text, images, audio, or even code, which is often indistinguishable from human-created content. Powered by advances in deep learning and neural networks, GenAI models learn patterns from vast datasets and use that knowledge to generate novel outputs. A defining feature of recent GenAI is the use of large language models (LLMs) and other transformer-based architectures. For instance, OpenAI's GPT-series (Generative Pre-trained Transformer) models like GPT-4.5 and GPT-4o have been trained on hundreds of billions of words from the internet to predict and compose text coherently. These models operate by analysing the statistical structure of language; given a prompt, they predict the most likely continuation one word at a time, which enables them to compose essays, answer questions, or have conversations. As a 2025 study explains, GenAI leverages deep learning and natural language processing to "create diverse content such as text, images, and audio by analysing vast datasets" (Zhang et al., 2025). In practical terms, this means a GenAI system can take an input (e.g., "Explain the significance of charity in Islam") and produce a human-like answer by drawing on the patterns it learned during training.

Several core technologies underlie GenAI's capabilities. First, the transformer architecture (introduced in 2017) revolutionised how AI models handle language by allowing efficient attention to context, making it possible to train extremely large models that maintain coherence over long passages of text (Alqarni, 2024). Transformers enabled LLMs like BERT, GPT-2, and GPT-3 to thrive (Antoun et al., 2020). Second, neural network advances and hardware improvements have allowed models with tens of billions of parameters, which imbue them with an almost uncanny ability to capture nuances of language and knowledge. Third, techniques like few-shot learning and fine-tuning have made these models adaptable (Naveed et al., 2023) – for example, an LLM can be fine-tuned on Islamic texts so that it generates more context-specific religious content. Indeed, researchers have begun creating customised AI models using tools like GPT Builder that draw on authoritative Islamic sources (e.g., the Qur'ān or a ī al-Bukhari) to answer questions in an Islam-informed manner (El Ganadi et al., 2025). Lastly, on the image side, generative adversarial networks (GANs) and diffusion models allow AI to produce realistic images or art from text descriptions (for example, DALL·E generating a scene of a historic mosque based on a prompt). These technological advances form the backbone of GenAI tools that could be applied in educational settings.

Despite their impressive capabilities, GenAI systems have important limitations. One major issue is the tendency to "hallucinate" – that is, to produce incorrect or fabricated information that sounds plausible. Large language models do not truly understand facts; they rely on pattern prediction, so if prompted with a question to which they have not learned a correct answer, they may generate a convincing-sounding but false answer. In general education contexts, this can lead to misinformation or factual errors being given to students. In a religious context, the stakes are even higher: an AI might confidently generate a hadith or Quran verse that in reality does not exist, or misquote an Islamic ruling, thus misleading learners. Early experiments with Islamic Q&A bots have indeed shown "significant limitations, including hallucinations and reference inaccuracies, which undermine [AI's] reliability for handling sensitive religious content" (El Ganadi et al., 2025). A 2025 study proposing an EMAN framework (Embedding Methodology for Authentic Narrations) noted that naive use of GPT-4 on hadith questions produced answers with bogus citations, prompting the need for grounding the AI in verified databases to ensure accuracy (El Ganadi et al., 2025). Another limitation is bias: AI models can inherit biases present in their training data. For example, if much online content links certain negative terms with Islam, the model might unconsciously reproduce those associations. Some research found that AI text generators associated Islam with concepts of violence 1.7 times more frequently than they did for other religions, while referencing positive terms like "love" and "forgiveness" more often in other religious groups (Abid et al., 2021). Such biases can reinforce harmful stereotypes if not addressed (Abubakari, 2025b; Kuck, 2023). GenAI also lacks true moral judgment or context awareness – it cannot gauge the spiritual appropriateness of an answer, and it has no intent or conscience behind its words. This means it might respond to a sensitive question (say, about theological doctrine or ethical dilemmas) in a way that a human scholar never would, simply because it does not grasp the deeper significance or potential impact on a believer's mindset.

GenAI in General and Religious Education

Understanding the strengths and weaknesses is crucial before applying GenAI to education. In general education, teachers are beginning to use AI for tasks like automated grading, generating practice problems, or even as conversational tutors. GenAI can personalise learning by adapting content to each learner's pace and style – for instance, simplifying explanations for a beginner or offering deeper analysis for an advanced student (Yan et al., 2024). It can also broaden resources: a history class could ask an AI to generate diary entries from the perspective of a historical figure to enrich understanding. In assessment, AI can provide immediate feedback on student essays or solutions, helping students learn from mistakes in real time. There are also creative uses, such as language learning chatbots that simulate immersion or art generation tools for design classes (Yang et al., 2022; Yassine & Gammoudi, 2023). Educational research acknowledges these benefits but also highlights "critical issues such as model imperfections and the disruption of traditional assessments" (Abubakari & Suprapto, 2021; Yan et al., 2024). For example, if students rely on AI to do their homework, it becomes harder to assess their true abilities, raising questions about academic integrity. Thus, schools and universities are developing policies around AI use – some encourage it as a learning aid, others restrict it to prevent plagiarism.

When it comes to religious content creation and pedagogy, GenAI's role is only beginning to be explored. Early signs show both promise and caution. On the positive side, AI can help make religious knowledge more accessible. By "tailoring content to individual learners", an AI tutor could engage youth with personalised examples and stories relevant to their lives, potentially fostering a deeper understanding of Islamic doctrines and values (Abubakari, Zakaria, & Musa, 2023; Abubakari, Shafik, et al., 2024; Zhang et al., 2025). AI might also assist in clarifying complex theological concepts: for instance, by breaking down a dense classical text into simpler language, or by answering follow-up questions at any hour, something a human teacher might not always be available to do. Studies suggest AI can "clarify ambiguities in religious texts, enhancing their interpretability" for students. Additionally, AI can introduce novel metaphors or narratives that spark reflection, thereby encouraging learners to think creatively about religious teachings (Syafitri et al., 2024; Zhang et al., 2025). These potential benefits align well with Islamic pedagogy's goals of tadabbur (deep reflection on texts) and make it conceivable that GenAI could act as a helpful study companion for learners memorising Qur'ān or studying fiqh.

However, the challenges in a religious setting are amplified. Any AI-generated religious guidance must be scrutinised for authenticity against trusted sources, as the margin for error is slim when sacred teachings are involved. The presence of bias or inappropriate content is a serious concern – an AI lacking a moral compass might, if asked a controversial question, produce an answer that deviates from accepted Islamic positions or that offers an overly secular interpretation of a spiritual matter. The Scientific Reports study notes that generative AI, by reflecting user prompts and data biases, can exploit cognitive biases, distorting individuals' perceptions of religious truths (Zhang et al., 2025). For example, if a student consistently asks leading questions, the AI might reinforce that student's preconceived notions (confirmation bias) instead of challenging them with a more balanced perspective (Jain & Menon, 2023). There is also the issue of spiritual nuance – AI can generate the text of a supplication (*du ā'*) or a sermon, but can it capture the *ruhānīyah* (spiritual essence) that a learned, God-conscious teacher would imbue in those words? Most would argue it cannot, at least not in any intentional way. These concerns underline why the integration of GenAI into IRE must be handled with extreme care, guided by scholars and ethicists.

In summary, GenAI is a powerful new tool in the educational arsenal, capable of generating human-like content and tailoring learning experiences at scale. It holds clear relevance for IRE, from translating classical texts to potentially answering students' questions about faith. Yet, because IRE deals with sacred knowledge, the bar for accuracy and appropriateness is much higher than in secular subjects. As we proceed, we will explore concrete applications of GenAI in Islamic education (the "what is possible" part), followed by an in-depth discussion of pedagogical and theological considerations (the "what is appropriate" part). This structure will help ensure we not only imagine the potential of GenAI but also critically examine its fit within the Islamic educational paradigm.

APPLICATIONS OF GENAI IN ISLAMIC RELIGIOUS EDUCATION (IRE)

GenAI's versatility means it can be applied in various aspects of Islamic Religious Education, whether in formal settings (schools, universities, *madāris*) or informal learning (personal study, community programs). In the following points, we explore some of the emerging and potential applications of GenAI in IRE, as identified in recent research and pilot projects:

- **AI-Generated Qur'ān Summaries and Exegesis**: One promising use of GenAI is to assist with understanding the Qur'ān by providing summaries, explanations (tafsīr), or contextual information about verses. For example, an AI language model fine-tuned on classical Quranic commentaries could generate a summary of the main points of *Sūrah Yāsīn* or answer a student's question like "What is the lesson of the story of Prophet Joseph in the Qur'ān?" Some tools already allow users to query Quranic content in natural language. Researchers have experimented with custom LLMs that ingest authoritative sources like the Qur'ān and Hadith collections to provide answers grounded in those texts (El Ganadi et al., 2025). The goal is that when a learner asks, say, "What does Islam say about forgiveness?" the AI can draw from relevant verses and hadith rather than general internet text. By generating on-the-fly explanations, such an AI could function as a virtual *mufassir* (exegete) at a basic level, highlighting key interpretations or differences of opinion from classical scholars. However, accuracy and bias control are critical here. The AI must not stray from authentic interpretations or fabricate sources. Scholars have proposed strategies like embedding-based retrieval, where the AI pulls in actual quotes from tafsīr works to support its output, thereby reducing the chance of hallucination. Early results show this approach can anchor AI outputs in a structured knowledge base, significantly improving reliability for Quranic Q&A (El Ganadi et al., 2025). In practice, this means a teacher or student using the system could always cross-verify the AI's answer with the cited sources (e.g., Ibn *Kathīr*'s commentary on a verse). Over time, such tools might evolve into sophisticated Qur'ān study aids – imagine an app where you highlight an *āyah (*A Qur'anic verse*)* and the AI provides linguistic analysis, historical context, and tafsīr insights, all curated from reputable works.
- **Hadith Analysis and Verification Tools**: Another area is using GenAI for Hadith studies. Given the massive corpus of hadith literature, students often find it challenging to know the authenticity and context of particular narrations. AI can be used to quickly retrieve hadiths related to a topic or even to check the reported authenticity class. For instance, an AI could function as a Hadith bot where one asks, "Is this saying a hadith, and if so, is it authentic?" By cross-referencing databases like those of Bukhārī or Muslim, the AI can provide an answer along with the source. Moreover, GenAI can assist in hadith commentary: explaining the meaning of a hadith or reconciling apparent contradictions between different narrations. A cutting-edge study

introduced the EMAN framework specifically for mitigating GPT's hallucinations in Islamic text generation, focusing on hadith (El Ganadi et al., 2025). It demonstrated that grounding the AI in a verified hadith database (through embedding techniques) "significantly improves performance by anchoring outputs in a structured knowledge base, reducing hallucination rates, and increasing accuracy." This indicates AI can be a useful tool to navigate hadith literature, so long as it is kept on a tight leash of authenticity. Beyond verification, we also have the concept of conversational fatwā bots. These are AI-driven chatbots that attempt to answer juristic questions. For example, a user might ask an app, "What are the requirements for Zakāt on my income?" and the AI could provide an answer drawn from fiqh sources. The appeal is obvious – instant answers any time. However, this application is perhaps the most controversial. Fatwā (religious rulings) often require a deep understanding of context, the questioner's circumstances, and the objectives of Shariah. No AI today truly understands context or metaphysical aims; it can only regurgitate what is in its training data. Scholars warn that one cannot simply "use AI to give a fatwa" because AI lacks comprehensive knowledge of sources and the human wisdom to apply them. As a result, any fatwa chatbot must be heavily supervised by qualified scholars. A more viable near-term use is AI as a support tool for muftis – for example, quickly gathering relevant scriptural and legal references for a human mufti to review (Munshi et al., 2021).

- **Virtual Tutors for Qur'ān Memorisation and Tajwīd**: Learning to recite the Qur'ān correctly (with proper tajwīd) and memorising passages is a core part of IRE, especially for children. GenAI coupled with speech recognition can function as a tireless Qur'ān tutor. Already, apps exist where a student recites verses and an AI evaluates the pronunciation, detecting errors in the articulation of Arabic letters or the rules of elongation and nasalisation. AI can give adaptive feedback: for instance, highlighting a word where the pronunciation was off and demonstrating the correct way. A case study of Islamic elementary schools found that AI integration "enhances Quranic learning ... by providing adaptive feedback, interactive learning tools, and automated assessments" (Djazilan et al., 2024). Students can get immediate correction rather than waiting for the next session with a human teacher. Moreover, the AI can personalise the learning plan, focusing on the specific verses a student struggles with, or adjusting the speed of recitation for practice. Gamification can be layered on top: the AI might generate quizzes on memorised verses or even simple games (e.g., ordering the jumbled verses correctly) to make memorisation engaging for young learners. However, educators insist that such AI tools must augment, not replace, the traditional teacher-student relationship in Qur'ān learning (Abubakari, Shafik, et al., 2024; Djazilan et al., 2024). The human Qur'ān teacher (*Qāri'* or Shaykh) provides not just technical correction but also spiritual encouragement and ensures the student learns with proper reverence. The concept of *sanad* (a certified chain of reciters) in Qur'ān memorisation cannot be fulfilled by an AI; you still ultimately need a qualified human to certify that a student has recited the entire Qur'ān correctly. Thus, virtual tutors are best used for practice and reinforcement at home, while final assessment and guidance remain with human experts. Even so, these AI tutors could help many learners who do not have easy access to a teacher daily, a common situation in non-Muslim majority countries.

- **Gamified Islamic Learning Content**: GenAI can dynamically create content that makes learning about Islam fun and interactive. For example, an AI could generate role-play scenarios or stories that teach moral lessons from the Sīrah (Prophetic biography). It might craft a choose-your-own-adventure game where students virtually accompany historical figures like Salahuddin Ayyubi or visit ancient Muslim civilisations, learning history and ethics along the way. With advances in natural language generation and even image creation, these scenarios could be customised to the learner's choices in real time. Educators have suggested that Virtual Reality (VR), combined with AI, could simulate events like the Hajj or historical moments, giving students an immersive experience of Islamic history (Norman et al., 2025). While VR in Islamic education is still in its infancy, such approaches carry a lot of appeal for Gen Z learners who are digital natives. Gamification through AI might include an app that quizzes students on duʿās or 99 Names of God but adjusts difficulty based on the student's performance, or a chatbot that plays the role of a companion quizzing the student about daily prayer times and giving gentle reminders. Research from a 2025 study in West Java noted that "AI and gamification can be effective tools in personalising Islamic learning, such as in Qur'ān memorisation and interactive-based simulations of Islamic history" (Norman et al., 2025). However, scholars caution that gamification must retain substance – it should not cross into trivialising sacred content as mere entertainment. Balance is needed so that while students are engaged, they also understand the seriousness and sanctity of what they learn (for instance, a game involving Qur'ān verses must still respect the etiquette due to those verses). With carefully crafted boundaries (e.g., avoiding depiction of Prophet Muhammad or other prophets in any interactive media, in line with Islamic sensitivities), generative AI-driven gamification can open creative avenues for instilling knowledge and love of Islam in the young.

In highlighting these applications, it becomes clear that GenAI can permeate nearly every facet of IRE: from personal ibādah (worship, like Qur'ān reading) to academic religious studies, from elementary madrasa education to adult learning. The potential benefits are increased accessibility, personalisation, and engagement. A student in a remote area can access an AI tutor for tajwīd practice where a human teacher is not available daily. A curious young Muslim can ask an app dozens of questions about Islam in private, which they might be too shy to ask an imam, thus satiating their curiosity and guiding them. A classroom teacher can bring abstract concepts to life with AI-created stories or get administrative help in grading.

Yet, these very applications also raise serious pedagogical and theological questions. For each use case, one must ask: Are we preserving the integrity of Islamic teachings? Are we respecting the boundaries of what is appropriate for a machine to do versus what requires human spiritual insight? How do we prevent errors or misuse? The next section will delve into those questions, examining the risks of automating sacred knowledge, the role of intention and authenticity, and how to balance the advantages of GenAI with the irreplaceable elements of human-based religious education.

PEDAGOGICAL AND THEOLOGICAL CONSIDERATIONS

Any incorporation of GenAI into Islamic Religious Education must contend with a host of pedagogical and theological considerations. These go to the heart of what Islamic education is about – not merely information transfer, but the nurturing of faith, character, and a connection to the divine. In the following subsections, we discuss several key considerations.

Risks of Over-Automation in Sacred Knowledge

There is an inherent risk in automating what has traditionally been a very human-centric, heart-centric process. Islamic learning has always been conveyed "heart-to-heart" and "handed down" through personal mentorship – think of the Prophet teaching his companions, or scholars transmitting knowledge in person to their students with *tarbiyah* (holistic upbringing). If AI tools start taking over tasks like answering fatwā questions or leading study circles, we risk reducing sacred knowledge to a mechanical exchange. There is a worry about the loss of *barakah* (blessing) and spiritual depth when a machine mediates learning. A chatbot can give a technically correct answer about how to pray, but will the student feel the same reverence as when learning from a devout teacher who embodies the prayer? This concern is echoed by many educators who stress that AI should never replace the human teacher in IRE, but only assist (Djazilan et al., 2024). The teacher in Islam (*mu'allim* or *murabbi*) is not just a fact-deliverer but a moral and spiritual exemplar.

A hadith states, "Verily, the scholars are the heirs of the Prophets," underlining the almost sacred role of a teacher. No matter how advanced, an AI cannot inherit that prophetic legacy. It cannot model sincerity (ikhlā), compassion, or piety.

Thus, a heavy reliance on AI could inadvertently promote an attitude that religious learning is just like any other subject – something to be mastered with rote Q&A – whereas traditionally it is also about spiritual refinement under guidance. The automation concern also includes the scenario of students becoming passive consumers of AI-delivered knowledge, instead of actively engaging, memorising, and reflecting. If a student knows they can always ask the AI for a Quranic verse or fatwā, will they still put in the effort to memorise that verse or internalise the fiqh reasoning process? The process of learning in Islam (e.g., wrestling with a difficult text, repeating recitations until perfected, consulting a teacher, and gradually increasing in wisdom) has its value beyond the outcome. Over-automation might short-circuit that process, potentially leading to shallower understanding.

Authenticity, Bias, and Misinformation

As noted earlier, GenAI systems can introduce errors or biases in religious content, which is a grave concern. From a theological perspective, attributing false statements to God or the Prophet (even unintentionally via AI) is problematic. If an AI-generated hadith is fabricated (*maw ūʿ*) but a student believes it is real, that is a misinformation issue with spiritual consequences. Maintaining authenticity is paramount. Any AI tool used in IRE must undergo rigorous validation by experts. This could involve scholars being part of the AI development cycle, curating the training data, and testing outputs (Abubakari, 2024; Jain & Menon, 2023). It may also require AI systems to be limited in scope – for example, a Quran tutor AI should probably only answer questions about Quran wording and tajwīd rules, not broad theological questions, unless it has a verified knowledge base for those.

Bias is another subtle issue: AI might inadvertently reflect sectarian bias if trained on one school of thought's literature more than another. This could skew a student's perspective without them realising alternatives exist. For instance, an AI trained mostly on Sunni sources might answer a question about an Ashʿarī vs Salafi interpretation in a one-sided manner. Or if trained largely in Arabic-English texts, it might under-represent perspectives from non-English speaking Muslim scholars. Ethically, designers of AI in IRE should strive for balance and diversity of input, or clearly label the orientation of the AI (e.g., "trained on Sunni fiqh of the Shafi'i school" or such). The issue of algorithmic bias extends to how Islam and Muslims are portrayed. As mentioned, researchers found GenAI could amplify negative biases, like associating Islam with violence more than other religions (Abid et al., 2021;

Abubakari, 2025b; Zhang et al., 2025). If Muslim students detect such bias in an educational tool, it can be demoralising and may reinforce internalised stereotypes.

Furthermore, biased outputs could mislead non-Muslim users or students about Islamic teachings. To combat this, one study recommends "identifying and mitigating biases in training data to prevent amplification during content generation", using techniques like adversarial training (Zhang et al., 2025). In practice, this might mean filtering out or counterbalancing Islamophobic content in the AI's corpus or fine-tuning the model on texts that emphasise Islam's true values of peace and mercy, thereby nudging it toward impartiality. On misinformation, an additional strategy is ensuring transparency – the AI should ideally cite its sources so that users can verify. An AI that says, *"According to Imam al-Nawawi's Riyā al- āli īn, doing X is recommended"* and provides the reference is far more trustworthy than one that asserts the ruling. This aligns with the Islamic emphasis on isnād – even our AI should come with an isnād of sorts!

Delegating Interpretation to Non-Sentient Entities

Interpretation of Islamic texts (tafsīr of Qur'ān, or ijtihād in law) is a deeply intellectual and spiritual exercise. Classical scholars approach interpretation with not only knowledge of language and precedent, but also with spiritual intuition (*fiqh al-qalb*) and fear of God, often beginning works with invoking Allah's guidance. Handing this role to an AI – a non-sentient entity with no belief or consciousness – raises the question: *Can true understanding or valid ijtihād come from something that does not actually believe or have moral agency?* Most would argue no. AI might simulate an interpretation based on patterns from existing commentaries, but it cannot exercise wisdom (*hikmah*) or truly weigh ethical implications in light of conscience. There is also no accountability – if a human mufti gives a wrong fatwa, he bears the sin and the community can correct him; if an AI gives a wrong fatwa, who is responsible? Perhaps the programmers or the institution deploying it, but this is a grey area. Some studies even debate whether AI could be considered to "have opinions" in religion (Putrawan, 2025; Tsuria & Tsuria, 2024), which verges on absurd from an Islamic viewpoint since it lacks a soul and accountability on Judgment Day.

Moreover, Islamic tradition sometimes values silence or withholding judgment in ambiguous cases – an AI, by design, will attempt an answer to virtually any question, because it is programmed to respond. This could lead to overconfidence in uncertain matters. For example, issues of theology or eschatology that are not fully resolved in Islamic scholarship might nonetheless get a confident answer from a bot, potentially shutting down the healthy space of ambiguity that exists in human teaching (where a scholar might say "*Allahu a lam*, God knows best, there are multiple views on this"). Delegating interpretation to AI could thus impoverish the discourse by giving an illusion of certainty where there is none. To address this, one proposal is that AI in IRE be limited to informational and retrieval functions, not authoritative interpretation or rulings. AI can fetch what has been said by scholars but not decide what should be said anew. Theologically, many would maintain that only humans can be valid interpreters of God's will, because interpretation is an act of worship (ijtihād can be rewarded even if the scholar errs, per hadith). A machine cannot earn a reward or sin; hence, it operates outside the moral framework that gives interpretation its legitimacy.

Islamic Educational Philosophy vs. Algorithmic Learning

Islamic pedagogy is traditionally holistic, emphasising not just the intellect (*aql*) but also the soul (*rū*) and manners (*adab*) of the student. Education (*tarbiyah*) is about shaping a person who not only knows the information but also lives it in character, embodying virtues like honesty, humility, and patience. This is why so much of Islamic learning happens in person, with students observing how the teacher behaves, how they treat others, and how they practice what they preach. There is an oft-cited Islamic maxim, *"adab* (proper conduct) precedes knowledge." A computer algorithm has no conduct to demonstrate; it cannot mentor a student in akhlāq (ethics) through example. Furthermore, algorithmic learning tends to emphasise efficiency, performance metrics, and what can be measured (quiz scores, content coverage). Islamic education, on the other hand, values the immeasurable – the sincerity in one's heart, the improvement in one's behaviour, the spiritual experiences along the way. There is a concern that introducing AI and data-driven methods could push IRE toward a more utilitarian model ("how many juz' memorised, how many hadith learned") at the expense of tacit spiritual formation. "The halaqah and talaqqī methods are still dominant in some Islamic boarding schools", precisely because they involve intimate mentorship and collective learning circles which are hard to quantify (Norman et al., 2025). Some teachers and parents may resist AI for fear it dilutes this personal touch and the ethos of *adab-based learning*.

There is also the concept of knowledge as light – a traditional notion that knowledge (*ilm*) is not merely information but a light that God places in the heart of the sincere. How would an AI fit into this paradigm? Could reliance on AI even be seen as contrary to the idea that one should strive and struggle (*mujāhada*) for knowledge to earn that light truly? These are philosophical questions educators in IRE should debate. The practical upshot is that IRE must ensure that algorithmic tools remain servants to the pedagogical goals, not drivers of them. If a particular AI application does not align with the higher objectives of Islamic education (for instance, if it promotes superficial learning or individual isolation), then perhaps it should be avoided or reworked. On the other hand, if AI can free teachers from rote tasks so they can spend more time on mentorship and moral guidance, then it could be seen as serving the Islamic philosophy of education by giving teachers more bandwidth to do what humans do best.

The Role of the Teacher (Murabbī/Mu'allim)

In Islamic tradition, the teacher holds a very honoured status, often likened to a spiritual parent. The teacher is called *murabbī* (nurturer) when focusing on character building, and *mu'allim* (instructor) when focusing on imparting knowledge; in many cases, the same person fulfils both roles. No matter how advanced technology becomes, the role of the teacher is indispensable in IRE. Educators from the aforementioned 2024 study in Indonesia unanimously emphasised that AI can "support religious education" and even improve academic outcomes; however, AI must complement rather than replace traditional teacher-led instruction to maintain the spiritual and moral aspects of Islamic education (Djazilan et al., 2024). This underscores that teachers are the guardians of the ethos and atmosphere in which learning occurs. An AI cannot lead a heartfelt duʿā' at the end of class, cannot notice a troubled look in a student's eyes and provide counsel, and cannot tailor an approach knowing that a certain student comes from a difficult home environment. The teacher's empathy and personal relationship with students foster love of learning and of the faith.

There is also a concept of *ijaza* in Islamic learning – a teacher authorises a student, indicating a chain of learning. While not all IRE contexts use formal *ijazah*, the idea is that knowledge is sanctioned and blessed through a human chain. We cannot (or should not) have "AI-issued ijazas"! What we might see is teachers themselves leveraging AI to become even better guides. For example, an ustādh who is well-trained in using AI could quickly pull up different scholarly viewpoints or interesting facts during a lesson, enriching the discussion. This way, the teacher remains at the centre, orchestrating the learning, but with AI as a resource at their fingertips (akin to how some teachers use internet searches or multimedia today, but more powerful). The teacher's role may evolve to include being a digital curator and ethics coach, teaching students not just Islamic knowledge, but also how to use AI tools responsibly in their quest for knowledge. In essence, the presence of AI in the classroom might add a new responsibility to the teacher: ensuring that the *adab* of using knowledge tools is observed (for instance, not letting students cheat via AI, teaching them to verify AI answers, reminding them of the intention behind seeking knowledge). Far from diminishing the teacher's role, GenAI could make it even more crucial, because someone has to mediate between the vast information AI provides and the student's understanding. The teacher becomes the one who contextualises, corrects, and provides the human touch that frames AI-provided information within a moral and spiritual narrative.

Personalised vs. Collective Learning

GenAI excels at personalisation – adapting to the individual learner. However, Islamic learning has a strong collective dimension. From childhood, Muslims learn in group settings: maktab classes, mosque circles, Ramadan dars, and so on. There is wisdom in learning together – it builds brotherhood/sisterhood, encourages mutual learning (students correct and motivate each other), and prevents isolation. Collective rituals like congregational prayer (*alāh*) and group recitation are as much about community as education. If education were to become too personalised (everyone with their AI tutor, isolated in a VR headset or on their phone), we risk undermining the *ummah* (community) spirit in learning. As one observation noted, in many pesantren (Islamic boarding schools), traditional group study and face-to-face interactions remain central, and even technology use is curbed (some ban smartphones) to preserve this ethos (Norman et al., 2025). On the flip side, personalisation can help address different learning paces – not every student thrives in a one-size-fits-all lecture. AI could allow advanced students to go further and help slower students review fundamentals without embarrassment. The key will be to balance individual and group learning. Perhaps the model could be students do certain tasks individually with AI at home (flipped-classroom style), then come together in class to discuss or practice as a group. That way, each has learned according to their ability, but they still engage collectively, learning cooperation and humility.

Collective learning also serves as a check on errors – peers and teachers can immediately spot if someone got the wrong idea from an AI, whereas a lone learner might go down the wrong path without realising. Additionally, many Islamic practices (like memorisation) encourage healthy competition in groups (*musābaqa*), which might be less motivating if one only competes against an AI app. Educators might use AI to form study groups intelligently: e.g., pairing students who are weak in certain areas with those who are strong, as identified by AI assessments, thereby enhancing peer tutoring. In any case, preserving social interaction and communal bonds in learning will be important. Otherwise, we might produce technically knowledgeable individuals who lack the soft skills and communal ties that come from traditional study circles and mentorship. The concept of *u bah* (companionship) in seeking knowledge, where being in the company of the righteous is itself transformative, cannot be replicated by studying alone with a gadget.

Niyyah (Intention) and Spiritual Context

Finally, a consideration often raised by Muslim educators is ensuring that the use of technology does not erode the purity of intention (niyyah) with which knowledge is sought (Abubakari, Zakaria, et al., 2024; Abubakari, 2025a). In Islam, actions are judged by intentions (as per a famous hadith). A student is encouraged to seek knowledge *"for the sake of Allah,"* to benefit themselves and others, not for showing off or merely worldly gain. There is a subtle worry that using AI might make things "too easy" and thus students may not develop the same depth of sincerity or work ethic. For example, a student might use an AI to do their Islamic studies homework and get a good grade, but in the process, they bypass the personal effort that might instil deeper appreciation or humility. The intent shifted from understanding to simply completing a task efficiently. Teachers will need to remind students about niyyah in the context of AI: "Why are you learning this? If you use AI, is it helping you learn or just shortcutting? Remember to use it as a tool, but the goal is to understand and come closer to Allah truly."

Similarly, the spiritual state in which one learns is important – traditionally, adab would include doing *wu ū* (ablution) before a Quran class, sitting respectfully, maybe starting with duʿā' for seeking knowledge. If students are casually querying a religious AI bot while multitasking or lounging, that outward behaviour might reflect a less attentive inner state. It is not that the AI causes this, but the convenience of it might lead to a lessening of formality that, in turn, could lessen reverence. Educators might thus integrate some spiritual disciplines around AI usage: for instance, advising students to treat the content with respect still (if an AI Quran app shows verses, one should treat those verses like one would the mushaf, not just swipe them off casually). The concept of *urmah* (sanctity) of knowledge should extend to the digital realm. Additionally, intention applies to creators of AI content: a teacher using AI to generate materials should also reflect, "Am I using this to enhance student learning or just to reduce my workload? Am I vigilant that the output is correct? Am I praying for guidance in how I deploy this tool?" By keeping intentions aligned with serving the educational mission, teachers and developers can help ensure the technology remains a means of attaining God's pleasure, not an end that distracts from it.

In light of these considerations, it is evident that the integration of GenAI in IRE is not purely a technical or curricular matter – it strikes at the core values and methods of Islamic education. Safeguards and guidelines are needed to address these concerns. Some immediate ideas include requiring scholar oversight for any AI-generated religious content, using AI primarily for supplementary purposes rather than core teaching, training both teachers and students in AI literacy (so they understand what the AI can/cannot do), and fostering a culture where AI is seen as a collaborative tool rather than an authoritative source. Encouragingly, research voices are calling for exactly this measured approach. One paper notes that the ethical use of AI in religious education demands "ethical guidelines and oversight mechanisms" so that AI becomes a tool for inclusion and unbiased learning rather than a source of distortion (Zhang et al., 2025). The next section, on ethical and legal challenges, will continue this thread, focusing more on policy-level and societal issues in Muslim contexts that influence how GenAI might be adopted in education.

ETHICAL AND LEGAL CHALLENGES IN GENAI IMPLEMENTATION

Deploying generative AI in Islamic educational settings not only raises pedagogical concerns but also broader ethical and legal issues that vary across Muslim societies. These challenges stem from the need to align AI technology with Islamic moral values, legal principles (Sharīʿah compliance), and cultural sensitivities. In the following sections, we examine some key challenges.

AI Alignment with Islamic Values

Muslim communities expect technology, especially one involved in teaching religion, to uphold values such as modesty, honesty, justice, and respect for the sacred (Abubakari, Zakaria, et al., 2024; Abubakari, 2025a; Abubakari & Kalinaki, 2024). A foremost concern is content morality. For example, generative image AIs must be constrained not to produce indecent images or depictions of revered figures, as Islam prohibits the portrayal of prophets and emphasises modesty in the representation of humans. An unguided AI image generator might create illustrations that conflict with Islamic dress codes or sanctities (imagine an AI inadvertently generating an image of a mosque with inappropriate elements or disrespectfully mixing religious symbols). Therefore, any AI tools for Muslim learners should have filters reflecting Islamic norms, similar to how mainstream AI ethics filters block extreme violence or sexual content; here, they would also block blasphemous or immodest outputs. In terms of truthfulness, AI must be aligned with the value of idq (truth). Hallucinations or confidently false statements contravene the principle of speaking truthfully, so the AI's propensity to fabricate is not just a technical flaw but an ethical one in an Islamic view (El Ganadi et al., 2025). One could argue that unleashing an AI that often lies (even unintentionally) into an educational setting violates the Quranic injunction "And do not mix truth with falsehood or conceal the truth while you know [it]" (Qur'ān 2:42). Thus, developers have an ethical imperative to minimise AI falsehoods for these contexts – through rigorous testing and conservative design where the AI says "I do not know" rather than guess, when confidence is low.

Justice and fairness are also crucial values. Islam strongly emphasises *adl* (justice) and i sān (doing good/initiative-taking justice). Example of bias: if an AI favours one ethnicity or gender implicitly, that is unjust. For instance, if an AI tutor only presents examples of Muslim men in leadership roles and not women, it could subtly perpetuate a bias that Islam does not endorse (since capable women have held important roles historically). Or if an AI always uses Arab culture examples, non-Arab students might feel marginalised, contrary to the Islamic ideal of egalitarianism among ethnic groups. Researchers like Elmahjub (2023) advocate for pluralistic ethical benchmarking, meaning AI ethics in the Muslim world should draw on Islamic principles like ma la a (public welfare) and not just Western AI ethics codes. In practice, this means AI deployed in Muslim contexts should be evaluated on how well it preserves human dignity, prevents harm, and promotes welfare – essentially a Maqā id al-Sharīʿah approach to AI governance. For example, one could map the five maqā id (religion, life, intellect, lineage, property) to AI guidelines: does the AI protect religion (e.g., avoid weakening faith or spreading heresy), protect life (e.g., health/safety of students), protect intellect (e.g., encourage critical thinking rather than intellectual laziness), protect lineage/honour (e.g., avoid content that disrespects family values), and protect property (e.g., handle personal data responsibly, which relates to rights over one's information). These are abstract but provide a moral compass. Encouragingly, some Muslim-majority nations are explicitly incorporating Islamic values in their AI strategies. A comparative study on Saudi Arabia and the UAE notes that these governments aim to "harmonise [AI] security and privacy with Islamic principles," integrating cultural and ethical values into AI frameworks (Gorian & Osman, 2024). They recognise that technology policy must reflect the society's moral fabric – for instance, Saudi Arabia's AI Ethics principles reference human dignity, which resonates with Islam's teachings on honouring humankind (Qur'ān 17:70).

Fatwas and Institutional Responses to AI-Generated Content

The introduction of GenAI in Islamic education is prompting responses from religious authorities and institutions. Questions are being raised to muftis and councils: Is it permissible to use ChatGPT to get answers about Islam? Can an AI-written khutba (sermon) be delivered? Is it acceptable to use AI translations of the Qur'ān? These new issues often require formal guidance (fatāwā). Early indications show a cautious but open attitude: many scholars say AI is a tool – its permissibility lies in how it is used and the content it produces. If it is used to aid learning and the content is verified and good, it is permissible; if it produces un-Islamic or erroneous content and people follow it unthinkingly, then it is problematic. For instance, the Jordanian Fatwa Department's article in January 2024 acknowledged the benefit of AI in drafting fatwā research but warned against unsupervised use for final rulings (Za`atreh, 2024). We may soon see guidelines or codes from Islamic organisations about AI. Possibly, something akin to "When using AI for Islamic content: ensure a scholar reviews outputs; do not use AI as the sole source for religious decisions; and do not allow AI to transgress Shariah limits in content generation."

There may also be fatwas addressing specific cases: for instance, ruling on whether an AI's recitation (using synthesized voice) can be used for prayer (probably not, since imam needs to be an adult human in congregational prayer); or whether using AI to generate Islamic art with verses is allowed (with conditions to maintain respect). Institutional responses are not just prohibitive – some are initiative-taking in leveraging AI. Legal frameworks might also evolve- education ministries in Muslim countries could issue rules about AI. For instance, a ministry might require that any AI tools used in schools be certified for content accuracy and cultural appropriateness. There could be laws around data privacy in line with Islamic ethics, since privacy is strongly protected in Islam (Gorian & Osman, 2024), misuse of student data by AI would be seen as violating both secular and religious principles.

Privacy, Data Protection, and Surveillance Concerns

Privacy is a core concept in Islamic ethics – the Qur'ān and Hadith place great emphasis on respecting personal boundaries, not spying, and protecting personal information (e.g., the Prophet forbade eavesdropping or looking into someone's house without permission). In the digital age, data privacy takes on new meaning. AI in education typically collects a lot of data about students: their performance, their questions, even potentially voice or video data if it is a tutor app. In an Islamic school context, administrators and parents will be concerned about how that data is stored and used. Is it being kept confidential? Could third parties access it? For example, if an AI app for Quran memorisation records a child's recitation, uploads it to the cloud, is that okay? It might inadvertently expose the child's voice to strangers if not secured.

More broadly, some fear a scenario of surveillance: governments or companies might use AI in schools not just for education but to monitor students. An extreme hypothetical: AI analysing students' speech in class could be used to flag "ideologically deviant" opinions. Given the varied politics of the Muslim world, one can imagine both secular-leaning regimes and conservative ones might have an interest in tracking what is being taught or said in religious classes. This raises legal and ethical red flags. The ideal approach, consistent with Islamic values of trust and privacy, is informed consent and minimal intrusion. If AI is used, students (or guardians) should know what data is collected and have a say. Data should only be used for educational benefit, not sold or misused. Some Muslim countries may refer to the concept of amānah (trust) – handling personal data is an *amānah*; violating it is a sin (analogous to how gossip or revealing someone's secret is considered sinful). Interestingly, the recent work on AI ethics in KSA and UAE highlighted that the

Islamic concept of privacy has unique aspects, emphasising clear moral guidelines even in ambiguous cases (Gorian & Osman, 2024). This suggests that legal regulations in those countries aim to infuse that clarity, possibly imposing stricter rules on AI regarding what data can be collected (e.g., biometric data might be sensitive because of concerns about dignity and misuse). In practice, educational institutions adopting AI might implement policies like: no AI recordings without permission, anonymisation of student data when processed by AI, and no AI cameras in private spaces (aligning with the Islamic ethos that people's private lives should not be intruded upon). Furthermore, transparency of AI algorithms might be sought – parents may want to know how an AI makes decisions about their child's learning path (e.g., is there any bias or error affecting it?).

Cultural Sensitivities and Representational Fairness

The Muslim world is culturally diverse, and educational content must be culturally sensitive. GenAI trained predominantly on Western or non-Muslim data might produce examples or scenarios that are tone-deaf or offensive in a Muslim context (Abubakari, 2024, 2025b). Simple example: an AI drafting a story problem might mention a family drinking wine at dinner, normal in some cultures but offensive in a Muslim classroom. Or it might generate names and always use non-Muslim names for "good" characters and Muslim names for villains if trained on bias-tainted fiction, which can reinforce negative tropes. Representational fairness means ensuring that the AI's outputs represent different cultures fairly and avoid stereotypes. In Islamic education, one might want the AI to sometimes provide examples from various Muslim cultures – Arab, Malay, Turkish, African, etc., to reflect the ummah's diversity. Without intentional design, an American-trained model might give every example from American life, which overseas students cannot relate to, or worse, slip in culturally inappropriate references. Another sensitivity is sectarian differences. The AI should be careful in contexts where Shīʿa and Sunnī practices differ (for instance, how prayer is taught). If it is not sect-aware, it could confuse students or seem to take sides. Ideally, an AI application would clarify its context or be customizable (a Madrasa in Iran might configure it for Jaʿfari fiqh answers, whereas a school in Morocco for Mālikī answers).

Language is also a factor – a lot of AI tools support English and maybe Arabic, but what about Urdu, Bahasa, or Hausa? Lack of language support for some Muslim-majority languages is a fairness issue. While translation tech can help, true accessibility means AI should directly handle content in those languages. On the legal side, some countries might regulate this by requiring local data sets or local training to imbue the right cultural context. For example, there could be a push to develop specifically "Islamic world-trained" models to reduce reliance on those trained on mainly Western internet data. Indeed, initiatives like Turkic or Arabic large models are underway. From an ethical viewpoint, this is about preserving cultural identity and ensuring AI does not become a vector of cultural homogenization or subtle Westernisation. Educational use of AI should reinforce students' cultural and religious identity, not undermine it (Abubakari, Zakaria, et al., 2024; Abubakari, 2025a). An interesting cultural sensitivity is also voice and persona: if an AI tutor speaks, what accent or gender voice does it use? Would a female-voiced assistant be preferred for girls in some conservative contexts (or conversely, would some object to any "feminine" persona teaching mixed classes)? These are nuanced matters. Perhaps giving users a choice in the AI's persona could help – e.g., choosing a voice that pronounces Arabic terms correctly and feels culturally familiar.

Legal Compliance with Sharīʿah and National Laws

Beyond ethics, there is the question of Sharīʿah compliance for AI itself. While classical fiqh did not discuss AI, scholars can extrapolate principles. For instance, consider intellectual property: if an AI generates an Islamic textbook chapter, who owns it? Sharīʿah has concepts of authorship and stewardship of knowledge. Plagiarism is morally frowned upon (it is a form of dishonesty). Thus, if AI produces content by training on someone else's work, is that fair use or a violation of the original author's rights? This is being debated in Western IP law and would equally interest Islamic jurists, who might draw analogies to quoting without attribution (allowed if moderate and for benefit) vs wholesale copying. Another area is liability: If an AI tool gives incorrect religious advice and someone acts on it to their detriment, is there a legal case? Secular law is figuring this out, but in Islamic law, notions of gharar (uncertainty) and amān (liability for harm) could be invoked. Providers might need to have clear disclaimers (as indeed many do, e.g., "This is not a fatwa service, always consult a scholar for serious matters"). Government regulation in some Muslim countries might classify educational AI under certain oversight regimes, especially if it is delivering religious content. For instance, some countries require religious teachers to be certified; would they require AI to be "certified" by the religious authority as well? It is conceivable. Already, printed religious material often goes through censorship or approval in certain places (like Al-Azhar inspects books in Egypt for orthodoxy). If an AI is effectively "producing" new text, regulators might try to extend that process – an AI service, for example, has to undergo review or get a license. Technically, that is challenging, but legally, it might be on the agenda.

In conclusion, the ethical-legal landscape for GenAI in Muslim contexts is complex, intertwining universal AI issues with specific Islamic values and social norms. A recurring theme is the need for responsible AI governance that involves religious scholars, tech experts, and policymakers. Cross-disciplinary collaboration can help ensure that standards are set so AI usage "is not only innovative but also morally and religiously acceptable" (Gorian & Osman, 2024). This might result in guidelines or even an "Islamic AI Ethics" framework that parallels existing AI ethics principles, but with an added layer of Sharīʿah considerations (Mohadi & Tarshany, 2023). For example, where general AI ethics says, "Do not harm," the Islamic version might enumerate the Maqā id to specifically ensure no harm to faith, life, intellect, and so on. Therefore, the challenges are significant, but not insurmountable. By addressing privacy through strong data protections, bias through inclusive training data and oversight, and cultural missteps through localisation, educators and developers can create AI tools that respect and enrich the Islamic educational experience. The next section will propose a more concrete framework for integrating GenAI into Islamic education, building on both the opportunities and cautions we have discussed.

FRAMEWORK FOR INTEGRATING GENAI IN ISLAMIC EDUCATION

To harness the benefits of generative AI in Islamic education while mitigating its risks, a clear framework is needed. In the next points, we outline a multi-faceted framework grounded in Islamic principles (especially Maqā id al-Sharīʿah, the objectives of Islamic law) and best practices in educational technology (like training, digital literacy, and institutional policies). Consequently, we name this framework as Shariah-Guided GenAI Integration Framework for Islamic Education (SG-GAIIE Framework). This framework can guide policymakers, school administrators, and educators in responsibly integrating GenAI into IRE. We now describe the core elements of the SG-GAIIE Framework as follows:

1. **Shariah-Aligned Guiding Principles:** All use of GenAI in IRE should be governed by principles that ensure alignment with the higher objectives of Islam. The five universally recognised *Maqā id al-Sharī ah* provide an excellent scaffold:
   - ***Protection of Dīn (Religion)***: AI tools must preserve and enhance the learner's understanding and practice of Islam, not confuse or dilute it. This means prioritising accuracy in religious content and ensuring that AI reinforces authentic beliefs and values. For example, an AI Quran tutor should improve one's recitation and appreciation of the Qur'ān, thus strengthening their dīn. Any feature that could misguide in creed or practice should be off-limits. As one study concluded, we must incorporate ethical considerations into the development and usage of AI,

with Islamic ethics offering a constructive contribution to global AI ethics (Mohadi & Tarshany, 2023). Practically, this could entail having a *Shariah board* or advisory council review AI educational content and updates (similar to how Islamic banks have Shariah boards for products).

- ***Protection of Aql (Intellect)***: The framework should ensure AI truly educates and stimulates the intellect rather than making students intellectually lazy. Responsible use of GenAI means using it to *augment critical thinking*, not replace it. Teachers can use strategies like having students verify AI answers or critique them. Effective education models can incorporate AI if they still emphasise understanding and reasoning (Berberich et al., 2020). The goal is an AI-integrated pedagogy that "creatively integrates critical thinking into religious education environments" rather than spoon-feeding answers (Zhang et al., 2025). Furthermore, this objective includes mental well-being – AI should not mentally harm students (e.g., by exposing them to distressing content or by overloading them with information).
- ***Protection of Nafs (Life/Self)***: While not as directly relevant in a classroom as in, say, healthcare AI, this principle reminds us to consider the holistic well-being of students. AI use should not cause excessive stress, isolation, or dependency that might harm a student's personal development. Balance screen time and ensure human interaction so that students' social and emotional needs (part of "self") are protected. In some cases, AI can help – for example, if a student is too shy to ask questions, an AI chat can provide a safe space, improving their educational experience. The framework would encourage such supportive uses.
- ***Protection of Nasl (Lineage) and Ird (Honour)***: In educational terms, this ties to protecting students' rights and dignity. The framework should enforce privacy (not exposing student data or images improperly) (Gorian & Osman, 2024). It also means AI content should respect family values and not overstep into areas parents or the community might consider their domain (for example, discussions on sensitive topics should be handled with parental awareness). AI should complement, not clash with, the moral upbringing from family. Some Islamic schools might incorporate a policy that AI must not contradict what is taught at home in key moral matters – or at least, if such a sensitive question arises, it defers to asking a teacher or parent (like parental controls).
- ***Protection of Māl (Property)***: Ensure that the introduction of AI is a justified investment that does not waste resources. This objective in context might translate to cost-effectiveness – choosing AI solutions that

provide real value for money and broad benefit. Also, intellectual property could be considered: avoid pirated software or violating others' rights, as that would be a form of unjust appropriation of property. If the school develops its own AI content, open-sourcing some tools could be a *sadaqah jāriyah* (continuing charity) to benefit others, aligning with the Islamic spirit of knowledge sharing.

Thus, by explicitly stating these principles in an integration policy, educators create a moral benchmark. One paper on Islamic AI ethics notes that using *ma la a* (public good) as a guide allows balancing utility with moral constraints (Elmahjub, 2023). For example, suppose an AI feature is very useful but carries a small risk of misguiding. In that case, the principle of protecting dīn may override pure utility and lead to dropping that feature. Conversely, if an AI feature significantly helps preserve intellect (like an accessibility tool for special-needs learners), that ma la a might justify extra effort to implement it. Figure 1 demonstrates the elements of the SG-GAIIE Framework.

Figure 1. Shariah-guided genAI integration framework for Islamic education

Framework for Integrating GenAI in Islamic Education

Characteristic	Shariah-Aligned Guiding Principles	Educator Training and Digital Literacy	Institutional Guidelines and Fatwa Board Collaboration
Protection of Dīn (Religion)	Prioritise accuracy and reinforce authentic beliefs.	Worldview and ethics training is crucial.	Content verification process is essential.
Protection of ʿAql (Intellect)	Augment critical thinking, not replace it.	Teachers need Islamic pedagogy with AI	Acceptable use policy is very important.
Protection of Nafs (Life/Self)	Balance screen time and ensure human interaction.	Continuous support is very important for teachers.	Data and privacy measures are critical.
Protection of Nasl (Lineage) and ʿIrd (Honour)	Enforce privacy and respect family values.	Training per needs	Cultural & religious sensitivity checks are crucial.
Protection of Māl (Property)	Ensure cost-effectiveness and avoid violating rights.	Technical and AI literacy is very important.	Training compliance is crucial for teachers.
Other Considerations	Use maṣlaḥa (public good) as a guide.	Training per needs	Collaboration with fatwa boards is critical.

2. **Educator Training and Digital Literacy:** The success of GenAI in Islamic education hinges on teachers being competent, pedagogically and technologically. A well-trained teacher can mediate between AI and students, making the experience positive; an untrained teacher might misuse or mistrust the AI, leading to problems. Ironically, studies indicate most individuals in higher ed-

ucation, including IRE, possess low levels of digital competency (Abubakari, Zakaria, Musa, et al., 2023; Abubakari et al., 2025; Abubakari & Kalinaki, 2024). Therefore, comprehensive professional development is crucial. This training should cover technical skills, pedagogical methods, and Islamic content awareness:

- **Technical and AI Literacy:** Teachers should understand how GenAI works at a conceptual level (its strengths, limitations, and why it might err). They should learn the tools available (e.g., how to prompt ChatGPT effectively, or how to use an AI grading assistant). Training can involve firsthand workshops using actual classroom scenarios. Considering current trends, an ideal training outcome is that teachers become comfortable co-designing lessons with AI assistance (like generating quiz questions which they then "filter" for Islamically appropriateness). Recent research emphasises nurturing AI-based literacy and adaptive-driven skills in educators to facilitate informed engagement with GenAI (Yan et al., 2024).
- **Islamic Pedagogy with AI:** Teachers need guidance on blending traditional Islamic teaching methods with AI tools. For example, how to use AI for drill practice (like memorisation) while still applying the tarbiyah approach? Or how to have students do collaborative work when each might have access to AI. Perhaps new pedagogical models will emerge, like "AI-augmented halaqah," where a group uses an AI to gather information and then discusses it together. Teachers could simulate some strategies during training. They should also be trained to detect AI-generated content in student work to address academic honesty (for instance, if a student submits an essay, teachers should know clues of AI writing or use AI-detection tools, so that students are discouraged from simply outsourcing reflective assignments to AI).
- **Worldview and Ethics Training:** Crucially, teacher training must incorporate an Islamic worldview component. This means helping teachers frame AI as a tool within an Islamic understanding of knowledge. They should discuss scenarios like: What do I do if the AI gives an answer that conflicts with what I know to be Islamic teaching? How do I explain to students why the AI said that and what the correct understanding is? Teachers essentially become AI ethics moderators in the classroom. They should be equipped to have conversations with students about why certain AI output might be wrong or biased (turning it into a teachable moment about both the subject matter and critical thinking). Training can involve case studies (e.g., showing a mistaken AI answer to a fiqh question and walking through how to correct it using

Islamic sources). Additionally, teachers should be aware of fiqh issues related to AI use. For instance, if using a text-to-speech that recites the Quran, what is the ruling on listening to it? (Most likely it is fine, but one should still show respect as with any Quran recitation.) Or if using AI to produce practice Islamic quiz questions, verifying that none are disrespectful or trivialising sacred matters.

- **Continuous Support:** Given the rapid evolution of AI, training should not be one-off. There should be ongoing support communities – perhaps online forums or workshops where Islamic educators share tips and experiences. This can be facilitated by organisations like Islamic education networks or even ministries. It may lead to developing an "IRE AI Integration Manual" that gets updated annually.

The need for such training is supported by studies that identified instructor readiness as a challenge in AI adoption (Djazilan et al., 2024). Investing in building confidence and competence among teachers is thus non-negotiable. When teachers are adept, they can ensure AI is used purposefully, enhancing learning while maintaining the Islamic ethos.

3. **Institutional Guidelines and Fatwa Board Collaboration:** Schools, madrassahs, universities, and educational boards should develop clear policies and guidelines for GenAI usage. These can be informed by collaborative input from tech experts, education specialists, and Islamic scholars (e.g., local Ulema council or fatwa board members). Guidelines might include:
    - **Acceptable Use Policy:** Define what AI can and cannot be used for in the institution. For example: "AI may be used for supplementary tutoring, generating practice materials, language assistance, etc. AI should not be used as the final authority on Islamic rulings taught in class – all answers should be cross-checked with approved texts." Or an exam policy: "Using AI tools during exams or for graded assignments is considered cheating unless explicitly allowed." Having it in writing sets expectations for students and staff alike.
    - **Content Verification Process:** Establish a process where any new substantial content introduced via AI (like a study handout entirely generated by AI) is reviewed by a knowledgeable teacher or scholar before distribution. Perhaps require a "human in the loop" sign-off for content that is religious or sensitive. This echoes what researchers have called for: oversight mechanisms in deploying GenAI within religious contexts (Zhang et al., 2025).

- **Data and Privacy Measures:** Institutions should state how student data with AI is handled, aligning with legal and Islamic standards of privacy. For instance, if using a third-party AI platform, perhaps avoid inputting full student names or personal details into it. If the school builds its own AI (say, a custom chatbot on local servers), ensure it is secure. Parents should be informed and consent to their children's data being used in AI systems, where applicable.
- **Cultural & Religious Sensitivity Checks:** The guidelines can specify that any AI content that will be shared broadly (like something on the school's website or publications) undergo a sensitivity check, perhaps by someone aware of common cultural pitfalls or sectarian nuances.
- **Training Compliance:** Make it a policy that teachers must undergo the training to use AI in teaching. Possibly, a certification could be given (e.g., "Certified Islamic EdTech Educator") to those who complete courses on AI integration, ensuring quality control.

Finally, collaboration with fatwa boards or local scholars is important for legitimacy and community acceptance. If a prominent mufti or Islamic education authority endorses the institution's approach to AI, it alleviates many concerns from parents or other stakeholders. Fatwa boards could issue statements like: "It is permissible to use AI in teaching Islamic subjects provided X, Y, Z conditions are met." We already see the beginnings of such discourse; formalising it bridges the gap between religious authority and technological innovation. Additionally, scholars on a consultative board can help address new fiqh questions as they arise. For example, if a question emerges like "Can AI be used to simulate an imam's voice to lead prayer recordings?" the board can discuss and issue a timely guideline. Essentially, *shura* (consultation) between tech implementers and Islamic scholars should be an ongoing part of the integration framework, ensuring AI usage remains under the moral compass of the community.

RECOMMENDATIONS AND FUTURE DIRECTIONS

Practical Recommendations

Recommendations for various stakeholders emerge from our discussion. In the following highlighted points, the chapter recommends strategies for educational stakeholders, policymakers, and technologists, advocating cautious optimism in balancing tradition with innovations.

- **For Policymakers and Educational Authorities:** Develop and endorse guidelines that integrate ethical and religious oversight for AI in curricula. Invest in capacity building – for example, funding teacher training programs on AI usage in Islamic education and supporting the creation of localised Islamic datasets so that global AI tools can be fine-tuned to Muslim contexts (thus reducing cultural bias). Consider forming interdisciplinary committees (involving *ulama*, technologists, and educators, among others) that periodically review new AI tools entering the market for compliance with cultural and religious norms (similar to how some countries review school textbooks). Encourage knowledge exchange between countries – a successful pilot of AI integration in, say, Malaysia's Islamic schools could be shared with schools in the Middle East or Africa, with necessary adaptations. Ultimately, policymakers should aim to create an environment where AI can be adopted safely, meaning maximising benefits while instituting checks and support systems to manage risks (Djazilan et al., 2024).
- **For Educators and School Leaders:** Embrace AI as a tool to enhance your teaching but do so deliberately. Start small – identify specific pain points in your teaching that AI might alleviate (grading, generating materials, extra tutoring for struggling students) and pilot an AI solution there, monitoring outcomes closely. Always keep the teacher's role central; use AI to free up time for what teachers do best (mentoring, inspiring, imparting values). Foster a school culture where AI is discussed openly – have sessions with students about what AI can and cannot do, so they set realistic expectations and do not become over-reliant. Incorporate AI into the curriculum of related subjects (ICT or even Islamic studies) so students learn about it through an Islamic ethical lens. Remain vigilant about content – just as teachers would not bring unknown books into class without reviewing them, they should not deploy AI content unchecked. One practical tip is to maintain a repository of vetted prompts and outputs that teachers have found useful, effectively a library of AI-generated content that has been human-reviewed for accuracy and appropriateness. This saves time and ensures quality. Above all, educators should maintain agency: if an AI tool is not meeting your educational or ethical standards, tweak it or abandon it. The goal is not to use AI for its own sake, but to enrich learning in the service of Islamic educational goals.
- **For Technologists and AI Developers:** There is a tremendous opportunity and need for developing AI solutions tailored to Islamic educational needs. This could range from better Arabic NLP for classical texts, to algorithms that can incorporate the rulings of different madhhabs when answering questions, to knowledge-based graphs of Qur'anic and hadith data that improve answer accuracy (like the EMAN framework attempted for hadith (El

Ganadi et al., 2025). Technologists should collaborate with Islamic scholars and educators from the design phase – a form of co-design that ensures the product meets real classroom needs and respects religious constraints. When fine-tuning models, consider including data from Islamic sources (Qur'ān, Sunnah, scholarly works) in a way that does not violate copyrights but gives the AI a genuine grounding in the tradition. Implement features that allow transparency and user control: for example, a "source mode" where the AI can display which book or fatwa its answer likely came from (El Ganadi et al., 2025). Moreover, be mindful of languages – there is a bias in AI development towards English; investing in Arabic, Urdu, Turkish, Malay, and other languages spoken by large Muslim populations is vital for equity. On the ethical side, developers should incorporate Islamic ethical checks in their models, akin to how OpenAI has moral guidelines; one could have an added layer for Islamic contexts (for instance, a content filter that catches and blocks the generation of Islamically objectionable material). The concept of *"Islamic AI ethics"* is emerging, and developers can pioneer it, possibly in partnership with institutions like the International Institute of Islamic Thought (IIIT) or departments of Islamic studies interested in technology (Elmahjub, 2023; Mohadi & Tarshany, 2023). This might lead to new research and innovation that not only benefits Muslim learners but also contributes to the global discourse on AI ethics by adding a rich civilizational perspective.

Future Outlook and Directions

Looking ahead, several emerging research areas present themselves at the intersection of AI and Islamic education/ethics:

- **AI-Islamic Ethics Co-Design:** Scholars like Elmahjub (2023) have begun articulating how Islamic ethical principles like ma la a can inform global AI norms. Future research could involve concrete experiments: designing an AI system with an "Islamic ethical agent" that adjusts outputs based on ethical rules (for example, refusing to engage with slander or backbiting if a user attempts it, citing Islamic reasons). Does this improve user outcomes in Muslim populations? How do non-Muslim users react to an AI that has a values stance (there's potential for broader application in making AIs that are values-sensitive to any community)?
- **Cross-Cultural AI in Islamic Education:** Comparative studies can be done on how different Muslim-majority regions implement AI in education. For example, a study might compare a madrasa in Indonesia using AI tools with a maktab in the UK doing the same – what cultural or pedagogical differences

emerge? Early glimpses show differences in adoption rates (with "modern Islamic schools" vs traditional ones having varied uptake (Norman et al., 2025). By examining multiple contexts, we can gather best practices that are generalizable as well as those that are culture-specific. Such research would guide how to adapt AI interventions to local needs.

- **Long-term Impacts on Religious Learning and Practice:** A crucial area is to track over time whether students who learned with AI assistance differ in their religious knowledge retention, understanding, and practice compared to those who learned traditionally. Do they end up with a weaker or stronger connection to the material? Are they more prone to questioning and critical thinking (potentially positive), or do they take things less seriously because a machine was involved (potentially negative)? Longitudinal studies would be valuable here. One study urged exploration of "long-term impacts of AI on moral education" in faith-based environments (Djazilan et al., 2024), which is a call to action for researchers to follow cohorts of learners over the years.
- **Augmented Scholars:** Outside of K-12 or basic education, think about how AI might assist Islamic scholars, imams, and muftis. Tools that rapidly search and summarise across thousands of fatwa archives or hadith could accelerate scholarly work. How might that change the process of issuing a *fatwā* or authoring an academic paper in Islamic studies? Will it lead to a new kind of scholarship or *ijtihād*? Studying this (perhaps by pilot testing AI research assistants in a seminary context) can be fascinating.
- **Ethnographic and Theological Reflections:** There is room for more qualitative research – how do teachers feel about AI after using it? Do they find it threatens their role or enhances it? How do students perceive the "authority" of an AI answer vs a teacher's answer? There may be theological reflections as well: for instance, if an AI can mimic styles of Islamic literature, what does that say about human creativity, which Islam sees as a gift from God? Such questions border on philosophy of mind and theology of technology, and Muslim theologians might join the conversation that other religious thinkers have started.

In concluding, we return to the image of *"Revelation meets Algorithm."* This meeting need not be a clash; it can be a conversation – one where timeless wisdom guides cutting-edge innovation. The chapter has aimed to demonstrate that by leaning on our rich Islamic intellectual heritage, we can approach GenAI neither with blind acceptance nor with fear, but with critical engagement. We saw how historical Muslim scholars integrated new knowledge and tools in their eras; today's challenge is similar in spirit, if different in form. As we step into a future where AI becomes ubiquitous, the Islamic education community has the opportunity to lead by example in ethical tech integration. By doing so, we honour both the trust of knowledge passed down from our predecessors and the creative intellect bestowed on us to solve unfamiliar problems. Hopefully, with wise implementation, GenAI will not become a threat to Islamic education but a means to further illuminate the minds and hearts of students, helping them read, reflect, and ultimately live the message of Islam in an ever-changing world.

CONCLUSION

In this chapter, we have explored the integration of GenAI in contemporary Islamic Religious Education, exploring the intersections between Islamic theology, pedagogy, and AI. The chapter began by addressing foundational Islamic epistemology, highlighting historical precedents of technological assimilation in Muslim scholarship, followed by a technical overview of GenAI capabilities and limitations. Practical applications in IRE, such as AI-assisted Qur'anic exegesis, hadith verification, personalised virtual tutoring, and gamified learning, were critically discussed. The chapter further dove into pedagogical and theological considerations by emphasising that human touch and roles are irreplaceable, ethical authenticity, and the spiritual dimensions of education are critical. Ethical and legal challenges within IRE contexts were also highlighted, proposing a Shariah-aligned framework for responsible AI integration.

Generative AI is poised to become an integral part of education worldwide, and as this chapter has explored, it holds both promise and peril for Islamic Religious Education. In summary, GenAI offers powerful tools that can revolutionise learning experiences – from AI tutors that make Qur'ān memorisation more efficient, to intelligent search systems that help students navigate the vast ocean of Islamic scholarship. It can cater to individual learning needs and spark creative engagement with religious material, potentially making Islamic studies more accessible and appealing to the digital generation. However, alongside these advantages, we have identified significant challenges and cautions. The sanctity and authenticity of sacred knowledge can be compromised if AI is used naively; biases in AI outputs can misrepresent Islamic teachings and cultures; and an over-reliance on automation could erode the spiritual teacher-student bond that lies at the heart of traditional Islamic pedagogy. The key insight is that GenAI is a double-edged sword – it can be a "powerful ally in the pursuit of knowledge" or a crutch that undermines genuine understanding, depending on how we wield it.

Our exploration through the lens of Islamic theology and pedagogy reveals a path of cautious optimism. Islam's epistemological framework, which once enabled Muslims to assimilate Greek philosophy and pioneer algebra, can likewise engage with AI proactively yet critically. By treating AI as *khādim* (servant) rather than *muwajjih* (director) of the educational process, we can balance innovation with tradition. Classical principles like *ma la a* (public interest) and *istihsān* (equity) can guide decisions on when AI's benefits outweigh its risks. For instance, if an AI app significantly helps dyslexic students learn the Qur'ān (a clear ma la a for intellect and religion), that is a strong point in its favour, as long as it is implemented in a way that upholds respect for the Qur'ān. On the other hand, if an AI feature trivialises a sacred concept, an educator might exercise *istihsān* to avoid it even if technically useful, erring on the side of reverence. This balanced mindset – neither techno-utopian nor alarmist – is in line with Islam's general approach of moderation (*wasatiyya*).

REFERENCES

Abid, A., Farooqi, M., & Zou, J. (2021). Persistent Anti-Muslim Bias in Large Language Models. *Proceedings of the 2021 AAAI/ACM Conference on AI, Ethics, and Society*, 298–306. DOI: 10.1145/3461702.3462624

Abubakari, M. S. (2024). Overviewing the Maze of Research Integrity and False Positives Within AI-Enabled Detectors: Grammarly Dilemma in Academic Writing. In Mutawa, A. (Ed.), *Impacts of Generative AI on the Future of Research and Education* (pp. 335–366). IGI Global., DOI: 10.4018/979-8-3693-0884-4.ch013

Abubakari, M. S. (2025a). Digital Technologies Adoption in Islamic Education for Fostering Lifelong Learning Culture: Pilot Survey Preliminary Insights. In Anshari, M., Almunawar, M. N., & Ordóñez de Pablos, P. (Eds.), *Multi-Industry Digitalization and Technological Governance in the AI Era* (pp. 103–126). IGI Global., DOI: 10.4018/979-8-3373-1681-9.ch005

Abubakari, M. S. (2025b). Overviewing Biases in Generative AI-Powered Models in the Arabic Language: AI Fairness for Sustainable Future. In Syafrudin, M., Fitriyani, N. L., & Anshari, M. (Eds.), *Achieving Sustainability in Multi-Industry Settings With AI* (pp. 361–390). IGI Global., DOI: 10.4018/979-8-3373-2530-9.ch013

Abubakari, M. S., & Kalinaki, K. (2024). Digital Competence in Islamic Education for Lifelong Learning: Preliminary Analysis Using DigComp 2.1 Framework. In Hawamdeh, M. M. K., & Abdelhafid, F. (Eds.), *Embracing Technological Advancements for Lifelong Learning* (pp. 1–31). IGI Global., DOI: 10.4018/979-8-3693-1410-4.ch001

Abubakari, M. S., Shafik, W., & Hidayatullah, A. F. (2024). Evaluating the Potential of Artificial Intelligence in Islamic Religious Education: A SWOT Analysis Overview. In *AI-Enhanced Teaching Methods* (pp. 216–239). IGI Global. DOI: 10.4018/979-8-3693-2728-9.ch010

Abubakari, M. S., & Suprapto, S. (2021). Educational Data Mining to Predict Students Performance Based on Deep Learning Neural Network. *Proceeding International Conference On Health, Social Sciences And Technology, 1*(1), 13–16. https://ojs.poltekkespalembang.ac.id/index.php/icohsst/article/view/697

Abubakari, M. S., Zakaria, G. A. N., & Musa, J. (2023). Digital Learning Acceptance in Islamic Education: Validity and Reliability Testing of the Modified Technology Acceptance Model. *Canadian Journal of Educational and Social Studies, 3*(6), 27–42. DOI: 10.53103/cjess.v6i1.185

Abubakari, M. S., Zakaria, G. A. N., & Musa, J. (2024). Perceived compatibility and students' intention to adopt digital technologies in Islamic education institutions. *Cogent Education, 11*(1), 2430869. DOI: 10.1080/2331186X.2024.2430869

Abubakari, M. S., Zakaria, G. A. N., & Musa, J. (2025). Validating the DigComp framework among university students across different educational systems. *Discover Education, 4*(1), 200. DOI: 10.1007/s44217-025-00652-x

Abubakari, M. S., Zakaria, G. A. N., Musa, J., & Kalinaki, K. (2023). Assessing Digital Competence in Higher Education: A Gender Analysis of DigComp 2.1 Framework in Uganda. *SAGA: Journal of Technology and Information System, 1*(4), 114–120. DOI: 10.58905/saga.v1i4.210

Achruh, A., Rapi, M., Rusdi, M., & Idris, R. (2024). Challenges and Opportunities of Artificial Intelligence Adoption in Islamic Education in Indonesian Higher Education Institutions. *International Journal of Learning. Teaching and Educational Research, 23*(11), 423–443. DOI: 10.26803/ijlter.23.11.22

Alqarni, M. (2024). Embedding Search for Quranic Texts based on Large Language Models. *The International Arab Journal of Information Technology, 21*(2), 243–256. DOI: 10.34028/iajit/21/2/7

Antoun, W., Baly, F., & Hajj, H. (2020). *AraBERT: Transformer-based Model for Arabic Language Understanding*. https://doi.org//arXiv.2003.00104DOI: 10.48550

Berberich, N., Nishida, T., & Suzuki, S. (2020). Harmonizing Artificial Intelligence for Social Good. *Philosophy & Technology, 33*(4), 613–638. DOI: 10.1007/s13347-020-00421-8

Butt, N. A., Basharat, A., & Kamran, A. B. (2024). Semantic Enrichment of Hadith Corpus - Knowledge Graph Generation from Islamic Text. *Semantic Web Journal*. https://www.semantic-web-journal.net/system/files/swj3651.pdf

Daun, H., & Arjmand, R. (2018). *Handbook of Islamic Education* (Daun, H., & Arjmand, R., Eds.). Vol. 7). Springer International Publishing., DOI: 10.1007/978-3-319-64683-1

Daun, H., & Arjmand, R. (2021). Globalisation and Islamic Education. In Zajda, J. (Ed.), *Third International Handbook of Globalisation, Education and Policy Research* (pp. 451–463). Springer International Publishing., DOI: 10.1007/978-3-030-66003-1_25

Djazilan, M. S., Rulyansah, A., & Rihlah, J. (2024). Why AI is Essential for the Future of Islamic Education: A Call for Ethical and Effective Implementation. *EDUKASIA: Jurnal Pendidikan Dan Pembelajaran*, *5*(2), 201–216. DOI: 10.62775/edukasia.v5i2.1373

El Ganadi, A., Aftar, S., Gagliardelli, L., & Ruozzi, F. (2025). Generative AI for Islamic Texts: The EMAN Framework for Mitigating GPT Hallucinations. *Proceedings of the 17th International Conference on Agents and Artificial Intelligence*, 1221–1228. DOI: 10.5220/0013312800003890

Elmahjub, E. (2023). Artificial Intelligence (AI) in Islamic Ethics: Towards Pluralist Ethical Benchmarking for AI. *Philosophy & Technology*, *36*(4), 73. DOI: 10.1007/s13347-023-00668-x

Gorian, E., & Osman, N. D. (2024). Digital Ethics of Artificial Intelligence (AI) in Saudi Arabia and United Arab Emirates. *Malaysian Journal of Syariah and Law*, *12*(3), 583–597. DOI: 10.33102/mjsl.vol12no3.798

Gyagenda, A. (2024). The Contribution Of Muslim Scholars Towards Science, Technology And Knowledge: A Historical Perspective. *Journal of Islamic Studies and Arabic Language*, *3*(2), 85–104.

Hidayat, M. C., & Arifin, S., Asrori, & Rusman. (2020). Integration Science Technology with Islamic Values: Empowering Education Model. *Proceedings of the 1st Borobudur International Symposium on Humanities, Economics and Social Sciences (BIS-HESS 2019), 436*, 966–970. DOI: 10.2991/assehr.k.200529.202

Jain, L. R., & Menon, V. (2023). AI Algorithmic Bias: Understanding its Causes, Ethical and Social Implications. *2023 IEEE 35th International Conference on Tools with Artificial Intelligence (ICTAI)*, 460–467. DOI: 10.1109/ICTAI59109.2023.00073

Karagözoğlu, B. (2017). Contribution of Muslim Scholars to Science and Technology. In *Science and Technology from Global and Historical Perspectives* (pp. 137–184). Springer International Publishing., DOI: 10.1007/978-3-319-52890-8_6

Kuck, K. (2023). Generative Artificial Intelligence: A Double-Edged Sword. *2023 World Engineering Education Forum - Global Engineering Deans Council (WEEF-GEDC)*, 1–10. DOI: 10.1109/WEEF-GEDC59520.2023.10343638

Mghari, M., Bouras, O., & El Hibaoui, A. (2022). Sanadset 650K: Data on Hadith narrators. *Data in Brief*, *44*, 108540. DOI: 10.1016/j.dib.2022.108540 PMID: 36065202

Mohadi, M., & Tarshany, Y. (2023). Maqasid Al-Shari'ah and the Ethics of Artificial Intelligence. *Journal of Contemporary Maqasid Studies*, *2*(2), 79–102. DOI: 10.52100/jcms.v2i2.107

Munshi, A. A., AlSabban, W. H., Farag, A. T., Rakha, O. E., Al Sallab, A. A., & Alotaibi, M. (2021). Towards an Automated Islamic Fatwa System: Survey, Dataset and Benchmarks. *International Journal of Computer Science and Mobile Computing*, *10*(4), 118–131. DOI: 10.47760/ijcsmc.2021.v10i04.017

Naveed, H., Khan, A. U., Qiu, S., Saqib, M., Anwar, S., Usman, M., Akhtar, N., Barnes, N., & Mian, A. (2023). *A Comprehensive Overview of Large Language Models*. https://doi.org//arXiv.2307.06435DOI: 10.48550

Norman, E., Pahlawati, E., Siregar, M. L., & Damayanthy, D. (2025). Digital Transformation of Islamic Education: AI, Gamification, and Pedagogical Adaptation for Generation Z. *Medina-Te: Jurnal Studi Islam*, *21*(1), 37–49. DOI: 10.19109/medinate.v21i1.27952

Putrawan, B. K. (2025). From Prayer to Data: The Transformation of Theology in the Age of Artificial Intelligence and its Implications for Religious Practice. *Transformation: An International Journal of Holistic Mission Studies*, *0*(0), 02653788241312229. Advance online publication. DOI: 10.1177/02653788241312229

Syafitri, A., Efriyanti, L., & Devi, I. (2024). The Role of Artificial Intelligence in Encouraging Innovation and Creativity in Islamic Education. *Nizham Journal of Islamic Studies*, *12*(01), 1–10. DOI: 10.32332/nizham.v12i01.8602

Tamuri, A. H. (2021). Teaching Practices of Islamic Education Teachers Based on 5 Mim Concept in Religious Secondary Schools in Indonesia. *International Journal of Islam and Contemporary Affairs*, *1*(1), 1–24. DOI: 10.61465/jurnalyadim.v1i1.37

Tsuria, R., & Tsuria, Y. (2024). Artificial Intelligence's Understanding of Religion: Investigating the Moralistic Approaches Presented by Generative Artificial Intelligence Tools. *Religions*, *15*(3), 375. DOI: 10.3390/rel15030375

Yan, L., Greiff, S., Teuber, Z., & Gašević, D. (2024). Promises and challenges of generative artificial intelligence for human learning. *Nature Human Behaviour*, *8*(10), 1839–1850. DOI: 10.1038/s41562-024-02004-5 PMID: 39438686

Yang, H., Kim, H., Lee, J. H., & Shin, D. (2022). Implementation of an AI chatbot as an English conversation partner in EFL speaking classes. *ReCALL*, *34*(3), 327–343. DOI: 10.1017/S0958344022000039

Yassine, S., & Gammoudi, M. M. (2023). Trends and Challenges of Arabic Chatbots : Literature Review. *Jordanian Journal of Computers and Information Technology*, *09*(03), 261–286.

Za'atreh, M. (2024). *The Impact of Artificial Intelligence on Drafting Religious Edicts (Fatwas)*. The Fatwa Department of the Hashemite Kingdom of Jordan. https://aliftaa.jo/article-en/5743/Article.aspx?ArticleId=5858#:~:text=The Impact of Artificial Intelligence,Fatwas

Zhang, J., Song, W., & Liu, Y. (2025). Cognitive bias in generative AI influences religious education. *Scientific Reports*, *15*(1), 15720. DOI: 10.1038/s41598-025-99121-6 PMID: 40325105

Chapter 8
Faith, Freedom, and Artificial Intelligence:
An Economic Perspective on Digital Rights and Religious Expression

Supratik Guha
https://orcid.org/0000-0001-7447-4469
Shahid Matangini Hazra Government General Degree College for Women, India

ABSTRACT

The pervasive integration of artificial intelligence (AI) into digital platforms profoundly reshapes societal structures, including the landscape of religious expression. This chapter outlines a comprehensive study examining the intricate economic interplay among faith, digital rights, and AI. It investigates the quantifiable economic impacts of AI-driven content moderation on religious expression, including the costs associated with misinformation, censorship, and algorithmic bias, as well as the economic opportunities and challenges for religious institutions adopting AI. By applying economic frameworks such as public goods theory and transaction cost economics, this study aims to inform the development of equitable AI governance models that uphold fundamental digital rights and religious freedom. The anticipated findings will provide a critical, data-driven rationale for policy interventions and technological solutions, fostering a digital environment that supports diverse religious expression while mitigating economic and societal harms.

DOI: 10.4018/979-8-3373-3830-9.ch008

INTRODUCTION

Background: The Digital Transformation of Society and Religion

The digital transformation of society has fundamentally reshaped human interaction, access to information, and economic activity. This profound shift extends significantly to religious expression, which has evolved from traditional, structured environments to dynamic online platforms. The internet and various digital tools have democratized access to theological discourse, enabling global connectivity and fostering new forms of community that transcend traditional geographical boundaries. This evolution has also led to the emergence of a substantial "spiritual services market," valued at hundreds of billions of dollars (ProfileTree, 2025), and significant economic contributions from religious organizations through their online engagement.

The digital transformation, however, presents an inherent duality for religious expression. While it offers unprecedented opportunities for enhanced accessibility, new forms of community, and streamlined spiritual engagement, it simultaneously introduces significant risks. The mechanisms that enable positive transformation, such as the democratization of content, rapid dissemination, and personalized engagement, are precisely those that can be exploited to facilitate negative outcomes. For instance, the open access to information can lead to the proliferation of unverified or misinterpreted teachings, theological distortions, and the promotion of divisive ideologies. This suggests a fundamental tension and a double-edged sword effect rather than simply discrete good and bad uses. This inherent tension complicates the development of effective governance and policy frameworks, as measures designed to curb harmful content might inadvertently stifle legitimate religious expression, innovation, or community building. It underscores the need for nuanced technological design and regulatory approaches that can differentiate between beneficial and detrimental uses within the complex and sensitive domain of religious discourse.

In the digital age, artificial intelligence (AI) has emerged as one of the most transformative forces reshaping society. From healthcare and finance to law enforcement and communication, AI systems increasingly influence how people live, interact, and make decisions. Amid this technological revolution, a pressing and often overlooked issue lies at the intersection of AI, digital rights, and religious expression. While AI promises economic efficiency and personalized services, it also raises critical concerns about fairness, inclusion, and freedom—especially the freedom of religion or belief (FoRB).

Religious expression, once limited to physical spaces like places of worship or community gatherings, now flourishes—or flounders—on digital platforms. Social media, content-sharing sites, and AI-driven recommendation engines determine which voices are heard and which are silenced. In this context, AI becomes a gatekeeper of religious visibility, shaping who can share their beliefs and how widely their messages spread. The economic dimensions of this dynamic are profound: religious content creators may find opportunities for monetization or face unjust demonetization; faith-based organizations may gain reach or be marginalized by algorithmic filters.

The convergence of artificial intelligence (AI) and human rights in the digital age introduces new dimensions of opportunity and concern. While AI technologies are revolutionizing economies, societies, and governance, they also intersect with core human freedoms, notably the freedom of religion or belief (FoRB). As AI systems mediate more of our interactions—online and offline—they play a growing role in shaping the environment in which religious identities are expressed, suppressed, or commodified.

This chapter explores these intersections through an economic lens, examining how AI technologies affect digital religious expression, access to religious content, algorithmic bias, and surveillance, and how these in turn impact economic opportunities and constraints for individuals and religious communities. It contends that the future of inclusive digital economies depends on how AI systems are governed to uphold not just efficiency and innovation, but also fundamental freedoms, especially the right to religious expression. The proposal highlights the dual role of AI as both an enabler and a threat to FoRB, with economic implications that merit deeper scholarly and policy-oriented inquiry.

Problem Statement: The Interplay of AI, Digital Rights, and Religious Expression in the Digital Economy

The rapid advancement and integration of Artificial Intelligence (AI) into digital platforms introduce new layers of complexity to this ongoing digital transformation. AI offers promising opportunities for religious organizations, including personalized spiritual content, enhanced accessibility of sacred texts, and administrative support for clergy. However, it simultaneously poses significant ethical and economic challenges. These include algorithmic biases, profound privacy concerns, the erosion of epistemic trust, and the potential for AI-generated misinformation to distort religious discourse, trivialize sacred traditions, and even incite real-world violence.

Digital rights are understood as the fundamental freedoms and entitlements that individuals possess and should be able to exercise in the digital environment (American Library Association, 2021). Nevertheless, AI-driven content moderation systems, often deployed by platforms operating under strong economic incentives to maximize user engagement and advertising revenue, frequently create friction with these fundamental rights, particularly in the sensitive domain of religious content. This tension can lead to concerns about over-censorship of legitimate religious expression, misinterpretation of nuanced content, and the disproportionate silencing of marginalized religious voices.

The economic perspective is not merely an analytical lens but a critical determinant of these dynamics. The economic imperative driving algorithmic bias and rights infringement is evident in how platforms operate. Algorithms are often designed to maximize user engagement and advertising revenue. When these profit-driven algorithms are combined with opaque AI systems trained on biased data and lacking cultural context, the result is a disproportionate restriction of free expression and marginalization of users, particularly in the Global South. The causal chain is clear: the pursuit of profit leads to the design of engagement-optimizing AI algorithms. These algorithms, inherently biased due to training data and a lack of contextual understanding, then lead to algorithmic discrimination and content moderation errors, which in turn infringe upon digital rights such as freedom of expression and non-discrimination. This also generates negative economic externalities. This indicates that the economic model of digital platforms, specifically ad-revenue maximization, is not merely a backdrop but a direct, causal driver of the technical limitations and ethical failures of AI content moderation, leading to systemic violations of digital rights, rather than these being isolated technical or ethical issues. This implies that purely technical solutions for AI bias or content moderation failures will be insufficient without addressing the underlying economic incentives of the platforms. Effective regulatory frameworks must therefore consider these economic drivers and potentially introduce disincentives for harmful practices or incentives for rights-respecting AI development to truly protect digital rights.

Misinformation, hate speech, and censorship incur quantifiable financial costs, impacting financial markets, eroding public trust, and disrupting economic stability. Conversely, religious institutions represent a substantial economic force, contributing trillions to national economies, and AI adoption presents both significant economic opportunities and challenges for their operations and outreach. The current regulatory landscape for AI is fragmented and inconsistent, highlighting an urgent need for dynamic governance models that can balance technological innovation with accountability and the protection of fundamental digital rights.

This chapter explores the transformative intersection of artificial intelligence (AI), digital rights, and religious expression through an economic lens. As digital platforms increasingly mediate faith-based discourse, AI-driven content moderation has emerged as both an enabler and suppressor of religious freedom.

Research Questions and Objectives

Research Questions

1. What are the quantifiable economic impacts (costs and benefits) of AI-driven content moderation on religious expression and digital rights, particularly concerning misinformation, censorship, and algorithmic bias?
2. How do the economic incentives of digital platforms influence the development and application of AI content moderation policies, and what are the resulting economic externalities on religious communities and their digital rights?
3. What economic frameworks (e.g., public goods theory, transaction cost economics, regulatory economics) can inform the development of more equitable and rights-respecting AI governance models for religious expression in the digital sphere?
4. How can privacy-preserving AI technologies, such as federated learning, be economically incentivized and implemented to safeguard sensitive religious data while promoting beneficial online religious engagement?

Objectives

- To conduct a comprehensive economic analysis of the financial costs associated with religious misinformation, hate speech, and censorship on digital platforms.
- To evaluate the economic opportunities and challenges for religious organizations in adopting AI technologies for ministry, outreach, and community engagement.
- To analyze the economic motivations of social media platforms in their content moderation strategies and their impact on digital rights and religious freedom.
- To explore the applicability of economic theories (e.g., public goods, externalities, transaction costs) to conceptualize and protect digital rights and religious expression in the AI era.
- To propose economically viable and ethically sound policy recommendations and technological solutions, including privacy-preserving AI, for fostering a digital environment that upholds faith and freedom.

Significance of the Study: Economic, Societal, and Ethical Implications

This research is critical given the increasing global reliance on digital platforms for religious expression and the pervasive, often opaque, influence of AI on online discourse. It aims to provide a novel, interdisciplinary economic lens to understand the complex interplay of faith, freedom, and AI, moving beyond purely technical, legal, or sociological analyses.

Economic Significance

Quantifying the substantial economic costs of misinformation and censorship will provide a clear, data-driven rationale for increased investment in ethical AI development and robust governance mechanisms. Understanding the tangible Return on Investment (ROI) of AI adoption for religious organizations can guide strategic resource allocation and foster responsible technological integration within the religious sector. Analyzing the economic motivations and incentives of digital platforms is crucial for designing effective regulatory frameworks that align private interests with public good.

Societal Significance

The study will contribute to fostering a more inclusive, equitable, and trustworthy digital public sphere where diverse religious expression can flourish without undue suppression or distortion. By specifically addressing algorithmic bias, it aims to mitigate the disproportionate harms faced by marginalized religious communities, ensuring their equitable participation and voice in online spaces.

Ethical Significance

The research will directly inform the development of more ethical AI by highlighting the critical importance of human dignity, justice, fairness, and transparency in the design, deployment, and governance of AI systems. It will underscore the complex ethical imperative of balancing freedom of expression with the prevention of harm, especially concerning religious content, which often involves deeply held beliefs and cultural nuances.

This study investigates the economic dimensions of this dynamic, analyzing how platform incentives, algorithmic bias, and censorship impact the rights and visibility of religious communities—especially in the Global South. It examines the financial costs of religious misinformation, over-moderation, and digital exclusion, while highlighting the growing economic footprint of digital religious engagement and the spiritual services market. Drawing on public goods theory, transaction cost economics, and regulatory frameworks, the chapter provides a novel economic rationale for rights-respecting AI governance. It proposes actionable policy and technological solutions—including federated learning and hybrid moderation models—that align ethical imperatives with economic incentives. Ultimately, the chapter argues that safeguarding digital religious expression is not only a moral and legal necessity but also a strategic economic imperative for inclusive digital development.

LITERATURE REVIEW: INTERSECTING DOMAINS

Digital Rights and Religious Freedom in the Online Environment

Digital rights are understood as the fundamental freedoms and entitlements that individuals possess and should be able to exercise in the digital environment. These rights encompass a broad range of issues, including freedom of expression, access to information from diverse sources, privacy, and the right to non-discrimination. They are recognized as crucial for individuals to fully participate in the digital economy and society, enabling democratic processes, fostering public debate, and facilitating online activism and mobilization. The digital rights movement itself emerged from early efforts against online censorship and surveillance.

Religious liberty is not merely a policy preference but a fundamental right, enshrined in constitutional texts, such as the U.S. First Amendment, and numerous federal statutes. It protects the right of individuals to exercise their religion freely, including performing or abstaining from physical acts in accordance with beliefs, and expressing religious beliefs, subject to narrow, universally applicable limits. The Universal Declaration of Human Rights (Article 18) further affirms freedom of thought, conscience, and religion, including the freedom to change belief and practice it alone or in community. While digital technologies offer immense opportunities to strengthen these human rights, they also present growing threats, such as targeted persecution of religious or belief minorities and the misuse of technology for surveillance and censorship. Governments have a direct obligation to protect human rights, and the private sector has a responsibility to respect them, engaging in due diligence to ensure their products and services do not infringe upon these rights.

The protection of digital rights and religious freedom yields a significant economic multiplier effect. The evidence indicates that robust protection of digital rights is essential for economic growth, and similarly, religious freedom demonstrably leads to economic growth. This occurs by empowering individuals to engage in entrepreneurial behaviours, contribute to innovation, and attract human capital. Furthermore, religious freedom is linked to reduced corruption, enhanced peace, and greater societal stability, all of which are fundamental preconditions for sustained economic development. The causal chain suggests that robust protection of digital rights and religious freedom fosters increased individual participation, trust, and innovation in the digital economy, which in turn reduces social friction and conflict, attracts human and financial capital, and ultimately drives overall economic growth and prosperity. This perspective reframes the debate around digital rights and religious freedom from solely a human rights or ethical concern to a pragmatic economic imperative. Their protection constitutes a public good that generates positive externalities across the economy. Conversely, the absence of these protections leads to negative welfare consequences, deterring investment and disrupting critical economic sectors. This provides a strong, quantifiable argument for governments and corporations to invest in protecting these rights, as neglecting them incurs significant opportunity costs in terms of foregone economic development and increased societal instability.

The Digital Landscape of Religious Expression

Digital platforms have fundamentally transformed religious practices and community engagement. They offer innovative avenues such as virtual sermons, AI-generated prayers, and personalized spiritual guidance tailored to individual preferences. AI tools, for instance, can assist clergy in creating custom messages, streamlining sermon preparation, and enhancing outreach and community engagement through digital platforms. This digital shift facilitates global connectivity, allowing religious communities to transcend traditional geographical boundaries and foster new, often more accessible, forms of spiritual connection. The COVID-19 pandemic significantly accelerated the adoption of online worship and digital ministry, demonstrating the remarkable resilience and transformative potential of faith in a digital era.

Despite these opportunities, the democratization of religious content online introduces significant risks. Digital media can lead to theological distortions, the proliferation of unverified or misinterpreted teachings, and the promotion of divisive ideologies. AI, in particular, can distort sacred traditions or culturally significant materials when it remixes them without adequate understanding or contextual awareness, leading to doctrinal confusion, trivialization, or misrepresentation (Al-Zaman, 2021). This can manifest as AI tools generating content that conflates theological categories or simulates prophetic or divine voices, risking spiritual manipulation and fostering an uncritical dependence on technology rather than genuine spiritual guidance. Furthermore, extremist groups effectively leverage online platforms and their algorithms to broadcast their ideologies globally and create "echo chambers,"

A reinforcing existing beliefs, fostering a sense of community among like-minded individuals, and potentially leading to radicalization and interreligious violence.

This phenomenon, termed the "synthetic sacred," carries significant economic and epistemic erosion. AI's advanced generative capabilities, coupled with a lack of inherent understanding or contextual awareness, enable the mass production of plausible but distorted or fabricated religious content. This undermines traditional religious authority and authentic spiritual experiences, leading to an erosion of epistemic trust in all online religious information. The proliferation of synthetic content blurs the line between authentic and fake, leading to widespread skepticism even towards truthful information, a phenomenon known as the "liar's dividend". This is not merely about factual misinformation; it represents a profound challenge to the very nature of religious truth, authority, and spiritual experience in the digital age, with long-term societal, theological, and economic consequences. These consequences can include reduced engagement with online religious platforms, decreased participation in the spiritual economy, and a potential market failure where authentic religious content struggles to compete with AI-generated "synthetic sacred" content. This calls for not only technical solutions for misinformation detection but also robust educational and theological responses to cultivate digital discernment among religious adherents and to reaffirm the value of human-mediated spiritual experiences.

ECONOMIC ANALYSIS OF DIGITAL RIGHTS AND RELIGIOUS EXPRESSION IN THE AI ERA

Economic Value and Opportunities of Digital Religious Engagement

The global spiritual services market represents a significant and growing economic sector. It was valued at US$376.0 billion in 2024 and is projected to reach US$787.4 billion by 2035, demonstrating a robust Compound Annual Growth Rate (CAGR) of 7.0% (ProfileTree, 2025). This substantial growth is primarily driven by the increasing adoption of mind-body practices and the profound influence of digital platforms on cultural and spiritual engagement. Parallelly, the market size of religious organizations is also experiencing consistent growth, predicted to expand from $373.48 billion in 2023 to $463.78 billion by 2028. The rise of online religious services and digital ministry is explicitly identified as a key factor contributing to this market expansion.

Religion contributes substantially to national economies, with the U.S. religious economy alone contributing nearly $1.2 trillion annually (ProfileTree, 2025), placing it ahead of many national economies globally. This multifaceted contribution stems from congregations (e.g., $418 billion annually in the U.S. through operations, services, education, and "magnet effects" from events like weddings and tourism), religious institutions (e.g., hospitals, universities, charities contributing another $303 billion), and faith-based businesses. Online platforms have become indispensable for religious organizations to maintain community, deliver services, and engage members, especially during periods of crisis like the COVID-19 pandemic. The increased accessibility enabled by digital engagement is a direct driver of continued market growth in spiritual services.

The digital economy has emerged as a new frontier for religious entrepreneurship and value creation. The substantial and growing economic value generated by religious organizations and the spiritual services market is directly linked to how digital platforms enable new forms of religious expression, outreach, and community building. Online religious services and digital ministry are explicit drivers of this economic expansion. This fundamentally transforms how faith interacts with the market, moving beyond traditional models of religious economy. AI adoption further amplifies this, with non-profit and grassroots organizations, including religious non-profits, increasingly experimenting with and adopting generative AI tools to enhance productivity and achieve labor cost savings (Balidemaj, 2024), particularly in response to rising economic pressures and service demands. AI can automate repetitive administrative tasks such as donor research, new donor stewardship, and content development, thereby freeing up staff time for higher-value, relationship-driven work. Case studies demonstrate significant potential ROI, including a 252% increase in average monthly ad spend, 107 new donations, and 935 new email subscribers for one ministry. However, concerns persist regarding data privacy and security, accuracy of AI outputs, potential biases in AI systems, and the long-term sustainability of short-term efficiency gains. This suggests that public policies promoting digital inclusion, digital literacy, and ethical AI development specifically tailored for religious organizations can unlock significant untapped economic and social benefits. It also implies that existing economic models of religious behavior need to be updated to account for digital engagement as a distinct, powerful, and growing dimension of the religious economy.

The following table provides a balanced and empirically grounded cost-benefit analysis of AI adoption for religious organizations. By clearly presenting both the quantifiable benefits, such as financial gains and efficiency metrics, and the significant, often overlooked, challenges, including ethical concerns, operational complexities, and sustainability issues, it offers a holistic perspective. This directly informs strategic decision-making for religious leaders, non-profit managers, and policymakers, highlighting not only where investment is economically beneficial but also where caution, ethical oversight, and resource allocation for risk mitigation are paramount. It transforms abstract discussions of AI's potential into concrete, actionable insights relevant to an economic perspective.

Table 1. ROI of AI adoption in religious organizations/non-profits

Aspect	Benefits	Challenges
Productivity/Efficiency	Increased productivity (e.g., 10-15 hours/week saved); 30% reduction in proposal development time; Labor cost savings	Unforeseen time needed to monitor outputs and manage compliance/ quality issues
Financial Gains	Increased donations (e.g., 107 new donations); Increased ad spend (e.g., 252% increase); $1.41 in returns for every dollar spent (41% ROI) for early adopters	Continued competition in funding cycles (AI does not generate extra funding); Potential for rising tool prices once embedded
Outreach/Engagement	New email subscribers (e.g., 935 new subscribers); Improved communication/ outreach; Better targeting of donors; More meaningful interactions	Potential undermining of organizational cohesion, trust, and internal values
Ethical Concerns	Ethical AI development can align with human dignity, justice, and common good	Data privacy and security concerns (70% of organizations concerned); Accuracy concerns (63% worried); Representation and biases (57% concerned); Lack of governance
Overall Success	92% of early adopters see ROI from AI investments	Short-term efficiency gains may not be sustainable long-term

This table provides a balanced and empirically grounded cost-benefit analysis of AI adoption for religious organizations. By clearly presenting both the quantifiable benefits, such as financial gains and efficiency metrics, and the significant, often overlooked, challenges, including ethical concerns, operational complexities, and sustainability issues, it offers a holistic perspective. This directly informs strategic decision-making for religious leaders, non-profit managers, and policymakers, highlighting not only where investment is economically beneficial but also where caution, ethical oversight, and resource allocation for risk mitigation are paramount. It transforms abstract discussions of AI's potential into concrete, actionable insights relevant to an economic perspective.

Economic Costs of Misinformation, Hate Speech, and Censorship

Financial Losses from Online Misinformation

Misinformation, especially religious misinformation, carries substantial and quantifiable economic costs across various sectors. Globally, the total losses induced by disinformation reached a staggering US$78.2 billion in 2019 (Al-Zaman, 2021). This figure includes significant annual impacts such as stock market losses amounting to approximately US$39 billion, investor losses of around US$17 billion due to decisions influenced by misinformation, and reputation management costs for targeted companies reaching about US$9.54 billion. The healthcare sector alone incurs roughly US$9 billion in annual expenditure to address false information, with major costs tied to combating fake news about anti-vaccine campaigns and climate change. The advancement of AI technology makes the spread of false information increasingly challenging to identify, as journalists report growing difficulty in distinguishing disinformation from accurate information due to AI's role. This technological facilitation contributes to the rampant production and dissemination of information, which can influence personal behavior and investment decisions, potentially inciting panic in society and the market, and leading to a credibility crisis.

Economic Impact of Censorship and Internet Shutdowns

Internet censorship, particularly in the form of internet shutdowns, has significant economic costs and directly restricts civil liberties (American Library Association, 2021). In 2015, the estimated cost of 81 internet shutdowns for 19 countries was $2.4 billion, with India being among the top five countries experiencing economic loss due to such events. These disruptions affect various economic sectors, including education, finance, manufacturing, and agriculture, impacting a nation's digital economy. Beyond direct financial losses, censorship can dampen economic productivity by segregating cyberspace and stopping information flows, leading to labor productivity loss. Even increased latency due to censorship can significantly distort the labor market. The economic impact of content moderation errors, such as false positives (over-removal) and false negatives (under-removal), also contributes to these costs. Over-removal of legitimate content, including religious expression, can stifle free speech and disproportionately impact marginalized communities.

Financial Consequences of Algorithmic Bias

Algorithmic bias in AI systems, particularly in sensitive domains like financial services, carries significant financial consequences. Research shows that AI-generated financial advice can exhibit religious biases, leading to personalized responses that may alienate clients or introduce ideological friction. This can diminish client trust and lead to disengagement from financial strategies. More broadly, biased outcomes in finance can cause pecuniary losses, societal disparities, and legal challenges. For example, African American and Latinx borrowers have been charged significantly higher interest rates in fintech lending, amounting to hundreds of millions in extra interest annually, even with equivalent credit scores (Balendra, 2025).

AI can perpetuate existing inequities by reflecting biases present in training data, operating as "black boxes" that hide discrimination, exploiting systemic challenges (e.g., limited access to credit for certain communities), and even through "group fairness" metrics that appear fair overall but lead to unfair outcomes within subgroups.[1] This indicates that AI, without conscious oversight and commitments against potential biases, can exacerbate existing inequities for economically vulnerable communities.[1] Addressing religious biases in AI-driven financial advice is essential to preserve the integrity of financial decision-making and foster fairness, inclusivity, and trust in a digital ecosystem that respects diverse cultural and religious identities.

Algorithmic Colonialism: A Systemic Economic Harm

The economic and social costs of "algorithmic colonialism" in content moderation are substantial (Balendra, 2025). Historical colonial power dynamics and economic disparities have led to a Western-centric development of Natural Language Processing (NLP) and AI models, coupled with underinvestment in diverse languages and cultural contexts. This results in biased AI models that fail to understand nuances in non-Western languages and cultures, leading to a discriminatory impact and systematic marginalization of users in the Global South. This manifests as disproportionate censorship (over-removal) or ineffective moderation (slow-removal) of content from Majority World/Global South users, including religious minorities, perpetuating inequality, hindering free speech, and leading to economic disempowerment for these communities.

This indicates that AI's technical limitations and ethical failures in content moderation are not merely accidental but are deeply rooted in historical power imbalances and economic disparities, effectively extending a form of "algorithmic colonialism" into the digital sphere.[1] This results in significant economic and social costs for the already marginalized, including missed opportunities for digital inclusion and equitable participation.[1] This perspective elevates the discussion beyond individual instances of bias to a systemic issue, demonstrating that the economic benefits of AI are unequally distributed, and its harms are disproportionately borne by those who are already economically and socially disadvantaged. This calls for a fundamental shift from a universal "one-size-fits-all" AI moderation approach to culturally and linguistically sensitive, localized models, requiring substantial and equitable investment, capacity building, and genuine collaboration with Majority World researchers and communities.

The following table provides a balanced and empirically grounded assessment of AI's practical performance in content moderation. By clearly outlining both its strengths and inherent weaknesses, it directly supports the argument that AI's limitations are not just technical but have profound economic and social consequences, especially when combined with biased training data and profit-driven platform incentives. It helps to illustrate why algorithmic bias and moderation errors occur, providing a concrete basis for understanding the costs discussed in this section and highlighting the need for human oversight and culturally sensitive models.

Table 2. Comparison of AI content moderation capabilities and limitations

Aspect	Capabilities	Limitations
Speed	Real-time processing, faster responses	Rapid content generation outpaces AI adaptation
Scale	Processes vast data volumes (e.g., 3M+ posts/day on Facebook)	Overwhelmed by sheer volume, increasing likelihood of harmful content slipping through
Pattern Recognition	Identifies patterns, trends, virality, and sources of disinformation	Struggles with evolving slang, coded language, and new forms of harmful content
Nuance Detection	Advanced NLP (emoji decoding, semantic embeddings, topic modeling) for some nuance	Fails to grasp sarcasm, irony, idioms, cultural context, and true intent
Bias	Can be designed with fairness-aware algorithms and regular audits	Inherits and amplifies biases from training data, human annotators, and developers; disproportionately affects marginalized groups
Transparency	Potential for Explainable AI (XAI) to clarify decisions	Often "black boxes," lacking clear decision-making processes and accountability
Data Requirements	Requires large, representative datasets for training	Data scarcity for low-resource languages, specific contexts, and nuanced hate speech types
Support	Assists human fact-checkers, reduces exposure to graphic content	Cannot fully automate effective moderation; human oversight remains indispensable

PROPOSED METHODOLOGY

This research proposal advocates for a mixed-methods approach, combining quantitative economic modeling with qualitative analysis of AI systems and religious discourse.

Phase 1: Economic Modeling and Data Analysis

- **Quantifying Costs of Misinformation and Censorship:** This phase will involve developing econometric models to estimate the direct and indirect economic costs of religious misinformation, hate speech, and content censorship. Data sources will include publicly available reports on financial losses due to disinformation, analyses of internet shutdown impact on GDP, and studies on the economic effects of algorithmic bias in financial contexts. The models will account for variables such as lost revenue, reduced investment, reputational damage, and the costs associated with dispute resolution and appeals processes.
- **Analyzing ROI of AI in Religious Organizations:** A cost-benefit analysis framework will be applied to assess the Return on Investment (ROI) of AI adoption by religious organizations. This will involve collecting data through surveys and case studies of religious non-profits and institutions that have implemented AI tools. Metrics will include time saved, cost reductions, increases in donations or outreach, and qualitative benefits such as enhanced community engagement and service delivery.
- **Platform Economic Incentives:** Economic models of platform behavior will be developed to analyze how revenue models (e.g., advertising-based vs. subscription-based) and market structures influence content moderation policies and their impact on digital rights. This will involve examining the trade-offs platforms face between maximizing user engagement and mitigating harmful content, and how these decisions create economic externalities.

Phase 2: Qualitative Analysis of AI Systems and Religious Content

- **Algorithmic Bias in Religious Contexts:** This phase will involve a detailed qualitative analysis of AI-driven content moderation systems, focusing on their performance with religious content. This will include examining how AI struggles with linguistic nuance, cultural context, and intent in religious discourse. Case studies of content moderation errors affecting religious expression will be analyzed to identify patterns of over-removal or under-removal, particularly impacting marginalized religious communities.

- **Ethical Implications and Governance:** This will involve reviewing existing ethical guidelines and regulatory frameworks for AI, particularly those addressing content moderation and data privacy. The analysis will identify gaps in current governance models concerning religious freedom and propose how economic incentives can be leveraged to promote more equitable and rights-respecting AI development.
- **Privacy-Preserving AI for Sensitive Data:** The study will explore the technical feasibility and economic viability of privacy-preserving AI technologies, such as federated learning, for handling sensitive religious data. This will involve assessing their potential to safeguard individual privacy and religious beliefs while enabling beneficial online religious engagement, considering the consent challenges and regulatory gaps in current frameworks.

Phase 3: Policy Recommendations and Framework Development

- Synthesize findings from Phases 1 and 2 to develop concrete, economically informed policy recommendations for governments, tech companies, and religious organizations.
- Propose new or adapted economic frameworks (e.g., digital public goods, common pool resources) to conceptualize and protect digital rights and religious expression in the AI era.
- Outline strategies for incentivizing ethical AI development and deployment, including market-based mechanisms for audit and compliance, and liability frameworks.

EXPECTED OUTCOMES AND CONTRIBUTIONS

This research is expected to yield several significant outcomes and contributions:

- **Quantifiable Economic Evidence:** The study will provide robust, data-driven estimates of the economic costs associated with religious misinformation, hate speech, and censorship, offering a compelling economic rationale for investing in ethical AI and robust content moderation. It will also quantify the ROI for religious organizations adopting AI, guiding their strategic investments.

- **Enhanced Understanding of Platform Incentives:** The research will illuminate the complex economic incentives driving digital platforms' content moderation decisions, explaining how these motivations can lead to unintended consequences for digital rights and religious expression. This understanding is crucial for designing effective regulatory interventions.
- **Novel Economic Frameworks:** The study will contribute to the academic literature by applying and potentially extending economic theories (e.g., public goods, externalities, transaction costs, information asymmetry) to the nascent field of digital rights and religious expression in the AI era. This will offer new conceptual tools for policymakers and scholars.
- **Policy Recommendations:** Concrete, actionable policy recommendations will be developed for governments, tech companies, and religious institutions. These recommendations will focus on fostering a digital environment that balances freedom of expression with the prevention of harm, promotes equitable digital participation, and safeguards sensitive religious data.
- **Promotion of Ethical AI Development:** By highlighting the economic and societal harms of algorithmic bias and lack of transparency, the research will advocate for the development of more ethical, culturally sensitive, and privacy-preserving AI systems, particularly for religious content. This includes promoting hybrid human-AI moderation models and federated learning approaches.
- **Empowerment of Marginalized Communities:** The study's focus on algorithmic colonialism and its disproportionate impact on marginalized religious communities will contribute to efforts aimed at ensuring their equitable voice and participation in the digital sphere, fostering digital inclusion and justice.

CASE STUDIES: FAITH AND AI IN PRACTICE

Case 1: YouTube's Algorithm and Christian Influencers in the U.S.

Several U.S.-based Christian creators have reported that videos addressing topics like abortion, gender, or prophecy are demonetized despite high engagement. In many cases, AI moderation misinterprets theological critique as hate speech or misinformation. The economic effect is significant: lower ad revenue, fewer sponsorships, and reduced content output.

Case 2: Muslim Content Creators and TikTok

Muslim influencers in the UK and South Asia have faced challenges when posting content about Ramadan, Palestine, or Islamic teachings. Posts are either shadow banned or removed without explanation. Given that many of these influencers rely on digital platforms for income through brand collaborations, such actions limit economic participation and public religious engagement.

Case 3: Jewish Communities and Online Hate

Jewish creators face another dimension of economic harm: online hate. Even when platforms do not suppress Jewish content, algorithmic amplification of antisemitic hate speech creates an unsafe digital environment, discouraging participation. Some creators have opted out of monetization or deleted content entirely, resulting in a loss of livelihood and voice.

THE POLITICAL ECONOMY OF ALGORITHMIC RELIGIOUS VISIBILITY

AI platforms are not neutral tools—they are commercial enterprises with political implications. Algorithms are optimized for engagement, not equality. Content that provokes outrage, fear, or tribal loyalty tends to perform better, including religious extremism or sensationalism. This rewards divisive religious narratives and punishes contemplative, pluralistic, or minority views.

Moreover, most AI systems are developed by a handful of powerful tech firms—Meta, Google, Microsoft, OpenAI—primarily based in the Global North. The economic logic of these firms often neglects the cultural and religious diversity of users in the Global South, where faith plays a larger role in public life. This digital colonialism risks exporting homogenized content standards and monetization models ill-suited for global pluralism.

POLICY AND ETHICAL CONSIDERATIONS

Transparency and Accountability in AI Moderation

Platforms must disclose how AI systems make decisions regarding religious content (Bioni, Rielli, & Zanatta, 2025). This includes flagging mechanisms, training datasets, and appeals processes. Transparent systems would allow religious creators to understand and adapt their content without compromising their faith or financial sustainability.

Pluralism in Training Data

AI models should be trained on diverse, multilingual, and multicultural data that reflects global religious expressions. Including scholars of religion and interfaith dialogue experts in the AI development process can improve system sensitivity and reduce false positives.

Digital Rights as Economic Rights

Freedom of religion in digital spaces must be recognized not only as a civil liberty but also as an economic right. Just as the right to free trade or employment is protected, so too should digital religious labor be safeguarded from algorithmic discrimination.

Inclusion in AI Governance

Faith-based organizations, especially from the Global South, must be included in global conversations on AI ethics, such as those led by the UN, EU, or national AI task forces. A multi-stakeholder governance model ensures that AI serves diverse values, not just market-driven imperatives.

CONCLUSION

The intersection of faith, freedom, and artificial intelligence in the digital economy presents a complex and evolving landscape.[1] While AI offers transformative opportunities for religious expression and community engagement, its current deployment by digital platforms, often driven by economic incentives to maximize engagement and advertising revenue, introduces significant risks.[1] These risks manifest as quantifiable economic costs stemming from misinformation, hate speech, censorship, and pervasive algorithmic biases that disproportionately affect marginalized religious communities.

The analysis presented in this report underscores that the challenges in AI-driven content moderation are not merely technical or ethical but are deeply rooted in economic structures and incentives. The economic model of digital platforms can inadvertently perpetuate algorithmic colonialism, where historical power imbalances and underinvestment in diverse linguistic and cultural contexts lead to biased AI systems and unjust moderation outcomes. This results in substantial economic and social costs, including foregone opportunities for digital inclusion and equitable participation.

Conversely, protecting digital rights and religious freedom acts as a powerful economic multiplier, fostering innovation, attracting human capital, reducing social friction, and driving overall economic growth. Religious institutions themselves represent a significant economic force, and strategic, ethical AI adoption can unlock further economic and social benefits for them. This reinforces the interconnectedness of economic, ethical, and societal well-being in the AI era. The report's core argument is that a holistic, interdisciplinary approach is not just academically sound but practically necessary for effective governance. Neglecting any one dimension (economic, ethical, or social) will inevitably undermine progress in the others. For policymakers, this means that investments in digital rights and ethical AI are not just optional considerations but fundamental to long-term economic prosperity and social cohesion, framing the issue as a strategic imperative for national development and global stability.

Therefore, effective governance of AI in this domain requires a comprehensive approach that transcends purely technical or legal solutions. It necessitates the integration of economic frameworks to understand platform behavior, quantify harms, and identify incentives for rights-respecting AI development. This implies that the digital environment, particularly the spaces where religious expression and interaction occur, should be treated as a "digital public good" or "digital commons" rather than solely a private market. This mindset shift would necessitate collective responsibility from governments, tech companies, civil society, and religious organizations to co-create and maintain a digital infrastructure that serves the common good (Bühler et al., 2023). It suggests moving beyond a purely profit-driven model to one that prioritizes shared prosperity, equitable access, and the flourishing of diverse expressions, requiring innovative governance models that may include public-private partnerships, data cooperatives, or new regulatory bodies focused on digital welfare.

Future efforts must focus on developing culturally and linguistically sensitive AI models, ensuring transparency and accountability in algorithmic decision-making, and exploring privacy-preserving technologies like federated learning for sensitive religious data. This research aims to provide the critical economic evidence and theoretical foundations necessary to guide policymakers, tech companies, and religious communities toward building a digital future where faith can flourish, freedom is upheld, and economic prosperity is equitably shared.

REFERENCES

Al-Zaman, M. S. (2021, February). *A content analysis of social media users' reaction to religious disinformation in Bangladesh.* DigitalCommons@University of Nebraska - Lincoln. https://digitalcommons.unl.edu/cgi/viewcontent.cgi?article=9100&context=libphilprac

American Library Association. (2021, October). *First Amendment and Censorship*. ALA. Retrieved June 11, 2025, from https://www.ala.org/advocacy/intfreedom/censorship

Balendra, S. (2025, May 16). Meta's AI moderation and free speech: Ongoing challenges in the Global South. *Cambridge Forum on AI: Law and Governance, 1*, e21. DOI: 10.1017/cfl.2025.5

Balidemaj, V. (2024, August). *Artificial Intelligence Integration, Concerns, Benefits, and the Need for Ethical Policies for Community Foundations and Nonprofit Organizations*. Clemson OPEN. https://open.clemson.edu/cgi/viewcontent.cgi?article=4768&context=all_dissertations

Bioni, B., Rielli, M., & Zanatta, R. (2025, February 28). *Beyond Digital Rights: Towards a Fair Information Ecosystem?* TechPolicy.Press. Retrieved June 11, 2025, from https://www.techpolicy.press/beyond-digital-rights-towards-a-fair-information-ecosystem/

Bühler, M. M., Calzada, I., Cane, I., Jelinek, T., Kapoor, A., Mannan, M., Mehta, S., Mookerje, V., Nübel, K., Pentland, A., Scholz, T., Siddarth, D., Tait, J., Vaitla, B., & Zhu, J. (2023, June 29). Unlocking the Power of Digital Commons: Data Cooperatives as a Pathway for Data Sovereign, Innovative and Equitable Digital Communities. *MDPI, 3*(3), 11. https://www.mdpi.com/2673-6470/3/3/11

Chapter 9
Believing the Algorithm:
AI and the Transformation of Popular Belief in India

Mouparna Roy
Janki Devi Memorial College, University of Delhi, New Delhi, India

Nandini Basistha
https://orcid.org/0000-0002-8917-5979
Shree Guru Gobind Singh Tricentenary University, Gurugram, India

ABSTRACT

AI technologies in India are not only transforming digital habits but also reshaping belief systems. From religious chatbots to political propaganda and tools like ChatGPT, AI now mediates truth, tradition, and trust. Drawing on sociological and media theories, this chapter explores AI as a cultural actor in India's media ecology. Based on a mixed-methods survey of 150–300 respondents and analysis of AI-mediated content, it shows how algorithms reinforce dominant narratives across caste, gender, and religion. Using concepts like habitus and mediatization, it examines how repeated AI use reshapes understandings of knowledge and authority. The chapter calls for culturally rooted AI policies and critical digital literacy, arguing that AI is emerging as an ideological force shaping belief in an automated society.

INTRODUCTION

In contemporary India, the proliferation of artificial intelligence (AI) technologies has not only transformed digital consumption patterns but has begun to subtly and profoundly reshape the contours of popular belief systems. From AI-enabled religious chatbots and algorithm-driven political propaganda to AI-assisted knowl-

DOI: 10.4018/979-8-3373-3830-9.ch009

edge production tools like ChatGPT, the Indian public increasingly encounters AI as a mediator of truth, tradition, and trust. This chapter critically examines how AI technologies, embedded in everyday media practices, are influencing and reconfiguring belief systems in India through a socio - technological lens. Drawing on Berger and Luckmann's (1966) theory of the social construction of reality, the chapter argues that belief in contemporary India is not only socially produced but now increasingly algorithmically mediated. Through the lens of media studies, particularly the notion of algorithmic culture (Striphas, 2015), AI is conceptualized not merely as a technical apparatus but as a cultural actor one that shapes what is seen, said, and believed in digital spaces. The chapter explores how digital platforms and algorithmic affordances what content is surfaced, hidden, or recommended impact public understanding of religion, politics, identity, and truth.

Empirically, the chapter draws upon a mixed-methods online survey of 150–180 respondents across age, caste, gender, and region in India, supplemented by qualitative interviews and textual analysis of AI-mediated media content. Preliminary insights indicate that AI is reinforcing certain hegemonic narratives, particularly along caste, gender, and religious lines. For instance, devotional apps and AI-generated religious avatars have gained popularity, especially among urban youth, blending spiritual practices with algorithmic convenience. Simultaneously, AI-powered recommendation systems on platforms like YouTube and Instagram amplify politically polarized content, deepening belief silos and echo chambers (O'Neil, 2016). The chapter situates these developments within the broader framework of mediatization theory (Couldry &; Hepp, 2017), proposing that AI has become a central actor in the media ecology through which belief systems are negotiated, maintained, and transformed. It also utilizes Bourdieu's (1986) notion of habitus to interpret how repeated engagement with AI tools (e.g., Google search, ChatGPT, voice assistants) forms new dispositions towards knowledge, authority, and truth. In many cases, AI is not merely informing people's beliefs but co-creating them legitimizing or delegitimizing certain types of information through algorithmic filtering.

Ultimately, the chapter calls for critical digital literacy and culturally informed AI policy frameworks to prevent algorithmic biases from becoming naturalized belief systems. By highlighting the sociological consequences of machine-mediated meaning-making, the chapter contributes to growing interdisciplinary discourse on AI ethics, media cultures, and digital sociology in the Global South. It underscores the urgency of understanding AI not merely as infrastructure but as ideology an emerging digital force that is shaping how millions of Indians come to know, believe, and act in an increasingly automated society.

CONCEPTUAL ANALYSIS OF MEDIATIZATION

At present, the use of artificial intelligence (AI) is not limited to tech and industrial use. It has gradually become a part of our everyday life and is actively shaping the way we see things, speak, the way we search things on the internet and to an extent even the way we think or believe. From all the recommendations we get on the YouTube or the suggested Instagram reels, to the deepfake political or entertainment content, tools like ChatGPT, Google Search (Gemini), AI has situated itself in our lives to make sense of the world around us. This is a paradigm shift from the already existing digital platforms but not limited to the technological aspect, it is a cultural crossroad where AI has become an active agent in forming our opinions, beliefs and even how we construe truth. It is no longer a background infrastructure. In an era where everything is controlled by algorithms, it is important to understand McLuhan's (1964) *"the medium is the message"* where technologies do not only create or contain content but also plays a vital role in reshaping our perception.

The role of AI has now extended to guide, filter and even act as an authority rather than just being the medium of information. In India, the interaction between the users and AI through voice assistants, autofill, or recommended content through algorithms is not just content consumption rather engaging in the formation of a belief system by hidden systems. As Foucault (1980) stated, *"power produces knowledge"* becomes relevant here as the algorithm decides what content we watch, what should be in the foreground and what should fade away in the background. This system, on one hand, amplifies a certain type of content and, on the other hand, erases the other, deciding which voices should be heard.

Berger and Luckmann (1966) argued that reality itself is socially constructed through an institutional and mediated process. The digital landscape we are living in has increasingly shifted the mediation power from traditional institutions like religion, school or the press to the digital platforms driven by algorithms. The upcoming generation often turn to platforms like ChatGPT or YouTube for any knowledge on caste, gender, politics, history or even health, making it as their primary source of information. Striphas (2015) warned us about the functioning of algorithms in his work by stating that it is not merely neutral tool for information. It actively shapes our perception about culture by often reinforcing the dominant idea or the status quo while claiming to be a neutral or personalized, unbiased platform. In India, with multiple dimensions like caste, class, community, and gender, the mediated contents often reflect the bias through AI-generated recommendations and suggestions.

Bourdieu's (1986) concept of *habitus* helps us understand better how we develop our perception and internalize it while interpreting the world around us. The increase in the use of AI for forming knowledge has, in turn, created a new habitus for the Indian users while seeking validation from AI-curated suggestions and accepting the

AI-generated information while sidelining the traditional ways of lived knowledge and human expertise. The concept of *mediatization* given by Couldry and Hepp (2017) reiterates how the media not only reflect reality but also actively participate in construing and constructing it. Hence, when it comes to the mediation of the belief system in India with its embedded political polarization and social hierarchies, the algorithm actively works towards structuring it.

POWER, CULTURE, AND ALGORITHMS: THEORIZING AI-MEDIATED BELIEF

To actually understand the mechanism behind artificial intelligence and its role in re-shaping the belief system in India, we first need to see it as more than a technological tool. Rather, start seeing it as a cultural force or actively involved in our everyday communications, system of power and how we make sense of our surroundings. Nowadays, AI does not limit itself to processing the data given by us, but is also heavily involved in shaping our thoughts and belief systems. In the moments when we turn to platforms like ChatGPT, Google search, and Instagram for particular information or opinion, the algorithm is designed in a way to reinforce a curated output for us and, at times, distort the social values rather than just retrieving the information. This makes the AI an agent of how we accept a truth, which is organised, made visible and believed by it.

For a better understanding of this new formation of dynamics with AI, we must draw on interdisciplinary knowledge of sociology, media theory, digital humanities, and postcolonial studies. As it offers a lens and nuanced framework for analysing how our belief system is being altered or reinforced by AI, based on how it structures the knowledge itself. When caste, class, gender, politics, and religion merge with digital life, creating an intersection in a complex way, it becomes urgent for us to analyse its impact. It can be safely stated that AI is not neutral. It very well works within a given power structure and helps amplify it while subtly altering what we get to know and accept as reality.

From Media as Message to Media as Infrastructure

"The medium is the message" (McLuhan, 1964) is still relevant in our understanding of the media in the age of AI. It keeps reminding us that the form and structure of the media itself shape the content and its perception. When AI is integrated into digital platforms like ChatGPT, YouTube, WhatsApp, or Google, it not only functions as a medium but also configures visibility, legibility, and credibility of the

information. In turn, these platforms not just circulate belief but also algorithmically promote and prioritise one information over others.

As Chun (2016) elaborates, habitual media interactions shape our *"patterns of feeling,"* gradually aligning our behaviours with technological norms. This habituation becomes crucial when users begin to internalise algorithmically surfaced information as neutral or truthful.

Gitelman (2013), in her work, argues that media are not neutral vessels of communication but are instead socially constructed systems that are shaped by cultural and material contexts. She emphasises that the media's form and function are deeply intertwined with the social and cultural practices surrounding them. In a country like India, it must be understood from the complex postcolonial history of caste, class, language, religion, gender, and the digital infrastructure. If we take the emerging devotional apps like AstroBuddy or Sutradhar, for instance, they are not merely spiritual tools; in fact, they reinforce the religious practices in the disguise of technologically mediated content mainly directed and oriented toward the urban, upper-caste, middle-class susceptibility.

Gitelman (2013) argues that media are not neutral containers but *"socially realized structures of communication"* whose material and symbolic functions are deeply shaped by context. In India, these structures must be read in relation to the country's complex postcolonial history of caste, religion, language, and digital infrastructure. For instance, AI-powered devotional apps like AstroBuddy or Sutradhar are not merely spiritual tools they also recast religious practice as a form of technologically mediated consumption, often oriented toward middle-class, urban, and upper-caste sensibilities. But this transmutation of faith into an easy-to-use algorithmic interface is also the way it enshrines sacred rituals as quantifiable measures of devotion, how often you log in, how long you pray, how much you donate.

Algorithmic Culture and Platform Power

The conception of *"algorithm culture"* by Striphas (2015) becomes integral here as he states it as the *"ways in which the logic of big data and algorithmic recommendation systems influence cultural production and reception."* This can further be explained as the shaping of the cultural landscape by the algorithm as it decides what to show, hide or amplify. With the diverse languages in India, it further limits the access of traditional knowledge institutions. Thus, making the algorithm system a default source of information or *'truth'*.

Similarly, Bucher (2018) came forth with the notion of *"algorithmic imaginary"*, explaining the digital experience of the users and how they imagine and respond to the algorithm, which acts as an invisible force that inevitably shapes their insight. In the interviews conducted for this study, the respondents often expressed their conviction in the top-ranked results of Google search or YouTube recommendations, and their perception of it as an objective truth. One needs to understand that this trust is not the result of an epistemic evaluation by the user, but the belief in the power of the interface as an effective authority. But, as Nobel (2018) points out in her work, *Algorithms of Oppression,* this belief is far from being innocent and quite often perpetuates gendered, racial, and caste-based hierarchies under the pretext of neutrality.

Dispositions and the Digital Habitus

The concept of *habitus* (Bourdieu, 1986) becomes important to analyse the AI-driven content and how it assumes authority. Habitus explains the deeply embedded outlook that drives a person's perception, choices, and actions. The same applies to the repeated interaction with the AI interfaces in the digital life and forms *"algorithmic habitus"* which makes the user perceive the search results, recommendations, contents, or chat responses as an extension of their own thinking. Over the time, we start considering the interface as an extension of the self.

This is especially visible in how young people in India use AI-driven tools to form opinions on religion, caste, or politics. Students reported using ChatGPT or Quora to *"fact-check"* controversial social issues, often preferring these tools over traditional teachers or elders because the interface appears *"neutral"* or *"scientific."* However, as Bourdieu warns, the naturalisation of any epistemic authority without interrogating the conditions of its production risks reproducing existing power structures. In India, where social capital is unevenly distributed, those with digital fluency are more likely to shape and be shaped by these emerging forms of belief-making.

Mediatization and the Politics of Belief

Media is no longer a channel for communication and information rather has assumed the role of a social institution that also helps construct reality around us (Couldry & Hepp, 2017). Mediatization helps understand the media and its structural entanglement with the traditionally established social institutions like education, politics, religion, and every day-ness of life.

Mediation becomes a bit complex in India's context with the history of communalization, modernisation, and neoliberal globalisation. For instance, AI-generated avatars of Hindu gods used in devotional livestreams or holographic political campaigns blur the boundary between spectacle and faith, aesthetics, and truth. This further fits into the *"datafication of culture"* (van Dijck, 2013), as it defines how human practices become quantifiable digital outputs. Furthermore, it transforms the belief into quantifiable data that can be ranked, tracked, and monetised rather than a matter of conviction or tradition.

The technological shift has also transgressed into a cultural one. When asked a question about religion or history, the responses often reflect the mainstream narrative while conveniently leaving out the subaltern voices. This becomes a subtle way of altering or disciplining the belief, which can be explained through the Foucauldian process of normalisation, where the algorithm output becomes a defining boundary between the reliable knowledge and unreliable opinion. As Foucault writes, *"Truth is a thing of this world: it is produced only by multiple forms of constraint."*

Situated Algorithms: Postcolonial Contexts

It is crucial to shift the universal assumption that undermines the multi-dimensional AI discourse. As Benjamin (2019) and Arora (2019) argue, algorithmic systems are not neutral imports into the Global South; they are co-constituted with the socio-cultural environments in which they operate. In India, belief systems are already complex, contested, and stratified. Consequently, when AI enters this dynamic, it is not getting a blank slate rather a landscape with embedded caste hierarchies, historical violence, and linguistic plurality. A similar argument was put forth by Sundar (2008), as they stated that the intersection of algorithm systems with the pre-existing power structure in many ways, not even and discriminatory in nature. Thus, we need to engage with the postcolonial theory and subaltern studies to understand the true impact of AI on the belief system in India. We need to ask the question, who are the users whose beliefs are being validated by the AI? Or whose realities are made visible and whose are hidden? These are the central questions to understand the functioning of the algorithm and its cultural authority.

ALGORITHMIC ENCOUNTERS: EMPIRICAL INSIGHTS INTO AI AND BELIEF IN INDIA

The increasing use of AI in our everyday digital lives has made it a part of our cultural, political, and epistemic beliefs beyond functionality. In this section, the theoretical framework discussed before has been deliberated, grounded in the lived realities of the users and their exposure to AI-generated information. The empirical data has been drawn from a diverse set of Indian respondents, where we delve into the functioning of AI as not merely an informational tool but as an active actor in persuading, introspecting, and even transforming the belief system of the users.

The responses collected through the survey are analysed to give an insight into the sociological mapping of the authority of the algorithm and how it is internalised and perceived by the users across religious, regional, and gendered lines. AI platforms have become a catalyst for digitally mediated truth, from a subtle shift in the worldview to a dramatic reconsideration in personal or political views. Whether accepted, challenged, or critically navigated, these systems are no longer neutral utilities; they are co-constructors of belief in contemporary India.

This section tries to unpack the dynamics, beginning with an overview of the methodology and the demographic information, gradually moving towards a thematic analysis unveiling the statistical patterns outlining the emerging algorithmic culture in India.

Methodology and Demographic Profile of Respondents

The section presents the demographic profile of the empirical survey along with its methodological foundation used for the study. The research is based on a mixed-method approach that combines a structured online survey with open-ended questions and optional follow-up interviews. This approach was intentionally designed to triangulate both the qualitative and the quantitative contours of mediated beliefs and their transformation by AI. The study is based on the data drawn from the responses, which are not merely data points, but rather reflections situated in the cultural, emotional, and social life of the respondents embedded in the dependency on AI.

The survey collected 180 valid responses from across India, reflecting a demographically diverse population in terms of region, religion, caste, gender, and age group. The respondents were primarily engaged through Google Form, and it was circulated on Instagram, WhatsApp groups and academic mailing lists, giving access to the AI-exposed and digitally literate population. The survey consisted of both Likert-scale and multiple-choice questions, alongside open-ended text boxes that encouraged respondents to share personal stories, dilemmas, and reflections regarding AI's role in shaping their political, cultural, and spiritual beliefs.

Gender Distribution

Respondents included individuals across the gender spectrum. A notable majority identified as female, followed by male respondents, with a few choosing not to disclose or selecting *"other"* as their gender identity (for details, see, Figure 1). This distribution is particularly important when read against the narrative depth of the responses: female respondents consistently offered more affect-laden, relational, and emotionally nuanced accounts of their interactions with AI. This suggests a gendered interface with AI systems, where belief, emotion, and technology converge differently for different users.

Regional Distribution

For sociological clarity, the respondents were categorised into four geographic zones, broadly corresponding to linguistic, cultural, and political sensibilities:

- North India (e.g., Delhi, Uttar Pradesh, Rajasthan, Bihar, Haryana, Punjab, Himachal Pradesh, Jammu & Kashmir) – 79 respondents
- West India (e.g., Maharashtra, Gujarat, Madhya Pradesh) – 21 respondents
- East India (e.g., West Bengal, Jharkhand, Assam, Odisha) – 30 respondents
- South India (e.g., Tamil Nadu, Kerala, Andhra Pradesh, Telangana, Karnataka, Pondicherry) – 50 respondents

This more balanced dataset allows for a comparative regional analysis, where North India's overwhelming representation reflects both demographic density and higher digital outreach, while the substantial South Indian sample offers critical perspectives rooted in regional linguistic traditions, media ecologies, and religious worldviews. The regional distribution is especially relevant when tracing patterns of AI trust, belief reinforcement, and perceptions of bias (for details, see Figure 5).

Religious Affiliation

Religious self-identification among respondents displayed a diversity reflective of India's plural religious landscape, though skewed toward the majority Hindu population:

- Hindu – 129 respondents
- Christian – 18 respondents
- Muslim – 12 respondents
- Atheist/Agnostic – 9 respondents
- Other (Buddhist, Jain, Humanity, etc.) – 12 respondents (combined)

While the dataset is not statistically representative of India's religious demography, it offers insight into how different religious imaginaries intersect with algorithmic logics. Interestingly, respondents from minority religious groups, particularly Christians and Atheist/Agnostic individuals, reported higher rates of belief modification, suggesting a possibly greater openness to epistemic experimentation or dialogical engagement with AI systems (for details, see, Figure 4).

Caste and Class Profile

Though caste was not the primary axis of analysis, caste data was collected confidentially. Preliminary readings suggest that caste-privileged respondents (largely upper-caste Hindus) were more likely to state that AI reaffirmed their beliefs or provided *"rational clarity"*, whereas lower-caste respondents expressed either scepticism, ambivalence, or awe at AI's authority. This affirms Noble's (2018) contention that search algorithms often mirror and reinforce dominant social structures, albeit subtly and with localized variance.

In terms of class, most respondents were middle to upper-middle class, with access to smartphones, stable internet, and some level of English proficiency. This reflects an emerging techno-user base that is both a product and a subject of India's digital transformation.

Age Group

The majority of participants (approximately 87%) fell within the 18–35 age bracket, making them part of what may be called India's AI-native generation. These users are not merely passive consumers of AI but active interlocutors engaging with it for academic research, emotional support, job preparation, or even spiritual exploration. Their position at the intersection of algorithmic exposure and identity formation makes their responses especially valuable for studying belief plasticity in the digital age (for details, see Figure 1).

METHODOLOGICAL LIMITATIONS

As with all empirical research, this study comes with limitations:

- The sample, while large and diverse, is not statistically representative.
- The study disproportionately represents urban and digitally-connected populations, leaving out vast swathes of rural India where AI penetration is still uneven.
- Self-reporting biases may have shaped certain responses, particularly those reflecting aspirational uses of AI.
- Additionally, non-binary gender and lower caste voices, while present, remain numerically fewer and may need separate, focused inquiry.

Nevertheless, the richness of qualitative responses, from narratives of spiritual reawakening to algorithmic distrust, from expressions of emotional dependency to critiques of techno-authoritarianism, provides a revelatory map of how belief is being mediated, reshaped, and sometimes even generated by AI systems in contemporary India.

Age and Caste

Most respondents were between the ages of 18 to 35, representing a digitally literate, often urban, and largely English-speaking demography. Caste data, although collected, is treated with confidentiality and integrated in later intersectional analysis. Preliminary findings, however, suggest that caste-privileged respondents were more likely to report that AI affirmed or aligned with their beliefs, indicating possible algorithmic reinforcement of hegemonic narratives (Noble, 2018).

Limitations

While this study provides valuable insights, it is important to acknowledge limitations. First, the sample is not statistically generalizable. Second, digital reach constrained the survey to largely urban and digitally connected populations. Third, self-reporting bias and uneven regional participation may skew some data points. Nevertheless, the empirical richness, especially the qualitative responses, provides a vital window into the affective and cognitive role of AI in shaping popular belief systems in India.

In summary, the data set not merely represents but indicates the map of how the belief system in India is navigated in the digital public sphere, giving an insight about the intersection of machine logics into the cultural identity, political overview, and faith.

REGIONAL VARIATIONS IN AI-MEDIATED BELIEF FORMATION

India's sociological fabric is deeply regional shaped by its diverse languages, political traditions, religious landscapes, and uneven access to digital technologies. These differences do not just shape everyday life; they also influence how people engage with new tools like artificial intelligence (AI). In this section, we explore how AI interacts with belief systems across North, South, East, and West India. Drawing from responses of 180 survey participants, the analysis reveals that people's interactions with AI are not just technical they are shaped by their cultural environments and digital experiences, offering insight into how belief is increasingly mediated by algorithms. (For more detail, see Figure 5)

North India (n = 106 respondents, 58.9%)

North India, which had the largest share of respondents in our study, stands out as a region where artificial intelligence (AI) plays a paradoxical role both challenging and reinforcing existing belief systems. About 33.9% (36) of participants from this region said AI had influenced or changed their beliefs, while nearly 18% (19) felt it had strengthened what they already believed. This mix of responses mirrors the region's complex sociopolitical environment marked by strong religio-nationalist narratives and a high level of engagement with social media platforms.

Interestingly, 40.5% of respondents from this region said they had either believed something because AI told them so or were inclined to do so. This echoes Berger and Luckmann's (1966) idea that belief is not static, it is something we constantly build and rebuild through everyday interactions, which now increasingly include digital tools like AI.

Several responses revealed an emotional dimension to these interactions. One woman from Delhi shared that she often turned to AI when feeling overwhelmed, seeing it as a source of rational clarity. On the other hand, a male respondent from Uttar Pradesh noted that AI responses often carried what he perceived as *"leftist ideological framings"*, pointing to a sense of algorithmic bias. This perception reflects Seaver's (2018) argument that algorithms are not just passive channels they are shaped by broader cultural and institutional logics.

West India (n = 23 respondents, 12.8%)

West Indian respondents, largely from Maharashtra and Gujarat, displayed a more consolidative use of AI, more often reinforcing than altering beliefs. While only 17.4% (4) indicated belief modification, a notable 34.8% (8) reported that AI strengthened their beliefs. This pattern may point toward a rational-instrumental engagement with AI, consistent with the tech-forward ethos of states like Maharashtra.

39.1% of respondents acknowledged trusting AI-generated information as truth (*'Yes'* or *'Maybe'*), while 21.7% flagged AI's role in promoting dominant narratives. One respondent shared how AI helped sharpen arguments while writing about caste, indicating that AI serves as an epistemic scaffold (Striphas, 2015) through which individuals solidify and articulate complex socio-political positions.

The tendency for belief reinforcement over disruption here may be read through Pierre Bourdieu's (1986) notion of *habitus*, AI may provide information, but how that information is interpreted is contingent upon the existing cognitive structures, dispositions, and cultural capital of users.

East India (n = 37 respondents, 20.6%)

East Indian respondents (from West Bengal, Jharkhand, Assam, Odisha) displayed a high degree of belief fluidity. 32.4% (12) reported modification, and 16.2% (6) said AI strengthened their beliefs. A combined 48.6% thus showed tangible transformations in belief systems via AI.

Interestingly, 59.4% admitted they had believed or might believe something just because AI presented it, suggesting a high degree of epistemic reliance. This echo concerns raised by Robyn Caplan (2016), who suggests that AI systems may foster *"algorithmic trust"* by simulating objectivity and efficiency, often masking embedded cultural or political assumptions.

Narratives from the region include a respondent from Kolkata who reconsidered his stance on climate change after engaging with AI-generated simulations. Another respondent from Jharkhand found AI helpful in navigating tribal histories. These examples reaffirm Das's (2007) point that the everyday is a critical site of epistemological negotiation, where AI is now embedded as an interlocutor.

South India (n = 14 respondents, 7.8%)

Despite being the smallest sample, South Indian responses exhibited the highest proportional transformation in belief. 35.7% (5) experienced modification, and 21.4% (3) experienced strengthening, a combined 57.1% reporting some change due to AI.

42.9% stated that they accepted or might accept something as true because AI suggested it. Only 14.3% raised concerns about bias, suggesting relatively higher trust in AI systems compared to other regions.

Qualitative data included a female respondent from Chennai who reported using AI to connect scientific reasoning with her spiritual practices. Another respondent from Bangalore stated that AI helped shape his career trajectory and influenced his PhD topic choice. This suggests what José van Dijck (2013) calls *"datafication of selfhood"* where algorithmic systems do not merely reflect personal values but co-author them.

Table 1. Comparative insights across regions

Region	Modified Beliefs (%)	Strengthened Beliefs (%)	Trust in AI as Truth (%)	Perceived Bias (%)
North	33.9% (36)	17.9% (19)	40.5% (43)	19.8% (21)
West	17.4% (4)	34.8% (8)	39.1% (9)	21.7% (5)
East	32.4% (12)	16.2% (6)	59.4% (22)	24.3% (9)
South	35.7% (5)	21.4% (3)	42.9% (6)	14.3% (2)

Source: Survey thorough Google Form of 180 Respondents

The table underscores how belief modification is most prominent in South and East India, while belief reinforcement is higher in West India. Interestingly, respondents from East India showed the highest levels of trust in AI as a source of truth. This raises important questions about how digital tools are shaping what people consider reliable knowledge, and whether this points to deeper issues around digital literacy or dependence. At the same time, both North and East India reported strong concerns about bias and narrative control in AI outputs. This suggests that while AI is being embraced, there is also a growing awareness that its version of *'truth'* might not be politically or culturally neutral.

Regional responses show that AI's influence on belief varies widely across India. In North and East India, people both trust and question AI, treating it as a site of ideological tension. South India, though less represented, shows more introspective and transformative uses of AI. Meanwhile, West India displays a pragmatic approach, using AI to reinforce existing beliefs. These patterns suggest that regional culture and access shape how AI is interpreted not just as a tool, but as a mirror of local values.

What we see is not a flat, uniform spread of AI's influence, but a patchwork where belief is shaped by where people live, what media they consume, and how they relate to power. AI does not just offer information; it blends into people's everyday thinking, often quietly reinforcing or reshaping what they already believe. Banet-Weiser (2012) reminds us that belief itself is now something shaped and sold as part of how platforms operate. In India, this process plays out differently across regions, depending on who has access and whose voices dominate. AI, in this sense, is not neutral or passive; it is part of the cultural script, taking on the role of a storyteller, even a guide, in how belief is formed. (For more details, see Figure 5)

RELIGIOUS IDENTITY AND AI-MEDIATED BELIEF: DOMINANCE, DIVERGENCE, AND EPISTEMIC STRATIFICATION

Religion plays a deep and ongoing role in shaping belief systems in India, but its relationship with artificial intelligence (AI) is still a largely unexplored area. In our study, we found that religious identity was not just another demographic detail it shaped how people approached and interpreted AI. Out of the 180 participants, about 76% identified as Hindu, while the rest included Christians, Muslims, Atheists/ Agnostics, Buddhists, Jains, and other self-described affiliations. While this does not perfectly match the national religious breakdown, it highlights a crucial point: India's digital spaces are not equally accessible or inclusive. Who gets represented and heard online often reflects deeper social structures, including religion. (For details, see Figure 4)

Demographic Skew and Digital Access

The high proportion of Hindu respondents in the dataset reflects more than just religious demographics; it speaks to deeper structural patterns of access. As Payal Arora (2019) notes in her *"next billion users"* framework, digital participation in India is often filtered through layers of urban privilege, caste advantage, and linguistic accessibility. Building on this, Nishant Shah (2019) characterises the typical Indian digital user as middle-class, upper-caste, and Hindu, making digital spaces a mirror of existing offline hierarchies. So, the dominance of Hindu voices here is not a sign of religious bias, but a reflection of who gets seen and heard in a caste- and class-stratified digital world. (For details, see, Figure 4)

Epistemic Majoritarianism and Algorithmic Reinforcement

What the Hindu majority offers in this dataset is not just a matter of size; it opens a window into how AI subtly echoes dominant cultural scripts. Many Hindu respondents described feeling that AI content often mirrored or even reaffirmed their existing beliefs. Some mentioned moments of reflection, saying that AI had nudged them to reconsider certain views, while others felt more assured in what they already knew. About 27.7% shared that their beliefs had shifted, and 22.9% said those beliefs had been strengthened. This kind of engagement suggests both critical reflection and ideological reinforcement. Scholars like Noble (2018) and Benjamin (2019) have cautioned us about how algorithms can function as tools of social and cultural power, quietly privileging certain perspectives over others. In this case, AI does not merely provide information it curates belief in ways that often align with numerical and cultural dominance, a dynamic that could be understood as a form of epistemic majoritarianism.

This dynamic reflects what can be understood as *epistemic majoritarianism*, a condition in which communities with greater visibility on digital platforms are more likely to see their perspectives echoed back to them. Rather than merely providing information, AI systems subtly shape belief by reinforcing what is already widespread and culturally affirmed. (For details, see, Fig. 4)

Divergence Among Minoritised Faith Groups

Smaller faith-based groups in the dataset, Christians (9 respondents), Muslims (6), and Atheists/Agnostics (4), displayed distinct affective and cognitive relationships with AI. Among Christians, there was a noticeable openness to AI as a knowledge source, with 88.8% marking *'Yes'* or *'Maybe'* when asked if they believed AI-generated information. One Christian respondent described AI as *"a guide when there's no one around"*, highlighting the solitude and trust invested in digital tools. Muslim respondents, on the other hand, were more cautious. None reported outright belief in AI suggestions, although 66.7% selected *'Maybe'*. Their answers often reflected hesitation, framed by a sensitivity to how religious identities are misrepresented in public discourse and digital infrastructures. Atheist and agnostic participants showed the highest rate of belief transformation (75%), not as blind trust, but as a form of epistemic experimentation—using AI to make sense of hybrid truths involving science, wellness, ethics, and existential questioning.

These patterns contrast significantly with responses from many Hindu participants, who frequently saw AI as a mirror that reflected or reinforced pre-existing cultural frameworks. The differential is instructive. While AI served as a comfort zone or echo chamber for some, others approached it with a mix of curiosity, distrust, and critical engagement. For minority groups, belief through AI was not passive absorption but an active negotiation of visibility, voice, and safety in digitally coded spaces.

This variance aligns with Mignolo's (2009) concept of the *"coloniality of knowledge"*, where global systems AI included uphold hierarchies of what counts as credible knowledge. In India, these hierarchies are deeply entangled with caste and religious privilege, making it more likely for marginalised users to approach AI not as truth but as terrain, a space to be carefully navigated. For them, AI is less a destination and more a process of epistemic discernment, an arena where belief is continuously shaped by awareness of exclusion, history, and digital inequity

Simulacra, Spirituality, and Digital Orthodoxy

Some Hindu respondents said they turned to AI to make sense of spiritual traditions or question old beliefs, using it almost like a thinking companion. One woman mentioned it helped her *"move past some of the irrational aspects of religion"*, while others felt it deepened their connection to culture. These moments reflect what Baudrillard (2019) called simulacra when digital systems give the feeling of depth without being rooted in long-standing traditions. In that sense, AI starts to produce *"spiritual simulacra"*: belief systems that seem meaningful, not because they come from scripture, but because they come wrapped in data.

Moreover, when AI presents religious or cultural knowledge as *'neutral'* or 'objective,' it often masks built-in biases quietly reinforcing a digital orthodoxy that appears fact-based but reflects dominant perspectives. Respondents noted that AI occasionally promoted *'leftist'* or *'liberal'* values, while others said it aligned with "mainstream" perspectives. This ideological ambiguity mirrors what Bourdieu (1990) might call symbolic power, where the authority of the medium (AI) legitimises certain narratives without visible coercion.

Belief, Bias, and the Algorithmic Majority

Rather than removing or downplaying the religious analysis, this section uses the Hindu-majority composition of the dataset as a point of critical inquiry. It demonstrates that AI is not only being used within India's religious communities but is already embedded in how these communities reproduce, reform, or resist belief systems.

Through a combination of reinforcement, exploration, and scepticism, AI platforms are shown to mediate not just access to information but the affective and cognitive texture of belief itself. As India's digital landscape expands, so too will the algorithmic architectures that privilege certain identities, beliefs, and worldviews, making it imperative to track how religion, technology, and power co-constitute one another in the 21st century.

GENDERED PATTERNS OF AI-MEDIATED BELIEF: EMOTION, TRUST, AND COGNITIVE LABOR

The gendered dimension of AI-mediated belief systems reveals one of the most significant fault lines in the dataset. Across indicators ranging from trust in AI-generated information, perception of bias, belief modification, and affective reliance, female respondents consistently registered higher levels of engagement with, and impact from, AI technologies. Rather than viewing this as a monolithic trend, this section parses the patterns to show how emotional labour, epistemic trust, and sociotechnical positionality shape the gendered experience of AI.

This is particularly relevant when considered alongside the extensive scholarship on gendered technology use. Wajcman (2006) reminds us that technologies are never gender-neutral—they are shaped by, and in turn shape, existing power relations. In digital infrastructures such as AI, this is not merely about access, but about the nature of engagement: what is sought, how it is interpreted, and to what end it is used. Drawing on Haraway's (1988) idea of situated knowledges, the interaction of gender and AI-mediated belief suggests a different location from which truth and experience are accessed.

To contextualise these trends, the following table offers a quantitative summary of how male and female respondents (excluding the few non-disclosed entries) differed across various belief-related indicators.

Table 2. Gender-based distribution of AI influence across key dimensions (N = 153)

Dimension	Female (n = 79)	Male (n = 74)	Key Insight
Belief Modified	24.0% (19)	18.9% (14)	Women report more openness to belief revision through AI.
Belief Strengthened	19.0% (15)	12.1% (9)	Women also reflect higher belief reinforcement.
Total Impact on Belief (Modified + Strengthened)	43.0%	31.0%	Greater overall impact of AI on female belief systems.
Accepted AI as Truth ('Yes')	7.6% (6)	5.4% (4)	Higher willingness among women to affirm AI as truth.
Accepted AI as Truth ('Maybe')	11.4% (9)	4.0% (3)	Women show more epistemic hesitation rather than dismissal.
Total Influenced by AI as Truth (Yes + Maybe)	19.0%	9.5%	Almost double the susceptibility among women respondents.
Perceived Dominant Narrative Bias	19.0% (15)	8.1% (6)	Women more critically perceive hegemonic content in AI responses.
Perceived Caste/Religious Bias	12.7% (10)	8.1% (6)	Slightly higher perception of systemic bias among female respondents.
Emotion-Driven or Affective AI Usage	30.4% (24)	6.7% (5)	Women were nearly 5x more likely to use AI during emotionally charged moments.

Source: Survey thorough Google Form of 180 Respondents

This data challenges dominant assumptions about technological rationality and neutrality. Rather than confirming the masculinist notion of AI as a tool for pure logic or objective reasoning, female respondents tend to narrate their AI interactions in deeply personal and emotionally grounded terms. People turned to AI not just for answers, but for support in moments of doubt or stress. It became less of a tool and more like a thinking companion. (For details, see Figures 2, 7, and 9)

One female respondent shared that AI helped her *"decide certain things rationally when emotional enough to not take the correct decision"*. Another spoke about relying on AI to navigate a moral dilemma at work, saying it gave her *"a perspective that none of my friends or family could offer without judgement"*. This relational, trust-based mode of engagement reflects what Haraway (1991) describes as a *cyborg epistemology* a hybrid way of knowing that blends emotional vulnerability, rational thinking, and technological mediation.

In contrast, most male respondents described their use of AI in more functional terms asking for help with information, academic topics, or making practical choices with little emotional context attached. This difference echoes what Turkle (2011) observed: that our relationships with technology are often shaped by gender, with women tending to form more emotionally meaningful connections, while men often treat these tools in a more instrumental, task-oriented way.

Interestingly, even though women often described deeper emotional engagement with AI, they were also more attuned to its blind spots. Female respondents were quicker to point out caste biases, missing local histories, or political leanings in the answers they received. So, the same group that turns to AI for support does not do so blindly; they engage with it critically, holding both trust and doubt at once.

This mix of trust and doubt, what we might call a kind of double consciousness, is telling. As Banet-Weiser (2012) notes, digital life today is shaped by both branding and struggle, where belief and authenticity are always up for negotiation. For many women in our study, even a small moment of recognition through AI felt meaningful, given how often their histories are erased. Yet that did not stop them from noticing what was missing. The gendered reliance on AI for emotional support challenges narrow ideas of rationality. What if this is not about being less rational, but about a broader kind of intelligence one rooted in care, context, and lived experience?

In sum, gender shapes more than just access to AI it influences how it is used, trusted, and questioned. Feminised forms of engagement, grounded in emotion, narrative, and ethics, challenge the idea that belief is only about data consumption. Instead, they reveal that AI is part of an affective landscape, where care, conflict, and reflection all play a role in meaning-making. (For details, see Figures 10, 11, 12, and 16).

INTERSECTIONAL DIMENSIONS OF ALGORITHMIC INFLUENCE: CASTE, REGION, AND EPISTEMIC HIERARCHIES

While gender emerges as a significant axis of variation in responses to AI-mediated content, a more granular and intersectional reading of the data reveals deeper layers of algorithmic influence shaped by caste, religion, region, and educational access. These categories are not standalone silos but overlapping vectors of experience, each structuring how individuals receive, interpret, and internalise AI-generated outputs.

Charusheela's idea of intersectionality (2013), expanded by scholars like Hancock (2013), helps us see that belief is never shaped in isolation. When it comes to AI, people's interactions and trust are filtered through their social positions caste, gender, religion, class and often, those from subaltern backgrounds engage with AI differently than those in dominant groups

Caste and Epistemic Validation: Who Gets Reflected by the Algorithm?

Caste, while carefully navigated during data collection, still appeared as a quiet yet powerful force shaping how people related to AI. Respondents from Savarna backgrounds (inferred through names or institutions) more often felt that AI supported or reflected their beliefs. On the other hand, respondents from the marginalized communities (who self-identified in qualitative data) were more likely to question AI, pointing out how it echoed dominant perspectives and overlooked subaltern voices. One respondent noted: *"AI repeats what's on the internet and spreads the same bias further."* Another, a PhD scholar from a marginalised background, shared that she deliberately avoids using AI for belief clarification because *"It shows privilege and doesn't relate to what I've been through."* This perception resonates with Noble's (2018) thesis in *Algorithms of Oppression*, where she argues that algorithmic systems built on dominant datasets routinely marginalise or erase non-hegemonic perspectives. In the Indian context, this becomes even more charged, as caste is rarely visible in explicit metadata but always implicit in the structuring of content, what is deemed 'factual,' whose history is archived, and which narratives gain traction.

Thus, belief affirmation for dominant castes is not just a personal insight it is a form of epistemic validation, where the algorithm mirrors one's worldview, thereby reinforcing it. For others, the algorithm is either silent or oppositional, forcing users to navigate content critically or disengage entirely. (For details, see Figures 6, 10, 13, 15, 16, and 17)

Regional Variation and Linguistic Proximity

Geographic region emerged as a surprisingly important variable, not merely in terms of numerical representation but in how respondents framed their AI experiences.

- North Indian respondents (79 in total) overwhelmingly framed AI as a *"helpful tool"* for decision-making, content validation, and cultural interpretation. Many associated AI with enhanced productivity and information access, particularly in English-medium academic contexts.
- East Indian respondents (30), however, were more likely to express *ambivalence*, especially around religious content. A notable number raised concerns about AI's lack of recognition of regional deities, tribal traditions, or folk epistemologies.

- South Indian respondents (8) emphasized technical neutrality, focusing more on AI's limitations in language adaptability. One respondent pointed out that ChatGPT *"doesn't understand Dravidian philosophy"* or the specific moral universe in Tamil Sangam literature. This suggests a tension between regional knowledge systems and algorithmic flattening.
- West Indian respondents (21) leaned toward utilitarian usage, often praising AI for helping with business decisions, legal research, or technical writing. Their responses were less affective and more transactional, suggesting a class-inflected rationality (for details, see Figure 5)

The regional differences echo the notion of *pirate modernity*, where media circulates unevenly, producing differentiated experiences of the digital. Belief, in this case, is not just a cognitive category but a regionally inflected habitus (Bourdieu, 1986) one shaped by access to infrastructure, linguistic proximity to dominant knowledge systems, and historically sedimented modes of knowledge-making.

Religious Identity and Algorithmic Respectability

Religion is perhaps the most sensitive domain in which AI operates and where belief transformation or reinforcement has the most volatile potential. As noted earlier, the majority of respondents (83 out of 180) identified as Hindu. This overrepresentation does reflect a digital bias, Hindu users tend to dominate Indian social media spaces and academic networks, and they are more likely to encounter algorithmic platforms in English or Hindi.

This skew raises important questions. Rather than seeing it as a flaw in the dataset, we interpret it as an index of algorithmic centrality to majority belief formation. AI's engagement with Hinduism was often framed in terms of validation or interpretative help. Several Hindu respondents claimed that AI clarified misunderstood practices, offered *"scientific explanations"* for rituals, or helped them argue more confidently in public discourse, particularly online.

This tendency to rationalise belief through AI (e.g., explaining the *science behind a vrat*) mirrors what Chatterjee (2021) calls the *"respectabilization of belief"* in postcolonial publics, where religious expression must pass the test of modernity to be considered legitimate. AI, as a rational-seeming authority, becomes a bridge between traditional belief and contemporary knowledge systems, particularly for majority religions.

In contrast, minority religious respondents, Christians (9), Muslims (6), and Atheists/Agnostics (4) expressed more ambivalence or alienation. Some Muslim respondents noted that AI rarely understood *"nuances of Islam"* or offered politicised, biased answers. One Christian respondent highlighted how AI offered *"a sanitised version of belief"*, devoid of lived affect or community-specific theology. These responses echo Mignolo's (2009) idea of *"epistemic disobedience"*, where AI becomes a site of epistemic conflict rather than affirmation.

Educational Privilege and the Politics of Interpretation

While not always explicitly stated, a striking number of respondents were highly educated graduate or post-graduate students, often in English-medium institutions. This reflects the sample's digital privilege but also shapes how AI content is processed. Educated respondents were more likely to *critique AI outputs*, ask follow-up questions, or check for citation links. Yet this literacy did not always protect them from belief modification. As one respondent put it: *"Even when I know it could be biased, I still believe it sometimes because it sounds right."*

This paradox reflects what Striphas (2015) calls *algorithmic culture*, where belief is no longer a matter of faith or logic alone, but of interface trust the affective comfort one feels in navigating digital systems, even when they are opaque.

TOWARDS A SITUATED ALGORITHMIC SOCIOLOGY

Taken together, these intersectional insights push us to think beyond individual belief and toward a sociology of algorithmic interaction. Caste, region, religion, and educational access shape not only what people believe but how they believe how they question, trust, or resist digital information.

AI systems, rather than being mere tools, emerge as ideological terrains where privilege is reproduced and occasionally contested. They do not simply reflect beliefs; they participate in their construction selectively amplifying some, muting others, and asking all users to conform to their logics of readability.

Understanding AI-shaped belief is not just about what content is shown. It is also about the social, cultural, and unequal settings in which people interpret and trust that content.

AI as Myth, Memory, and Machine: Symbolic Authority in the Digital Age

Across India, people are increasingly turning to AI for everyday decisions, whether it is learning something new, dealing with a personal crisis, or even exploring spiritual questions. This is not just about convenience or efficiency anymore. What we are seeing is a deeper shift: AI beginning to take on the kind of authority we used to associate with religion, elders, or trusted media. While AI is often discussed as a smart tool or data assistant, many people now view it as something more, something that helps them make sense of the world. This section looks at how participants' stories reveal AI not as some emotionless machine, but as a deeply symbolic force, what McLuhan (1964) might call a *"hot medium"* that shapes not just what we know, but how we feel and believe.

AI as Myth-Maker and Interpretive Authority

Lévi-Strauss (1963) once observed that myths help make sense of life's contradictions by giving form to meaning. In many ways, AI seems to be taking on a similar role today, not just offering up information, but actively shaping how people understand what is true. Several respondents spoke of trusting AI outputs even when they were not entirely sure of the facts, suggesting that AI is moving beyond being a helpful tool. It is becoming something more of a source of belief, almost like the way people once turned to sacred texts or wise elders for guidance.

One respondent wrote: *"No one could tell me much about my husband's tribe, but AI gave me an answer right away."* Another noted: *"I used to think rituals were just superstitions. But AI explained them, and it made sense."* These kinds of responses show how AI ends up doing what Barthes (1972) called myth-making it takes complex cultural ideas and presents them as if they are simple, obvious, and outside politics. What gives AI its power is not just that it sounds accurate, but that it *feels* neutral. But as scholars like Noble (2018) and Benjamin (2019) have shown, that neutrality often hides the biases built into the data it learns from (for details, see Questions 13, 14, 15)

Memory Without History: Simulacra and Datafication

Baudrillard's (2019) idea of simulacra, where representations come to stand in for, and even replace, the real, feels particularly relevant when thinking about how AI is starting to influence how people remember and believe. Some respondents shared that they turned to AI to *"learn history"* or to *"understand facts"* better than they had through school or books. That ease of access is undeniably powerful. But it also raises a deeper question: when complex histories are reduced to clean, searchable answers, are we losing the messy, layered work of remembering? In such cases, AI is not just a tool for learning; it quietly reshapes how we think about what is real and what's worth knowing. One student shared: *"I trust AI more than the biased syllabus we are taught in school."* Here, the AI simulation of history becomes more trustworthy than embodied memory detached from context, politics, or intergenerational transmission. This simulation effect flattens nuance into a palatable output, privileging algorithmic logic over human contradiction.

Algorithmic Authority and Digital Rituals

What comes through in the data is more than just how people use AI it is how they relate to it. Many respondents described turning to AI not casually, but almost habitually, especially during moments of personal or emotional uncertainty. For some, it resembled the way one might turn to a trusted friend, a spiritual guide, or even a sacred text. As one participant put it: "*When I was angry, I asked AI how to handle it. It helped.*" Another recalled: "*I was confused about my PhD topic, and AI gave me new directions.*" These are not just tools being used; they are being consulted. In many of these interactions, there is something deeper at play than just trust in information; they reflect what Taussig (1993) describes as *"mimetic faith"*: a kind of belief that emerges not from verified truth but from the repeated, almost ritualistic, engagement with a system. This idea resonates with Appadurai's (1996) concept of the *'mediascape'*, where technologies like AI are not just about delivering content but about shaping what we imagine, aspire to, and internalise as possible futures.

McLuhan's (1964) distinction between hot and cold media offers a useful way to understand how AI is being experienced today. While we might assume AI, especially in its text-based form, would be a *'cold'* medium encouraging detached, analytical engagement, our data suggests otherwise. Many respondents described moments of emotional connection or even clarity through AI use, pointing to a more immersive and affective interaction. In this sense, AI takes on qualities of a *'hot'* medium: one that draws people in, offers closure, and simulates intimacy in ways that are both symbolic and deeply personal.

Trust, Aura, and the Logic of Belief

Benjamin's (2019) idea of *'aura'*, which he worried would fade with the rise of mechanical reproduction, seems to return in unexpected ways through AI. While mass media once dispersed and diffused authority, AI appears to do the opposite; it often reassembles it, giving back a sense of control, certainty, or even reverence to its outputs. The personalisation of AI answers, the immediacy of response, and the illusion of neutrality generate a new form of aura, one that feels tailored, sacred, and scientific at once.

This echoes Striphas's (2015) insight that algorithms do not just sort culture, they produce it. The beliefs formed or restructured through AI interactions are not merely reflections of existing social knowledge but new forms of algorithmically mediated belief. These beliefs may echo hegemonic ideologies, especially among caste-privileged, urban, English-speaking users, but they carry the emotional resonance of personal discovery.

Toward a Symbolic Sociology of AI

What the data reveals is not simply a population that uses AI, but one that is forming rituals, affective attachments, and belief systems around it. The machine, once merely a calculator or search engine, is now a semiotic structure one that mediates identity, history, and epistemology.

To understand AI's influence in India, then, we must move beyond instrumentalist accounts and ask: What kind of mythic authority does AI now hold? Whose histories does it retell, and whose does it erase? What beliefs does it consolidate, and which ones does it destabilise?

These are not technological questions; they are profoundly sociological and political ones, inviting a new grammar of belief for the algorithmic age.

The Future of Belief in an AI-Mediated Society

As India stands at the cusp of a digital revolution, the future of belief itself appears increasingly entangled with algorithmic mediation. While belief has historically been shaped by institutions such as religion, family, community, and mass media, the emergence of generative AI introduces a new epistemic actor one that is fast, scalable, personalized, and, crucially, opaque in its operations. This section draws on empirical data from our respondents and theoretical insights from media and technology scholars to explore how belief systems in India might evolve in an AI-saturated public sphere.

From Faith in Institutions to Trust in Code

A substantial portion of respondents, 57.7% admitted to either believing or *maybe* believing something was true because an AI system suggested it. This implies that AI has already begun to occupy the epistemic vacuum left by increasingly distrusted traditional institutions. In line with Couldry and Hepp's (2017) concept of *deep mediatization*, AI is not simply delivering content it is reorganizing the entire infrastructure of meaning-making. The locus of authority is shifting from priests, teachers, and even journalists to platforms and recommendation engines.

This transition raises an ontological question: what kind of 'truth' is being produced and legitimised by AI? As respondents themselves noted, AI is often perceived as *'neutral'* or *'factual'*, a perception that grants it epistemic authority. Yet, as Hong (2020) reminds us, the idea that algorithmic systems are neutral is more myth than fact. What often gets framed as 'objective' by AI is actually shaped by the biases in its training data, the assumptions of its developers, and the broader ideologies baked into the system.

AI AS A SIMULACRUM OF REASON AND BELIEF

The process of belief-making is no longer tethered to fixed, enduring institutions but instead formed within the fluid, real-time outputs of generative AI systems. This reflects what Baudrillard (2019) famously called the *simulacrum,* where signs no longer refer to reality but to other signs in an endless loop. Many respondents recounted turning to AI for clarity during emotional turmoil, spiritual doubt, or political confusion. In such moments, AI functions not merely as a tool but as a proxy for internal dialogue, mirroring one's worldview while subtly shaping it.

One female respondent mentioned: *"When I was emotionally overwhelmed, I asked ChatGPT for advice. The answer felt rational more rational than what my friends or parents would say."* This reveals the emergence of AI as a substitute confidante, a digital interlocutor that delivers answers without judgment. Yet, such simulations of reason lack context, emotion, and situated knowledge, suggesting a future where belief becomes detached from lived experience and embedded in code.

Generational Trust and Epistemic Offloading

Data shows the majority of respondents were between 18–35 years old, with high digital fluency and regular engagement with AI tools. For this generation, epistemic offloading, delegating belief validation and decision-making to AI is becoming normalized. As van Dijck (2013) argues, the platformization of knowledge leads to data-driven logics replacing deliberative or dialogic forms of knowledge production. This is a shift from *"I think therefore I am"* to *"It is suggested, therefore it must be."* A respondent from Bangalore noted: *"I didn't know what to do with my PhD topic. I kept asking ChatGPT to help me structure it. Eventually, I used what it generated. It felt right."* This kind of trust in generative plausibility over expert consultation or peer debate marks a profound transformation in how authority is constructed. In this future, the algorithm becomes the co-author of belief, not just its mediator.

Algorithmic Pluralism vs Cultural Homogenization

Despite the potential for AI to expose users to diverse perspectives, many respondents (especially Hindu respondents, who formed 80% of the sample) felt that AI platforms reinforced dominant narratives. 26% of all respondents believed that AI promotes majoritarian or mainstream viewpoints. This raises concerns about epistemic flattening, where minority perspectives are algorithmically sidelined, not through active censorship but through ranking, optimisation, and reinforcement learning.

As Udupa (2020) points out in her study of digital Hindu nationalism, algorithms do not just reflect online culture they often amplify dominant narratives, especially when user engagement drives what gets seen and shared. In India, this dynamic can easily turn AI into an echo chamber for castes, patriarchal, or communal ideologies unless there's active oversight and accountability built into the system.

Belief as a Platform Logic

Increasingly, belief itself may operate on platform logic dynamic, user-responsive, and gamified. Platforms like YouTube, Instagram, and now ChatGPT do not merely reflect existing beliefs but incentivize belief shifts that optimize attention and engagement. One respondent noted: *"The more I asked AI about spiritual topics, the more its answers matched how I was starting to see the world. It felt like it was getting to know me."* This personalization is precisely what makes belief fluid, modular, and post-traditional. As Striphas (2015) writes, algorithms are not neutral intermediaries but active agents of cultural production. AI-mediated belief is thus not fixed but continuously recalibrated to user preferences, eroding the stability of belief systems anchored in long-term spiritual, ethical, or ideological commitments.

Ethical Ambivalence and the Crisis of Meaning

While some respondents welcomed AI's rational clarity, others expressed fears about the erosion of critical thinking and excessive dependence. The ambivalence is clear:

- 57.7% believed AI to be mostly neutral.
- Yet over 26% were worried about bias and the loss of human agency.

This mirrors what Turkle (2011) described as the paradox of digital intimacy users feel 'seen' by machines but simultaneously displaced. The future of belief in an AI-driven society thus hinges on maintaining the human capacity for doubt, reflection, and ethical deliberation.

Toward a Contingent Future of Belief

Rather than forecasting a deterministic future, this chapter proposes that the future of belief in an AI-mediated society is contingently shaped by user agency, platform governance, cultural context, and digital literacy. Many respondents pointed to both the promise and the danger of AI: on one hand, easier access to knowledge, personalised suggestions, and better decision-making; on the other, the risk of misinformation, emotional detachment, and ideological manipulation.

In this shifting landscape, belief no longer seems rooted in the sacred, the inherited, or the communal. Instead, it is becoming something more fragmented, shaped by algorithms, validated through data, and held in private. Whether this shift will enrich democratic dialogue or shut it down remains an open question and one that urgently needs both sociological and ethical attention.

CONCLUSION

We now live in a time when algorithms shape not just what we see, but also how we know, feel, and believe. The real question is not whether AI influences our belief systems, that is already evident, but rather how deeply it does so, and in which directions. In this chapter, we have explored how belief is being shaped in socio-technical terms across contemporary India, drawing insights from 180 participants representing a range of regions, religions, castes, and genders.

Using a mixed-methods approach grounded in media theory, postcolonial critique, and the sociology of knowledge, we traced the contours of a shifting epistemic landscape. Here, AI is not simply delivering information; it is becoming an active agent in the formation of belief itself. This paradox reflects what many scholars have identified as the *"algorithmic condition"*, a state in which the authority of data supersedes older forms of moral, cultural, or religious authority (Rouvroy, Berns, & Carey-Libbrecht, 2013; Striphas, 2015). Respondents turned to AI not just for factual clarification but for emotional validation, career decisions, spiritual insight, and ideological reinforcement. Belief, it seems, is no longer solely tethered to inherited traditions or rational deliberation, but is increasingly performed, validated, and negotiated through machines.

Importantly, the study also unearthed the gendered, regional, and religious nuances of this transformation. Female respondents tended to articulate more affective and narrative-driven relationships with AI, while Hindu respondents, who constituted the majority, often engaged with AI as both a mirror and mediator of existing cultural frameworks. This unevenness is critical, not to be erased in the name of neutrality, but to be foregrounded as symptomatic of deeper sociotechnical hierarchies and digital inequalities.

From a theoretical standpoint, the chapter has moved beyond simplistic celebrations or critiques of AI. Drawing on McLuhan, Baudrillard, Noble, and others, we have tried to conceptualise AI not as a neutral intermediary but as a new media form, simultaneously cold and hot, simulacra and seductive, affective, and calculative. The algorithm, we argue, functions today as a techno-cultural subject, endowed with symbolic power to shape belief in subtle yet profound ways. The very conditions of belief, what counts as truth, what is emotionally resonant, and what is epistemically trustworthy are being restructured through platform logics. Yet the future is not predetermined. As several respondents themselves suggested, AI can be harnessed and critically used to challenge dominant narratives, democratize knowledge, and even bridge inter-generational or inter-religious understanding. But this requires what Foucault might call a *"critical ontology of ourselves"*: a willingness to examine how our engagements with AI shape not just what we believe, but how we believe.

In the end, this chapter does not offer closure but opens a field of inquiry. As AI becomes further entrenched in our cultural, religious, and political lifeworld, the sociology of belief must grapple with machines not as mere tools, but as co-constructors of meaning. To believe in the age of AI is to believe *with* the algorithm, not blindly, not passively, but with critical consciousness, cultural specificity, and epistemic care.

REFERENCES

Appadurai, A. (1996). *Modernity at Large: Cultural Dimensions of Globalization*. University of Minnesota Press.

Arora, P. (2019). *The Next Billion Users: Digital Life Beyond the West*. Harvard University Press. DOI: 10.4159/9780674238879

Banet-Weiser, S. (2012). Authentic™: The politics of ambivalence in a brand culture. In *Authentic*. New York University Press.

Baudrillard, J. (2019). Simulacra and simulations (1981). In *Crime and Media* (pp. 69–85). Routledge. DOI: 10.4324/9780367809195-8

Benjamin, R. (2019). *Race After Technology: Abolitionist Tools for the New Jim Code*. Polity Press.

Berger, P. L., & Luckmann, T. (1966). *The Social Construction of Reality: A Treatise in the Sociology of Knowledge*. Penguin Books.

Bourdieu, P. (1986). The forms of capital. In J. Richardson (Ed.), *Handbook of Theory and Research for the Sociology of Education* (pp. 241–258). Greenwood.

Bourdieu, P. (1990). *The Logic of Practice*. Stanford University Press. DOI: 10.1515/9781503621749

Bucher, T. (2018). *If... then: Algorithmic power and politics*. Oxford University Press. DOI: 10.1093/oso/9780190493028.001.0001

Charusheela, S. (2013). Intersectionality. *Handbook of research on gender and economic life*, 32-45.

Chatterjee, N. (2021). Translating Obligations: Tamassuk and Fārigh-kha ī in the Indo-Persian World. *Journal of Economic and Social History of the Orient*, *64*(5-6), 541–582. DOI: 10.1163/15685209-12341546

Chun, W. H. K. (2016). *Updating to remain the same: Habitual new media*. MIT press. DOI: 10.7551/mitpress/10483.001.0001

Couldry, N., & Hepp, A. (2017). *The Mediated Construction of Reality*. Polity Press.

Das, V. (2007). *Life and Words: Violence and the Descent into the Ordinary*. University of California Press.

Foucault, M. (1980). *Power/Knowledge: Selected Interviews and Other Writings, 1972–1977* (Gordon, C., Ed.). Pantheon.

Gitelman, L. (Ed.). (2013). *"Raw Data" is an Oxymoron*. MIT Press. DOI: 10.7551/mitpress/9302.001.0001

Hancock, A. M. (2013). Neurobiology, Intersectionality, and Politics: Paradigm Warriors in Arms? 1. *Perspectives on Politics, 11*(2), 504–507. DOI: 10.1017/S1537592713000959

Haraway, D. J. (1991). *Simians, Cyborgs, and Women: The Reinvention of Nature*. Routledge.

Hong, S. H. (2020). Technologies of speculation: The limits of knowledge in a data-driven society. In *Technologies of Speculation*. New York University Press. DOI: 10.18574/nyu/9781479860234.001.0001

Lévi-Strauss, C. (1963). Réponses à quelques questions. *Esprit (1940-)*, (322 (11), 628-653.

McLuhan, M. (1964). *Understanding Media: The Extensions of Man*. McGraw-Hill.

Mignolo, W. D. (2009). Epistemic disobedience, independent thought and decolonial freedom. *Theory, Culture & Society, 26*(7–8), 159–181. DOI: 10.1177/0263276409349275

Noble, S. U. (2018). *Algorithms of Oppression: How Search Engines Reinforce Racism*. NYU Press. DOI: 10.18574/nyu/9781479833641.001.0001

Rouvroy, A., Berns, T., & Carey-Libbrecht, L. (2013). Algorithmic governmentality and prospects of emancipation. *Reseaux (London), 177*(1), 163–196.

Seaver, N. (2018). What should an anthropology of algorithms do? *Cultural Anthropology, 33*(3), 375–385. DOI: 10.14506/ca33.3.04

Shah, N. (2019). Gender, algorithms, and affective labour: The case of online moderation. In McPherson, M. (Ed.), *Feminist in a Software Lab* (pp. 125–142). MIT Press.

Striphas, T. (2015). Algorithmic culture. *European Journal of Cultural Studies, 18*(4–5), 395–412. DOI: 10.1177/1367549415577392

Sundar, S. S. (2008). The MAIN model: A heuristic approach to understanding technology effects on credibility. In Metzger, M. J., & Flanagin, A. J. (Eds.), *Digital Media, Youth, and Credibility* (pp. 73–100). MIT Press.

Taussig, M. (1993). *The devil and the fetishism of the commodity in South America*. Editorial

Turkle, S. (2011). *Alone Together: Why We Expect More from Technology and Less from Each Other*. Basic Books.

Udupa, S. (2020). *Digital Hate: The Global Conjuncture of Extreme Speech*. Indiana University Press.

van Dijck, J. (2013). *The Culture of Connectivity: A Critical History of Social Media*. Oxford University Press. DOI: 10.1093/acprof:oso/9780199970773.001.0001

Wajcman, J. (2006). Technocapitalism meets technofeminism: women and technology in a wireless world. *Labour & Industry: a journal of the social and economic relations of work, 16*(3), 7-20.

Chapter 10
Harnessing Artificial Intelligence to Promote Religious Tolerance and Dialogue:
A Strategy to Detect and Counter Religious Hatred and Misinformation

Shyamashree Roy
https://orcid.org/0000-0001-7137-4534
Sister Nibedita Government General Degree College For Girls, Kolkata, India

ABSTRACT

The digital age presents a paradox where unprecedented connectivity fuels the spread of religious hatred and misinformation, threatening human rights and social cohesion. This chapter explores AI's strategic role in countering these harms by moving beyond reactive content removal toward a proactive, peacebuilding approach. It highlights the limitations of manual moderation and the necessity of scalable AI solutions. We review AI's advanced capabilities, including sophisticated NLP and multimodal analysis, which are crucial for detecting nuanced hate speech and misinformation. The chapter also discusses AI's potential to foster religious tolerance through counter-narratives and dialogue platforms. However, we examine ethical challenges such as algorithmic bias, the risk of over-moderation, and the complexities introduced by generative AI. The conclusion advocates for a multi-

DOI: 10.4018/979-8-3373-3830-9.ch010

stakeholder governance model, emphasizing "human-in-the-loop" oversight and international cooperation to ensure AI systems are technically robust, ethically sound, and culturally sensitive.

INTRODUCTION: THE DIGITAL CROSSROADS OF FAITH AND TECHNOLOGY

The advent of digital platforms has fundamentally reshaped global communication, offering unprecedented opportunities for cultural exchange and dialogue. However, this interconnectedness is simultaneously exploited for the rapid dissemination of harmful content, including religious hate speech, sectarian incitement, and malicious misinformation. Such content actively erodes trust, propagates harmful stereotypes, and directly contributes to real-world discrimination, persecution, and even violence against religious minorities or groups. The challenge is immense, spanning diverse languages, cultures, and myriad digital channels, often requiring nuanced contextual understanding that human moderators struggle to achieve at scale.

Public sentiment reflects this concern, with a significant majority of internet users expressing alarm over the prevalence of harmful content. Across surveyed countries, 68% of internet users believe that social media is the most widespread source of disinformation (UNESCO, 2023). Similarly, 67% of internet users report encountering hate speech online, a figure that rises to 74% among those under 35 years old (UNESCO, 2023). These statistics underscore the pervasive nature of the problem and its broad societal impact. The high prevalence rates of online disinformation and hate speech indicate that digital platforms are not merely passive conduits for content but rather active amplifiers of societal divisions. This phenomenon stems from underlying algorithmic designs that, while optimized for engagement, can inadvertently create "echo chambers," reinforcing existing biases and accelerating the spread of harmful narratives. This perspective shifts the focus from individual malicious actors to systemic vulnerabilities within platform design, highlighting the need for structural changes beyond just reactive content removal.

The imperative to address online religious intolerance cannot be overstated, as it directly undermines fundamental human rights, obstructs sustainable development goals, and poses a direct threat to international security. Recognizing this critical need, the United Nations General Assembly adopted a pivotal resolution in July 2021, titled "Promoting Inter-religious and Intercultural Dialogue and Tolerance in Countering Hate Speech" (UN General Assembly, 2021). This resolution urges all stakeholders, including States, to take stronger, coordinated action to confront hate, xenophobia, and discrimination, all within the boundaries of international human rights law. A significant outcome of this resolution was the establishment of June

18 as the International Day for Countering Hate Speech, marking the anniversary of the UN's comprehensive hate speech strategy launched in 2019. This strategy provides a system-wide framework for combating hate speech and offers essential guidance to enhance national efforts. The UN's explicit linkage of "Inter-religious and Intercultural Dialogue and Tolerance" with "Countering Hate Speech" signals a strategic evolution from purely reactive content moderation to a proactive, peacebuilding approach in the digital sphere. This combination suggests that the international community understands that merely suppressing harmful content is insufficient; true digital peace requires actively cultivating positive interactions, mutual understanding, and respect. Consequently, effective artificial intelligence (AI) solutions should not solely focus on detection and removal but also on fostering dialogue, amplifying positive narratives, and providing educational resources that promote religious tolerance, aligning with a broader peacebuilding mandate.

Current efforts to combat online hate speech are largely manual and reactive, frequently overwhelmed by the sheer volume and increasing sophistication of perpetrators who continuously adapt their tactics to evade detection. This paper champions the strategic application of AI as a powerful, scalable, and adaptable tool to augment human efforts in this critical fight. AI's advanced capabilities in data processing, pattern recognition, and semantic analysis offer a unique opportunity to shift from reactive moderation to proactive intervention. Crucially, AI can also be leveraged to cultivate spaces for positive dialogue and understanding. The overarching objective is to design, develop, and deploy an AI-driven system that not only identifies and flags harmful content but also actively supports the generation and promotion of counter-narratives and educational resources that foster religious tolerance and dialogue. The application of AI to fostering religious harmony remains an under-explored yet critically important field, despite AI technologies being increasingly employed in domains like healthcare, education, and law enforcement. The "under-explored" nature of AI for religious harmony highlights a significant research gap. This indicates that while AI is widely applied in general content moderation, its specific application to the nuanced and sensitive domain of religious tolerance requires dedicated, ethically-informed research. The unique cultural, linguistic, and theological specificities inherent in religious hatred and misinformation demand specialized approaches. This necessitates genuine interdisciplinary collaboration, where AI researchers work closely with religious scholars, ethicists, and social scientists to develop AI systems that are not only technically proficient in detection but also culturally sensitive, contextually aware, and ethically sound, specifically tailored for the complexities of religious discourse. This collaborative effort is essential to avoid unintended biases, over-moderation, or the suppression of legitimate religious expression.

This paper is structured to provide a comprehensive analysis of AI's role in promoting religious tolerance and dialogue. Following this introduction, Section 3 presents a brief review of the existing literature, Section 3 details the problem landscape of online religious hatred and misinformation. Section 4 explores current AI applications and case studies in combating online harms. Section 5 critically examines the ethical challenges and human rights implications of AI in this domain. Section 6 proposes strategic recommendations and discusses emerging AI trends for a responsible future. Finally, Section 7 concludes with a summary of key observations and a call for collaborative and ethical AI development.

LITERATURE REVIEW

The intersection of artificial intelligence (AI) and religious tolerance has emerged as a distinct field of inquiry within the broader domains of digital ethics, content moderation, and peacebuilding. Rapid advances in AI-driven natural language processing (NLP), sentiment analysis, and computer vision have given rise to new strategies for detecting and mitigating harmful content online, particularly hate speech, extremist propaganda, and misinformation targeting religious groups (UNESCO, 2023; Royal United Services Institute (RUSI), 2025). These technological interventions are situated within larger socio-political discourses about freedom of expression, algorithmic fairness, and the role of global digital platforms in fostering—or undermining—social cohesion (Meegle, 2025).

The concept of religious tolerance is historically rooted in philosophical traditions that emphasize respect for pluralism, non-discrimination, and peaceful coexistence (UNESCO, 2021). Interfaith dialogue, as a structured practice, has been promoted by institutions ranging from the United Nations Alliance of Civilizations to grassroots initiatives in multicultural societies (Balendra, 2025). The digital age has complicated these ideals, as platforms have become primary spaces for both dialogue and conflict (Perera et al., 2023).

From an AI ethics perspective, UNESCO's *Recommendation on the Ethics of Artificial Intelligence* provides a normative framework emphasizing inclusivity, transparency, and accountability (UNESCO, 2021). This aligns with the emphasis on classical ethics for AI governance, which advocates for socially beneficial design choices and respect for human dignity.

Recent studies demonstrate that AI-based hate speech detection models have evolved from simple keyword filters to sophisticated, context-aware systems employing deep learning architectures (Subramanian et al., 2023). Approaches such as multimodal hate speech detection leverage both textual and visual cues to identify harmful narratives that traditional methods might miss (Saeidnia et al., 2025).

Federated learning models, which allow collaborative training across multiple datasets without centralizing sensitive information, have shown promise in balancing privacy concerns with the need for robust moderation (Milvus, 2025). These techniques are increasingly being integrated into platform-level moderation policies, with notable examples including Meta's AI moderation systems, which seek to strike a balance between content control and protection of free expression (Mansur, Omar, & Tiun, 2023).

Studies have also examined AI's capacity to counter religious misinformation, which often blends factual distortion with emotive rhetoric to inflame tensions (Saikiran, Reddy, & Abhishek, 2024). The challenge is amplified in low-resource languages and culturally specific contexts where annotated datasets are limited, making the development of accurate models more complex (Fonseca et. al., 2024).

One of the most persistent challenges in AI-driven moderation is cultural and linguistic nuance. Hate speech detection models often underperform when applied to dialects, slang, or coded language used by specific communities (Global Survey, 2023). Moreover, religious intolerance online may manifest in subtle forms such as sarcasm, coded memes, or indirect denigration, which require not only linguistic but also socio-cultural contextualization (Perera et al., 2023).

Cross-cultural research highlights that perceptions of what constitutes "harmful" or "offensive" religious discourse vary widely (Malik, et. al. 2023). This makes the creation of universally applicable AI moderation systems difficult, as overly broad filtering may suppress legitimate expression, while overly narrow models may fail to intercept harmful content.

International policy frameworks increasingly recognize the dual imperative of safeguarding free expression and preventing the spread of online hate. The Global Digital Compact proposes multistakeholder governance mechanisms to ensure that AI systems are deployed ethically and inclusively (Author, Year). At the national level, countries have adopted varying approaches—ranging from Germany's *NetzDG* law mandating content takedown within strict time limits to India's IT Rules emphasizing platform accountability.

Scholars argue that effective governance must be both *proactive*—through upstream design of inclusive AI systems—and *reactive*—through rapid response to emerging threats (Khera et. al., 2025). Public-private partnerships, such as those seen in collaborative counter-speech initiatives, are increasingly viewed as essential.

While AI offers unprecedented scale and speed in detecting harmful content, it raises ethical questions about surveillance, bias, and autonomy. Algorithmic bias can result in disproportionate targeting of minority communities, leading to digital marginalization rather than protection. Privacy concerns are heightened when AI systems monitor encrypted or private communications under the justification of preventing harm (Jahan & Oussalah, 2023).

The balance between freedom of expression and protection from harm remains contentious. Civil society organizations have cautioned that opaque moderation algorithms risk chilling legitimate religious discourse, especially for minority faith groups that may already face systemic marginalization (Das et. al., 2023).

Identified Gaps in Literature

Despite significant advances, several gaps persist in the literature:

1. **Limited longitudinal studies** – Few works have examined the long-term impacts of AI moderation on religious tolerance in digital spaces.
2. **Underrepresentation of non-Western contexts** – Much of the empirical evidence is drawn from English-speaking or Western settings, limiting cross-cultural applicability.
3. **Evaluation of counter-speech effectiveness** – While counter-speech is promoted as an alternative to takedown, rigorous evaluation of its success in religious contexts remains scarce.
4. **Integration of interfaith dialogue frameworks into AI systems** – Current models rarely embed structured dialogue principles, missing opportunities for positive engagement.

The literature underscores AI's potential to function as both a shield against harmful religious discourse and a facilitator of constructive interfaith engagement. However, technological sophistication alone is insufficient without ethical guardrails, cultural competence, and inclusive governance structures. As AI continues to evolve, the next generation of systems must be designed not only to detect and remove harmful content but also to actively promote digital environments where diverse religious expressions can coexist respectfully.

THE PROBLEM LANDSCAPE: ONLINE RELIGIOUS HATRED AND MISINFORMATION

The digital environment provides fertile ground for the rapid and widespread dissemination of religious intolerance. Several inherent characteristics of online platforms exacerbate this issue, creating a complex and pervasive challenge.

Characteristics of the Digital Scourge: Scale, Speed, Anonymity, Echo Chambers

Online content can achieve global virality within minutes, reaching millions before any human intervention can occur, making it exceedingly difficult to contain harmful narratives once they are unleashed. This unprecedented scale and speed of dissemination mean that malicious content can cause significant damage before traditional moderation efforts can respond.

Furthermore, the perceived anonymity afforded by the internet emboldens individuals to express extreme views that they might otherwise refrain from voicing in offline settings, often without fear of immediate repercussion. This lack of accountability can lower the barrier for individuals to engage in hateful or inflammatory discourse.

Algorithmic content recommendations, while designed for engagement, can inadvertently create "echo chambers." These digital spaces reinforce existing biases and primarily expose users to information that aligns with their pre-existing beliefs, thereby intensifying polarization and rendering them more susceptible to extremist views. The confluence of anonymity and algorithmic echo chambers creates a self-reinforcing feedback loop that accelerates radicalization and makes it harder for individuals to encounter diverse perspectives. Anonymity reduces the social accountability that might temper extreme expressions, while echo chambers ensure that these uninhibited, often extreme views are amplified and constantly reinforced to a receptive, like-minded audience. This process can create a "radicalization pipeline" where users are increasingly exposed only to content that confirms their biases, leading to a faster, more entrenched adoption of extremist ideologies, including religious hatred. This highlights a systemic design flaw in digital platforms that needs to be addressed through structural changes, not just reactive content removal.

Sophistication of Harmful Content and Cultural/Linguistic Nuances

Hate speech and misinformation are not always overt or easily identifiable. They can be subtle, employing coded language, sarcasm, dog-whistling, visual cues, and sophisticated psychological manipulation to evade detection by both human and automated systems (Royal United Services Institute (RUSI), 2025). State and non-state actors increasingly engage in coordinated disinformation campaigns specifically aimed at sowing discord and manipulating public opinion. These campaigns often leverage advanced techniques to appear credible and bypass detection.

A critical challenge lies in the fact that what constitutes hate speech or misinformation can vary significantly across cultures, languages, and religious contexts. A statement that might be innocuous in one context could be deeply offensive or inciting in another, making universal detection and moderation exceptionally challenging. The evolving sophistication of harmful content, particularly the use of coded language and multimodal tactics, creates an adversarial AI problem where detection systems must constantly adapt. The dynamic and adaptive nature of hate speech, where tactics continuously evolve to bypass existing moderation efforts, means that static or infrequently updated AI models will quickly become obsolete. This necessitates a continuous learning and adaptation loop for AI systems, rather than a one-time deployment. This "arms race" dynamic implies that relying solely on AI for detection is insufficient; human expertise is crucial for identifying emerging tactics, understanding cultural nuances, and providing contextual insights that can then be used to train and refine AI models. This highlights the indispensable need for hybrid human-AI moderation systems, where human intelligence informs algorithmic development and adaptation, rather than AI attempting to fully replace human judgment.

Resource Constraints in Human Moderation and Real-World Consequences

Human content moderators face immense psychological strain due to exposure to harmful content, are inherently limited in the volume of content they can process, and require extensive, ongoing training to understand complex religious, cultural, and linguistic nuances. This makes manual moderation unsustainable for the vast scale of the problem. The existing gap in effective, scalable solutions for addressing this multi-faceted problem underscores the urgent need for innovative approaches where AI can play a transformative role.

The link between online hate speech and misinformation and real-world harm is clear and devastating. Such online content frequently translates into offline discrimination, harassment, violence, and even genocidal acts. Empirical evidence confirms these impacts: exposure to hate content leads to negative attitudes, reduced intergroup trust, increased victimization, and significant psychological harm, including depressive symptoms, reduced life satisfaction, and increased social fear. The societal impact is quantifiable; police-recorded hate crimes in England and Wales, for instance, rose by 252% between 2012 and 2023, with over 50% of the population routinely exposed to hateful content online (Royal United Services Institute (RUSI), 2025). The unsustainability of manual moderation coupled with the severe and quantifiable real-world impacts of online hate creates an urgent societal imperative for scalable, effective AI solutions, despite their inherent challenges. The inability of human moderators to cope with the sheer volume and complexity of harmful content directly contributes to the escalation of online hate into real-world suffering and societal instability. This establishes a clear causal link between the technological problem of scale and the urgent human rights crisis. It underscores that AI is not merely a technological enhancement for efficiency but a necessary tool for public safety, mental well-being, and the protection of vulnerable groups in the digital age, provided its ethical deployment is carefully managed.

The following table summarizes the key drivers and impacts of online religious hatred and misinformation, providing a consolidated view of the problem landscape.

Table 1. Drivers and impacts of online religious hatred and misinformation

Category	Drivers of Online Religious Hatred and Misinformation	Documented Impacts on Individuals and Society
Digital Platform Characteristics	Scale and Speed of Dissemination	Erosion of Trust
	Anonymity and Impunity	Propagation of Stereotypes
	Echo Chambers and Polarization	Discrimination and Persecution
Content Nature	Sophistication of Harmful Content (coded language, multimodal, psychological manipulation)	Violence (offline, including genocidal acts)
	Cultural and Linguistic Nuances	Psychological Harm (depressive symptoms, reduced life satisfaction, increased social fear)
Moderation Challenges	Resource Constraints for Human Moderation	Reduced Intergroup Trust
		Increased Online Victimization
		Amplification of Hate Crime (e.g., 252% rise in police-recorded hate crimes in England and Wales 2012-2023)

This table visually consolidates and presents the complex, multifaceted problem statement surrounding online religious hatred and misinformation. It offers a clear, concise, and easily digestible overview of the intricate interplay between the various drivers and their severe impacts, enhancing the report's accessibility. By synthesizing critical information from multiple sources, it highlights the causal and correlational relationships between factors like algorithmic amplification, the psychological toll on individuals, and the escalation of online hate into real-world violence. This clear delineation of the problem serves as a robust empirical foundation for the subsequent sections of the paper, logically justifying the urgent need for AI intervention and providing a clear baseline against which proposed AI solutions, their effectiveness, and their inherent challenges can be rigorously discussed and evaluated.

AI'S ROLE IN COMBATING ONLINE HARMS: CURRENT APPLICATIONS AND CASE STUDIES

Artificial intelligence is increasingly playing a critical role in recognizing and reducing hate speech across online platforms. Its capabilities extend beyond mere detection to proactive intervention and the cultivation of positive dialogue.

AI for Detection and Identification

Natural Language Processing (NLP) and Deep Learning for Hate Speech Detection

AI systems, particularly those leveraging advanced Natural Language Processing (NLP) models such as BERT and GPT variants, are trained on vast datasets of text (and increasingly, images and audio). These models learn to identify intricate patterns, linguistic cues, and subtle nuances that indicate hate speech, even when the harmful content is disguised with sarcasm, irony, or coded language. Unlike older, simpler keyword-based filters, modern AI systems possess the capability to analyze the *context* in which words are used. This allows them to differentiate between a word that might be acceptable in one context but hateful in another, by assessing sentiment and emotional tone to distinguish legitimate discussion from inflammatory rhetoric.

Deep learning models, including Convolutional Neural Networks (CNNs), Recurrent Neural Networks (RNNs), and transformer-based architectures, have consistently demonstrated strong performance on various hate speech detection benchmarks. Recent advancements include novel prompt-based neural architectures for few-shot hate speech detection, such as MS-FSLHate. This framework integrates prompt-enhanced embeddings with a lightweight CNN-BiLSTM backbone and attention pooling. It has shown to outperform competitive baselines in precision, recall, and F1-score, particularly addressing performance deterioration in few-shot or low-resource settings that typically rely on large annotated corpora. The advancement from rudimentary keyword-based filters to sophisticated, context-aware NLP and deep learning models signifies a critical maturation in AI's ability to understand the *intent* and *nuance* behind language. This evolution moves beyond superficial detection to more profound semantic analysis, which is indispensable for navigating the complexities of religious discourse. The shift from simple keyword matching to contextual and semantic analysis is profoundly significant because religious hate speech often does not rely on explicit slurs but rather on subtle cues, dog-whistling, reinterpretation of sacred texts, or culturally specific derogatory terms. These nuanced forms of hatred cannot be accurately identified by basic filters. AI's ability to grasp context and intent allows it to better navigate the inherent ambiguity and cultural specificity of religious content, making it a far more viable and ethically responsible tool for promoting religious tolerance.

Multimodal Analysis: Integrating Text, Image, and Audio

Hate speech is not confined to text alone; it increasingly manifests across multiple modalities. AI systems are now capable of analyzing images (e.g., symbols, memes), videos (e.g., deepfakes), and audio for harmful content, combining insights from these different modalities for more robust and comprehensive detection. An example is the University of Waterloo's "Multi-Modal Discussion Transformer (mDT)," which detects hate speech by understanding the complex relationship between text and images within online discussions.

A flexible deep learning model for multimodal hate speech detection has been developed to integrate features from visual, audio, and textual modalities in videos. This model demonstrates strong performance gains over unimodal baselines and, crucially, is designed to remain functional and reliable even when one or more modalities are missing or noisy, enhancing its practical applicability in real-world scenarios. Further research proposes a novel Multi-modal Hate Speech Detection Framework (MHSDF) that combines Convolutional Neural Networks (CNNs) and Recurrent Neural Networks (RNNs) to analyze complex, heterogeneous data streams. This hybrid approach leverages CNNs for spatial feature extraction (e.g., visual cues, local text patterns) and Long Short-Term Memory (LSTM) for modeling temporal dependencies in text and audio. This framework has achieved high detection accuracy (98.53%), robustness, and interpretability compared to existing models. The transition to multimodal AI is a direct, necessary response to perpetrators' evolving tactics that increasingly blend synthetic and real elements across different media types. This represents a proactive technological adaptation in the ongoing "arms race" between malicious actors and content moderation systems. The development of multimodal detection capabilities is a critical counter-tactic against the increasing sophistication of harmful content, particularly the rise of AI-generated deepfakes, manipulated images, and memes that combine visual and textual cues. This directly addresses the challenge of content that blurs the line between authentic and artificially created imagery. This signifies a crucial step in building more resilient and comprehensive detection systems. However, it also highlights the continuous challenge of staying ahead of malicious actors who constantly innovate their methods of evasion. The design of "flexible" models that can gracefully handle missing modalities during inference further emphasizes the practical complexities of real-world content moderation, where complete data across all modalities is often unavailable.

Misinformation and Disinformation Detection: Fact-Checking and Source Credibility

AI can effectively cross-reference claims against established fact-checking databases to identify known false narratives, including those with religious themes. Advanced AI algorithms can assess the credibility of information sources by analyzing publication history, reputation, and patterns of bias, helping to determine if content originates from a reliable or a malicious source. AI can also track the propagation of misinformation, enabling the identification of bot networks or coordinated campaigns specifically designed to amplify hateful or false religious narratives. A systematic review covering 2014 to 2024 emphasizes AI's capacity to enhance information verification through sophisticated algorithms and Natural Language Processing (NLP). The review highlights AI's strengths in adaptability, scalability, pattern recognition, automation, and real-time monitoring for combating misinformation.

While fine-tuned BERT transformers demonstrate high effectiveness (84-90% accuracy) at classifying AI-generated fake news, they show significantly lower accuracy (49% for real Kaggle articles, 21% for real AI-generated articles) in classifying real news articles. This disparity suggests potential bias in the model or insufficient training data for authentic content. The differential accuracy of AI in detecting *fake* versus *real* news implies a potential for AI to inadvertently suppress legitimate content or contribute to a "truth deficit" if models are not meticulously balanced and regularly retrained on diverse, unbiased datasets. This observed imbalance in performance reveals a critical vulnerability. If AI systems are more adept at identifying falsehoods than at authenticating truth, there is a risk of "over-removal" of legitimate content or, conversely, a failure to adequately verify genuine information. This is particularly problematic in sensitive religious contexts where "truth" can be subjective, deeply held, and easily misconstrued. This highlights an ethical imperative for developers to ensure that AI models are equally proficient in authenticating real information as they are in identifying false narratives, to prevent unintended censorship and maintain trust in reliable sources.

Illustrative Cases

Real-world deployments showcase AI's growing impact in content moderation:

- **Meta's Fight Against Religious Hate Speech (India):** In 2020, following internal documents leaked to The Wall Street Journal that revealed failures to remove hate speech in India targeting Muslims, Facebook (now Meta) implemented stricter AI content moderation mechanisms. Within six months, Meta's AI proactively flagged over 90% of hate speech content before users reported it, focusing specifically on Hindi, Urdu, and English content targeting religious minorities.

- **YouTube's Algorithm & Religious Polarization (Brazil):** A 2019 University of São Paulo study found that YouTube's recommendation algorithm often steered users toward more radical and anti-religious content. In response, YouTube implemented AI-based moderation tools, leading to the demonetization and de-amplification of over 30,000 extremist channels related to religious hate, which reduced their reach by nearly 70%.
- **The Rohingya Crisis and Facebook in Myanmar:** In 2018, the UN accused Facebook of playing a role in inciting violence against the Rohingya Muslim community in Myanmar, with over 1,000 posts promoting hate going unchecked. Following international backlash, Facebook introduced AI filters in Burmese, resulting in the removal of over 64,000 hate posts in a year and proactively flagging 90% of such content.
- **Jigsaw's "Perspective":** A notable example of AI in this space is "Perspective," a tool developed by Jigsaw, a division of Alphabet, in partnership with Google. This tool utilizes machine learning and NLP to evaluate the "toxicity" of an online comment, providing platforms with a score indicating the potential harmfulness of content. This assists platforms in moderating discussions more effectively and reducing harmful interactions.

The recurring pattern of tech companies implementing significant AI moderation improvements *after* experiencing substantial public backlash and documented real-world harm (as seen with Meta in India/Myanmar and YouTube in Brazil) suggests a reactive rather than proactive ethical development cycle. This indicates a systemic failure in embedding human rights considerations *by design* from the early stages of platform development. While these cases demonstrate AI's potential, they also highlight that the impetus for robust ethical AI deployment often arises from external pressure and crisis rather than inherent organizational foresight.

AI for Proactive Counter-Narratives and Dialogue Promotion

Beyond detection and removal, AI offers significant potential for actively fostering religious tolerance and dialogue. This involves shifting from a purely defensive posture to one that cultivates positive online environments.

Strategies for Intelligent Content Suggestions and Positive Discourse Amplification

AI can analyze conversations to identify "intervention points"—moments where a discussion is veering towards conflict or where an opportunity exists to introduce positive, accurate information. Intelligent content suggestion systems can then be employed to recommend:

- **Educational resources:** Links to verified facts, scholarly articles, or theological explanations to correct misunderstandings and counter misinformation.
- **Empathy-building narratives:** Stories or testimonials that highlight shared values and positive interfaith interactions, fostering greater understanding and reducing prejudice.
- **Factual corrections:** Providing concise, evidence-based rebuttals to misinformation, directly addressing false narratives.

Furthermore, AI can actively boost the visibility of content that promotes tolerance, respect, and accurate information about different faiths, helping to "drown out" harmful narratives. This moves beyond merely removing hate speech to actively cultivating positive alternatives and promoting constructive discourse. AI can also identify and disable malicious accounts, such as bots, that are often used to spread hate speech and disinformation at scale by analyzing suspicious behavior patterns like rapid posting or repetitive content.

The United Nations Strategy and Plan of Action on Hate Speech describes hate speech as any expression that targets or discriminates against people based on aspects of their identity, such as religion, ethnicity, or gender. Although a universally accepted legal definition is still being developed, there are growing efforts by governments, civil society, and individuals to tackle the problem, particularly in the digital space.

The Plan of Action emphasizes the importance of collaboration—especially with technology and social media companies—in addressing hate speech. AI technologies are highlighted as powerful tools for early detection and prevention of conflict, but their use must be guided by strong human rights protections to avoid potential misuse. In this context, UN Member States have reaffirmed their dedication to regulating AI responsibly under frameworks like the Global Digital Compact, while also reinforcing their commitment to fighting online hate speech.

In July 2021, the UN General Assembly voiced global concern about the alarming increase in hate speech worldwide. As a result, it adopted a resolution titled "Promoting Inter-religious and Intercultural Dialogue and Tolerance in Countering Hate Speech." This resolution urges all stakeholders—including States—to take stronger action to confront hate, xenophobia, and discrimination, all within the boundaries of international human rights law.

One significant outcome of the resolution was the establishment of June 18 as the International Day for Countering Hate Speech, marking the anniversary of the launch of the UN's comprehensive hate speech strategy in 2019. On this day, the UN encourages governments, civil society, international bodies, and individuals to organize initiatives that raise awareness, identify sources of hate speech, and develop proactive strategies to address them. This strategy represents the first system-wide framework from the UN aimed specifically at combating hate speech, offering essential guidance on how it can support and enhance national efforts.

Whether it's state actors, technology firms, media outlets, educators, religious leaders, activists, youth, or individuals directly affected by hate, there is a shared moral obligation to oppose hate speech firmly and to contribute meaningfully to its prevention.

Artificial Intelligence and the Fight Against Hate Speech

- AI now plays a critical role in recognizing and reducing hate speech across online platforms. Through Natural Language Processing (NLP), AI systems can detect offensive, dehumanizing, or threatening content and take timely action. However, one of the most complex challenges lies in distinguishing hate speech from legally protected free expression.
- A notable example of AI in this space is "Perspective", a tool developed by Jigsaw, a division of Alphabet, in partnership with Google. This tool uses machine learning and NLP to evaluate how "toxic" an online comment might be. It provides platforms with a score indicating the potential harmfulness of content, helping them moderate discussions more effectively and reduce harmful interactions.

Bots and AI-Fueled Disinformation

- AI-driven bots are another significant concern, as they can rapidly distribute hateful content and manipulate public discourse. These automated accounts have the capacity to flood social platforms with large volumes of hate messages, escalating tensions. A clear example of this occurred during the 2016 U.S. presidential election, when bots were widely used on platforms like Twitter (now X) and Facebook to spread disinformation and hate-fueled narratives. Many of these automated campaigns aimed to sway public opinion and amplify societal divides.

- To tackle this, companies such as Facebook have invested in AI tools designed to identify and curb bot activity. These tools analyze unusual patterns like excessive posting, repetitive interactions, and suspicious account origins to flag potential automated behavior.
- Overall, technology—and AI in particular—can be an effective ally in curbing hate speech. Social media platforms already use advanced AI systems to monitor content, intervene proactively, and prevent harm. These same technologies, which have proven highly successful in other areas like fraud prevention in finance, can also be adapted to monitor online speech. With the ability to not only detect but also prevent potentially harmful discourse, AI stands as a proactive force in reducing hate before it escalates into real-world consequences.

Case Studies: AI in Religious Practice and Community Engagement

AI is increasingly being integrated into religious contexts to facilitate spiritual growth, interfaith dialogue, and community engagement:

- **St. Paul University Philippines' Interfaith Initiatives:** St. Paul University Philippines (SPUP) has integrated AI into its interfaith initiatives to enhance dialogue, inclusivity, and spiritual understanding among students from diverse religious backgrounds. This integration spans learning environments, policies, and programs. Specific AI tools include:
    - **Chatbots and Virtual Dialogue Platforms:** These facilitate real-time interfaith communication, extending outreach beyond the physical campus and providing personalized spiritual counseling and Q&A.
    - **Sentiment Analysis:** This tool analyzes dialogue tone and intent in real-time, helping identify implicit bias or misunderstanding and offering faculty actionable feedback. AI moderation in online interfaith discussions, supported by sentiment analysis, enhances respectful communication.
    - **Adaptive Learning Systems:** These systems customize content delivery to reflect diverse religious perspectives, fostering comprehensive and empathetic understanding. They provide personalized learning pathways and interactive modules. The impact includes enhanced student participation through increased accessibility and interactive tools, fostering empathy via virtual reality simulations and empathy prompts, and promoting respectful communication by guiding civil discussions.

- **AI in Broader Religious Practice and Community Engagement:** Religious leaders worldwide are leveraging social media and AI-powered assistants to connect with followers and other religious communities globally, broadcasting messages of optimism, peace, and solidarity.
  - Examples include the Pope's use of digital channels for global discourse, AI-powered applications providing real-time access to Islamic teachings for humanitarian initiatives, and platforms like Brahma Gyaan guiding Hindus through ancient scriptures, enhancing access for minority groups.
  - AI is facilitating cross-border relationships and international peace discussions among interfaith leaders. At the UN Climate Action Summit, religious groups used AI-powered platforms to offer spiritual perspectives on climate justice, complementing diplomatic efforts. AI-enabled technology has also assisted faith-based organizations in organizing petitions, mobilizing communities for protests, and fostering discussions about environmental responsibility.
  - Virtual interfaith prayer circles, where individuals from diverse religious backgrounds convene in real-time to pray for peace or discuss conflict resolution, exemplify a new form of global collaboration transcending traditional boundaries.

NAVIGATING THE ETHICAL MINEFIELD: CHALLENGES AND HUMAN RIGHTS IMPLICATIONS

While AI offers immense potential, its application in sensitive areas like religious content moderation and dialogue promotion is fraught with significant ethical challenges and human rights implications. These concerns necessitate careful consideration and robust safeguards.

Algorithmic Bias and Data Inequities

Bias in Training Data and its Disproportionate Impact on Minorities

A major limitation of AI systems stems from biases and flaws inherent in their training data. If the data used to train the AI contains existing human biases, the AI might inadvertently discriminate against certain groups or misclassify legitimate speech as hate speech. This can lead to skewed outcomes, disproportionately affecting marginalized communities, as seen in applications like facial recognition and predictive policing. There is often a lack of diversity in training data, which limits nuanced understanding of marginalized communities' experiences, and smaller languages are less understood by AI systems.

Challenges in Contextual Understanding and Evolving Language

AI may struggle to understand complex nuances and context in language, leading to misinterpretations of information, including sarcasm, idiomatic expressions, and culturally specific references. Hate speech tactics continuously evolve, and AI must adapt to new slang, memes, and cultural contexts. The distinction between satire, criticism, and genuine hate speech remains a complex challenge for AI, often resulting in false positives or negatives.

The Global South Perspective: Over-removal and Slow Removal

AI-driven content moderation on social media platforms has a discriminatory impact, particularly in the Global South, where it often clashes with cultural and linguistic diversity. This reliance on AI algorithms by platforms like Meta leads to "over-removal" (censorship of lawful content) and "slow removal" (failure to address harmful material), both of which perpetuate inequality and hinder free speech. This phenomenon illustrates systemic biases and inequalities in AI deployment.

The disparities stem from several factors:

- **Cultural Prejudices and Economic Inequalities:** Content moderation practices are largely shaped by Western cultural norms, despite the Global South being a rapidly emerging market for social media. This imbalance leads to inequality and arbitrary practices, as tech companies often underinvest in moderation for poorer nations, considering them marginal markets.
- **Language Barriers and Inadequate Language Training:** High-resource languages benefit from extensive digitized content and advanced NLP tools, while low-resource languages face significant challenges due to limited data and poor translation tools. Tech companies frequently rely on machine translation instead of investing in native language resources, leading to errors, cultural inaccuracies, and biases. This disproportionately impacts minority and local languages, allowing misinformation and hate speech to go unchecked in languages like Burmese, Amharic, and Sinhala/Tamil.
- **Political and Corporate Biases:** Meta, for example, has been criticized for underinvesting in content moderation for non-English speaking markets, contributing to the proliferation of hate speech and incitement to violence. Algorithmic decisions often reflect inherent biases, producing inconsistent and discriminatory outcomes across global demographics.

- **Lack of Contextual Awareness:** AI systems often fail to understand the nuances of local idioms, sarcasm, or cultural connotations, leading to "over-removal" of legitimate posts. Conversely, the limitations of AI in low-resource languages mean that harmful content can go unchecked for longer periods, as seen in Myanmar during the Rohingya crisis and in Bangladesh with religious tensions.

The Tension Between Freedom of Expression and Harm Prevention

AI's intervention in online discourse must strike a delicate balance to avoid over-moderation and ensure legitimate expression is not suppressed. The growing reliance on AI in content moderation raises critical questions about its impact on human rights, particularly the right to freedom of expression, privacy, and the prohibition of discrimination.

Risks of Over-Moderation, Censorship, and Silencing Marginalized Voices

A key concern is that AI-driven moderation, especially for hate speech, often lacks the ability to grasp linguistic nuance, cultural context, and intent. This can lead to over-removal, censorship, and the disproportionate silencing of marginalized voices. Biased datasets and insufficient training data contribute to discriminatory enforcement, disproportionately affecting minority communities and raising serious concerns about violations of free speech. The tension between free speech and harm prevention is exacerbated by AI's limitations in understanding nuance, necessitating clear ethical frameworks and robust human oversight. Without these, AI systems risk becoming instruments of unintended censorship, particularly for vulnerable groups whose expressions might be misclassified due to cultural or linguistic specificities.

Ethical Principles for AI Content Moderation: Transparency, Fairness, Cultural Sensitivity

Ethical content moderation involves monitoring and controlling user-generated content in alignment with moral standards and principles, balancing a safe online environment with freedom of speech. Key principles include:

- **Privacy:** Policies must ensure user privacy is protected.
- **Consistency:** Standards should be applied uniformly to all community members.

- **Transparency:** Platforms must be open about their content moderation guidelines, ensuring users can access and understand them. This includes algorithmic transparency, providing clarity on how AI systems make decisions.
- **Fairness:** Moderators must exercise impartiality, refraining from prejudice based on ethnicity, faith, or political views. AI systems need to be created and trained in an unprejudiced way, avoiding discrimination against any users based on protected attributes.
- **Cultural Sensitivity:** Those monitoring online material should be trained to understand and appreciate cultural nuances to avoid incorrect evaluations.
- **Explainability:** AI models should provide clarity and interpretability regarding content moderation choices, fostering confidence and allowing users to comprehend why specific material is identified or removed.

Privacy, Accountability, and the “Black Box” Dilemma

Data Collection Concerns and User Rights in AI Systems

AI-driven content moderation presents privacy risks, as it often requires large-scale data collection that may infringe on users’ rights under laws like the General Data Protection Regulation (GDPR). The immense computational power required by AI systems also raises environmental impact concerns.

Addressing Lack of Transparency and Ensuring Accountability

Some AI algorithms are often referred to as “black boxes,” making it difficult to understand how they arrive at their decisions. This lack of transparency is problematic for accountability and oversight. When content moderation is outsourced to third-party vendors, tech companies may not fully understand their algorithms' training data or functioning. This opacity hinders the ability to identify and rectify biases or errors.

The Crucial Role of Human Oversight

Human oversight is crucial to ensure ethical decision-making remains integral to AI efforts. AI should complement human decision-making rather than replacing it, especially given the risk of false positives and negatives and the ability of malicious actors to circumvent moderation. Humans are essential for verifying and contextualizing information, fine-tuning models as tactics evolve, and ensuring that AI systems do not suppress legitimate expression.

The Double-Edged Sword of Generative AI

The emergence of generative AI (GenAI) models has introduced new complexities and amplified existing threats.

New Avenues for Propaganda, Deepfakes, and Radicalization

Generative AI enables terrorist and extremist actors to produce propaganda on a larger scale, more quickly, and with greater reach. This includes high-quality and high-volume material, making detection and moderation challenging for tech companies. GenAI facilitates the spread of false or inaccurate information with greater speed and sophistication, making it difficult for tech companies and regulators to respond. Deepfakes are a major concern, eroding trust in official information sources and mainstream media, and enabling public figures to deny real statements by attributing them to deepfake technology. There is also concern about AI influencing large datasets by flooding forums with misinformation to mainstream extremist narratives.

The combined effects of increased propaganda and disinformation can lead to significant consequences for radicalization and recruitment. Chatbots, like the one involved in the Windsor Castle attacker's radicalization, can create a false impression of support ("astroturfing") and reinforce radical beliefs, potentially encouraging violence. GenAI also allows for highly personalized recruitment by exploiting personal grievances and targeting propaganda based on language and information preferences. Furthermore, terrorist and extremist actors can use generative AI for operational purposes, such as attack planning and learning new tactics like malicious codes for cyberattacks or the use of drones.

Challenges in Detection and Mitigation of AI-Generated Harmful Content

Advances in AI allow individuals and groups to create highly realistic hate-filled images, videos, and convincing text designed to exploit prejudices, reinforce stereotypes, or sow division. These AI tools no longer require advanced technical skills, making it easy for a wide range of actors to produce tailored content with minimal effort. AI-generated content can mimic the style and appearance of legitimate news sources or impersonate trusted public figures, lending added credibility to harmful and misleading messages.

AI technologies act as a significant force multiplier for the spread of online hate. The simplicity and speed with which AI can generate large volumes of text, images, or videos allow for rapid and wide-scale dissemination, making it difficult for moderators, platforms, and researchers to keep pace. This dynamic is referred to as a 'tsunami' of radical and harmful content. Users also adapt tactics to bypass moderation, employing euphemistic phrases, hybrid content manipulation (combining AI-generated visuals with manual editing), algorithmic gaming (e.g., 'Vernetzungstweets'), and cross-platform adaptation to increase the visibility and reach of hateful content.[3] Generative AI fundamentally shifts the landscape of online harms, lowering the barrier for malicious content creation and acting as a force multiplier. This demands a paradigm shift in detection strategies, moving beyond reactive removal to proactive identification of generative patterns and a deeper understanding of how synthetic content manipulates human perception.

TOWARDS A RESPONSIBLE FUTURE: STRATEGIC RECOMMENDATIONS AND EMERGING TRENDS

Addressing the complex challenges posed by online religious hatred and misinformation requires a multi-pronged approach that leverages advanced AI capabilities, fosters ethical AI design, and establishes robust multi-stakeholder governance frameworks.

Advancing AI Capabilities for Enhanced Detection and Mitigation

Continued innovation in AI is essential to stay ahead of evolving threats.

Innovations in Few-Shot Learning and Multimodal AI

Few-shot learning, as exemplified by prompt-enhanced deep learning frameworks like MS-FSLHate, is crucial for improving hate speech detection in low-resource settings or for newly emerging forms of hate speech where large, annotated datasets are unavailable. These models can achieve high precision, recall, and F1-scores even with limited training data.

The development of robust multimodal AI systems, capable of analyzing text, images, and audio in conjunction, is also critical. Such systems, like the flexible deep learning model for multimodal hate speech detection or the MHSDF, demonstrate superior performance over unimodal baselines and can adapt to scenarios where certain modalities are missing or noisy. This comprehensive approach is vital given the increasingly complex and multi-layered nature of online harmful content.

Explainable AI (XAI) for Interpretability and Trust

The "black box" nature of many deep learning models poses a significant challenge to their adoption, particularly in sensitive domains like content moderation where transparency and accountability are paramount. Explainable AI (XAI) addresses this by designing protocols that make AI algorithms more understandable and interpretable. XAI techniques, such as Shapley value estimation and attention-based visualization, provide insights into how AI models arrive at their decisions, enhancing user trust and enabling human oversight. For instance, frameworks like SemFedXAI, while primarily for healthcare, illustrate how semantic web technologies can enrich AI models with domain knowledge to provide contextualized, multi-level explanations that are more comprehensible to human users.

Federated Learning (FL) for Privacy-Preserving Content Moderation

Traditional AI models often rely on centralized data collection, raising significant privacy concerns. Federated Learning (FL) offers a transformative paradigm by enabling decentralized model training across multiple nodes without sharing raw data. This approach significantly enhances privacy and data security, as only model updates, not the sensitive content itself, are transmitted.

FL also contributes to improved model inclusivity and reduced bias. By training across diverse datasets from different locations and user groups, FL can create models that perform better for broader populations, including those speaking low-resource languages or from underrepresented demographics. Furthermore, FL can reduce the environmental footprint of AI systems by minimizing data transfer and distributing computation, thereby lowering energy consumption associated with large centralized data centers. The integration of XAI and FL is critical for overcoming privacy and transparency challenges, building trust, and ensuring ethical deployment in sensitive domains such as religious content moderation. This hybrid approach allows for the benefits of AI to be harnessed while mitigating the risks associated with data centralization and algorithmic opacity.

Fostering Religious Tolerance and Dialogue through Ethical AI Design

AI's potential extends beyond merely detecting and removing harmful content to actively cultivating environments conducive to religious tolerance and interfaith dialogue.

Developing AI-Driven Platforms for Empathetic and Inclusive Interfaith Engagement

AI can be leveraged to design, develop, and deploy systems that actively support the generation and promotion of counter-narratives and educational resources fostering religious tolerance and dialogue. This involves creating intelligent content suggestions, promoting positive discourse, and identifying intervention points in online conversations.

Case studies demonstrate the practical application of AI in this domain. St. Paul University Philippines (SPUP) has successfully integrated AI into its interfaith initiatives, utilizing tools like chatbots, sentiment analysis, and virtual dialogue platforms to enhance student participation, empathy, and respectful communication. These tools facilitate real-time interfaith communication, provide personalized spiritual counseling, and analyze dialogue tone to identify implicit biases, offering faculty actionable feedback. Virtual and augmented reality applications can offer immersive experiences that simulate interreligious interactions, deepening cognitive and emotional engagement.

Leveraging AI for Personalized Religious Education and Resource Access

AI can personalize learning pathways and curate spiritual development resources, facilitating reflective learning experiences. Adaptive learning systems can customize content delivery to reflect diverse religious perspectives, fostering a more comprehensive and empathetic understanding of different faiths. Beyond academic settings, AI-powered applications can provide real-time access to religious teachings, making them significant in humanitarian initiatives and social campaigning, and enhancing religious access for minority groups who might have been excluded from traditional platforms.

The application of AI can move beyond reactive moderation to the active cultivation of positive interfaith relations. This transformation in religious practice and education involves creating digital spaces where mutual understanding, empathy, and respect are actively fostered, rather than merely protecting against harm. This represents a proactive and constructive role for AI in building a more pluralistic and harmonious digital society.

Table 2. Opportunities for AI in promoting religious tolerance and dialogue

Category	Specific AI Applications	Benefits for Religious Tolerance and Dialogue
Content & Discourse	Intelligent Content Suggestions (educational resources, empathy-building narratives, factual corrections)	Corrects misunderstandings, fosters empathy, provides evidence-based rebuttals.
	Positive Discourse Amplification	Actively cultivates positive online environments, drowns out harmful narratives.
	Counter-Narrative Generation	Provides alternative perspectives, challenges extremist ideologies.
Dialogue & Engagement	AI-driven Interfaith Dialogue Platforms (chatbots, virtual spaces)	Facilitates real-time, respectful communication across faiths; extends outreach beyond physical spaces.
	Sentiment Analysis in Discussions	Identifies implicit bias, guides civil discussions, offers faculty feedback for student well-being.
Education & Practice	Personalized Religious Education (adaptive learning systems, resource curation)	Customizes content to diverse religious perspectives, enhances comprehensive and empathetic understanding.
	Immersive Experiences (VR/AR for interreligious interactions)	Deepens cognitive and emotional engagement with diverse spiritual traditions.
	Real-time Access to Religious Teachings	Enhances religious access for minorities, supports humanitarian and social campaigning.
Community & Peacebuilding	Identification of "Intervention Points" in conversations	Allows for timely introduction of positive information, redirects discussions from conflict.
	Cross-border Interfaith Collaboration	Facilitates international peace discussions, supports joint advocacy on global issues (e.g., climate justice).
	Identification and Disabling of Malicious Accounts (bots)	Curbs automated spread of hate speech and disinformation.

Table 2 provides a structured overview of the proactive applications of AI that can actively contribute to fostering religious tolerance and dialogue. By presenting these opportunities, the table highlights AI's potential to move beyond merely detecting and removing harmful content. It underscores how AI can be strategically designed to cultivate positive online environments, facilitate meaningful interfaith engagement, and support personalized religious education, thereby actively contributing to peacebuilding efforts in the digital age.

Multi-Stakeholder Governance and Policy Frameworks

The effective and ethical deployment of AI in promoting religious tolerance necessitates robust governance frameworks and collaborative efforts across various stakeholders.

The Crucial Role of Human Oversight and "Human-in-the-Loop" Approaches

Human oversight is paramount in AI systems, especially in content moderation. AI should augment, not replace, human judgment, ensuring that ultimate human responsibility and accountability are maintained. Effective oversight requires human involvement to address the risks of false positives and negatives, which are particularly sensitive in religious contexts. Humans are essential for verifying and contextualizing information, identifying emerging tactics used by malicious actors, and continuously fine-tuning AI models. This "human-in-the-loop" approach ensures that ethical considerations and nuanced understanding of religious and cultural contexts remain central to AI deployment.

International Cooperation and Standards: UN, UNESCO, IEEE Guidelines

Addressing online religious hatred and misinformation requires a concerted global effort. International bodies are developing frameworks to guide responsible AI use:

- **United Nations Strategy and Global Digital Compact:** The UN Strategy and Plan of Action on Hate Speech emphasizes collaboration, particularly with technology and social media companies, in addressing hate speech. AI technologies are highlighted as powerful tools for early detection and conflict prevention, but their use must be guided by strong human rights protections to avoid potential misuse. UN Member States have reaffirmed their dedication to regulating AI responsibly under frameworks like the Global Digital Compact (GDC). The GDC is a comprehensive framework affirming governments' commitment to creating a safe, inclusive, and people-centered digital environment, highlighting the importance of digital public infrastructure (DPI) in closing connectivity and data gaps while supporting an inclusive digital ecosystem that respects human rights. The UN's cohesive framework for AI is driven by the High-Level Committee on Management Task Force on the Use of Artificial Intelligence in the United Nations System (HLCM TF-

AI), which aims to develop normative guidance and promote mechanisms for pooling technical capacity and knowledge sharing on AI.

- **UNESCO Recommendation on the Ethics of AI:** UNESCO produced the first-ever global standard on AI ethics in November 2021, applicable to all 194 member states. This recommendation emphasizes the protection of human rights and dignity as its cornerstone, based on principles such as transparency, fairness, and human oversight. It includes extensive Policy Action Areas to translate core values into action across various domains, including data governance, education, and social well-being.
- **IEEE AI Ethics Guidelines:** Organizations like the IEEE are exploring established ethics systems, including religious approaches, to address algorithmic design in autonomous and intelligent systems. Their work focuses on ensuring AI systems align with human values, addressing issues like algorithmic biases, fairness, accountability, and privacy.

Recommendations for Governments, Tech Companies, Civil Society, and Religious Leaders

- **Governments and Regulatory Bodies:**
    - Develop and enforce clear, adaptable legal and policy frameworks for AI content moderation that balance freedom of expression with harm prevention, ensuring cultural and linguistic sensitivity.
    - Invest in digital literacy and AI literacy campaigns to empower citizens to critically assess online information and identify harmful content.
    - Promote and fund interdisciplinary research into AI for religious tolerance, ensuring ethical considerations are embedded from design to deployment.
    - Require greater transparency from tech companies regarding their AI moderation algorithms and data practices, especially in the Global South.
- **Technology Companies:**
    - Prioritize "safety by design" in AI development, embedding ethical considerations and human rights protections from the outset, rather than reacting to crises.
    - Invest significantly in diverse, high-quality training datasets that reflect global linguistic and cultural nuances, particularly for low-resource languages, to mitigate algorithmic bias.
    - Implement robust human-in-the-loop systems that integrate human moderators' expertise for complex, nuanced content and provide mechanisms for user appeal and redress.

    - Collaborate with civil society organizations, academic institutions, and religious leaders to develop culturally sensitive AI solutions and community-specific moderation guidelines.
- **Civil Society Organizations and Human Rights Activists:**
    - Advocate for stronger regulatory frameworks and greater accountability from tech companies regarding AI content moderation and its human rights impact.
    - Engage in "red-teaming" exercises to identify potential misuses of generative AI by extremist groups and inform developers of emerging threats.
    - Develop and promote counter-narratives and educational resources, leveraging AI tools to amplify positive messages and foster interfaith dialogue.
- **Religious Leaders and Communities:**
    - Actively engage in the discourse around AI governance and development, ensuring that religious and ethical perspectives inform policy and technological design.
    - Utilize AI-powered platforms and social media to promote messages of peace, interfaith collaboration, and human rights, extending their reach globally.
    - Develop theological guidelines on AI use within their communities, promoting digital discernment among congregants, and using AI to enhance, not replace, spiritual development and pastoral care.

CONCLUSION: CHARTING A PATH FOR AI IN A PLURALISTIC WORLD

The digital age presents a profound paradox: while offering unprecedented connectivity, it has also become a fertile ground for the rapid and pervasive spread of religious hatred and misinformation. This phenomenon, fueled by the scale, speed, and anonymity of online platforms, exacerbated by algorithmic echo chambers, and complicated by the evolving sophistication and cultural nuances of harmful content, poses a direct threat to human rights, social cohesion, and international security. The unsustainability of manual content moderation, coupled with the demonstrable real-world impacts of online hate, underscores an urgent societal imperative for scalable and effective solutions.

Artificial intelligence has emerged as an indispensable tool in this critical fight. Advanced NLP and deep learning models, capable of contextual understanding and multimodal analysis, are proving increasingly effective in detecting nuanced hate speech and misinformation across diverse digital formats. Illustrative cases from major tech platforms demonstrate AI's capacity to proactively flag and reduce harmful content, although these significant improvements often follow periods of public scrutiny and documented harm. Beyond detection, AI offers transformative potential for actively promoting religious tolerance and dialogue through intelligent content suggestions, amplification of positive narratives, and the development of platforms for empathetic interfaith engagement.

However, the deployment of AI in such sensitive domains is fraught with ethical complexities. Algorithmic biases, stemming from non-representative training data and a lack of cultural nuance, can lead to discriminatory outcomes, particularly in the Global South, where "over-removal" of legitimate content and "slow removal" of harmful material are prevalent. The fundamental tension between freedom of expression and harm prevention is exacerbated by AI's limitations in understanding human intent and context, necessitating adherence to principles of transparency, fairness, and cultural sensitivity. Furthermore, the rise of generative AI introduces a new layer of challenge, lowering the barrier for malicious content creation and acting as a force multiplier for propaganda and deepfakes.

Towards a responsible future, continuous innovation in AI capabilities, including few-shot learning, explainable AI (XAI), and federated learning (FL), is crucial. XAI enhances interpretability and trust, while FL offers privacy-preserving solutions for collaborative content moderation. These advancements, coupled with ethical AI design, can foster positive interfaith relations by enabling AI-driven dialogue platforms and personalized religious education. Ultimately, charting a path for AI in a pluralistic world demands a multi-stakeholder approach. Human oversight remains paramount, ensuring that AI augments, rather than replaces, human judgment and responsibility. International cooperation, guided by frameworks from organizations like the UN and UNESCO, is essential for developing global standards. Governments, tech companies, civil society, and religious leaders must collaborate to develop and deploy AI systems that are technically robust, ethically sound, culturally sensitive, and truly serve the common good, safeguarding religious freedom and fostering a more tolerant and harmonious digital society.

Future research should focus on developing specific metrics for evaluating AI's effectiveness in reducing religious hate speech, exploring the long-term impacts of AI on religious identity and community formation, and conducting cross-cultural studies to inform the development of globally equitable AI ethics frameworks. A deeper understanding of how AI can be designed to proactively bridge divides, rather than merely detect them, will be central to realizing its full potential in promoting religious tolerance and dialogue.

REFERENCES

Balendra, S. (2025). Meta's AI moderation and free speech: Ongoing challenges in the Global South. *Cambridge Forum on AI: Law and Governance*, *1*, e21. Advance online publication. DOI: 10.1017/cfl.2025.5

Das, M., Raj, R., Saha, P., Mathew, B., Gupta, M., & Mukherjee, A. (2023). HateMM: A multi-modal dataset for hate video classification. *arXiv*. https://doi.org//arXiv.2305.03915DOI: 10.48550

Fonseca, A., Perera, S., Meedin, N., Caldera, M., Perera, I., & Ahangama, S. (2024). Analyzing hate speech dynamics on Twitter/X: Insights from conversational data and the impact of user interaction patterns.

Jahan, M. S., & Oussalah, M. (2023). A systematic review of hate speech automatic detection using natural language processing. *Neurocomputing*, *546*, 126232. Advance online publication. DOI: 10.1016/j.neucom.2023.126232

Khera, S. Anuradha, Singh, A., & Singh, K. K. (2025). Exploring multimodal hate speech detection using machine learning and deep learning models. In A. Singh & K. K. Singh (Eds.), *Multimodal generative AI*. Springer. https://doi.org/DOI: 10.1007/978-981-96-2355-6_11

Malik, J. S., Qiao, H., Pang, G., & van den Hengel, A. (2023). *Deep Learning for Hate Speech Detection: A Comparative Study*. arXiv. https://arxiv.org/abs/2202.09517

Mansur, Z., Omar, N., & Tiun, S. (2023). Twitter Hate Speech Detection: A Systematic Review of Methods, Taxonomy Analysis, Challenges, and Opportunities. *IEEE Access : Practical Innovations, Open Solutions*, *11*, 14065–14094. DOI: 10.1109/ACCESS.2023.3239375

Meegle. (2025). AI Ethics And Content Moderation. https://www.meegle.com/en_us/topics/ai-ethics/ai-ethics-and-content-moderation

Milvus. (2025). What are the societal benefits of federated learning? https://milvus.io/ai-quick-reference/what-are-the-societal-benefits-of-federated-learning

Perera, S., Meedin, N., Caldera, M., Perera, I., & Ahangama, S. (2023). A Comparative Study of the Characteristics of Hate Speech Propagators and Their Behaviours Over Twitter Social Media Platform. *Heliyon*, *9*(8), e19097. DOI: 10.1016/j.heliyon.2023.e19097 PMID: 37636360

Royal United Services Institute (RUSI). (2025). *Online Hate Speech and Discrimination in the Age of AI*. https://static.rusi.org/online-hate-speech-and-discrimination-in-the-age-of-ai-june-2025.pdf

Saeidnia, H. R., Hosseini, E., Lund, B., Tehrani, M. A., Zaker, S., & Molaei, S. (2025). Artificial intelligence in the battle against disinformation and misinformation: A systematic review of challenges and approaches. *Knowledge and Information Systems*, *67*(4), 3139–3158. Advance online publication. DOI: 10.1007/s10115-024-02337-7

Subramanian, M., Sathiskumar, V. E., Deepalakshmi, G., Cho, J., & Manikandan, G. (2023). A survey on hate speech detection and sentiment analysis using machine learning and deep learning models.

UN General Assembly. (2021). *Recommendation on the ethics of artificial intelligence*. https://digitallibrary.un.org/record/4062376?v=pdf

UNESCO. (2023). *Global Survey on the Impact of Online Disinformation on Democratic Processes and Human Rights*. https://www.unesco.org/sites/default/files/medias/fichiers/2023/11/unesco_ipsos_survey.pdf

Chapter 11
From Belief to Bandwidth: Navigating Freedom of Religion or Belief in the Age of Algorithms

Mishika Malik
https://orcid.org/0009-0002-0060-0965
Christ University, India

ABSTRACT

As our lives become increasingly intertwined with digital technology and way people experience and express religion is also continuously evolving. This one chapter explores how idea of FoRB is evolving in digital world over course of time, where smartphones, social media, algorithms have become everyday tools for faith, connection, control. While digital spaces can open up new opportunities for interfaith dialogue, spiritual exploration, community-building, they can also pose serious risks. Issues like online hate speech, digital surveillance, content moderation, algorithmic bias often challenge free expression of belief. This chapter will have a closer look at how FoRB operates in online environments by combining insights from international human rights law, digital sociology, case studies from around world. We here focus on examining how free belief truly is in age of internet, considering what it takes to protect that freedom when technology both connects and controls.

INTRODUCTION

In our hyper-connected world today, digital technology guides almost every aspect of everyday life, from communication and work to identity and community building and thus religion is no exception. From livestreamed church services and algorithm-driven devotionals to spiritual reels and AI-composed prayers, individuals are consistently interacting with religion through digital platforms. What was tra-

DOI: 10.4018/979-8-3373-3830-9.ch011

ditionally practiced mostly in material spaces such as temples, mosques, churches, and gurudwaras has now been carried over into cyberspaces, individual phones, public feeds, and international livestreams. This has widened the scope of religion and belief systems but made it more difficult to practice and also protect Freedom of Religion or Belief (FoRB) than most had envisaged at the same time.

FoRB is identified universally as a basic human fundamental right contained in Article 18 of the Universal Declaration of Human Rights and reaffirmed by the International Covenant on Civil and Political Rights. It ensures that all individuals have the freedom to adopt, convert from one religion or belief to another, or profess and practice a religion or belief of their choice alone or in community, in public or in private. These protections were initially intended for a world where systems of belief were practiced mostly offline and subject to physical laws, institutional hierarchies, and state regulation. Now, though, the central acts of belief,worship, preaching, meditation, religious instruction, proselytizing, are occurring on digital platforms subject to private tech firms and algorithmic regimes.

The internet has democratized religious practice in profound ways. Anyone with a smartphone and an internet connection can preach, pray, or engage in religious rituals without geographic limits and one thing that is coming to the surface with internet emerging trends is cross-cultural and cross-religion practices. These technologies have opened up sidelined or geographically fragmented communities to find visibility and spiritual fraternity. Research has observed that digital religiosity, particularly for the younger populations, provides a feeling of autonomy, curiosity, and malleable identity construction (Campbell, 2020).

However, the same platforms that provide freedom pose new risks as religious content is subject to ambiguous and inconsistent moderation norms. Social media posts are removed, hashtags get ghosted, and whole accounts are suspended under "hate speech" or "extremism." These tactics have an out of proportion impact on religious minorities, particularly in situations of political or ethnic conflict. For instance, in India, some Instagram users complained of the mysterious blocking of the #MuslimLivesMatter hashtag during protests in 2020. In China, Uyghur Muslim surveillance even reaches tracking Quran-reading applications and WeChat religious group conversations (Cheong, 2021). In these instances, online spaces intended for expression become areas of control, silence, and risk.

Meanwhile, religious practitioners on these sites undergo algorithmic curation meaning what they are allowed to see, what is advertised, and what is obscured is influenced by recommendation algorithms, trending scores, and engagement patterns. These mechanisms are not created with religious liberty in mind, and their central aim is not to advance pluralism or defend rights, but to maximize attention, advertising dollars, and site "safety." Consequently, religious content that is subtle, minority-oriented, or politically charged can be relegated, and religious material users can be steered into polarizing or commercialized content (Leibold, 2019).

The outcome is a paradox which is that the same digital infrastructure that opens windows for religious expression can also constrict and twist such expressions. They can facilitate the illusion of freedom meaning that because everyone can say something, but not everyone is being heard equally.

The virtual world has also dissolved the line between spiritual and profane. Religious memes, reels, and influencers combine divine messages with entertainment media. AI chatbots learning on religious scriptures now provide prayer recommendations and spiritual "advice." While these changes can facilitate the accessibility of spiritual practices, they also increase concern about appropriation, dilution, and commercialization of belief.

This changing dynamic between faith and technology also influences how people connect with their own spirituality. Digital religion tends to be personalized, on-demand, and performative. Believers can participate in virtual rituals with no communal participation, browse between multiple belief systems at once, or construct a spiritual identity that fits their online persona whereas others are fragmented or stripped of depth. Religious leaders and institutions also have new questions to address like how to retain authority when faith is crowdsourced or how to shape spiritual formation in a time of consumer spirituality.

FoRB in the digital age needs to be seen not only in legal or political terms, but also in cultural and technological terms (Bowring, 2010) No longer is it simply a matter of whether one can practice a religion, but of whether that practice is seen, safeguarded, and valued in the rapidly moving, commercially driven world of online platforms. Experts contend that more conventional human rights frameworks require immediate revision to capture these new realities and above all the expanding role of technology corporations in managing speech concerning belief (Bielefeldt, Pinto, & Petersen, 2022).

This chapter attempts to explore these intricate dynamics. It interrogates how FoRB is being recast in an era in which belief is streamed, monitored, and selectively boosted by machine learning algorithms. According to theoretical paradigms from digital sociology, human rights law, and platform governance, the chapter unmasks how digital life both facilitates and constrains freedom of belief.

In the end, this question is not a question about religion or technology but a question about power and who possesses it, how it is wielded, and who gets marginalized. By mapping the shift from sacred texts to screens, this chapter aims to shed light on the changing landscape of religious freedom in the digital age.

EVOLVING MEANING OF FREEDOM OF RELIGION OR BELIEF

Freedom of Religion or Belief (FoRB) is arguably the most universally accepted human right, though also among the least understood and most disparately secured. As societies increasingly become digitized and data-driven, the original and authentic meaning of FoRB is in the process of being remapped. No longer a matter of the right to practice in temples, mosques, churches, or homes, FoRB now has the immense plausibility to reach out and encompass cyberspace, platform-regulated spaces, and AI-mediated expression. The transition away from physical altars to digital feeds tells us something more profound that a belief itself is being transformed by the very frameworks that now transmit it (Cheong, 2021).

Historically, FoRB emerged in reaction to coercive religious governance under empires, monarchies, and colonial powers. The Treaty of Westphalia (1648) brought an end to Europe's religious conflicts and, meanwhile, also established the doctrine of state sovereignty in matters of religion. Subsequently, the famous Enlightenment philosophers such as John Locke and Voltaire have pinned their views on individual moral freedom in matters of conscience, a foundation for contemporary protections of religious liberty. These concepts found their culmination in the Universal Declaration of Human Rights, where Article 18 establishes the right to freedom of thought, conscience, and religion; moreover, the right to alter religion and manifest it in teaching, practice, and observance. The International Covenant on Civil and Political Rights brought these protections into binding international law.

Modern concepts of FoRB take it one step beyond and highlight dignity, non-coercion, and freedom to live one's belief in its entirety, even in pluralistic or hostile environments. The core of FoRB lies not only in tolerating religion but also in guaranteeing that people, whatever their majority, minority, indigenous group, or non-believing status, can live and express their faith meaningfully (Bielefeldt, Pinto, & Petersen, 2022).

Yet the legal framework that shaped FoRB was designed for an analog world. It was constructed to guard physical manifestations of belief: religious icons, physical congregations, printed books, and formal communities. Now, all those manifestations have drifted mainly online and towards the screens. People nowadays go to virtual prayers, broadcast religious sermons, and participate in spiritual discussions through social media platforms. These platforms are now the new public square regulated not by international law, but by terms of service, shadowy community guidelines, and increasingly, AI systems trained on partial or biased data (Grandinetti, 2020).

This is a significant change in who regulates religious expression. Once, states were the main enforcers or abusers of FoRB. Today, private technology firms and AI systems are global gatekeepers. Social media platforms such as Meta, TikTok, and YouTube determine what types of religious content are permissible, what is promoted, and what is taken down. These choices are applied through a combination of human moderators and AI-driven automated systems (Binns, 2020).

Although AI moderation is programmed to detect hate speech and disinformation, it poses severe concerns in the context of FoRB. AI has no concept of religious nuance and has no way of consistently distinguishing between a call to violence and a religious term that is used in the context of debating theology. For instance, words like jihad, martyrdom, or conversion are usually flagged, blacklisted or deleted even when used in permissible religious learning or discourse (Binns, 2020). This has resulted in instances where Islamic scholars have had their sermons deleted, or where Christian pages giving an overview of missionary work were inadvertently classified as hate content.

Well-driven research showed that more than 40% of religious YouTubers reported experiencing algorithmic censorship or demonetization, particularly when speaking of politically charged or misunderstood religious subjects. Most described feeling censored not out of malice, but out of ignorance and which was considered as digital marginalization according to them (Grandinetti,2020).

AI not only moderates but also curates. Algorithms determine what shows up in your feed, which accounts are suggested, and what gets relegated to the edges. Research with experiments on algorithmic bias reveals that search results for religion tend to mirror commercial, sensationalist, or even discriminatory trends, particularly when searching for marginalized or non-Western religions. (Noble, 2018). This builds user expectations about what constitutes "authentic" faith, favoring mainstream narratives and pushing aside quieter, more nuanced expressions of religiosity.

The confluence of state authority, AI, and surveillance is even more troubling. In nations such as China, artificial intelligence has made the systematic monitoring of religious activities possible. Facial monitoring cameras at mosques, keyword surveillance on apps and app data collection from Quran apps are utilized to develop profiles of "risky" believers (UNHRC, 2018). Algorithms might label a person as a potential extremist based on prayer routines or religious app usage, without any human intervention. That terrifying degree of surveillance compels people into self-censorship, undermining not only FoRB but also trust, community, and faith.

But it's not just authoritarian governments. Spirituality itself is being rebranded by algorithmic means. AI chatbots educated on religious literature now provide prayer recommendations and theological musings. Meditation apps base recommendations on biometric information on mantras, or scripture. Although such technology can improve access, particularly for the disabled or geographically remote, it also threatens to fragment religion into pieces, commodifying spiritual rituals into measured, gamified content (Campbell, 2020). In making belief convenient, there is a risk of making it superficial.

This intersection of FoRB and AI leads to an important question: Will religious freedom be able to persist in systems that are designed not to support belief in any way? Legal systems are constructed to defend pluralism, compassion, and conscience, and AI is made to maximize interaction, impose generalized "safety," and serve commercial purposes. Without intentional ethical oversight, such systems have the potential to misrepresent, stifle, or unwittingly penalize certain types of belief, particularly those that are not Western, secular, or mainstream in character.

There is however a growing concern, and thus resistance steps in. Civil society groups, online rights campaigners, and faith communities are calling for faith-sensitive algorithmic ethics. Recommendations range from training AI on religiously diverse data, engaging faith scholars in content moderation design, and requiring platforms to submit transparency reports detailing how they manage religious content. A particular interest is the potential case of Mozilla's Responsible AI Challenge, where one proposal had guidelines specifically for safeguarding spiritual and indigenous expressions of data in tech contexts.

Finally, charting the path of FoRB spaces to the internet, and now into AI-determined structures, sheds light on the fact that we are not merely moving beliefs from one medium to another but recreating them. In this environment, the query is not merely "Are you free to speak your truth?" but also "Will your truth be heard, visible, or silenced by a machine? As systems of belief increasingly set in line with code, computation, and commercial platforms, there is a high necessity for FoRB to develop not just as a legal protection, but as a digital and ethical design principle.

EXPRESSION OF FAITH IN A DIGITAL ERA

The Internet was once envisioned as a zone of absolute freedom, meaning one where individuals might speak their ideas, identities, and beliefs unobstructed by boundaries. But in practice, things are more complex and complicated, particularly when it comes to living out our faith on the Internet. For many people today, the articulation of belief is more than simply showing up for a service or reading religious texts and expanding more into a developing culture like sharing a prayer on Instagram, attending a virtual satsang, listening to a sermon on YouTube, or posing theological queries anonymously on Reddit. Religion has moved online and so have the manners in which individuals experience and are restricted in freedom of religion or belief (FoRB) have shifted.

To a great extent, this online shift has opened up access to religion. For instance, now a young girl in a conservative town can be part of an interfaith prayer circle on an online meeting platform or a Dalit Christian young person in India can listen to sermons without any bias or class or caste differences. Tales are not uncommon anymore for an artist to upload their respective content and connect with various people on different continents and moreover from diverse religious backgrounds or with distinct sets of belief. This phenomenon has been referred to as "networked religion," whereby religion is no longer restricted to a physical or geographical location, but digital visibility through the means of hashtags, followers, and livestreams (Campbell & Tsuria,2021)

By referring to a particular case of how popular the Ram Mandir virtual darshan campaign was during the COVID-19 lockdown as an example we witnessed an inflated surge in practicing religion through digitalization even during the time of world crisis. While temples closed their gates, millions went to YouTube, Facebook Live, and specialized apps to view rituals live in real time, rekindling a sense of community in a period of confinement. In the same vein, international Muslim communities observed Taraweeh prayers live from Mecca, streamed into their living rooms via Ramadan. These weren't mere videos, but they were spiritual lifelines for many individuals and moreover for various communities, (Campbell, 2020).

But while online communities provide fertile ground for deep religious participation, they are also seen as breeding ground for new obstacles as well. Sites reward with visibility the content that is liked, shared, and commented on but not the content that is theologically astute or spiritually enriching. And so, religious artists tend to be forced to produce click-it spirituality and walk on a path that is more entertaining rather than informative. Simultaneously, there are new concepts that are arising with the trends of digitalization, for illustration, a few churches now hire full production crews for Sunday broadcasts. Consequently, many Muslim influencers find it difficult to balance modesty with platform visibility. It can be said that many personal moments, such as prayer or sorrow, are sometimes constructed based on what works online (Hutchings, 2017).

Even more disturbing are instances where platform regulations directly conflict with religious expression. In India, a number of short videos featuring women speaking about their right to hijab were taken down under the "hate speech" policy of the platform, despite of the fact that the videos were non-violent and individual. This was amidst the wider national discussion around banning hijabs in schools across the country in 2022, leaving many Muslim women subjected to online silencing when they wanted to be heard. The concerned application then explained that portions of the content had been identified by automated filters, and it misinterpreted the political and religious context (Binns, 2020).

Other upscale examples are the removal of Zakir Naik's videos from Facebook and YouTube where some of Naik's videos were appropriately targeted for hate speech, but others were taken down as well that had harmless theological debates, which included religious words such as "jihad" that AI-based content filtering tools misinterpreted. The risk here isn't merely censorship but is misunderstanding, and this misunderstanding is being implemented into the algorithms that mediate what the world views online (Naudts, 2021).

These problems are not just for believers but also ex-believers and religion critics alike who take online spaces to speak their minds and sometimes consider it as the only place to do so safely. In nations such as Saudi Arabia, Iran, or Pakistan, visiting or commenting in such spaces is risky and it is also noted that Middle Eastern nations have even actively blocked subreddits related to religion in the name of "extremism" and others monitor these spaces through surveillance software. For many users, remaining anonymous online isn't just a preference but is a survival (Bielefeldt, Pinto, & Petersen, 2022).

So, ultimately, we're left with a paradox wherein on one hand, the Internet amplifies religious diversity like never before but on the other, it also gives rise to new gatekeepers, that is, private tech companies and AI systems which decide what gets seen, what gets suppressed, and what gets flagged. And these systems are not necessarily culturally competent. They tend to perform based on training data that is lacking in representation from non-Western, non-Christian religious contexts (Noble, 2018). That is, material from Hindu rituals, Islamic debates, or indigenous ceremonies is more likely to be misinterpreted or deleted.

This tension is worked out most clearly on religious minorities and vulnerable groups in the sense that their work is frequently flagged, shadow-banned, or overwhelmed by more moderate religious voices. And when there is harassment such as prostitution, queer spiritual leaders or trolling progressive theologians, social media platforms act slowly, if at all. These protection gaps can make individuals feel as though their freedom to believe or disbelieve is contingent on conforming to the algorithm.

But in all this complexity, there are also tales of hope, resilience, and ingenuity as seen at the time of the second wave of the COVID-19 pandemic in India where Instagram was filled with interfaith healing prayers. Using hashtags such as #InThisTogether and #PrayForIndia, Muslims, Hindus, Sikhs, Christians, and atheists shared their prayers from across religions and no religion, bound together in virtual solidarity. It wasn't institutionalized by any organization but was grassroots, digital spirituality in practice. It plainly demonstrated how faith can bridge lines when platforms facilitate not constrain (Cheong, 2021).

Another heartening trend is the emergence of AI-enabled religious apps when used responsibly. Hindu "Sadhana," Muslim "Qalbox," and Christian "Pray.com" apps provide personalized religious content, such as prayers, chants, and reminders. Ethically designed, these apps aid accessibility, particularly for populations that include the elderly, disabled, or geographically separated. But they also pose difficult yet serious questions about whether we are over-automating faith or are we commodifying sacred experience as data entry and notifications. (Campbell, 2020)

Still, it would be unfair to suggest tech is the villain here. Many platform developers simply aren't aware of how deeply FoRB intersects with design choices. That's why digital rights activists have begun pushing for faith-aware moderation policies which are heard by some platforms, for example, in 2022, Instagram reviewed its nudity policy after Hindu and Pagan communities protested the removal of sacred art and similarly Twitter (now X) introduced optional filters to protect religious content from misclassification. Religious thinkers, technology innovators, human rights attorneys, and community activists need to collaborate to make platforms safe for belief, doubt, dissent, and ritual.

Ultimately, the online world is not just a mirror of religion but is a part of it. The issue isn't if you can freely practice your faith online, however, whether or not that practice is viewed, comprehended, and honored by the platforms that harbor it. Conclusively, it's about seeing the holy in the digital and making sure that faith, in all its iterations, has room to breathe even in code.

ALGORITHMIC DILEMMA

As artificial intelligence silently becomes the digital world's nervous system, it more and more influences how beliefs are expressed, tracked, and sometimes suppressed. This quiet but profound transformation asks pressing questions which include will religious freedom be able to coexist in systems never intended to preserve it, what occurs when belief meets machine logic and most importantly how do we protect FoRB when threats aren't ever-present but insidiously embedded in code.

The first architects of AI systems could never have dreamed that their tools would ever shape religious rights. AI was meant to optimize traffic, automate factories, and make search engines better. But now it is AI that decides what religious content is flagged, whose religious posts are deleted, and whose online rituals discover their people. It doesn't patrol in uniform or wear a badge. It simply makes a decision.

Consider, for example, the symbiotic relationship between content moderation and AI. Various social media platforms nowadays all depend heavily on machine learning algorithms to identify and remove "harmful" or "violating" content. While this has been successful in lessening online extremism, it has also resulted in the wrongful removal of legitimate religious speech. Terms such as "jihad," "martyrdom," or "conversion" are frequently classified as hate speech or terror-related terms irrespective of theological context. It has been established that automated moderation disproportionately affects religious minorities, particularly those from Muslim and indigenous communities, whose language and practices do not meet Western algorithmic standards (Basu & Sen, 2023).

Worst of all is how AI impacts not only content but visibility. Algorithms decide which posts get promoted, which get buried. Studies on algorithmic bias show that search engines tend to reinforce stereotypes, displaying Islam-related items as radical or Hindu rituals as superstitious even when neutral or positive items are available (Noble,2018). Effectively, religious expression is no longer merely the right to speak but about having the right to be heard and discovered.

However, the stakes increase when we look beyond platforms to state AI use. In despotic states, AI-powered surveillance systems are used to monitor religious activity in bone-chilling detail. The most-widely cited example is the case of Uyghur Muslims in Xinjiang, China, where mosques are watched by facial recognition cameras, AI-sorted phone data, and predictive policing algorithms monitor who prays, when, and how frequently. Those found to be "too pious" can be sent to re-education camps (UNHRC, 2018). Most Uyghurs don't realize they're being monitored until repercussions come. Their FoRB is violated not at the time of act but in the unseeing eyes upon it.

Even in democratic nations, the convergence of religion and AI creates ethical alarms. For instance, India's Aadhaar system, while not an AI per se, is frequently utilized with AI-powered surveillance tools and questions about how religious profiling might occur through data collection. In the midst of communal tensions, the tools may be used to target certain communities. All these indicate that AI is no longer neutral infrastructure but is seen as a political ground.

But AI extends beyond surveillance or oppression. It remakes the practice of belief, too. AI-driven apps such as Qalbox, Bible AI, or Sadhana provide individuals with personalized faith experiences: personalized prayers, spiritual prompts, and even AI-computed interpretations of scriptures. Although it is convenient, perhaps, but dangerously at risk of reducing religion to an algorithmic regimen. Users might be more likely to depend on recommendation than introspection, and belief can then be a passive scroll instead of an active exploration. The digitalization of piety has the power to transform spirituality from a richly experienced process into a sequence of maximized habits (Campbell,2020).

This leads to the ethical conundrum that AI is designed to be efficient and not empathetic. It has no comprehension of intention, context, or conscience. Legal instruments such as the Universal Declaration of Human Rights and the ICCPR were authored for the preservation of human dignity rather than to be interpreted by computers. Therefore, what happens when AI becomes the de facto interpreter of FoRB?

One possibility would be to insert human rights principles into algorithms directly.That involves integrating FoRB experts, theologians, and ethicists into the design of AI systems—particularly for moderation, search, and recommendation. For instance, it has been suggested that there needs to be "human-in-the-loop" models where contentious content is identified by AI but evaluated by human moderators who are trained in cultural and religious literacy (Cheong, 2021). Twitter's (now X) 2022 pilot program, in which it introduced optional religious-sensitivity filters for its moderation boots, is an early step in that direction.

The second solution is algorithmic transparency. Sites must release frequent reports about how religious material is censored, what words get censored, and what system of appeal exists. The same way that governments must be transparent about freedom-of-religion abuse, so now must technology giants whose choices determine global discourse.

Furthermore, we require regulatory authorities that are familiar with both technology and rights. Governments have started establishing AI ethics committees, but few of them have FoRB as a category of concern. In the absence of this, religious material can be an easy casualty in "safety" policies of wider scope. In a surveillance capitalism world, freedom needs to be fought for not only from states but also from systems designed to anticipate and manipulate human behavior.

Notably, there is increasing resistance. In India, local digital literacy movements are empowering tribal and Dalit groups to stake out online religious space. Underground feminist theologians in Iran are producing encrypted podcasts. In the United States, AI ethics researchers are collaborating with interfaith organizations to chart biases in language models. They are tiny movements, but they indicate a moral imagination coming up against techno-determinism. At its essence, the problem of FoRB in the AI era is this: Machines are being asked to make sense of belief, but belief is not data. It is emotion, tradition, dissent, community, and mystery. It resists categorization. Any system that wishes to be respectful of FoRB must be adaptive, open, and humble. It must be able to see that faith is lived, not logged.

The AI revolution does not need to eradicate religious freedom, but it will, if we fail to act urgently and in advance. We are at a fork in the road: either belief is another goal to be optimized, or it is a sacred liberty to be safeguarded even in tomorrow's circuits and codes.

RESISTANCE, RECLAMATION, AND REFORM

At a time when digital systems more and more determine what we are able to say, share, and believe, faith and conscience communities are not just passive consumers of technology. They are becoming proactive actors of resistance and innovation. On different continents and belief traditions, people and institutions are taking back their right to Freedom of Religion or Belief (FoRB) in digital contexts not simply by resisting algorithmic injustices, but by rethinking how belief can thrive in an AI-made world.

Resistance is about awareness. The public is unaware of how much algorithms are influencing religious expression. However digital rights campaigners, interfaith organizations, and researchers are raising alarms about this silent censorship. For example, the Internet Freedom Foundation in India has complained about how religious hashtags of minority festivals during sensitive times are algorithmically downranked. Similarly, organizations like Access Now and ARTICLE 19 have indicated that minority religions' online content is disproportionately censored, particularly in war zones. They call for greater transparency about content moderation as well as algorithmic audits, considering religious bias.

Another dramatic instance of grassroots resistance was in 2021, when Instagram continuously deleted artwork posted by Hindu and indigenous artists based on its "nudity" policy. The photos were of deities that were presented traditionally in a culturally revered way. In response, a global campaign tagged #DontDeleteMyGod became viral in which different users resort to sharing their holy images, challenging the algorithmic erasure of culture and religion. The campaign eventually led Instagram to clarify its policies and establish a review process for culturally sensitive content (Cheong, 2021).

Alongside reactive resistance, there are also proactive movements of reclamation. Religious publics are establishing their own online spaces, safe from the atrocities of commercial algorithms. Platforms such as UmmahHub (a Muslim social network app), Faithlife (for Christians), and Sangha Live (for Buddhists) for instance allow users to engage in faith-based content without fear of shadow banning or decontextualized censorship. Such websites prioritize things such as privacy, purposeful engagement, and theological integrity over virality.

Reclamation also involves educating believers about their online rights. Interfaith tech literacy workshops are being planned in the likes of Nairobi, Jakarta, and Sao Paulo to help users learn when their content is being unfairly censored, how to appeal platform decisions, and how to use encryption tools to discuss sensitive matters of belief securely. In other areas, including Sub-Saharan Africa and Latin America, the workshops are also arenas of religious solidarity, where individuals from different religious backgrounds share moments of digital exclusion.

The legal sector is not lagging behind. It is increasingly realized that international human rights law must be adapted to reflect AI's influence on FoRB.Certain legal thinkers have started to start advocating for Article 18 of the ICCPR to be amended in express terms to provide protection for online religious expression and algorithmic nondiscrimination. In 2023, certain NGOs and legal thinkers made an application to the UN Special Rapporteur on FoRB to request that the General Assembly adopt a new General Comment on the interpretation of how FoRB is implemented in the digital era. The remark is sure to encompass such topics as content moderation, platform accountability, and states' use of predictive technologies.

Tech developers themselves are becoming part of the solution in the process. The new discipline of "faith-aware design" calls upon platforms to embed ethical controls that take religion into account. Others are testing AI models that can flag religious-sensitive content to be reviewed by humans, rather than deleted. Meta's Oversight Board, while still contentious, has ruled on cases of religious speech and is establishing precedents that take worldwide cultural contexts into consideration.

There also exist new examples of faith communities and tech entrepreneurs collaborating. Code together with Conscience, a pilot initiative in Germany, brought together Muslim, Jewish, and Christian religious leaders with software developers to collaborate on content moderation standards respectful of religious speech. Digital rights attorneys in India have collaborated with Dalit and Adivasi religious leaders on tracking algorithmic discrimination against local language content.

Young people are at the center of much of this upheaval. On college campuses and in internet forums, young believers and doubters alike are calling to account technology companies. They're employing the very technologies of the era, be it podcasts, hashtags, open letters, code repositories to claim their right to believe, to doubt, to question, and to speak.

These mobilizations are not easy. It requires resources, scale, and user trust to build independent religion-based platforms. Legal reform is slow and often resisted by entrenched tech lobbies and moreover not all communities enjoy equal access to digital literacy or legal advocacy. But still, despite these barriers, the momentum is undeniable.

What we are seeing is not only a call for digital equality, but a more profound redefinition of religious freedom itself. FoRB in this era needs to go beyond tolerance and be about inclusion, representation, and empowerment. The right to believe cannot be properly safeguarded unless it encompasses the right to voice that belief in terms that are understood, heard, and respectfully mediated.

In some sense, these acts of resistance and reclamation are sacred in and of themselves. They inform us that belief is not fixed but it constantly changes, evolves, and sometimes it pushes back. And in an age when lines of code can determine the parameters of conscience, the act of declaring one's faith or skepticism in cyberspace becomes a spiritual and political act.

The challenge at hand is transparent: to envision systems that not only tolerate belief but positively protect it. Systems that view religious expression not as a threat to be contained, but as right to be upheld. And to make that happen, we're going to require a union of clerics and coders, activists and engineers, believers and atheists, working together to make certain that freedom to believe endures, even in the age of the algorithm.

REPROGRAMMING THE BELIEF

The last sections before this have led to the implication that the virtual world doesn't merely mimic the freedoms and the limitations of the real one. It remakes them. And nowhere is this as evident as in the instance of Freedom of Religion or Belief (FoRB). Now, what we can do differently for all the dilemmas that have been mentioned below.

The good news is that we're not beginning at square one. Globally, a variety of actors are already building the framework for a technology future that honors FoRB, however, what we require now is a clear map which is a dynamic, evolving, rights-centered approach that recognizes the richness of belief in the digital world and constructs systems that enable it.

Design with Dignity in Mind

Technology is not existent in some sort of vacuum. Each line of code has the values of its developers on it. That's why designers and developers need to be educated to think about FoRB not as a principle of law, but as lived experience. Faith-aware design is knowing that "one-size-fits-all" moderation doesn't apply to religion. It's creating moderation systems that account for cultural context, theological language, and minority representation. We've already witnessed tiny glimpses: Meta's in-house teams advising interfaith communities; Instagram modifying its nudity policy following removals of sacred art; Google collaborating with Hindi and Tamil language theologians to minimize algorithmic misclassification. But these can't be solitary gestures. We want worldwide, institutionalized efforts that integrate human rights into the tech pipeline from ideation to launch.

Shift from Control to Care

Existing platform models view religious content mainly as a liability, something that could potentially break rules or cause controversy. Moreover, we could invert this point of view and also view it from a different angle altogether exploring the main concerns like what if platforms viewed expression of faith as care work, community development, and meaning making about how to live in the world. Instead of simply erasing or concealing religious posts, sites might bring in tiered tools: context labels, voluntary content warnings (not auto-bans), and peer review networks composed of skilled faith advisors. This method is more care ethics than compliance ethics and it views belief not as a "risk factor" but as a human condition to be held gently and wisely.

Bridge Technologists and Theologians

One of the most promising ways forward is co-creation. Picture hackathons with software developers sitting next to monks, rabbis, atheists, and indigenous scholars. Not to argue theology, but to construct tools that function across belief systems. Picture AI systems learning not merely from linguistic data, but from narratives, parables, psalms, and proverbs from traditions worldwide. These collaborative projects would not merely produce superior tech but they'd produce mutual understanding. Already, there are pilot initiatives doing just that. In South Africa, a group of Zulu Christian developers and sangoma elders have introduced a translation app that honors biblical and ancestral linguistic specifics. In Indonesia, Islamic AI research centers are working on how to develop bots that can describe Shariah concepts without activating moderation flags. These aren't regarded as some fringe tests but the future in action.

Create Digital Sanctuary Zones

FoRB in the digital era also requires spatial metaphors: sanctuaries. Like temples and mosques serve as spiritual havens, we require virtual spaces where individuals are able to venture and express their faith without monitoring, derision, or algorithmic invisibility. These might be in the form of encrypted communities, alternative social networks, or even time-based virtual spaces that are organized around religious festivals. Crucially, they have to be accessible not only to the tech elite but also to those with slow bandwidth, education, or mobility. This is an issue of both digital justice and spiritual equity (Krüger & Oliver, 2023).

Legal Evolution, Not Just Protection

Lastly, law needs to change. not in response, but in anticipation. As environmental rights transitioned from marginal issues to core precept, so too will FoRB in technological regulation. This involves: Amending the ICCPR's General Comment 22 to add digital FoRB by name, establishing international algorithmic auditing frameworks on the basis of religious prejudice, requiring platforms to publish content removal transparency reports. None of this will be simple. But legal innovation has trailed cultural change. The digital realm has transformed our cultures, and our laws must now follow.

This isn't a matter of romanticizing faith or demonizing technology. It's the acknowledgment that both have an influence over who we are, and who we can be. A rights-based future for tech isn't about creating perfect systems. It's about creating better ones, ones that grasp belief not as spam to be blocked, but as a signal to be boosted because ultimately, to defend FoRB is not to save religion. It is to save our common right to meaning.

FROM MARGINS TO MOVEMENTS

Whereas most of the debate about digital FoRB is policy or surveillance, there is a lesser-acknowledged, often unremarked reality: not all believers move in virtual spaces the same way. For individuals at faith/margin intersections: minority faiths, LGBTQ+ faiths, women's faiths, indigenous peoples, the internet is both lifeline and minefield.

Intersectionality teaches us that religious freedom is a phenomenon influenced by variables beyond belief. Gender, caste, ethnicity, sexuality, economic status, and geography all play a role in the ability to engage in religious expression. Despite FoRB being legally enshrined, its online expression is anything but equal, and the divide between theory and reality is widening in an increasingly algorithm-driven world.

Minority religious groups such as Ahmadiyya Muslims, Baha'is, and Sikhs tend to be algorithmically suppressed, made invisible, or subject to targeted abuse. Their material may be taken down, downranked, or mass-reported and therefore they would engage in self-censorship. Dalit Christians and Dalit Hindus in South Asia get de-platformed and harassed online when they challenge dominant caste interpretations or advocate for justice within faith regimes. Their visibility gets interpreted as provocation and not expression, and this offline exclusion only reinforces offline discrimination.

LGBTQ+ theists are uniquely at risk. Social media allows queer theology investigation and community building, but also views such content widely flagged by moderation algorithms as "sensitive," "controversial," or "viating" community standards based on heteronormative religious interpretation (Binns, 2020).

In a study conducted in 2022, the Digital Rights Foundation discovered that queer religious content creators are far more likely to be targeted by hate speech and platform take-downs. Terms such as "queer Muslim" or "trans pastor" become algorithmic flags for warning despite their validity. Not only do these failures affect freedom of speech but also the psychological and spiritual welfare of such groups, locking them further into a sense of isolation from both conventional religious contexts and online public domains.

Women of faith, particularly within patriarchal religious worlds, are harassed online when they take on reinterpretation, leadership, or visibility regarding topics such as menstruation, clergy roles, or spiritual authority. Platforms label abusive interaction as "debate" rather than offering protection, leading to silencing instead of support (Campbell, 2020). Their work is policed in manners that reflect their off-line marginalization, and for most, on-line participation is an emotionally draining play-off between empowerment and backlash. Despite this, many women are leading vibrant on-line movements, reclaiming hallowed texts and roles using feminist theology, narrative, and collective activism.

Native practitioners also face another barrier—epistemic misrecognition. Their visual, oral, and ritualistic religious practices are poorly understood by text-based, Western-coded AI systems. Algorithms are likely to label their practices as "superstition" or "misinformation," blocking preservation and transmission of native religions on-line. Moreover, commercialization of indigenous rituals on the part of influencers and promotional websites truncates spiritual meaning and feeding cultural appropriation. The erasure enacted online is further exacerbated by a lack of infrastructure and voice in platform decision-making, which gives indigenous communities little leverage or visibility.

And yet, in the midst of all this, resistance blooms. In Myanmar, Buddhist peace activists created encrypted Telegram groups to push back against the wave of anti-Rohingya discourse on Facebook. By drawing empathetic scripture and ethical narratives, they reconstituted portions of the digital sangha centered on peace. Their work demonstrates the potential of theological literacy as a counter-narrative to extremism.

In the US, Black churches used livestreaming, TikTok theology, and interfaith town halls to incorporate worship and activism during the pandemic and the years following. Their messages and sermons addressed systemic racism, spiritual rebirth, and intergenerational conversations utilizing technology as a pulpit for change. Numerous well-known leaders have taught millions, using virtual faith as a force of empowerment and public witness.

In Iran, underground Zoroastrian and Christian networks use encrypted services such as ProtonMail and Signal to read Scripture, exchange devotionals, and coordinate spiritual support under the peak of state surveillance. Such virtual communities are sacred spaces, they resist state oppression by secure communication and demonstrate the importance of digital independence in dictatorial environments.

Faith communities like Faith for the Web, Sacred Cyberspace, and the Muslim Tech Collective are pioneering this work. They create open-source repositories and decentralized networks that allow diverse people to access theology, co-create digital rituals, and record lived religious experience. These groups seek not only to guard belief but to code sanctity into digital space design. They refuse the concept of tech religious neutrality and advocate for design justice based on spiritual diversity.

Artistic activism is critical to reimaging FoRB. Hashtags such as #MyFaithMyVoice, #DigitalSutras, and #QueerQuran translate scripture into spoken word, protest art, and music video. They push back against erasure by making theology a public performance, reclaiming visibility through voice, movement, and metaphor.

For example, the online arts collective "Sacred Rebellion" produces immersive digital exhibitions navigating spiritual trauma and healing from marginalized viewpoints, integrating visual culture and theology.

What is common to these movements is a common refusal to be deleted. Whether through end-to-end encrypted worship or algorithmic resistance, excluded believers are not simply conforming to present systems, rebuilding them. Digital FoRB is now less a matter of permission than participation. These communities will not wait for platforms or policies to invite them in. Rather, they are fashioning alternative, spiritually dense ecosystems that celebrate complexity and collective strength.

To support this momentum, key interventions are required. Moderation systems need to be audited for not just hate speech accuracy but also for bias against underrepresented forms of belief. Faith literacy education must be incorporated into algorithm creation with advisory boards made up of an assortment of traditions. Appeals systems must make themselves multilingual and culture-aware to serve users globally. Empowerment-centered digital literacy programs are a pragmatic necessity—educating queer believers in online protection, defending women religious leaders from cyber-attack, and enabling indigenous people to maintain their culture with dignity. Investment must be made in digital sanctuaries not driven by profit-generating algorithms, community-driven platforms emphasizing access, privacy, and fidelity integrity.

Governments and international organizations need to make tech companies accountable, not only for free speech, but for spiritual safety. Seminaries and religious educators also have a role to play in creating curricula on digital ethics so that the next generation of faith leaders can appreciate the digital aspects of FoRB.

FoRB in the digital era is not simply about protecting the right to hold beliefs but about creating the conditions to express, share, and live out those beliefs in a genuine way. It's about taking back voice, space, and sacred presence within spaces that were never meant for such a degree of diversity.

It is, in the end, not a story of loss. It is a story of tenuous, revolutionary hope. When code and conscience intersect with faith, something akin to alchemy occurs: practice of shared revolt, an inclusive canvas, and a journey toward digital holiness. The excluded believers are not awaiting inclusion; they are constructing what they require. By doing so, they are redefining freedom of belief in the age of the algorithm.

CONCLUSION

The path through intersections of religion, technology, and power reveals both extreme threats and unprecedented opportunities. Freedom of Religion or Belief is no longer limited to physical locations or classic legal defenses; it instead plays out on algorithmic timelines, in hidden chat rooms, and across global networks where human and artificial actors construct religious visibility and vulnerability.

We have seen how minority religions, LGBTQ+ faith believers, women of faith, and indigenous religious followers navigate virtual spaces differently and consistently encounter new forms of suppression, harassment, or misrepresentation. But through such adversity is a strong center of self-determination and innovation. Communities are not just existing in virtual realms, they are recharting them, bringing along values of spirituality, dignity, and inclusivity.

If FoRB is going to flourish within this new world, it must be reimagined in a positive direction. Legal frameworks must be addressed to take a deeper look at the problem of algorithmic bias and speech regulation by corporations. Technology companies moreover must integrate faith literacy into their design and moderation processes, and civil society must have open accountability. Religious leaders, scholars, and human rights activists also must engage with one another to make sure digital literacy incorporates the capacity to protect and express faith online.

The digital world, with all its imperfections, is still an uncharted platform for intercultural conversation, theological innovation, and community formation. The query is not if FoRB may flourish in the algorithm age, but it is if we have the courage, vision, and collective will to enable it to do so. By making the voices of marginalized communities central, challenging structural injustices, and integrating human rights into the core of our social media platforms, we can build online communities where faith is not just tolerated but valued.

Ultimately, ensuring FoRB online is not a technical challenge in isolation, instead it is a moral calling. It challenges us on the grounds of empathy, to legislate with humanity, and to envision a digital common where all consciences, philosophies, and faiths may have space to exist. The rewards are great, but so are the risks, a universe in which the right to believe, doubt, worship, or dissent is as ordinary online as it is offline, and as well-entrenched in the cloud as it is in the cathedral.

REFERENCES

Basu, S., & Sen, S. (2023). Silenced voices: Unravelling India's dissent crisis through historical and contemporary analysis of free speech and suppression. *Information & Communications Technology Law*, *33*(1), 42–65. DOI: 10.1080/13600834.2023.2249780

Bielefeldt, H., Pinto, T. A., & Petersen, M. J. (2022). Introduction: Freedom of Religion or Belief as a Human Right. *The Review of Faith & International Affairs*, *20*(2), 1–12. DOI: 10.1080/15570274.2022.2065799

Binns, R. (2020). Human Judgment in algorithmic loops: Individual justice and automated decision-making. *Regulation & Governance*. Advance online publication. DOI: 10.1111/rego.12358

Bowring, B. (2010). *Manual on the Wearing of Religious Symbols in Public Areas*. Security and Human Rights., DOI: 10.1163/187502310791305927

Campbell, H. A., & Evolvi, G. (2020). Contextualizing current digital religion research on emerging technologies. *Human Behavior and Emerging Technologies*, *2*(1), 5–17. DOI: 10.1002/hbe2.149

Campbell, H. A., & Tsuria, R. (Eds.). (2021). *Digital Religion: Understanding Religious Practice in Digital Media* (2nd ed.). Routledge., DOI: 10.4324/9780429295683

Cheong, P. H. (2021). Bounded Religious Automation at Work: Communicating Human Authority in Artificial Intelligence Networks. *The Journal of Communication Inquiry*, *45*(1), 5–23. DOI: 10.1177/0196859920977133

Digital Rights Foundation. (2022). *Gendered disinformation and online violence in South Asia*. https://digitalrightsfoundation.pk

Grandinetti, J. (2020). Examining embedded apparatuses of AI in Facebook and TikTok. *AI & Soc* 38, 1273–1286 (2023). https://doi.org/DOI: 10.1007/s00146-021-01270-5

Hutchings, T. (2017). *Creating Church Online: Ritual, Community and New Media* (1st ed.). Routledge., DOI: 10.4324/9780203111093

Krüger. (2023). *Oliver*. Posthumanism and Digital Religion., DOI: 10.1093/oxfordhb/9780197549803.013.26

Leibold, J. (2019). Surveillance in China's Xinjiang Region: Ethnic Sorting, Coercion, and Inducement. [Surveillance in China's Xinjiang Region: Ethnic Sorting, Coercion, and Inducement]. *Journal of Contemporary China, 29*(121), 1–15. DOI: 10.1080/10670564.2019.1621529

Naudts, M. (2021). Thinking Outside the [Black] Box: Rethinking Power and Agency in the Relationship Between Facebook's Users and Its Recommender System Algorithm. DOI: 10.13140/RG.2.2.25275.63529

Noble, S. U. (2018). *Algorithms of Oppression: How Search Engines Reinforce Racism*. NYU Press., DOI: 10.18574/nyu/9781479833641.001.0001

United Nations Human Rights Council. (2018). *Report of the Office of the United Nations High Commissioner for Human Rights: The situation of human rights in the Xinjiang Uyghur Autonomous Region, People's Republic of China*. https://www.ohchr.org

KEY TERMS AND DEFINITIONS

Algorithmic Bias: Algorithmic bias happens when AI systems inadvertently privilege or disadvantage some content or communities because of biased training data or inherent assumptions within the system. In the context of FoRB, this might result in the silencing of minority religious voices or mislabeling of religious conversation as extremist speech.

Content Moderation: Content moderation is the system by which online sites apply community standards, employing human moderators as well as AI-based systems. Although it seeks to censor offensive language, moderation fails to be culturally and religiously sensitive in its evaluation, often removing harmless or educational content. Religious words can be misconstrued, and content gets deleted.

Digital Activism: Digital activism is a term used to describe the utilization of digital resources for organizing, campaigning, and mobilizing on social or political issues. In the FoRB community, it can mean pushing back against religious discrimination, campaigning for faith rights, or promoting interfaith dialogue.

Digital Religion: Digital religion is the integration of religious belief, ritual, and communal life into digital technology. It is more than "religion that just so happens to be online" and is a complete change in the way that faith is lived, accessed, and understood. Digital religion enables believers to transcend spatial distances, interact instantaneously, and engage in rituals from a distance. At the same time, it poses questions related to authenticity, authority, and surveillance.

Ethical AI Design: Ethical AI design incorporates fairness, transparency, and accountability into AI systems so they honor cultural and religious diversity. For FoRB, this requires developing moderation algorithms that can differentiate between hate speech and valid theological debate, and offer transparent appeal processes.

Freedom of Religion or Belief (FoRB): Freedom of Religion or Belief is a fundamental human and inherent right enshrined in Article 18 of the Universal Declaration of Human Rights. It safeguards the freedom of an individual to adopt, modify, or abandon any religion or belief without fear of coercion, discrimination, or punishment. That is, it grants someone the right to practice and declare any religion he or she wishes or no religion at all simultaneously. In the cyber age, FoRB goes beyond material places of worship to the virtual space, from sharing verses of scripture on Instagram, participating in online prayer groups on Zoom, or viewing online sacred texts.

Intersectionality: Intersectionality, examines how intersecting identities like religion, gender, sexuality, and ethnicity, influence different experiences of privilege or oppression. In the online FoRB environment, intersectionality is used to clarify why particular groups have compounded disadvantages.

Platform Governance: Platform governance includes the rules, policies, and enforcement methods platforms employ to manage speech and conduct. These choices control what religious content is on view, what is silenced, and how conflicts are mediated.

Religious Digital Literacy: Religious digital literacy is a skill to interact with religious material online in a secure, educated, and critical manner. This involves familiarity with privacy settings, awareness of algorithmic bias, and confirmation of authenticity of religious information

Surveillance Capitalism: Surveillance capitalism is an economic system where personal information is reaped, processed, and sold, usually without complete knowledge of the user. In religious terms, this might involve monitoring attendance at religious events, use of an app to read scriptures, or donations online, generating a profile that may be used for commercial or political gains.

Compilation of References

Abdullah, M. A. (2022). Islamic Religious Education Based on Religious Intersubjectivity: Philosophical Perspectives and Phenomenology of Religion. *Jurnal Pendidikan Agama Islam, 19*(1), 141–164. DOI: 10.14421/jpai.2022.191-11

Abid, A., Farooqi, M., & Zou, J. (2021). Persistent Anti-Muslim Bias in Large Language Models. *Proceedings of the 2021 AAAI/ACM Conference on AI, Ethics, and Society*, 298–306. DOI: 10.1145/3461702.3462624

Abiri, G. (2024). Public Constitutional AI. *ArXiv (Cornell University), 2*(1). Cornell University. /arxiv.2406.16696DOI: 10.2139/ssrn.4874670

Abubakari, M. S., & Suprapto, S. (2021). Educational Data Mining to Predict Students Performance Based on Deep Learning Neural Network. *Proceeding International Conference On Health, Social Sciences And Technology, 1*(1), 13–16. https://ojs.poltekkespalembang.ac.id/index.php/icohsst/article/view/697

Abubakari, M. S., Shafik, W., & Hidayatullah, A. F. (2024). Evaluating the Potential of Artificial Intelligence in Islamic Religious Education: A SWOT Analysis Overview. In *AI-Enhanced Teaching Methods* (pp. 216–239). IGI Global. DOI: 10.4018/979-8-3693-2728-9.ch010

Abubakari, M. S. (2024). Overviewing the Maze of Research Integrity and False Positives Within AI-Enabled Detectors: Grammarly Dilemma in Academic Writing. In Mutawa, A. (Ed.), *Impacts of Generative AI on the Future of Research and Education* (pp. 335–366). IGI Global., DOI: 10.4018/979-8-3693-0884-4.ch013

Abubakari, M. S. (2025a). Digital Technologies Adoption in Islamic Education for Fostering Lifelong Learning Culture: Pilot Survey Preliminary Insights. In Anshari, M., Almunawar, M. N., & Ordóñez de Pablos, P. (Eds.), *Multi-Industry Digitalization and Technological Governance in the AI Era* (pp. 103–126). IGI Global., DOI: 10.4018/979-8-3373-1681-9.ch005

Abubakari, M. S. (2025b). Overviewing Biases in Generative AI-Powered Models in the Arabic Language: AI Fairness for Sustainable Future. In Syafrudin, M., Fitriyani, N. L., & Anshari, M. (Eds.), *Achieving Sustainability in Multi-Industry Settings With AI* (pp. 361–390). IGI Global., DOI: 10.4018/979-8-3373-2530-9.ch013

Abubakari, M. S., & Kalinaki, K. (2024). Digital Competence in Islamic Education for Lifelong Learning: Preliminary Analysis Using DigComp 2.1 Framework. In Hawamdeh, M. M. K., & Abdelhafid, F. (Eds.), *Embracing Technological Advancements for Lifelong Learning* (pp. 1–31). IGI Global., DOI: 10.4018/979-8-3693-1410-4.ch001

Abubakari, M. S., Zakaria, G. A. N., & Musa, J. (2023). Digital Learning Acceptance in Islamic Education: Validity and Reliability Testing of the Modified Technology Acceptance Model. *Canadian Journal of Educational and Social Studies*, *3*(6), 27–42. DOI: 10.53103/cjess.v6i1.185

Abubakari, M. S., Zakaria, G. A. N., & Musa, J. (2024). Perceived compatibility and students' intention to adopt digital technologies in Islamic education institutions. *Cogent Education*, *11*(1), 2430869. DOI: 10.1080/2331186X.2024.2430869

Abubakari, M. S., Zakaria, G. A. N., & Musa, J. (2025). Validating the DigComp framework among university students across different educational systems. *Discover Education*, *4*(1), 200. DOI: 10.1007/s44217-025-00652-x

Abubakari, M. S., Zakaria, G. A. N., Musa, J., & Kalinaki, K. (2023). Assessing Digital Competence in Higher Education: A Gender Analysis of DigComp 2.1 Framework in Uganda. *SAGA: Journal of Technology and Information System*, *1*(4), 114–120. DOI: 10.58905/saga.v1i4.210

Achruh, A., Rapi, M., Rusdi, M., & Idris, R. (2024). Challenges and Opportunities of Artificial Intelligence Adoption in Islamic Education in Indonesian Higher Education Institutions. *International Journal of Learning. Teaching and Educational Research*, *23*(11), 423–443. DOI: 10.26803/ijlter.23.11.22

Agbese, M., Alanen, H.-K., Antikainen, J., ... (2023). Governance in ethical and trustworthy AI systems: Extension of the ECCOLA method for AI ethics governance using GARP. *e-Informatyka*. https://www.e-informatyka.pl/index.php/einformatica/volumes/volume-2023/issue-1/article-1/

Ahmed, S., Sumi, A. A., & Aziz, N. A. (2024). Exploring Multi-Religious Perspective of Artificial Intelligence. *Theology and Science, 23*(1), 1–25. Taylor & Francis online. DOI: 10.1080/14746700.2024.2436783

Ali, M., Sapiezynski, P., Bogen, M., Korolova, A., Mislove, A., & Rieke, A. (2021). Discrimination through optimization: How Facebook's ad delivery can lead to skewed outcomes. *Proceedings of the ACM on Human-Computer Interaction*. DOI: 10.1145/3479598

Alqarni, M. (2024). Embedding Search for Quranic Texts based on Large Language Models. *The International Arab Journal of Information Technology*, *21*(2), 243–256. DOI: 10.34028/iajit/21/2/7

Al-Zaman, M. S. (2021, February). *A content analysis of social media users' reaction to religious disinformation in Bangladesh*. DigitalCommons@University of Nebraska - Lincoln. https://digitalcommons.unl.edu/cgi/viewcontent.cgi?article=9100&context=libphilprac

American Library Association. (2021, October). *First Amendment and Censorship*. ALA. Retrieved June 11, 2025, from https://www.ala.org/advocacy/intfreedom/censorship

Antoun, W., Baly, F., & Hajj, H. (2020). *AraBERT: Transformer-based Model for Arabic Language Understanding*. https://doi.org//arXiv.2003.00104DOI: 10.48550

Appadurai, A. (1996). *Modernity at Large: Cultural Dimensions of Globalization*. University of Minnesota Press.

Arora, P. (2019). *The Next Billion Users: Digital Life Beyond the West*. Harvard University Press. DOI: 10.4159/9780674238879

Ashraf, C. (2021). Exploring the impacts of artificial intelligence on freedom of religion or belief online. *The International Journal of Human Rights, 26*(5), 1–35. Taylor & Francis online. DOI: 10.1080/13642987.2021.1968376

Ashraf, Z. A., & Mustafa, N. (2024). AI Standards and Regulations. *Advances in Healthcare Information Systems and Administration Book Series*, 325–352. DOI: 10.4018/979-8-3693-7051-3.ch014

Azenkot, S., Prasain, S., Borning, A., ... (2011) Enhancing independence and safety for blind and deaf-blind public transit riders. In: Proceedings of the 2011 annual conference on Human factors in computing systems - CHI '11, New York, NY, 2011, pp.3247–3256. New York: ACM. DOI: 10.1145/1978942.1979424

Balendra, S. (2025, May 16). Meta's AI moderation and free speech: Ongoing challenges in the Global South. *Cambridge Forum on AI: Law and Governance, 1*, e21. DOI: 10.1017/cfl.2025.5

Balidemaj, V. (2024, August). *Artificial Intelligence Integration, Concerns, Benefits, and the Need for Ethical Policies for Community Foundations and Nonprofit Organizations*. Clemson OPEN. https://open.clemson.edu/cgi/viewcontent.cgi?article=4768&context=all_dissertations

Banet-Weiser, S. (2012). Authentic™: The politics of ambivalence in a brand culture. In *Authentic*. New York University Press.

Barbara, J., Koenitz, H., & Bakk, Á. K. (2021). *The Ethics of Virtual Reality Interactive Digital Narratives in Cultural Heritage*. DOI: 10.1007/978-3-030-92300-6_27

Barocas, S., & Selbst, A. D. (2016). Big Data's disparate impact. *California Law Review*, *104*(3), 671–732.

Basu, S., & Sen, S. (2023). Silenced voices: Unravelling India's dissent crisis through historical and contemporary analysis of free speech and suppression. *Information & Communications Technology Law*, *33*(1), 42–65. DOI: 10.1080/13600834.2023.2249780

Baudrillard, J. (2019). Simulacra and simulations (1981). In *Crime and Media* (pp. 69–85). Routledge. DOI: 10.4324/9780367809195-8

Beck, K., Beedle, M., Van Bennekum, A., ... (2001) Manifesto for Agile Software Development. Available at: https://agilemanifesto.org/ (accessed 16 August 2019).

Bender, E. M., Gebru, T., McMillan-Major, A., & Shmitchell, S. (2021). On the dangers of stochastic parrots: Can language models be too big? In *Proceedings of the 2021 ACM Conference on Fairness, Accountability, and Transparency* (pp. 610–623). DOI: 10.1145/3442188.3445922

Benjamin, R. (2019). *Race After Technology: Abolitionist Tools for the New Jim Code*. Polity Press.

Berberich, N., Nishida, T., & Suzuki, S. (2020). Harmonizing Artificial Intelligence for Social Good. *Philosophy & Technology*, *33*(4), 613–638. DOI: 10.1007/s13347-020-00421-8

Berger, P. L., & Luckmann, T. (1966). *The Social Construction of Reality: A Treatise in the Sociology of Knowledge*. Penguin Books.

Bielefeldt, H., Ghanea, N., & Wiener, M. (2016). *Freedom of religion or belief: An international law commentary*. Oxford University Press. DOI: 10.1093/law/9780198703983.001.0001

Bielefeldt, H., Pinto, T. A., & Petersen, M. J. (2022). Introduction: Freedom of Religion or Belief as a Human Right. *The Review of Faith & International Affairs*, *20*(2), 1–12. DOI: 10.1080/15570274.2022.2065799

Binns, R. (2018). Fairness in machine learning: Lessons from political philosophy. *Proceedings of the 2018 Conference on Fairness, Accountability and Transparency*, 149–159.

Binns, R. (2020). Human Judgment in algorithmic loops: Individual justice and automated decision-making. *Regulation & Governance*. Advance online publication. DOI: 10.1111/rego.12358

Bioni, B., Rielli, M., & Zanatta, R. (2025, February 28). *Beyond Digital Rights: Towards a Fair Information Ecosystem?* TechPolicy.Press. Retrieved June 11, 2025, from https://www.techpolicy.press/beyond-digital-rights-towards-a-fair-information-ecosystem/

Boddington, P., & Černý, D. (2024). The moral machines: How generative AI challenges freedom of thought and conscience. *Minds and Machines*. https://link.springer.com/journal/11023/volumes-and-issues/34-3

Boddington, P. (2017). *Towards a code of ethics for artificial intelligence*. Springer. DOI: 10.1007/978-3-319-60648-4

Bostrom, N. (2014). *Superintelligence: Paths, dangers, strategies*. Oxford University Press.

Bourdieu, P. (1986). The forms of capital. In J. Richardson (Ed.), *Handbook of Theory and Research for the Sociology of Education* (pp. 241–258). Greenwood.

Bourdieu, P. (1990). *The Logic of Practice*. Stanford University Press. DOI: 10.1515/9781503621749

Bowring, B. (2010). *Manual on the Wearing of Religious Symbols in Public Areas*. Security and Human Rights., DOI: 10.1163/187502310791305927

Brkan, M. (2019). Artificial intelligence and human rights: A business and human rights perspective. *Cambridge International Law Journal*, *8*(2), 241–258.

Broeders, D., Schrijvers, E., & Hirsch Ballin, E. (2017) Big Data and security policies: Serving security, protecting freedom. Available at: https://english.wrr.nl/binaries/wrr-eng/documents/policy-briefs/2017/01/31/big-data-and-security-policies-serving-security-protecting-freedom/WRR_PB6_BigDataAndSecurityPolicies.pdf (accessed 31 July 2019).

Bucher, T. (2018). *If... then: Algorithmic power and politics*. Oxford University Press. DOI: 10.1093/oso/9780190493028.001.0001

Bühler, M. M., Calzada, I., Cane, I., Jelinek, T., Kapoor, A., Mannan, M., Mehta, S., Mookerje, V., Nübel, K., Pentland, A., Scholz, T., Siddarth, D., Tait, J., Vaitla, B., & Zhu, J. (2023, June 29). Unlocking the Power of Digital Commons: Data Cooperatives as a Pathway for Data Sovereign, Innovative and Equitable Digital Communities. *MDPI, 3*(3), 11. https://www.mdpi.com/2673-6470/3/3/11

Buolamwini, J., & Gebru, T. (2018). Gender shades: Intersectional accuracy disparities in commercial gender classification. *Proceedings of Machine Learning Research*. http://proceedings.mlr.press/v81/buolamwini18a/buolamwini18a.pdf

Butt, N. A., Basharat, A., & Kamran, A. B. (2024). Semantic Enrichment of Hadith Corpus - Knowledge Graph Generation from Islamic Text. *Semantic Web Journal*. https://www.semantic-web-journal.net/system/files/swj3651.pdf

Campbell, H. A. (2017). *Digital religion: Understanding religious practice in new media worlds*. Routledge.

Campbell, H. A., & Evolvi, G. (2020). Contextualizing current digital religion research on emerging technologies. *Human Behavior and Emerging Technologies*, *2*(1), 5–17. DOI: 10.1002/hbe2.149

Campbell, H. A., & Tsuria, R. (2021). *Digital religion: Understanding religious practice in digital media*. Routledge. DOI: 10.4324/9780429295683

Çapar, G. (2024). Global Constitutionalism and Legitimate International Authority. *Jus Cogens*, *6*(3), 223–243. Advance online publication. DOI: 10.1007/s42439-024-00093-4

Cavoukian, A. (2008). Privacy in the clouds. *Identity in the Information Society*, *1*(1), 89–108. DOI: 10.1007/s12394-008-0005-z

Charusheela, S. (2013). Intersectionality. *Handbook of research on gender and economic life*, 32-45.

Chatterjee, N. (2021). Translating Obligations: Tamassuk and Fārigh-kha ī in the Indo-Persian World. *Journal of Economic and Social History of the Orient*, *64*(5-6), 541–582. DOI: 10.1163/15685209-12341546

Chaudhary, M. Y. (2024). *Augmented Reality*. Virtual Reality, and Religion., DOI: 10.1093/oxfordhb/9780197549803.013.28

Cheong, P. H. (2021). Bounded Religious Automation at Work: Communicating Human Authority in Artificial Intelligence Networks. *The Journal of Communication Inquiry*, *45*(1), 5–23. DOI: 10.1177/0196859920977133

Chowdhury, R., & Williams, J. (2024). Artificial intelligence and socioeconomic forces: Transforming the landscape of religion. *Humanities & Social Sciences Communications*, *11*(1), 602. Advance online publication. DOI: 10.1057/s41599-024-03137-8

Chun, W. H. K. (2016). *Updating to remain the same: Habitual new media*. MIT press. DOI: 10.7551/mitpress/10483.001.0001

Citron, D. K., & Pasquale, F. A. (2014). The scored society: Due process for automated predictions. *Washington Law Review (Seattle, Wash.)*, *89*, 1–33.

Coeckelbergh, M. (2020). *AI ethics*. MIT Press. DOI: 10.7551/mitpress/12549.001.0001

Condell, J., McShane, N., Alvarez, J., & Miller, A. (2021). *Virtual Community Heritage – An Immersive Approach to Community Heritage*. DOI: 10.5617/jomi.8791

Connelly, L. (2022). *Internet - Based Practices*. DOI: 10.1093/oxfordhb/9780190632922.013.33

Couldry, N., & Hepp, A. (2017). *The Mediated Construction of Reality*. Polity Press.

Covucci, C., Confetto, M. G., Ključnikov, A., & Panait, M. (2024). Unrevealing the nexus between digital sustainability and corporate digital responsibility: A dual-track systematic literature review towards a framework of corporate digital sustainability. *Technology in Society*, *79*, 102743. DOI: 10.1016/j.techsoc.2024.102743

Crawford, K. (2021). The atlas of AI: Power, politics, and the planetary costs of artificial intelligence. *AI & Society*. Advance online publication. DOI: 10.1007/s00146-021-01349-z

Crawford, K. (2021). *The Atlas of AI: Power, politics, and the planetary costs of artificial intelligence*. Yale University Press.

Daruwala, N. A. (2025). Social media, expression, and online engagement: A psychological analysis of digital communication and the chilling effect in the UK. *Frontiers in Communication*, *10*, 1565289. Advance online publication. DOI: 10.3389/fcomm.2025.1565289

Das, V. (2007). *Life and Words: Violence and the Descent into the Ordinary*. University of California Press.

Daun, H., & Arjmand, R. (2018). *Handbook of Islamic Education* (Daun, H., & Arjmand, R., Eds.). Vol. 7). Springer International Publishing., DOI: 10.1007/978-3-319-64683-1

Daun, H., & Arjmand, R. (2021). Globalisation and Islamic Education. In Zajda, J. (Ed.), *Third International Handbook of Globalisation, Education and Policy Research* (pp. 451–463). Springer International Publishing., DOI: 10.1007/978-3-030-66003-1_25

Davis, J., & Nathan, L. P. (2015). Value Sensitive Design: Applications, adaptations, and critiques. In Van den Hoven, J., Vermaas, P. E., & Van de Poel, I. (Eds.), *Handbook of Ethics, Values, and Technological Design* (pp. 11–40). Springer. DOI: 10.1007/978-94-007-6970-0_3

Digital Rights Foundation. (2022). *Gendered disinformation and online violence in South Asia*. https://digitalrightsfoundation.pk

Dignum, V. (2020). Responsibility and artificial intelligence. *Oxford Handbook of Ethics of AI*, 215–231. DOI: 10.1093/oxfordhb/9780190067397.013.12

Ding-Yang, H. (2024). Virtual Realities in Spiritual Practices: Exploring Immersive Technologies in Digital Rituals. *International Journal of Religion*, *5*(12), 2051–2059. DOI: 10.61707/4yam2a55

Djazilan, M. S., Rulyansah, A., & Rihlah, J. (2024). Why AI is Essential for the Future of Islamic Education: A Call for Ethical and Effective Implementation. *EDUKASIA: Jurnal Pendidikan Dan Pembelajaran*, *5*(2), 201–216. DOI: 10.62775/edukasia.v5i2.1373

Doukianou, S., & Lalioti, V. (2024, October). Ethical Extended Reality: Bridging Technology and Cultural Heritage. In *2024 IEEE International Conference on Metrology for eXtended Reality, Artificial Intelligence and Neural Engineering (MetroXRAINE)* (pp. 301-306). IEEE. doi:DOI: 10.1109/MetroXRAINE62247.2024.10796742

Dwivedi, P. S., & Narula, A. (2020). Religious communities in simulated sacred spaces: A study of pilgrimages in digital media. Journal of Content. *Community and Communication*, *11*(10), 260–267. DOI: 10.31620/JCCC.06.20/19

Eisenstein, E. L. (1979). *The printing press as an agent of change*. Cambridge University Press.

El Ganadi, A., Aftar, S., Gagliardelli, L., & Ruozzi, F. (2025). Generative AI for Islamic Texts: The EMAN Framework for Mitigating GPT Hallucinations. *Proceedings of the 17th International Conference on Agents and Artificial Intelligence*, 1221–1228. DOI: 10.5220/0013312800003890

Elmahjub, E. (2023). Artificial Intelligence (AI) in Islamic Ethics: Towards Pluralist Ethical Benchmarking for AI. *Philosophy & Technology*, *36*(4), 73. DOI: 10.1007/s13347-023-00668-x

Eubanks, V. (2018). *Automating inequality: How high-tech tools profile, police, and punish the poor.* St. Martin's Press.

Eykholt, K., Evtimov, I., Fernandes, E., ... (2018) Robust physical-world attacks on deep learning models. In: 2018 IEEE/CVF conference on computer vision and pattern recognition, Salt Lake City, UT, 18–22 June 2018, pp.1625–1634. IEEE.

Feldstein, S. (2019). *The global expansion of AI surveillance.* Carnegie Endowment for International Peace.

Fjeld, J., Achten, N., Hilligoss, H., Nagy, A., & Srikumar, M. (2020). Principled artificial intelligence: Mapping consensus in ethical and rights-based approaches. *Berkeley Journal of Law & Technology.* https://doi.org/DOI: 10.15779/Z38M32N851

Flanagan, M., Howe, D. C., & Nissenbaum, H. (2008). Embodying values in technology: Theory and practice. In Van den Hoven, J., & Weckert, J. (Eds.), *Information Technology and Moral Philosophy* (pp. 322–353). Cambridge University Press. DOI: 10.1017/CBO9780511498725.017

Floridi, L., Cowls, J., Beltrametti, M., Chatila, R., Chazerand, P., Dignum, V., Luetge, C., Madelin, R., Pagallo, U., Rossi, F., Schafer, B., Valcke, P., & Vayena, E. (2018). AI4People—An ethical framework for a good AI society: Opportunities, risks, principles, and recommendations. *Minds and Machines*, *28*(4), 689–707. DOI: 10.1007/s11023-018-9482-5

Floridi, L., & Taddeo, M. (2016). What is data ethics? *Philosophical Transactions. Series A, Mathematical, Physical, and Engineering Sciences*, *374*(2083), 20160360. DOI: 10.1098/rsta.2016.0360 PMID: 28336805

Fonseca, A., Perera, S., Meedin, N., Caldera, M., Perera, I., & Ahangama, S. (2024). Analyzing hate speech dynamics on Twitter/X: Insights from conversational data and the impact of user interaction patterns.

Foucault, M. (1980). *Power/Knowledge: Selected Interviews and Other Writings, 1972–1977* (Gordon, C., Ed.). Pantheon.

Franzke, A. S. (2016). *Big Data Ethicist - What Will the Role of the Ethicist Be in Advising Governments in the Field of Big Data?* Utrecht University.

Gerards, J. (2019). The fundamental rights challenges of algorithms. *Netherlands Quarterly of Human Rights*, *37*(3), 205–209. DOI: 10.1177/0924051919861773

Gitelman, L. (Ed.). (2013). *"Raw Data" is an Oxymoron.* MIT Press. DOI: 10.7551/mitpress/9302.001.0001

Goertzel, B., & Pennachin, C. (Eds.). (2007). *Artificial general intelligence.* Springer. DOI: 10.1007/978-3-540-68677-4

Gómez, O. A. (2025). The State as a Humanitarian Actor: Opportunities and Challenges in Decolonizing Humanitarianism. *Yearbook of International Humanitarian Law*, 43–73. DOI: 10.1007/978-94-6265-663-5_2

González, F. (2020). Robot priests and funeral rituals: When technology meets religion. *Religion and Digital Society*, *12*(1), 21–35.

Gorian, E., & Osman, N. D. (2024). Digital Ethics of Artificial Intelligence (AI) in Saudi Arabia and United Arab Emirates. *Malaysian Journal of Syariah and Law*, *12*(3), 583–597. DOI: 10.33102/mjsl.vol12no3.798

Gorwa, R., Binns, R., & Katzenbach, C. (2020). Algorithmic content moderation: Technical and political challenges in the automation of platform governance. *Big Data & Society*, *7*(1), 2053951719897945. DOI: 10.1177/2053951719897945

Grandinetti, J. (2020). Examining embedded apparatuses of AI in Facebook and TikTok. *AI & Soc* 38, 1273–1286 (2023). https://doi.org/DOI: 10.1007/s00146-021-01270-5

Gyagenda, A. (2024). The Contribution Of Muslim Scholars Towards Science, Technology And Knowledge: A Historical Perspective. *Journal of Islamic Studies and Arabic Language*, *3*(2), 85–104.

Halbertal, M. (2015) Three concepts of human dignity. Available at: https://youtu.be/FyEvREFZVvc (accessed 8 August 2019).

Hancock, A. M. (2013). Neurobiology, Intersectionality, and Politics: Paradigm Warriors in Arms? 1. *Perspectives on Politics*, *11*(2), 504–507. DOI: 10.1017/S1537592713000959

Handoko, A. (2024). Paradigm Of The Relationship Of Religion And The State. *Asian Journal of Engineering Social and Health*, *3*(2), 271–284. DOI: 10.46799/ajesh.v3i2.243

Harari, Y. N. (2018). *21 lessons for the 21st century.* Spiegel & Grau.

Haraway, D. J. (1991). *Simians, Cyborgs, and Women: The Reinvention of Nature.* Routledge.

Hartmann, D., de Pereira, J. R. L., Streitbörger, C., & Berendt, B. (2024). Addressing the regulatory gap: moving towards an EU AI audit ecosystem beyond the AI Act by including civil society. *AI and Ethics, 1*(1). Springer Nature Link. DOI: 10.1007/s43681-024-00595-3

Heidegger, M. (1977). *The question concerning technology and other essays* (W. Lovitt, Trans.). Harper & Row.

He, Y. (2024a). Artificial intelligence and religious freedom: Divergent paths converging on economic expansion. *Humanities and Social Sciences Communications, 11*(1), 1–12. *Humanities & Social Sciences Communications.* Advance online publication. DOI: 10.1057/s41599-024-02642-0

Hidayat, M. C., & Arifin, S., Asrori, & Rusman. (2020). Integration Science Technology with Islamic Values: Empowering Education Model. *Proceedings of the 1st Borobudur International Symposium on Humanities, Economics and Social Sciences (BIS-HESS 2019), 436*, 966–970. DOI: 10.2991/assehr.k.200529.202

Hong, S. H. (2020). Technologies of speculation: The limits of knowledge in a data-driven society. In *Technologies of Speculation.* New York University Press. DOI: 10.18574/nyu/9781479860234.001.0001

Hutchings, T. (2017). *Creating Church Online: Ritual, Community and New Media* (1st ed.). Routledge., DOI: 10.4324/9780203111093

Ienca, M., & Andorno, R. (2017). Towards new human rights in the age of neuroscience and neurotechnology. *Life Sciences, Society and Policy*, *13*(1), 5. DOI: 10.1186/s40504-017-0050-1

Jahan, M. S., & Oussalah, M. (2023). A systematic review of hate speech automatic detection using natural language processing. *Neurocomputing*, *546*, 126232. Advance online publication. DOI: 10.1016/j.neucom.2023.126232

Jain, L. R., & Menon, V. (2023). AI Algorithmic Bias: Understanding its Causes, Ethical and Social Implications. *2023 IEEE 35th International Conference on Tools with Artificial Intelligence (ICTAI)*, 460–467. DOI: 10.1109/ICTAI59109.2023.00073

Jeroen, T. (2023). Artificial intelligence and religious freedom. In Oxford University Press eBooks. DOI: 10.1093/law/9780192882486.003.0004

Jobin, A., Ienca, M., & Vayena, E. (2019). The global landscape of AI ethics guidelines. *Nature Machine Intelligence*, *1*(9), 389–399. DOI: 10.1038/s42256-019-0088-2

Jubba, H., Fernando, H., Larasati, Y. G., & Darus, M. R. (2024). *Between Reality and Virtuality: A Study of Muslim Perceptions of Metaverse Hajj as a Religious Practice*. Khazanah Theologia., DOI: 10.15575/kt.v6i1.33244

Karagözoğlu, B. (2017). Contribution of Muslim Scholars to Science and Technology. In *Science and Technology from Global and Historical Perspectives* (pp. 137–184). Springer International Publishing., DOI: 10.1007/978-3-319-52890-8_6

Khan, A., & Srinivasan, R. (2024). Algorithmic pluralism: Designing for religious diversity in public-service AI. *Journal of Social Computing*. Advance online publication. DOI: 10.23919/JSC.2024.0003

Khera, S. Anuradha, Singh, A., & Singh, K. K. (2025). Exploring multimodal hate speech detection using machine learning and deep learning models. In A. Singh & K. K. Singh (Eds.), *Multimodal generative AI*. Springer. https://doi.org/DOI: 10.1007/978-981-96-2355-6_11

Kosinski, M., Stillwell, D., & Graepel, T. (2013). Private traits and attributes are predictable from digital records of human behavior. *Proceedings of the National Academy of Sciences of the United States of America*, *110*(15), 5802–5805. DOI: 10.1073/pnas.1218772110

Kosinski, M., & Wang, Y. (2018). Deep neural networks are more accurate than humans at detecting sexual orientation from facial images. *Journal of Personality and Social Psychology*, *114*(2), 246–257. DOI: 10.1037/pspa0000098

Krüger. (2023). *Oliver*. Posthumanism and Digital Religion., DOI: 10.1093/oxfordhb/9780197549803.013.26

Kuck, K. (2023). Generative Artificial Intelligence: A Double-Edged Sword. *2023 World Engineering Education Forum - Global Engineering Deans Council (WEEF-GEDC)*, 1–10. DOI: 10.1109/WEEF-GEDC59520.2023.10343638

Kumar, A. B., & Mohanty, A. (2024). Artificial Intelligence. *Advances in Human and Social Aspects of Technology Book Series*, 35–62. DOI: 10.4018/979-8-3693-3334-1.ch002

Kumar, A. B., & Sanjaya, K. (2025). Advances in Social Networking and Online Communities Book Series. AI and Social Justice., DOI: 10.4018/979-8-3693-9904-0.ch008

Kumar, A. B., Sanjaya, K., & Saleem, M. (2025). Justice in the Age of Algorithms. *Advances in Computational Intelligence and Robotics*, •••, 191–210. DOI: 10.4018/979-8-3693-9395-6.ch009

Kurzweil, R. (2005). *The singularity is near: When humans transcend biology*. Viking.

Latif, S., Qayyum, A., Usama, M., Qadir, J., & Williams, M. J. (2021). Artificial intelligence for religious studies: The potential and the risks. *AI & Society*, *36*(1), 123–135.

Latonero, M. (2018). *Governing artificial intelligence: Upholding human rights & dignity*. Data & Society Research Institute.

Lauser, A. (2008). Zwischen Heldenverehrung und Geisterkultur: Politik und Religion im gegenwärtigen spätkommunistischen Vietnam. *Zeitschrift für Ethnologie*.

Lebedev, M. A., & Nicolelis, M. A. (2017). Brain-machine interfaces: From basic science to neuroprostheses and neurorehabilitation. *Physiological Reviews*, *97*(2), 767–837. DOI: 10.1152/physrev.00027.2016

Leese, M. (2014). The new profiling: Algorithms, black boxes, and the failure of anti-discriminatory safeguards in the European Union. *Security Dialogue*, *45*(5), 494–511. DOI: 10.1177/0967010614544204

Leibold, J. (2019). Surveillance in China's Xinjiang Region: Ethnic Sorting, Coercion, and Inducement. [Surveillance in China's Xinjiang Region: Ethnic Sorting, Coercion, and Inducement]. *Journal of Contemporary China*, *29*(121), 1–15. DOI: 10.1080/10670564.2019.1621529

Lévi-Strauss, C. (1963). Réponses à quelques questions. *Esprit (1940-)*, (322 (11), 628-653.

Lim, Y.-K., Stolterman, E., & Tenenberg, J. (2008). The anatomy of prototypes: Prototypes as filters, prototypes as manifestations of design ideas. *ACM Transactions on Computer-Human Interaction*, *15*(2), 1–27. DOI: 10.1145/1375761.1375762

Li, X.-Z., Chen, C.-C., & Kang, X. (2023). Religious diversity education: Raising children's awareness of religious diversity through augmented reality. *Humanities & Social Sciences Communications*, *10*(1), 708. Advance online publication. DOI: 10.1057/s41599-023-02123-w

Logan, W. (2005).*Dien Bien Phu: development and conservation in a Vietnamese cultural landscape*.

Lu, Y., Cao, Y., Wang, B., & Yang, S. (2025). AI governance: A systematic literature review. *AI and Ethics*, *5*(3), 3265–3279. Advance online publication. DOI: 10.1007/s43681-024-00653-w

Madgule, M., Vinayaka, N., Sonkhaskar, Y. M., Patel, D. R., Karthikeyan, R., & Selvakumar, P. (2023). Mechanical properties and microstructure of activated TIG welded similar joints of Inconel alloys by desirability approaches. *Materials Today: Proceedings*, *77*, 528–533.

Makridakis, S. (2017). The Forthcoming Artificial Intelligence (AI) revolution: Its Impact on Society and Firms. *Futures*, *90*(90), 46–60. DOI: 10.1016/j.futures.2017.03.006

Malik, J. S., Qiao, H., Pang, G., & van den Hengel, A. (2023). *Deep Learning for Hate Speech Detection: A Comparative Study*. arXiv. https://arxiv.org/abs/2202.09517

Mann, M., & Matzner, T. (2019). Challenging algorithmic profiling: The limits of data protection and anti-discrimination in responding to emergent discrimination. *Big Data & Society*, *6*(2), 1–11. DOI: 10.1177/2053951719895805

Mansur, Z., Omar, N., & Tiun, S. (2023). Twitter Hate Speech Detection: A Systematic Review of Methods, Taxonomy Analysis, Challenges, and Opportunities. *IEEE Access : Practical Innovations, Open Solutions*, *11*, 14065–14094. DOI: 10.1109/ACCESS.2023.3239375

Mantelero, A. (2018). AI and Big Data: A blueprint for a human rights, social and ethical impact assessment. *Computer Law & Security Review*, *34*(4), 754–772. DOI: 10.1016/j.clsr.2018.05.017

McCormack, J., Gifford, T., & Hutchings, P. (2022). The Rise of AI Religions: Spiritual Implications of Autonomous Text and Ritual. *AI & Society*.

McLuhan, M. (1964). *Understanding Media: The Extensions of Man*. McGraw-Hill.

McStay, A. (2020). *Emotional AI: The rise of empathic media*. SAGE Publications.

Meegle. (2025). AI Ethics And Content Moderation. https://www.meegle.com/en_us/topics/ai-ethics/ai-ethics-and-content-moderation

Menkel-Meadow, C. J., & Schneider, A. K. (2025). International Conflict Resolution Processes. SSRN *Electronic Journal*. SSRN. DOI: 10.2139/ssrn.5168799

Mghari, M., Bouras, O., & El Hibaoui, A. (2022). Sanadset 650K: Data on Hadith narrators. *Data in Brief*, *44*, 108540. DOI: 10.1016/j.dib.2022.108540 PMID: 36065202

Mignolo, W. D. (2009). Epistemic disobedience, independent thought and decolonial freedom. *Theory, Culture & Society*, *26*(7–8), 159–181. DOI: 10.1177/0263276409349275

Milvus. (2025). What are the societal benefits of federated learning? https://milvus.io/ai-quick-reference/what-are-the-societal-benefits-of-federated-learning

Mohadi, M., & Tarshany, Y. (2023). Maqasid Al-Shari'ah and the Ethics of Artificial Intelligence. *Journal of Contemporary Maqasid Studies*, *2*(2), 79–102. DOI: 10.52100/jcms.v2i2.107

Mohamed, S., Png, M. T., & Isaac, W. (2020). Decolonial AI: Decolonial theory as sociotechnical foresight in artificial intelligence. *Philosophy & Technology*, *33*(4), 659–684. Advance online publication. DOI: 10.1007/s13347-020-00405-8

Mozur, P. (2019). One month, 500,000 face scans: How China is using A.I. to profile a minority. *The New York Times*. https://www.nytimes.com

Munir, B. (2025). Islamophobic Artificial Intelligence in the USA: A Critical Analysis of Religious Bias in Datasets. *The Law Library Journal, 1*(1). *SSRN*. DOI: 10.2139/ssrn.5265355

Munshi, A. A., AlSabban, W. H., Farag, A. T., Rakha, O. E., Al Sallab, A. A., & Alotaibi, M. (2021). Towards an Automated Islamic Fatwa System: Survey, Dataset and Benchmarks. *International Journal of Computer Science and Mobile Computing*, *10*(4), 118–131. DOI: 10.47760/ijcsmc.2021.v10i04.017

Mylenka, H., & Anhelova, A. (2021). Augmented reality in contemporary religious practice. The Journal of v N Karazin Kharkiv National University Series Philosophy Philosophical Peripeteias, 64, 104-112. DOI: 10.26565/2226-0994-2021-64-9

Naudts, M. (2021). Thinking Outside the [Black] Box: Rethinking Power and Agency in the Relationship Between Facebook's Users and Its Recommender System Algorithm. DOI: 10.13140/RG.2.2.25275.63529

Nissenbaum, H. (2005). Values in technical design. In Mitcham, C. (Ed.), *Encyclopedia of Science, Technology and Ethics* (pp. lxvi–lxx). Macmillan.

Noble, S. U. (2018). *Algorithms of Oppression: How Search Engines Reinforce Racism*. NYU Press. DOI: 10.18574/nyu/9781479833641.001.0001

Norman, E., Pahlawati, E., Siregar, M. L., & Damayanthy, D. (2025). Digital Transformation of Islamic Education: AI, Gamification, and Pedagogical Adaptation for Generation Z. *Medina-Te: Jurnal Studi Islam*, *21*(1), 37–49. DOI: 10.19109/medinate.v21i1.27952

O'Callaghan, D., Greene, D., Conway, M., Carthy, J., & Cunningham, P. (2015). Down the (white) rabbit hole: The extreme right and online recommender systems. *Social Science Computer Review*, *33*(4), 459–478. DOI: 10.1177/0894439314555329

O'Neil, C. (2016). *Weapons of math destruction: How big data increases inequality and threatens democracy*. Crown Publishing.

OHCHR. (1966). *International Covenant on Civil and Political Rights*. United Nations. https://www.ohchr.org/en/instruments-mechanisms/instruments/international-covenant-civil-and-political-rights

Papadopoulos, T. (2025). Artificial intelligence in religious education: Ethical, pedagogical, and theological perspectives. *Religions*, *16*(5), 563. Advance online publication. DOI: 10.3390/rel16050563

Pariser, E. (2011). *The filter bubble: What the Internet is hiding from you*. Penguin Press.

Parmar, H., & Murari, U. K. (2025). Adapting AI Moderation. *Advances in Computational Intelligence and Robotics*, •••, 29–54. DOI: 10.4018/979-8-3373-0335-2.ch002

Paya, A. (2023). Is AI a threat to faith? How could we maintain human freedom, autonomy, and agency in the age of rising AI power? The Perspective of a Shi'a Muslim. *Journal of Shi'a Islamic Studies*, *16*(3-4), 185–208. DOI: 10.1353/isl.2023.a942954

Perera, S., Meedin, N., Caldera, M., Perera, I., & Ahangama, S. (2023). A Comparative Study of the Characteristics of Hate Speech Propagators and Their Behaviours Over Twitter Social Media Platform. *Heliyon*, *9*(8), e19097. DOI: 10.1016/j.heliyon.2023.e19097 PMID: 37636360

Picard, R. W. (1997). *Affective computing*. MIT Press. DOI: 10.7551/mitpress/1140.001.0001

Popova, B. (2023, January). Embracing the Metaverse: The Future of Islamic Teaching and Learning. In 2023 20th Learning and Technology Conference (L&T) (pp. 1-7). IEEE. DOI: 10.1109/lt58159.2023.10092367

Putrawan, B. K. (2025). From Prayer to Data: The Transformation of Theology in the Age of Artificial Intelligence and its Implications for Religious Practice. *Transformation: An International Journal of Holistic Mission Studies*, *0*(0), 02653788241312229. Advance online publication. DOI: 10.1177/02653788241312229

Rahwan, I. (2018). Society-in-the-loop: Programming the algorithmic social contract. *Ethics and Information Technology*, *20*(1), 5–14. Advance online publication. DOI: 10.1007/s10676-017-9430-8

Ramakrishnan, T., Mohan Gift, M. D., Chitradevi, S., Jegan, R., & Subha Hency Jose, P. Nagaraja, Rajneesh Sharma H.N., Selvakumar P., Sintayehu Mekuria Hailegiorgis, (2022). “Study of Numerous Resins Used in Polymer Matrix Composite Materials”, Advances in Materials Science and Engineering, vol. 2022, Article ID 1088926, 8 pages, 2022. DOI: 10.1155/2022/1088926

Raso, F., Hilligoss, H., Krishnamurthy, V., ... (2018) Artificial intelligence & human rights: Opportunities & risks. Available at: https://cyber.harvard.edu/publication/2018/artificial-intelligence-human-rights (accessed 22 August 2019).

Roffey, S. (2013). Inclusive and exclusive belonging: The impact on individual and community wellbeing. *Educational and Child Psychology*, *30*(1), 38–49. DOI: 10.53841/bpsecp.2013.30.1.38

Romana, F., & Santiago, F. (2024). A Comparative Analysis of Artificial Intelligence Regulatory Law in Asia, Europe, and America. *SHS Web of Conferences, 204*(1), 07006–07006. SHS Web of Conference. DOI: 10.1051/shsconf/202420407006

Rouvroy, A., Berns, T., & Carey-Libbrecht, L. (2013). Algorithmic governmentality and prospects of emancipation. *Reseaux (London)*, *177*(1), 163–196.

Royal United Services Institute (RUSI). (2025). *Online Hate Speech and Discrimination in the Age of AI*. https://static.rusi.org/online-hate-speech-and-discrimination-in-the-age-of-ai-june-2025.pdf

Russell, S., & Norvig, P. (2021). *Artificial intelligence: A modern approach* (4th ed.). Pearson.

Saeidnia, H. R., Hosseini, E., Lund, B., Tehrani, M. A., Zaker, S., & Molaei, S. (2025). Artificial intelligence in the battle against disinformation and misinformation: A systematic review of challenges and approaches. *Knowledge and Information Systems*, *67*(4), 3139–3158. Advance online publication. DOI: 10.1007/s10115-024-02337-7

Santoni de Sio, F., Robichaud, P., & Vincent, N. A. (2014). Who should enhance? Conceptual and normative dimensions of cognitive enhancement. HUMANA. *MENTE Journal of Philosophical Studies*, *7*(26), 179–197.

Scharffs, B. G. (2024). Building Bridges between Freedom of Religion and Belief and Other Fundamental Human Rights. *Routledge EBooks*, 117–128. DOI: 10.4324/9781003519188-9

Schlesinger, P. (2024). The Post-Public Sphere and Neo-Regulation of Digital Platforms. *Javnost (Ljubljana), 31*(1), 1–25. Taylor & Francis online. DOI: 10.1080/13183222.2024.2311010

Seaver, N. (2018). What should an anthropology of algorithms do? *Cultural Anthropology*, *33*(3), 375–385. DOI: 10.14506/ca33.3.04

Shah, N. (2019). Gender, algorithms, and affective labour: The case of online moderation. In McPherson, M. (Ed.), *Feminist in a Software Lab* (pp. 125–142). MIT Press.

Sheh Hamidulfuad, S. N. F. (2024, August). A Collaborative Social Design Framework for Designing Spiritual Technology: Empowering the Spiritual Experiences of the Indigenous Community Through Co-Creation. In Proceedings of the Participatory Design Conference 2024: Situated Actions, Doctoral Colloquium, PDC places, Communities-Volume 3 (pp. 92-95). doi:DOI: 10.1145/3661456.3666074

Srdanović, P., Skala, T., & Maričević, M. (2024). InHeritage—A Gamified Mobile Application with AR and VR for Cultural Heritage Preservation in the Metaverse. *Applied Sciences (Basel, Switzerland)*, *15*(1), 257. Advance online publication. DOI: 10.3390/app15010257

Sreenivasulu, A., & Manimozhi, T. Satheesh kumar P., Selvakumar P. and Singh P.,(2022). "The Model of Smart Sensing Device For Sensitive Nanoclusters Modification in Sensing Properties," 2022 2nd International Conference on Advance Computing and Innovative Technologies in Engineering (ICACITE), Greater Noida, India, 2022, pp. 1043-1047, DOI: 10.1109/ICACITE53722.2022.9823846

Striphas, T. (2015). Algorithmic culture. *European Journal of Cultural Studies*, *18*(4–5), 395–412. DOI: 10.1177/1367549415577392

Subrahmanyam, S. (2025a). Integrating AI and AR Into Teaching and Scholarly Communication. In Vrba, J., & Huynh, T. (Eds.), *Revolutionizing Academic Research With AI and Augmented Reality* (pp. 179–212). IGI Global Scientific Publishing. DOI: 10.4018/979-8-3373-1414-3.ch006

Subrahmanyam, S. (2025b). Qualitative Research Designs in Higher Education. In Mdikana, A. (Ed.), *Social Implications of Research in Higher Education* (pp. 263–296). IGI Global Scientific Publishing. DOI: 10.4018/979-8-3373-0654-4.ch010

Subramanian, M., Sathiskumar, V. E., Deepalakshmi, G., Cho, J., & Manikandan, G. (2023). A survey on hate speech detection and sentiment analysis using machine learning and deep learning models.

Sugumaran, K. M. D., Pandiyarajan V., Y. B S, Selvakumar P. and M. S, (2024). "Analysis of Electromyography Signals for Control of Mechanical Prosthesis using Machine Learning Techniques," 2024 2nd International Conference on Intelligent Data Communication Technologies and Internet of Things (IDCIoT), Bengaluru, India, 2024, pp. 1059-1067, DOI: 10.1109/IDCIoT59759.2024.10467707

Sundar, S. S. (2008). The MAIN model: A heuristic approach to understanding technology effects on credibility. In Metzger, M. J., & Flanagin, A. J. (Eds.), *Digital Media, Youth, and Credibility* (pp. 73–100). MIT Press.

Syafitri, A., Efriyanti, L., & Devi, I. (2024). The Role of Artificial Intelligence in Encouraging Innovation and Creativity in Islamic Education. *Nizham Journal of Islamic Studies, 12*(01), 1–10. DOI: 10.32332/nizham.v12i01.8602

Tamuri, A. H. (2021). Teaching Practices of Islamic Education Teachers Based on 5 Mim Concept in Religious Secondary Schools in Indonesia. *International Journal of Islam and Contemporary Affairs, 1*(1), 1–24. DOI: 10.61465/jurnalyadim.v1i1.37

Taussig, M. (1993). *The devil and the fetishism of the commodity in South America*. Editorial

Tegmark, M. (2017). *Life 3.0: Being human in the age of artificial intelligence*. Penguin.

Tsuria, R., & Yemini, A. (2024). Artificial intelligence's understanding of religion: Investigating the moralistic approaches presented by generative artificial intelligence tools. *Religions, 15*(3), 375. Advance online publication. DOI: 10.3390/rel15030375

Tubella, A. A., Theodorou, A., & Dignum, F.. (2019) Governance by glass-box: Implementing transparent moral bounds for AI behaviour. In: *Proceedings of the twenty-eighth international joint conference on artificial intelligence AI for improving human well-being*, 10–16 August 2019, pp.5787–5793. IJCAI.

Tufekci, Z. (2018). YouTube, the great radicalizer. *The New York Times*. https://www.nytimes.com

Turek, M. (2020). Theological ethics and artificial intelligence: New challenges and responses. *Ethics and Information Technology, 22*(3), 163–174.

Turkle, S. (2011). *Alone Together: Why We Expect More from Technology and Less from Each Other*. Basic Books.

Udupa, S. (2020). *Digital Hate: The Global Conjuncture of Extreme Speech*. Indiana University Press.

UN General Assembly. (2021). *Recommendation on the ethics of artificial intelligence*. https://digitallibrary.un.org/record/4062376?v=pdf

UN. (1948). *Universal Declaration of Human Rights*. United Nations General Assembly. https://www.un.org/en/about-us/universal-declaration-of-human-rights

UNESCO. (2021). *Recommendation on the ethics of artificial intelligence.* https://unesdoc.unesco.org

UNESCO. (2023). *Global Survey on the Impact of Online Disinformation on Democratic Processes and Human Rights.* https://www.unesco.org/sites/default/files/medias/fichiers/2023/11/unesco_ipsos_survey.pdf

UNHRC. (2020). *Freedom of thought report.* United Nations Human Rights Council.

United Nations Human Rights Council. (2018). *Report of the Office of the United Nations High Commissioner for Human Rights: The situation of human rights in the Xinjiang Uyghur Autonomous Region, People's Republic of China.* https://www.ohchr.org

United Nations. (1948). *Universal Declaration of Human Rights.* https://www.un.org/en/about-us/universal-declaration-of-human-rights

Van de Poel, I. (2013). Translating values into design requirements. In Michelfelder, D. P., McCarthy, N., & Goldberg, D. E. (Eds.), *Philosophy and Engineering: Reflections on Practice, Principles and Process* (pp. 253–266). Springer. DOI: 10.1007/978-94-007-7762-0_20

Van den Hoven, J., Stauch, M., Musiani, F., Ferrer, J. D., Ruggieri, S., Pratesi, F., Trasarti, R., & Comandé, G. (2024). Democracy in the Digital Age. *Hal.science.* DOI: 10.15488/18259

van Dijck, J. (2013). *The Culture of Connectivity: A Critical History of Social Media.* Oxford University Press. DOI: 10.1093/acprof:oso/9780199970773.001.0001

Van Sen, V., & Tho, N. N. (2020). Crossing boundaries and state-building: Harmonisation and tolerance in Vietnamese religions. *IJAPS, 16*(2), 59–83. DOI: 10.21315/IJAPS2020.16.2.4

Veale, M., & Binns, R. (2017). Fairer machine learning in the real world: Mitigating discrimination without collecting sensitive data. *Big Data & Society, 4*(2). Advance online publication. DOI: 10.1177/2053951717743530

Véliz, C., & Murphy, T. (2025). Artificial intelligence and its "slow violence" to human rights. *AI and Ethics, 5*(3), 2265–2280. Advance online publication. DOI: 10.1007/s43681-024-00547-x

Vijayakumar, G., Rajkumar, M., Rajiv Chandar, N., Selvakumar, P., & Duraisamy, R. (2024). Muniyandi Rajkumar, Rajiv Chandar N, Selvakumar P and Ramesh Duraisamy, (2024). Environmentally friendly TDS removal from waste water by electrochemical ion exchange batch-type recirculation (EIR) technique. *Environmental Science. Water Research & Technology*, *10*(4), 826–835. DOI: 10.1039/D3EW00793F

Wachter, S., Mittelstadt, B., & Floridi, L. (2017). Transparent, explainable, and accountable AI for the public sector. *Computer*, *50*(5), 56–65.

Wajcman, J. (2006). Technocapitalism meets technofeminism: women and technology in a wireless world. *Labour & Industry: a journal of the social and economic relations of work, 16*(3), 7-20.

Wakabayashi, D. (2018) Self-driving Uber car kills pedestrian in Arizona, where robots roam. The New York Times, 19 March.

Witte, J. (2020). The Right of Freedom of Religion: An Historical Perspective from the West. In Ferrari, S. (Eds.), *Routledge Handbook on Freedom of Religion and Belief.* SSRN Electronic Journal., DOI: 10.4324/9780203732625-4

Yang, H., Kim, H., Lee, J. H., & Shin, D. (2022). Implementation of an AI chatbot as an English conversation partner in EFL speaking classes. *ReCALL*, *34*(3), 327–343. DOI: 10.1017/S0958344022000039

Yan, L., Greiff, S., Teuber, Z., & Gašević, D. (2024). Promises and challenges of generative artificial intelligence for human learning. *Nature Human Behaviour*, *8*(10), 1839–1850. DOI: 10.1038/s41562-024-02004-5 PMID: 39438686

Yassine, S., & Gammoudi, M. M. (2023). Trends and Challenges of Arabic Chatbots : Literature Review. *Jordanian Journal of Computers and Information Technology*, *09*(03), 261–286.

Za'atreh, M. (2024). *The Impact of Artificial Intelligence on Drafting Religious Edicts (Fatwas).* The Fatwa Department of the Hashemite Kingdom of Jordan. https://aliftaa.jo/article-en/5743/Article.aspx?ArticleId=5858#:~:text=The Impact of Artificial Intelligence,Fatwas

Zhang, J., Song, W., & Liu, Y. (2025). Cognitive bias in generative AI influences religious education. *Scientific Reports*, *15*(1), 15720. DOI: 10.1038/s41598-025-99121-6 PMID: 40325105

Zhang, W., & Lee, M. K. (2025). Decolonizing AI ethics: Indigenous cosmologies and algorithmic bias mitigation. *AI & Society*. Advance online publication. DOI: 10.1007/s00146-024-01935-x

Zhu, H., Yu, B., Halfaker, A., & Terveen, L. (2018). Value-sensitive algorithm design. *Proceedings of the ACM on Human-Computer Interaction, 2*(CSCW), 1–23. DOI: 10.1145/3274463

Zuboff, S. (2019). *The age of surveillance capitalism: The fight for a human future at the new frontier of power*. PublicAffairs.

Zuiderveen Borgesius, F. (2018) Discrimination, artificial intelligence and algorithmic decision-making. Available at: https://rm.coe.int/discrimination-artificial-intelligence-and-algorithmic-decision-making/1680925d73 (accessed 17 August 2019).

About the Contributors

Swati Chakraborty is a Visiting faculty (Assistant Professor), at the Institute of Legal Studies and Research, GLA University. Dr. Chakraborty is associated as an Adjunct Faculty with Concordia University, Canada. Dr. Chakraborty is a Writing Fellow, at COMPOSE, Universitas Islam International Indonesia. She is an International Fellow of KAICIID in Lisbon, Portugal. She is the Founder of "Webplatform4Dialogue". Dr. Chakraborty is fellow of FoRB's Future.

***

Mussa S Abubakari, PhD, is an enthusiastic educational technology researcher and associate researcher with the Dig Connectivity Research Laboratory (DCRLab) in Kampala, Uganda, since 2024. He's an instructor in the Department of Physics and Mathematics at Kondoa Islamic Secondary School, Tanzania. He has a PhD in Educational Technology from Sultan Hassanal Bolkiah Institute of Education, Universiti Brunei Darussalam, and graduated in 2025. Dr. Mussa obtained a Master of Education degree in Electronics and Informatics Engineering at Yogyakarta State University, Indonesia, in July 2021. He obtained his BSc. in Telecommunications Engineering at the University of Dodoma in June 2016. His academic and research interests include educational technology, technology-enhanced learning, technology acceptance, open and distance learning, generative AI, and digital competence, among others. He has over 15 journal articles published in internationally reputable journals, several book chapters, and papers presented at international conferences.

Nandini Basistha [MA (Double), M.Phil., D.Phil., Post Doc] is working as Associate Professor, Department of Liberal Studies and Social Sciences, Faculty of Behavioural & Social Sciences, SGT University, Gurugram, Haryana. Previously, she was Executive Director, Interdisciplinary Institute of Human Security and Governance, New Delhi, India; Senior Assistant Professor at Amity Institute of

Liberal Arts, Amity University, Mumbai; ICSSR Post-Doctoral Fellow at Centre for North East Study & Policy Research, Jamia Milia Islamia; Assistant Professor of South Asian Studies, Kurukshetra University; Senior Fellow at Institute of Foreign Policy Studies, Calcutta University; UGC-SRF and UGC-JRF at Rajiv Gandhi Chair in Contemporary Studies, University of Allahabad; & Organiser at DRCSC, Kolkata. She authored 2 books - Narendra Modi & Northeast: Conflict Management through Development-Security Nexus (Delhi: Interdisciplinary Institute of Human Security and Governance, 2023) & Politics of Separatism (New Delhi: Vaibhav Publications, 2018) and edited 10 books on Gender Security-related topics. She published 33 research articles in Sage, Routledge and SCOPUS-Indexed and UGC-Care listed journal

Tridipa Sehanobis Das is an Assistant Professor of Law at Christ (Deemed to be University), Bangalore. She completed her Ph.D. and Master's in Constitutional Law from Rajiv Gandhi National University of Law, Punjab. Prior to joining Christ, she served as Assistant Professor of Law and LL.M. Coordinator at the Indian Institute of Legal Studies, West Bengal, for 4.5 years. She has authored a book on women's autonomy in reproductive choices and published extensively in peer-reviewed and Scopus-indexed journals. Her research interests include constitutional law, gender justice, reproductive rights, and human rights, with active participation in national and international conferences.

Supratik Guha is working as an Assistant Professor under WBES, Govt. of West Bengal. He has done B.SC Honours in Economics, MA in Economics from Jawaharlal Nehru University (with specialization in World Economy and Econometrics from CITD), New Delhi, completed M.Phil. in Economics from University of Calcutta and finally completed PhD from Jadavpur University. His area of interest and specialisation is Trade and Environment and Econometrics. He has published research articles and book chapters in reputed Scopus indexed journals, IGI Global, Emerald, Sage and Springer.

Kannan Kunnathully, specialize in International Trade Law and related advertising infringing fundamental rights, now focusing my research on the use of technology in the infringement of fundamental. I am now serving as an Assistant Professor at Vinayaka Mission's Law School, Vinayaka Mission's Research Foundation (DU) Chennai, Tamil Nadu. Here, I teach International law, Legal Research and Manuscript Writing. My passion for teaching and in-depth subject knowledge have earned me recognition as a dedicated educator. In addition to my academic role, I actively engage with corporate contract vetting together with utilisation of CSR funds for legal awareness programs. Looking forward, I aim to expand my research into emerging legal issues in the digital age, especially in privacy rights, while guiding aspiring law students and future legal scholars.

T.C. Manjunath was born on 6th February 1967. He did his BE from RV College of Engg. in 1989, ME in Robotics & Automation from LD College of Engg. in 1992 with First Rank and PhD in Systems & Control Engg. from IIT Bombay in the year 2007. He is currently working as the Dean Research R D and as Professor in the Dept. of Computer Science & Engineering with specialization in IoT, Cyber Security & Blockchain Technology in Rajarajeswari College of Engineering, Bengaluru, Karnataka. He has completed B.E. Degree from R.V. College of Engg., M.E. Govt.'s LD College of Engg., Gujarat Univ., Ahmedabad in First Rank and Ph.D. in Systems and Control Engineering from the Indian Institute of Technology Bombay IIT Bombay He has got a teaching academic, research and administrative experience of more than 35+ years 10 years as Principal, 8 years as HoD rest as faculty and has published more than 1200+ research papers in various national & international journals and conferences, with 175+ patents, 25 book-chapters, 25 awards and also published 25 text books in various field of science, engineering and technology, completed projects worth Rs. 9 Crores till date apart from guiding 10 PhD scholars. He is a member of 30 Professional Society Chapters and is a fellow of IE, IETE, AMIEE and a chartered engineer. He got the best research scholar award in 2006 in IIT Bombay amongst all the research scholars of the institute. He has got 10 awards in academics and research activities.

P. Selvakumar is currently an Associate Professor in the Department of Science and Humanities at Nehru Institute of Technology, Coimbatore, Tamil Nadu, India. Prior to joining Nehru Institute of Technology, he held positions as an Assistant Professor in the Department of Science and Humanities various engineering colleges in Coimbatore, Tamil Nadu, India, spanning from 2011 to 2023. Dr.P. Selvakumar's academic and research interests lie primarily in the field of phytochemistry. He has made significant contributions to his field, with an impressive record that includes 30 journal publications, 12 patents, and 20 conference papers. Additionally, he has organized 5 seminars and conferences, further demonstrating his commitment to academic and scientific exchange. Throughout his career, Dr. P.Selvakumar has been recognized for his dedication and excellence in teaching, having been honored with several awards, including the Best Teacher Awards. He holds a prominent position in the academic community, contributing actively to research.

Ganesh Pathak is an Associate Professor at Sri Balaji University, Pune (SBUP), where he plays a key role in delivering quality education and fostering academic excellence. With a strong background in management education and research, Dr.

Pathak is known for his insightful teaching, student mentorship, and contribution to curriculum development. His academic interests span across areas such as business strategy, operations, and organizational behavior. Dr. Pathak has contributed to various research publications and actively engages in seminars, workshops, and conferences at both national and international levels. His dedication to continuous learning and innovation makes him a valued member of the academic community at SBUP.

Pham Thi Hanh She's an invited lecturer at the University of Economics and Business, Vietnam National University, Hanoi; field Economics and Business Administration. She has a number of publications in reputed journals. Her research interest areas tourism, dark tourism, ecotourism. She has nearly 20 years of experience in research and teaching at units such as: Vietnam National University, Hanoi; Vietnam Women's Academy; Vietnam Academy of Social Sciences. Recognition from the the Ministry of Education and Training, Vietnam Women's Academy.

Mouparna Roy holds a PhD and an M.Phil. in Media Studies from the School of Social Sciences at Jawaharlal Nehru University (JNU). She also has a Master's degree in Sociology from JNU and a Bachelor's in Indigenous Culture Studies from Central University of Jharkhand. For two years, she worked as a Research Assistant for the University of Western Australia on the project "The Effect of Ambient Air Pollution on Altruistic Behavior - Field Experiment Evidence from China and India." With 5 years of research experience and 1 year of teaching experience, her PhD research explored the intricate aspects of dance writing. Her academic interests lie at the intersection of gender and media studies, focusing on performative studies and cultural narratives. Alongside her academic pursuits, she cultivated a deep appreciation for the arts and holds a degree in Bharatanatyam which has enriched her understanding of discipline, creativity, and cultural heritage. These experiences have also shaped her holistic perspective and enhanced her collaborative and expressive abilities reflected in her research interests.

Mohammad Saleem is currently serving as an Assistant Professor at the Faculty of Law, Marwadi University, Rajkot, Gujarat. He is pursuing his Ph.D. in Law from the Vellore Institute of Technology School of Law (VITSOL), Chennai, Tamil Nadu, and also holds a Post-Graduate Diploma in Cyber Laws from Bhartiya Vidyapeeth, Pune. Prior to joining Marwadi University, he worked as an Assistant Professor at the Faculty of Law, SRM University, Delhi-NCR, and also taught at the Aligarh Muslim University Centre, Murshidabad, West Bengal. An active scholar, he has authored the book Words of Hate: A Statutory Analysis of Hate Speech in

India and has presented numerous research papers at national and international conferences and seminars. His works have been published in reputed national and international journals on diverse areas of law. His academic interests primarily lie in Constitutional Law, Comparative Constitutional Law, Human Rights, Civil Liberties, Legal Philosophy, and Legal Reforms, through which he seeks to contribute to the empowerment of marginalized and underprivileged sections of society. His research areas span a wide spectrum, including rights related to women and children, freedom of speech and expression, preventive detention laws, election laws, democracy, and contemporary political developments at both national and international levels.

Karun Sanjaya is an Assistant Professor at Symbiosis Law School, Nagpur, specializing in Cyber Laws, Intellectual Property Laws, Artificial Intelligence, and allied fields. A two-time recipient of the Justice Krishna Iyer Memorial Merit Award (2019, 2022), he has also been honoured with the Adv. P.F. Thomas Memorial Gold Medal (2019) and the Dr. K.N. Chandrashekharan Pillai Gold Medal (2022) for his academic excellence. With over sixty research publications to his credit across diverse areas of law, he has established himself as a prolific scholar. He qualified UGC NET with JRF (Law) and is presently pursuing his PhD at VIT School of Law, Vellore Institute of Technology, Chennai, India. Prof. Karun also contributes to the global research community as part of the review team for Scopus-indexed journals, underscoring his commitment to advancing legal scholarship.

Pamarthi Satyanarayana, specialize in Constitutional Law and Legal Order, focusing my research on the interface between individual rights and public policy, with a strong emphasis on civil liberties, social justice, and the right to privacy. Over the past 36 months, I have served as an Assistant Professor of Law at Vel Tech Rangarajan Dr. Sagunthala R&D Institute of Science and Technology in Chennai, Tamil Nadu. Here, I teach courses such as Constitutional Law, Legal Research and Writing, and both Civil and Criminal Law. My passion for teaching and in-depth subject knowledge have earned me recognition as a dedicated educator. In addition to my academic role, I actively engage with the community, partnering with legal clinics to provide pro bono services to underprivileged individuals. Looking forward, I aim to expand my research into emerging legal issues in the digital age, especially in privacy rights, while guiding aspiring law students and future legal scholars.

Satya Subrahmanyam is a distinguished academic leader, researcher, and institutional strategist with over 27 years of experience in higher education, leadership, and research management. He holds two PhDs and a Postdoctoral qualification from the Polytechnic Institute of Leiria, Portugal. Currently serving as Professor and Dean (Research) at Holy Spirit University of Kaslik (USEK), Lebanon, he spearheads research initiatives that enhance academic excellence and institutional reputation. He played a pivotal role in the development of the Catholic University in Erbil, Kurdistan, where he established new departments, led research programs, and collaborated on international educational projects. As a founding member and Managing Partner of Vignan Institute of Technology and Management, India, he contributed to its transformation into a premier institution. With expertise in AI-driven business strategies, HR analytics, and leadership in technology adoption, he has published extensively, guided PhD research, and led training programs in corporate and academic settings.

Esther V is a law faculty at Tamil Nadu Dr. Ambedkar Law University, Chennai, and a Ph.D. scholar at Saveetha School of Law. She specializes in Intellectual Property Law, with research focused on patent law and public health. A gold medalist, University rank holder, published author, and active moot court judge, she has presented papers at national and international forums and taught a wide range of legal subjects at both UG and PG levels.

Index

A

B

C

D

E

F

G

H

I

M

O

P

R

www.ingramcontent.com/pod-product-compliance
Ingram Content Group UK Ltd.
Pitfield, Milton Keynes, MK11 3LW, UK
UKHW052002051026
15624UKWH00003B/526

9 798337 338309